From
HULL, HELL
AND HALIFAX

An Illustrated History of No.4 Group
1937-1948

From
HULL, HELL
AND HALIFAX

An Illustrated History of No.4 Group
1937-1948

CHRIS BLANCHETT

MIDLAND

An imprint of
Ian Allan Publishing

For those who failed to return . . .

From Hull, Hell and Halifax was first published in
1992 and all information was correct at that date.
Since then, sadly, a number of contributors have
passed away. It is to their memory that I would like
to dedicate this second edition.

First published 1992
Reprinted 2006

ISBN (10) 0 904597 81 4
ISBN (13) 978 0 904597 81 3

Published by Midland Publishing

an imprint of Ian Allan Publishing Ltd,
Hersham, Surrey KT12 4RG

Printed in England by
The Amadeus Press
Ezra House
West 26 Business Park
Cleckheaton
West Yorkshire
BD19 4TQ

Visit the Ian Allan Publishing website at
www.ianallanpublishing.com

North American trade distribution:
Specialty Press Publishers and Wholesalers Inc.
39966 Grand Avenue, North Branch,
MN 55056, USA
Tel: 651 277 1400   Fax: 651 277 1203
Toll free telephone: 800 895 4585
www.specialtypress.com

Photograph on previous page:
**Halifaxes of No.76 Squadron await their next
call for action, at Holme-on-Spalding Moor
during the summer of 1943 – a time when
the 'Battle of Hamburg' was about to
supersede the 'Battle of the Ruhr'.**
IWM, CH10227

Contents

Acknowledgements

Without the help of the following individuals, groups and organisations this book would never have been written.
It is with gratitude for their help, interest and encouragement
that I would like to take this opportunity to give them special mention.

Major contributors to *From Hull, Hell and Halifax*: Bill Day and fellow members of the No.4 Group Reunion Committee; Air Marshal Sir John Whitley, former AOC No.4 Group for his Tribute to No.4 Group; Squadron Leader Vernon Noble, ex-Public Relations Officer of No.4 Group for his Introduction to *From Hull, Hell and Halifax*; Bill Jacobs for early material of No.102 Squadron; Chuck Adams for much material on No.578 Squadron; Group Captain Ivor Easton; the late Air Chief Marshal Sir Augustus Walker; Wally Lashbrook; Wing Commander George Clapperton; Group Captain Sir Guy Lawrence; Sidney Pickles; Bernard Downs; Fred Hall; Matt Holiday; Doris Ikin; Des Moss; Arthur C.Smith for permission to use material from his book *Halifax Crew* published by Carlton Publications; Bill Plunkett; Phillip Brett; Ray Chance; Les Blanchard; Keith Lloyd photographer of Keighley; Wilf Baguley for help with photographs; Chaz Bowyer for permission to use material from *Pathfinders at War*, also help with photographs etc; Bill Chorley for permission to use material from *In Brave Company* No.158 Squadron History.

Special thanks to the following individuals who answered the call for assistance by providing interviews, stories and photographs etc: R.Albon; J.Allen; T.Allonby; A.R.Andrews; G.Barrett; Dorothy Beasty; R.L.Beckingham; S.Beckitt; K.Bolton; W.Boyes; G.Briggs; Len Broadhurst; R.Broad; J.Camm; G.Carver; the late General Jean Calmel; M.Chandler; L.Charlesworth; S.R.Cook; H.Coverley; R.Day; A.W.Davis; Group Captain Dixie Dean: A.P.Derrington; L.Donnelly; K.Dunham; G.Ellis-Wadsworth; W.Elvine; E.Fallen; N.Feury; P.Fitzgerald; E.Freeman; S.Freeman; D.Fullbrook; J.Greet; J.Harding; L.R.Harman; L.Harris; L.Henderson;

W.H.Higgs; Jock Hill; J.Hitchman; P.Hogan; G.Honey; G.Hubard; D.Hulbert; A.Hurst; Group Captain Hank Iveson; R.Jacquemier; E.Jarvis; B.Johnson; R.Jubb; R.Kilminster; H.King; W.Knott; P.Langsford; I.M.Lucas;

Graham Briggs joined the RAF in 1938: like many young men, he was keen to 'do his bit' for his country. After basic training he did a Wireless Course at Yatesbury followed by a short spell on Ground Signals with 77 Sqn. He then answered the call for more Air Gunners and with the necessary clearance 'chit' (no medical . .) he was soon off to 7 B&GS at Porthcawl where he trained on Whitley Is, Battles and Wallaces. Next it was to 10 OTU at Abingdon and after a brief 'hold' with 78 Squadron, the 4 Group Pool unit, in May 1940, he moved on to 58 Squadron. Still an AC2, he was soon to benefit from the decree that all aircrew should be at least of Sergeant rank, and as such he is seen here in his 'office', aboard Whitley 'K-Kitty' in August 1940. By the next March he had completed a tour and had been awarded a DFM. After 'screening' at 22 OTU Wellesbourne and later Wymeswold he went on to complete a second tour, with Don Charlwood's 103 Squadron Lancaster crew, in 1 Group, after which it was to 511 Squadron in Transport Command for 2½ years. Some 'bit'! Upon de-mob he returned to his native Leicestershire. *G.Briggs*

W.M.McDonald; S.McNeil; H.Mennell; H.Moore; D.Morrison; R.G.Moulton; Philip J.R.Moyes; the late Art Porter; I.Pacey; H.Pearce; D.Pugh; A.J.Ralph; M.Roberts; R.Runkine; G.Sanders; E.Sanderson; A.Schofield; R.Shallcross; G.Stear; G.Taverner; R.Thompson; R.Thurston; D.Waterman; A.Webb; A.D.Webb; A.White; J.Williams; R.Williamson; T.Wingham; Timber Wood.

Also, my grateful thanks to the following groups, organisations and individuals: the Royal Air Force Association; the Bomber Command Association; Aircrew Association; Captain W.McCash of the Falcon Field Association; Imperial War Museum Photographic Department; RAF Museum Photographic Section and Archives Department; Military Aircraft Photographs; Business Press International; Air Historical Branch (MoD); Ken Ellis, the Editor of *FlyPast*; Worth Photofinishers of Keighley; the staff of the Public Records Office, Kew; Eunice Wilson; Vincent Orange; Keith Woodcock; Chris Salter and Neil Lewis of Midland Counties; and I.Machell. My thanks are also due to the Editors of the many newspapers and magazines in the UK, Australia, Canada and New Zealand who kindly carried my appeals for help in contacting ex-members of No.4 Group.

Finally, to my wife Jennifer, my daughter Victoria and my son Neil, and to the other members of my family – thank you for your support and for being so patient over the last few years.

I acknowledge the Controller of HM Stationery Office for permission to quote from Crown Copyright documents in the Public Records Office. Copyright of all photographs (where known) is indicated. Other photographs are from the authors collection.

Foreword

*A tribute to the airmen of No.4 Group Bomber Command
from Air Marshal Sir John Whitley, KBE, CB, DSO, AFC,
Air Officer Commanding No.4 Group, 1945.*

I joined No.4 Group in May 1941 and, apart from a break of six weeks during which I was shot down but was fortunate to escape back to England, I was with the Group until the end of the war against Germany. As possibly the longest serving member in the Group, I saw at first hand the courage and dedication of the young men of Bomber Command. The casualty rate was horrific, particularly in the early years of the war, when a bomber crew rarely completed a tour of thirty operations.

It is fashionable for modern writers to decry Bomber Command's efforts during the Strategic Air Offensive against Nazi Germany. Admittedly, during the early stages of the war, bombing accuracy left much to be desired. It was not until we received the necessary electronic aids to navigation and target marking that we were then able to achieve such damaging effects on the enemy. Throughout the offensive No.4 Group played a leading role. Equipped initially with unsatisfactory aircraft types, the Group reached its full potential with the arrival of the later marks of the Halifax bomber.

This book, *From Hull, Hell and Halifax*, is the story of the incredible bravery of the aircrews of No.4 Group. The spirit of those men who went out night after night in their Whitleys, Wellingtons and Halifaxes was truly remarkable. Whilst the aircrews deserve our unstinting admiration, we must not forget the loyal ground staff. They worked long hours, sometimes in atrocious weather conditions, to back up those in the air magnificently.

John Whitley   October 1992.

Sir John Whitley served in Bomber Command from 1937 to 1945. He was Station Commander at Linton-on-Ouse, then became Commander of Driffield Base before being appointed AOC No.4 Group in February 1945. His distinguished postwar career included senior staff appointments in south east Asia, India and at the Air Ministry. He became AOC No.1 Bomber Group in 1953. He was appointed Inspector General of the RAF in 1959. He now lives in retirement in Hampshire.

Air Marshal Sir John Whitley, KBE, CB, DSO, AFC, Air Officer Commanding No.4 Group from 12th February to 7th May 1945. *J.R. Whitley*

Preface

Raincoat collar turned up against the biting wind and rain, I left the car and made my way along the narrow concrete path. I stepped gingerly to avoid the rain filled pot-holes and piles of broken concrete that littered the road before me. Up ahead, standing gaunt and desolate, was the control tower, once the throbbing heart of a busy bomber station. Now, some thirty years on, it was a gloomy deserted relic. Closer to, it was clear that the misguided youth of a later generation had been hard at work: mindless graffiti covered the outside walls. Undaunted I entered, broken glass crunched under my shoes as I climbed the wide concrete stairway leading to the main control room. Further evidence of the vandals handiwork greeted me as I forced back the creaking door and entered. What had been the vital nerve centre of an operational bomber station, with its constant day and night hum of human activity, was now cold, damp and deserted. On three sides of the room the glassless windows let in the wind and rain. Through the shattered panes could be seen a wide vista of the airfield with the main east-west runway just visible in the near distance. Weeds and stacks of sugar beet were doing their best to hide the evidence but the unmistakable pattern of runway and perimeter track was still discernible.

Suddenly, realising that I was being drenched by the rain sweeping in through the broken panes, I stepped back from the windows to examine the control room. Broken electrical sockets and dangling telephone cables hung from the decaying plaster. On the wall opposite the main windows hung a large blackboard. Faintly showing through the grime and graffiti I could just distinguish the shapes of letters and numbers recording the events of some long forgotten operation. What life and death dramas had been recorded on that board. Now, sadly, the ravages of time had hidden the evidence.

Cold and wet I decided that I had seen enough of this sad and desolate place. Outside the rain still swept across the deserted airfield, much as it must have done on many a day during those far off years of war, soaking the tireless ground crews as they laboured to prepare the bombers for their night's work.

In was my visit to the old wartime bomber station at Burn in Yorkshire, on a typically cold and damp Autumn day, that was to provide me with the spark of inspiration to write this history of No.4 Group. As I explored the remains of the former home of No.578 Squadron, I began to wonder what sort of men had flown and fought from places such as this? What part did they play in the overthrow of Nazi Germany? It was only after further research that I discovered that the airfield site at Burn was just one of many in the East Riding of Yorkshire used by the bombers of No.4 Group Bomber Command during the years 1937 to 1945.

The Group began its long association with the county of Yorkshire in the summer of 1937. The plan was to equip the Group with the new long-range heavy bombers then entering service as part of the expansion of Royal Air Force Bomber Command. Yorkshire was chosen as the location for the Group's stations because it was nearest to the potential enemy – Germany, and would allow the greatest penetration. The Vale of York, with its well drained areas of farmland and few large towns, was ideal for the siting of the large numbers of airfields that would be required.

From the beginning the Yorkshire character was to influence No.4 Group. Recognised characteristics of the county and its people – pride, stubbornness and self reliance – would become the hallmarks of the Group and would sustain it later through its darkest periods of heavy losses.

When operations commenced in September 1939, No.4 Group was the only specialist night bomber force possessed by any air force. Equipped initially with the Armstrong Whitworth Whitley twin-engined bomber, the Group's early contribution to the war effort, much to the chagrin of its crews, was the nightime dropping of 'Nickels' or propaganda leaflets. In those first few months of war such far flung locations as Hamburg, Munich, Vienna, Prague and even Warsaw were visited by the Whitleys of No.4 Group as they battled against their twin enemies, the Germans and the appalling elements.

From these humble beginnings the Group was to expand its activities and was involved in some notable 'firsts' during those early years. Whitleys from No.4 Group were the first British aircraft to drop bombs on German soil in World War II. No.4 Group aircraft were the first to fly over Berlin, much to the embarrassment of Herman Göring, the chief of the Luftwaffe, who had boasted that no enemy aircraft would fly over Reich territory.

It was Whitleys from No.4 Group that were the first to bomb Italy, making use of bases in the Channel Islands to reach their distant targets.

In later years, equipped exclusively with the Handley Page Halifax bomber No.4 Group took its place alongside those groups equipped with its more illustrious partner in the bombing offensive against Germany, the Lancaster. It is perhaps because the Lancaster bomber has been associated with the bombing of Germany, through such famous exploits as the attack on the Ruhr dams etc, that the Halifax-equipped groups have not received the recognition that they deserve. The deeds of No.4 Group may not have grabbed the headlines but night after night, throughout the war, the bombers from Yorkshire were out over Nazi occupied Europe delivering their lethal loads to the very heart of the enemy and on many occasions it was the crews of No.4 Group who bore the brunt of the losses.

I hope this account of the Group's activities, during those momentous years, and the stories of the men who flew and maintained the Whitleys, Wellingtons and Halifaxes, will in some way redress the balance.

Lord Halifax, speaking at the official christening ceremony of the Halifax bomber on 12th September 1941, used a few words of what has become a popular misquotation from an old Yorkshire prayer*. He went on to add that the time was not far distant when that prayer might be on all German and Italian lips. Strangely, no official badge for No.4 Group was ever authorised during the war. If there had been a badge I can think of no better motto for the Group than those words quoted by Lord Halifax on that day in September 1941, 'From Hull, Hell and Halifax, good Lord deliver us'.

Chris Blanchett,
Keighley   October 1992

The correct quotation from the prayer is given in Antiquities of Halifax *by Thomas Wright, published in 1738: 'From Hell, Hull and Halifax, good Lord deliver us'. During the 17th Century, the town of Halifax was very strict in enforcing the law against beggars and criminals, hence the birth of the proverb.*

Introduction

by Squadron Leader Vernon Noble
Public Relations Officer of No.4 Group 1940-43

After passing out from an Officers' Training Course at Loughborough at the end of 1940 I was posted to No.4 Group of Bomber Command where I remained for nearly three years, rising in rank from Pilot Officer to Squadron Leader. I regarded it as a privilege to serve with these gallant young crews whose average age was about 21 (and I felt like an old man at 32 when I joined). I shared their jubilation at attacks successfully carried out and their sadness about the very many comrades who never returned.

No.4 Group was the pioneer night bomber group, busily employed: in fact, it carried out its first raid in the evening of the day that war began, 3rd September 1939, but this was only to scatter leaflets on Germany: bombs soon followed. The Group was equipped with Whitleys and Wellingtons when I joined, soon to be converted to four-engined Halifaxes. Its airfields lay in and around the Vale of York, with headquarters at Heslington Hall where I was allocated a small room on the top floor across the corridor from the office of the Air Officer Commanding, Air Vice-Marshal Arthur Coningham. When he was appointed AOC Western Desert he was succeeded by Air Vice-Marshal C.R. Carr. I worked closely with both of them, because not only were they kindly disciplinarians as well as distinguished pilots of long experience but they had a helpful appreciation of public relations.

I spent little time in my office, and even less in my lodgings in the village. I was usually with the flying and ground crews on airfields during the day, and in the ops room at HQ during the night, waiting for signals from returning bombers which might give a clue to a follow-up story, or dozing in a chair in the Officers' Mess at Linton-on-Ouse. In this way, and with occasional flights, I shared the lives of these brilliant and brave wartime youths, but not their risks. I learned from them how to cope with the empty chairs at breakfast. I learned, too, the meaning of crew spirit and the brotherly closeness of all ranks in an aircraft. In my articles and reports of various kinds, and in my verses, I tried to explain the nature of this branch of war and the men who took part in it.

One of my first mentors was Leonard Cheshire who introduced me to the flying qualities of the Whitley and later the Halifax: even on circuits and bumps over the countryside you felt you were sharing an adventure with him. He had already begun to earn decorations: he had the DSO when I arrived, and later was to be awarded two bars to it, as well as the DFC and ultimately the VC. Before I left the group he became the youngest officer to command a station, Marston Moor. In addition to all his other abilities Cheshire had ambitions to become a writer himself, and he did in fact, write a book during 1943, entitled *Bomber Pilot*. The finest tribute I ever heard paid to anyone was when his Sergeant wireless operator remarked to me, 'If I have to die I'd rather die with Cheshire than anybody else'.

The Group had so many outstanding personalities – sergeants, warrant officers, officers – that it would be wrong to be selective. Names, faces, situations tumble from the memory . . . Wing Commander 'Willie' Tait, who was later to lead the successful attack on the *Tirpitz*, suddenly deciding on nights of no ops to change into his old patched tunic, which he called his 'drinking suit'; the Sergeant who persuaded his squadron commander to recall him from leave if there were any spectacular attack planned, and he rushed back to take part in the thousand bomber operation on Cologne – and was reported killed or missing; The late Wing Commander D.C.T. Bennett who was to found the Pathfinders and who was my severest critic, rebuking me for my report on a certain attack which, he said, 'glorified a bad show'; and that most remarkable lady, Baroness t'Serclaes.

It was the Baroness who unintentionally got me into trouble with royalty. She was the Squadron Officer, in charge of all the WAAF in the Group - nicknamed 'The Squo' - a heroine of the first World War with three rows of medal ribbons on her tunic. She toured the dozen or so stations on her motor-cycle at all hours of the day and night to visit her 'girls'; a strict but motherly commander, responsible for discipline and welfare.

In 1942 the King and Queen visited us. A spectacular diplay had been arranged for them at Dishforth because the King had expressed the wish to meet the men who had taken part in a daring and successful attack by paratroopers on a German radar station at Bruneval on the French coast. The Whitley Squadron carrying the paratroopers was led by Wing Commander P.C. Pickard: the men were commanded by Major Frost. On the day of the royal visit, nine Whitleys, each carrying ten soldiers, were to circle the airfield and then drop the men as the King and Queen arrived. The operation was carefully timed so that the paratroopers could descend as the royal party walked to the perimeter of the flying field, and then the soldiers could line-up for inspection near the hangars. On this occasion newspapers had been invited to send reporters and photographers, and the Air Ministry provided two limousines for them: I led the Press party in my humbler Ford, with two or three passengers. The tour started at Linton-on-Ouse and before the visit was completed I decided to take my party on to Dishforth to enable the cameramen to take-up good positions for the parachute drop. 'The Squo' also decided to get there early and proceeded me on her motor-bike, roaring along the deserted lanes.

When she arrived at Dishforth she told the Group Captain that the King and Queen would be here soon. The RAF Regiment guard at the gates was brought to attention, rifles ready for the present-arms salute. The RAF Sergeant spotted my entourage approaching in the distance, and following instructions he telephoned the control tower.

'They're here, sir!' he called; whereupon Pickard radioed to the circling Whitleys to formate in single line and drop their men.

When I slowed down at the gates and my Pressmen got the rare treatment of a full salute, bayonets flashing, I realised something was wrong. Then, to my horror, I saw the parachutes opening one after another like flowers in the sky and armed men descending, whereas the monarch for whom they were intended was still several miles away and out of sight.

I rushed to the control tower half-a-mile away, shouted an explanation to Pickard as he came down the steps. He hared back to contact the Whitleys, calling to the pilots, 'Keep 'em in! Hold back all you've got. Its premature - too bloody early'. He turned to me and grinned. Pickard the cheerful imperturbable!

By that time there were only three Whitleys with paratroopers aboard. They continued to circle. The Press photographers got excellent pictures, but King George VI and Queen Elizabeth saw only thirty paratroopers come down instead of the spectacular ninety.

I watched closely as Air Vice-Marshal Carr passed-on to the King my explanation of what had happened. I saw him smile. Then they all smiled, including Major Frost who by this time had assembled his men in lines. ready to introduce them to the King, whereas a few minutes earlier he had been justifiably angry. The misunderstanding was forgiven.

Another flap occurred in the same year when Winston Churchill and Deputy Prime Minister, Clement Attlee, visited No.4 Group. Everything went smoothly until the Prime Minister was ready to leave one of the northerly airfields. He was about to get into his car when he had a sudden thought. 'What would happen,' he asked the station commander, 'if Nazi paratroops landed in the fields over there?' The Group Captain promptly replied that the alarm would be given and the defence forces put into action. 'Good!' said the PM 'Sound the alarm. Let's see what happens.'

Chaos ensued. The couple of hundred airmen who were paraded at the entrance gates, ready to give the Prime Minister a rousing send-off, were surprised to hear the warning hooter sound; but they thought there must be a short-circuit and did nothing about it. They stood solidly in ranks – until an officer rode-up on a bicycle, shouting 'It's a mock invasion! Get cracking!'

Back at the airfield everyone seemed to be rushing hither and thither. The RAF Regiment manned the anti-aircraft guns, but other personnel could not obtain any weapons because the armoury was locked and the chief engineering officer had to be found to produce the key. WAAFs put on their tin helmets and took shelter in a trench.

Meanwhile, Mr Churchill, in the uniform of an Air Commodore and carrying a walking stick, strode impatiently about, asking each person he met what was his duty in such an emergency. He was obviously annoyed – but at the same time enjoying the fuss he'd caused. I stood with Mr Attlee and Air Vice-Marshal Carr, all of us keeping out of the PM's way and leaving the responsibility to the station commander, the unlucky Group Captain.

Eventually, everything and everybody were in place, but not before – as Mr Churchill so rightly pointed out – most of the aircraft would have by this time been destroyed if it had been the 'real thing'. It was perhaps unfair of Mr Churchill to put us to a test in this way because, if German paratroops had invaded our air space we should have had warning of their coming; but we admired his effort to keep us on our toes.

The Group was, in fact, attacked – at dawn one cloudy spring morning in 1941 when two German bombers accompanied our returning aircraft and were not detected until they were almost overhead. The signal 'Intruders' was given, runway lights were switched-off, guns manned. I happened to be on the airfield which they had made their target, waiting with the intelligence officers to interrogate crews. As sticks of incendiary bombs dropped, followed by high explosives, I dashed under a table beside the Group Captain and other officers. After the explosions there was gunfire from the ground and from the air: the enemy bombers had turned for yet another run and were shooting-up the airfield.

When it was all over we shakily emerged from under the table and went to the door. Here and there were small fires, but the largest came from the wooden hut which was the WAAF mess: this was still ablaze and girls were fighting the flames with hose-pipes, sand and extinguishers. While we, the officers, had been sheltering under a table the WAAFs had run out of their hostel (in peacetime the station's married quarters) and tackled the fires in their pyjamas. We heard how some had placed helmets over scattered incendiaries. Now they brought us cups of tea. 'And those are women, Noble!' exclaimed the Group Captain, a little shamefacedly.

VIPs pay a visit to the airfields of No.4 Group in the Summer of 1942. Pictured with Mr Churchill (in the uniform of an Air Commodore) at Linton-on-Ouse, left to right: Dr. H. V. Evatt, Australian Minister for External Affairs; Mr C. R. Attlee, Deputy Premier; and AV-M Carr. *IWM, CH5460*

There was another attack on the Group later, and the city of York itself was bombed, but when that happened some of our squadrons had moved to Lossiemouth for the big, concentrated assault on the *Tirpitz* in a Norwegian fjord, and I accompanied them. This was a murderous operation, Halifaxes going in low – some below the level of the cliffs – and Lancasters from Lincolnshire bombing from height. It was like the Charge of the Light Brigade, gunfire on all sides and ahead, and our losses were heavy. We only slightly damaged the big warship.

I think fondly of No.4 Group and those exciting years, the men and the machines in the Yorkshire countryside. When the memorial to the thousands of Allied airmen who died flying from Yorkshire airfields was unveiled in York Minster I made my testimony to their courage in a broadcast which included some of my verses: the following excerpt will revive the scene for many now-ageing airmen . . .

The music of the motors fades across the Wolds; the farms and fields of Yorkshire lie hazy in the dusk, and over on the coastline the trembling air receives the cavalcade of bombers as it marshals in the sky above the tongue of Flamborough that licks into the sea.

The flurry of the take-off has dwindled into calm on all the sprawling airfields across the Vale of York – Linton, Dishforth, Topcliffe, Leeming; Burn and Snaith and Marston Moor; Breighton, Leconfield, Rufforth, Dalton; Elvington and Middleton St George; Melbourne, Driffield, Riccall, Pocklington; Croft and Holme-on-Spalding Moor.

Deserted now the runways, like ribbons on the grass, wide and straight and dusty; the lamps have flickered off on hangars where the crew rooms are silent and alone; and dimly in the twilight the stations settle down to wait return of aircraft in the anxious yellow dawn.

People in the streets of York, familiar with the sound and sight of bombers overhead, glance upward in the fading light. Greyly stand the city walls, mysterious in the evening hours, and like an ancient tapestry, the sunset glows on Minster Towers.

Vernon Noble, Squadron Leader.

Squadron Leader Vernon Noble was Public Relations Officer for No.4 Group from 1940 to 1943. Recruited by the Air Ministry Directorate of Public Relations on the strength of his feature writing for national newspapers and as an author of magazine short stories, Vernon Noble was posted to No.4 Group at the end of 1940. His brief was to produce daily bulletins on operations, write articles for dissemination to the newspapers and broadcasting organisations at home and abroad, and conduct official visitors around airfields.

Chapter One

Roots in Expansion

'In air strength and in air power this country shall no longer be in a position inferior to any country within striking distance of our shores'. Prime Minister Stanley Baldwin's confident and reassuring statement to a crowded House of Commons was designed to allay fears and silence criticism. The date was 8th March 1934 and the Prime Minister, speaking during the debate on the air estimates, was listened to by an attentive House. Dark clouds were gathering on the horizon in the form of a menacingly resurgent Germany embarking on a rapid re-armament programme. Now at last the British Government and people realised that the time for complacency was over.

To meet the German threat Britain's armed forces were to be expanded and among the measures announced in July 1934 was a new expansion scheme for the Royal Air Force. Known as *Scheme A*, the plan envisaged the increase of the home based air forces from fifty to eighty-four squadrons by 1939. *Scheme A*, designed to counter the threat posed by the expanding German Air Force, was defensive in concept. Emphasis was on increasing the numbers of fighters by expanding the fighter force to twenty-eight squadrons. The weakness of the plan was that the offensive bomber element would only be increased to forty-one squadrons. A further inadequacy was that twenty-two of the bomber squadrons were planned to be equipped with light bombers lacking the range to strike at targets in Germany. If bombers were to play their predicted key role in any future conflict then the force that was being planned for the Royal Air Force in 1934 fell far short of that required to deter Hitler.

British hopes that *Scheme A* would act as a deterrent to the Germans were soon shattered by Hitler's announcement in March 1935 that the new German Luftwaffe was equal in strength to the Royal Air Force. The existence of a powerful German Air Force, in flagrant violation of the Versailles Treaty, was bad enough, but a force equal in strength to the Royal Air Force was alarming. It would later be proved that German claims to parity were false but at that time reports from Germany were causing concern in Britain. It was clear that earlier estimates of German air strength had been wide of the mark. In fact under Göring and his deputy Milch, the 'secret' German Luftwaffe had grown rapidly during 1934. During that year an average rate of production of 160 aircraft per month had

been achieved.

The realisation that *Scheme A* was inadequate in comparison with what the Germans were planning led the Air Staff to introduce two further schemes. In 1935 *Scheme C* proposed sixty-eight bomber squadrons of 816 aircraft and thirty-five fighter squadrons to be produced by 1937. *Scheme F* followed in February 1936 and was to produce 990 bombers.

During this period of crisis, specifications were issued by the Air Ministry to meet the requirements of the new bomber squadrons. The new bombers would need the qualities of long range, heavy bomb load and adequate defensive armament to carry out the sustained bombing operations then envisaged. The new heavy types – the Wellington, Hampden and Whitley – were then under development and would soon enter production but the Air Ministry were looking further ahead. By the end of 1936 specifications had been issued for the next generation of heavy bombers and from these would emerge the Stirling, Halifax and Lancaster.

As the Royal Air Force expanded it became necessary to form separate Fighter, Coastal and Bomber Commands as well as a separate organisation for training. In July 1936 Royal Air Force Bomber Command was established with its headquarters at Uxbridge and initially the command consisted of four bomber groups: Nos. 1, 2, 3 and 6. It was against this background of increasing international tension and the rapid expansion of the Royal Air Force that No.4 Group of Bomber Command came into being.

The group was formed as an offshoot of No.3 Group on 1st April 1937 at Mildenhall, Suffolk. Air Commodore A. T. Harris, later to become AOC-in-C Bomber Command, took up his command as the Group's first AOC on 12th June 1937.

The late Sir Arthur Harris, was one of the most controversial figures of the Second World War. A man of immense determination he was to bring to the fledgling No.4 Group a wealth of experience both in command and on the staff. Born in 1892, the son of an Indian civil servant, Albert Travers Harris saw service in the RFC during 1914-18. Granted a permanent commission in the new Royal Air Force he commanded No.45 Squadron in Iraq during 1922-24 flying Vickers Vernons. He later commanded No.58 Squadron, the first heavy bomber squadron reconstituted after the war, equipped with Vickers Virginias.

After a spell in Egypt as Senior Air Staff Officer he returned to England where he later became Deputy Director Operations/Intelligence at the Air Ministry. In 1934 he was appointed to head the Air Ministry Planning Department where he remained until his appointment as head of No.4 Group.

No.4 Group was to remain in Suffolk for only a short time for on the 29th June 1937 the headquarters was relocated at the newly opened airfield at Linton-on-Ouse near York. Linton had opened early in May of that year and construction work was still in progress when No.4 Group arrived. On that same day the group took over the following stations and squadrons from No.3 Group: Leconfield, Nos. 97 and 166; Driffield, Nos. 75 and 215; Dishforth, Nos. 10 and 78; Finningley, Nos. 7 and 76; and Linton-on-Ouse Nos. 51 and 58. The last two squadrons were actually located at Boscombe Down as flying was not possible at Linton due to construction work.

The equipment state of No.4 Group in the summer of 1937 reflects the transient stage to which the whole of Bomber Command, and indeed the Royal Air Force was subject too, at this time.

No.4 Group Bomber Command - 29th June 1937

Sqn	Equipment	Airfield
7	Heyford II/III	Finningley
10	Whitley I	Dishforth
51	Anson I, Virginia	Boscombe Down
58	Anson I, Virginia	Boscombe Down
75	Anson I, Virginia	Driffield
76	Wellesley	Finningley
78	Heyford II/III	Dishforth
97	Heyford II/III	Leconfield
166	Heyford III	Leconfield
215	Anson I, Virginia	Driffield

Only one squadron, No.10 based at Dishforth, had received the new Whitley bomber, then entering squadron service with Bomber Command. The Group's other nine squadrons were equipped with obsolete aircraft which included Virginia and Heyford biplanes and the outmoded Wellesley (see Appendix E). It was not until the late summer and autumn of 1937 that No.4 Group began to receive more Whitleys. Between July and October 78 Squadron became the second unit to re-equip with Whitley Mk.Is. Deliveries to the Group continued during October and November with 58 Squadron receiving the last of the Whitley Mk.I production run.

Above: **Handley Page Heyfords practising low-level formation flying.** *RAF Museum, 5606-5*

The first AOC of No.4 Group was Air Commodore A. T. Harris (12th June 1937 to 24th May 1938). Harris later went on to command No.5 Group and then, from 1942 to 1945, he was AOC-in-C Bomber Command. 'Bomber Harris' is pictured in a typically determined mood in his office at Bomber Command HQ during the war. *IWM, CH5493*

Opposite: **Whitley Mk.1 K7190 'A' of 10 Squadron at Dishforth in 1937. Just discernible on the nose is the squadron's winged arrow motif.** *RAF Museum, P2406*

Centre left and right: **Handley Page Heyford 1As of 10 Squadron. The Heyford was the mainstay of the RAF's heavy bomber force during the expansion period and was the last biplane bomber in service in the Royal Air Force.** *RAF Museum via MAP*

Bottom left: **Harrow Mk.II K6994 'O' of 75 Squadron prepares to take off from Driffield. The squadron received its first Harrows in September 1937, being fully equipped by November of that year.** *RAF Museum, P018124*

Bottom right: **Wellesleys of 76 Squadron photographed in 1937.** *RAF Museum via MAP*

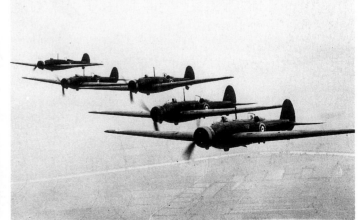

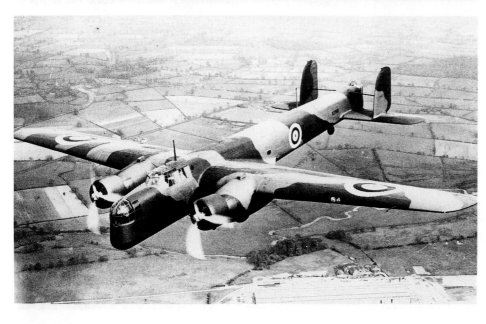

Air Commodore C.H.B. Blount (formerly in command of No.2 Group) was AOC No.4 Group from 25th May 1938 to 2nd July 1939. Upon leaving 4 Group, Blount was promoted to Air Vice Marshal and in September 1939 he took command of the Air Component Field Forces that moved to France in support of the British Expeditionary Force. Air Vice Marshal Blount is pictured in his office at HQ Air Component, late in 1939. *IWM, C228*

No.78 Squadron, based at Dishforth, began to receive Mk.1 Whitleys in July 1937. K7199 is one of the early deliveries, pictured at Dishforth in the late summer of 1937. The aircraft letter 'P' is on the nose side, in flight colour, possibly blue. *W. Baguley*

The ninth production Whitley Mk.1, K7191, served with No.10 Squadron from June 1937. A total of thirty-four Mk.1's were built, equipping Nos. 10, 58 and 78 Squadrons during the period 1937-38. *RAF Museum via MAP*

Opposite top: **Whitley Mk.II's began to reach the squadrons in January 1938 and this example, pictured on a pre-delivery flight, is K7222 that went to No.10 Squadron in that month; immaculately finished in Dark Green - Dark Earth - Night camouflage and Type A1 roundels with their bright yellow surround.** *RAF Museum, P4402*

The Whitley Prototype K4586 was flown for the first time at Baginton on 17th March 1936 and the first production Whitley Mk.1, K7183, was completed in March 1937. *Real Photographs*

Only thirty-four Whitley Mk.Is were completed (see Appendix J) before production gave way to the improved Mk.II, deliveries to the squadrons of No.4 Group commencing on 13th January 1938 when 58 Squadron received the second production aircraft (K7218). No.51 was the next squadron to convert to the Whitley whilst based at Boscombe Down, followed between March and May by 7 Squadron at Finningley.

It was in September 1938 – at the height of the Munich crisis with Europe on the brink of war – that the unpreparedness of Britain's armed forces became apparent: none more so than RAF Bomber Command as a glance at the equipment state of No.4 Group clearly shows. The re-equipment of squadrons with more modern aircraft was still far from complete and the 4 Group example was typical of the rest of Bomber Command.

No.4 Group Bomber Command - September 1938

Sqn	Equipment	Airfield
7	Whitley II	Finningley
10	Whitley I	Dishforth
51	Whitley II/III	Linton-on-Ouse
58	Whitley II	Linton-on-Ouse
76	Wellesley	Finningley
77	Wellesley	Driffield
78	Whitley I	Dishforth
97	Heyford II/III	Leconfield
102	Heyford III	Driffield
166	Heyford III	Leconfield

At the time of the Munich crisis, Bomber Command had mobilised forty-two squadrons, of which only twelve were equipped with bombers with sufficient range to attack Germany. Much of this force suffered from crippling shortages of pilots, spares and reserves of aircraft.

The rapid introduction into service of the new sophisticated aircraft, not surprisingly, caused many problems. Crashes were all too frequent as pilots struggled to cope with the faster and heavier new types. Squadron Leader Bill Jacobs recalls some of the difficulties.

'In November 1938 I joined No.102 Squadron at Driffield and was posted for duty with 'B' Flight. I had been posted straight from Electrical and Wireless School at Cranwell where I had been trained as a Wireless Operator under the Boy Entrant training scheme.

'At this time the squadron was in the process of conversion from the Handley Page Heyford, the last of the biplane heavy bombers, to the Whitley, a process which had commenced only the previous month. At the time of my arrival the Whitleys on charge were the new Mk.III version. The transition from the Heyford – really only a generation removed from its World War One predecessor – to the more advanced Whitley, was something of a problem and the need for specialised conversion training soon became apparent. Two incidents at Driffield in those early conversion days illustrate this need.

RAF personnel survey the burnt out wreck of a Whitley after a crash landing. It is possibly K7189 'L' a Whitley Mk.I of No.10 Squadron, that came down in a ploughed field during a cross country flight from Dishforth on 1st December 1937. *RAF Museum, P020336*

Heyford Mk.IIIs, K6889 'R' and K4029 'X', of 166 Squadron, photographed from a hanger roof at Leconfield. One of the original squadrons of 4 Group, No.166 became a Group Pool Squadron in May 1939. Together with 97 Squadron, these two units provided specialist conversion training for the Group. Date of photograph is believed late 1937 or early 1938. *RAF Museum, P1635*

The most serious involved a Whitley of 77 Squadron, then sharing Driffield with No.102 and just converting from Wellesleys to Whitley Mk.IIIs. On the night of 24th November 1938 this particular aircraft (K8963) was engaged in night circuits and landings when it crashed through the boundary fence on take-off and burst into flames. Pilot Officer Wood was killed in the fire and the only other occupant, Sergeant V. C. Otter, sustained severe burns. The cause of the accident was the premature raising of the flaps on take-off below the prescribed height and speed limits.

'The other incident involved an early Whitley of No.102 Squadron in which two senior officers were on a familiarisation flight. Coming in for their landing it seems they forgot about the undercarriage and proceeded to execute a perfect wheels up landing, no doubt wondering, for a brief moment, what had happened to the perfect three pointer they were going to display to their subordinates assembled on the apron. They were fortunate, though somewhat shaken.

'The need for specialised conversion training was satisfied initially by the introduction, in March 1939, of the Group Pool scheme whereby Nos.97 and 166 Squadrons at Leconfield became No.4 Group Pool. Similar pools were formed throughout Bomber Command. I was attached to No.4 Group Pool from 20th March to 15th April 1939, during which time I managed only two hours and five minutes day flying in Heyfords, which was something of a waste as I had already logged fifty-six hours in Whitleys. However, these were early days for the scheme which soon became most effective, particularly in orientating newly qualified pilots to the Whitley'.

The Air Staff had realised, at the time of the Munich crisis, that Bomber Command was in no condition to engage in battle with Germany. Insufficient numbers of aircraft, lacking range and bomb capacity, and crews not adequately trained in navigational skills, painted a depressing picture of a force unprepared for war. The Air Staff needed to buy time to develop the bomber force, but time was running out.

The Government was also pessimistic about the immediate future, with the prospect of air raids on Britain from German or occupied Belgian bases causing much concern. What strategy could Britain adopt in the event of war to avoid provoking the Germans into all out attacks on her cities and ports?

In Autumn 1937 thirteen directives, known as Western Air Plans, had been approved by the Air Ministry. Targets, in the event of war with Germany, were arranged in order of priority and included such wide-ranging alternatives as bombing German communications to hinder any advance into France or the Low Countries, to attacks on the German Fleet and its bases. One bizarre scheme suggested destroying large tracts of German forests by incendiary bombing.

After Munich it was realised that Bomber Command was unprepared to carry out most if not all of the Air Plans proposed. In addition, the British Government had declared, that in the event of war, only military targets would be attacked by the Royal Air Force. It was for this reason, as well as the need to preserve the nucleus of the bombing force, that in those final months of peace the only plans prosecuted with any enthusiasm were actions against the German fleet and the dropping of propaganda leaflets over Germany.

No.4 Group Bomber Command - September 1939

Sqn	Equipment	Airfield
10	Whitley IV	Dishforth
51	Whitley II/III	Linton-on-Ouse
58	Whitley III	Linton-on-Ouse
77	Whitley III	Driffield
78 (non-op)	Whitley IV, IVa	Dishforth
97	Whitley II/III, Anson	Leconfield
102	Whitley III	Driffield
166	Whitley I	Leconfield

Note: 97 and 166 were the Group Pool Squadrons

Whitley Mk.III K8936. This version had been introduced in August 1938, but by 1939 was already obsolete. *Armstrong Whitworth*

An early Whitley Mk.II, K7219 of No.58 Squadron, photographed in 1938. Shortages of gun turrets meant that early production Whitleys were flown with metal fairings fitted in place of front turrets.

A display of modern service aircraft at Northolt, 23rd May 1939, includes three Whitley Mk.III's of 58 Squadron.
Real Photographs

K9055 served with 78 Squadron in the early months of the war. The Mk.IVA differed from the standard Mk.IV Whitley in having Merlin X engines. This photograph was taken at Dishforth in August 1939. *Real Photographs*

Whitley Mk.III, K8957 of 'B' Flight No.102 Squadron at Driffield, August 1939. 'S-Sugar' wears the squadron's 'TQ' identity codes introduced at the time of the Munich crisis: these would later be changed to 'DY' at the

commencement of hostilities. Note the Type B fuselage and wing roundels and manually operated tail turret. K8957 later served with 10 OTU before being destroyed on a ferrying flight in April 1940. *W. Jacobs*

Chapter Two

Nickels in the Dark

The Summer of 1939 saw Europe hastily preparing for the inevitable conflict. The British and French now realised that their policy of appeasement towards Hitler had failed and the only way to halt the rampant dictator was by the use of force. During those last few months of peace the pace of training in the groups of Bomber Command began to intensify. Bill Jacobs of No.102 Squadron recalls that Summer and the confident mood that existed in the squadrons.

'On 11th June we went to Catfoss for the annual practice camp which extended into the early days of July. This was a very useful training session for all flying personnel. By August, with the situation in Europe looking very grave, we became involved in a short period of intense activity to test our Home Defence Organisation. I took part in what we called 'Dummy Raids' on 6th, 7th, 9th and 10th August. We were supposed to be friendly on the way out first time, enemy on the way in first time and second time out, and friendly on the second approach to our coast. Routing was east towards the Dutch coast which we were of course not allowed to cross. The Dutch made sure of this by identifying their coastline with brilliant illuminated letters which could be seen for miles from the air and quite unmistakeably 'NEDERLAND'. We were close to war and if it was to come let it. We were confident in our new equipment and in our ability to use it for the purpose of war'.

In July 1939, at the headquarters of No.4 Group, Air Vice Marshal Arthur Coningham took over as AOC from Air Commodore Blount, who had been in command since May 1938.

Born in Brisbane in 1895, and educated in New Zealand, Arthur Coningham had served in the army during the First World War before transferring to the Royal Flying Corps in 1916. From his army days, when he had served with New Zealand forces in Samoa and Egypt, he had gained the nickname 'Maori', inevitably changed to 'Mary'. Arthur Coningham was to prove a most popular and respected commander who always knew how far to stretch those under his command. Dynamic and young in outlook he was efficient and hard working with a shrewd eye for future leaders. It says much for his judgement that during his period of command of 4 Group there would emerge from its ranks many of the so called 'Bomber Barons', the future leaders, tactical innovators and personalities of Bomber Command.

On the eve of war, No.4 Group had become an all-Whitley force. The Mk.III version had been introduced in August 1938, but by 1939 this version was already obsolete, such had been the pace of development in bomber aircraft. The Whitley Mk.III differed from earlier versions in having a Nash and Thompson powered front turret in place of the manually operated Armstrong Whitworth version. In addition, a retractable ventral 'dustbin' turret, mounting twin 0.303-inch machine guns, had been installed. This installation, when lowered, had a drastic effect on performance, and consequently would be rarely used. By September 1939 the Whitley Mk.III equipped four squadrons within No.4 Group: Nos. 51, 58, 77 and 102.

Attempts to improve the Whitley performance had resulted in the Mk.IV, deliveries to 4 Group commencing early in 1939. The fitting of Rolls-Royce Merlin engines improved the Whitley's range and performance, and in addition, the replacement of the manually operated rear turret, with a power operated Nash and Thompson mounting – equipped with four 0.303-inch machine guns – meant that the Whitley Mk.IV had the most vicious sting in the tail of any bomber of its time. Another improvement was the fitting of a new plexiglas 'chin' extension on the nose, which greatly improved the bomb-aimer's view. At the outbreak of war the Whitley Mk.IV was in service at Dishforth with 10 Squadron and with 4 Group's reserve unit, No.78. This latter unit was a non-operational reserve, its role being to supplement the Group Pool by training crews and acting as a reservoir between the operational squadrons and the Group Pool.

On 1st September 1939 German forces smashed across the frontiers of Poland. Two days later Germany was at war with both the British Empire and France. Royal Air Force Bomber Command had been held in readiness to carry out its designated tasks under Air Plan No.7, (attacks on the German Fleet), and Air Plan No.14, (the dropping of propaganda leaflets). On the first afternoon of the war Wellingtons and Hampdens of Nos. 3 and 5 Groups carried out armed reconnaissance flights over the North Sea as far as the Heligoland Bight in search of German warships.

Meanwhile up in Yorkshire at Linton-on-Ouse there was intense activity as Nos.51 and 58 Squadrons prepared to carry out their part in Air Plan No.14, the propaganda war.

After making the short flight over to Leconfield, where half a million propaganda leaflets were loaded aboard each aircraft, the crews of 51 and 58 Squadrons awaited the order for take-off. The plan called for three Whitleys (K8938, K8941, K8982) from 51 Squadron to drop their leaflets on Hamburg while seven aircraft from 58 Squadron, (K8964 'R', K8969 'G', K8973 'K', K8990 'L', K9006 'E', K9009 'M', K9013 'W'), were to scatter their loads over Bremen and the Ruhr.

At 20.30 hours on that historic first evening of the war Flying Officer Milne of No.51 Squadron eased Whitley K8938 off the runway at Leconfield and climbed into the gathering darkness. The rest of the force followed at short intervals, the last aircraft leaving at 22.22 hours. No.4 Group were off to war!

Thick cloud cover over north western Germany hid the raiders and their intended targets and apart from the odd probing searchlight beam no opposition was encountered. However, three Whitleys from No.58 Squadron had problems on their return journeys: two suffered engine failures and one ran out of fuel. All three were forced to make landings in France. Flying Officer O'Neil in K8969 'G-George', was one pilot whose Whitley suffered engine failure and he had to crash-land his crippled aircraft near Amiens. Fortunately there were no casualties but the aircraft was wrecked.

As Monday 4th September dawned, the air and ground crews at Driffield began to prepare for another *Nickel* (the code word for leaflet operations) planned for that night, involving three Whitleys from 102 Squadron. The target was to be the Ruhr and the three aircraft from this unit were to be joined by seven aircraft from No.51 Squadron flying from their advanced airfield at Rheims in France.

Bill Jacobs, then a Leading Aircraftman Wireless Operator with 102 Squadron, was a member of one of the Whitley crews detailed for the squadron's first operation of the war:

'We had been standing by for several days and there was considerable activity in the hangars, particularly in altering the squadron identification letters on the aircraft from 'TQ' to 'DY'. Shortly after the official declaration of war was announced we had an air raid warning and took to the shelters but this was nothing more than a trial. The crews were restless, each wondering what we were waiting for, but the day passed without any indication of action, little different from any other

Above: **Air Marshal Sir Arthur Coningham (pictured in 1945), was AOC No.4 Group from 3rd July 1939 to 25th July 1941.** *IWM, CL1941*

Above right: **No.51 Squadron 3rd September 1939.** *W. Baguley*

Below: **The Sting in the Tail! An enemy fighter's view of the four 0.303-inch Browning machine guns fitted in the Nash and Thompson rear turret of the Whitley Mk.IV and later, as in this 78 Squadron example, the Whitley Mk.V.** *D. Webb*

Opposite: **A 102 Squadron Whitley crewman demonstrates the technique of leaflet dropping via the flare chute.** *IWM, C826*

Sunday apart from the enforced inactivity and an unusual quietness no doubt related to tension.

'The morning of Monday 4th September brought great activity in the Flights of both Nos.77 and 102 Squadrons, and it soon became apparent that we were to do our first show that night. Details of aircraft and crews were posted in the flight authorisation book during the afternoon: our details were –
Raid DM 82
Whitley III K8958 'DY-S'
Crew: Pilot Officer Bisset (Pilot)
      Pilot Officer Kierstead (Navigator)
      Sgt W. Lees (Observer/Front Gunner)
      LAC W. Jacobs (Wireless Op/Air Gunner)
      LAC C. Killingley (Rear Gunner).
Estimated time of departure 23.59 hours.

'Fuselages forward of the entry door were crammed with large parcels of leaflets wrapped in coarse brown paper tied with thick twine. Access, normally difficult enough because of the retracted ventral turret, was now extremely difficult through the narrow alley between the parcels on either side both fore and aft of the turret.

'At the evening briefing we were acquainted with the purpose of the mission and the reader will understand our feelings at not being called upon to deliver onto Germany's industrial heartland, anything more damaging than a good supply of paper and stout rubber bands. However, maintaining strict wireless silence, except in an emergency and until clear of enemy territory, we were to enter German airspace north of Holland and, avoiding neutral territory, fly southward distributing our leaflets down the Ruhr Valley, into France and home across the English Channel.

'By the time that we crossed the enemy coast we were flying at 15,000 feet and breathing oxygen. Visibility was good but ground features were obscured and navigation was by dead reckoning assisted by wireless bearings obtained by the Direction Finding loop aerial. Shortly before we commenced leaflet dropping we observed a beam of light apparently aimed in our direction from a point slightly below and to the right of our nose. We judged it to be airborne and Bill Lees gave it a burst from the front gun and the light immediately was extinguished.

'The lot of dropping the leaflets fell to Pilot Officer Kierstead and myself and what a wearisome business it was. At 15,000 feet the outside temperature was about fifteen degrees below freezing. We had to disconnect ourselves from the oxygen supply and we were soon bathed in sweat from the effort. The parcels nearest the flarechute were discharged first to clear the surrounding area. Soon the thick brown paper and string became a problem until space was cleared into which it could be condensed conveniently out of the way. The parcels aft of the turret could only be moved with difficulty over the raised turret, and to minimise the effort of moving them to the flarechute we had to partially lower the turret for a while with consequent effects on airspeed and fly-

ing characteristics. The whole process seemed interminably lengthy and we were quite exhausted by the effort at that height.

'I have read several accounts of leaflet dropping by writers who were not directly involved. These leaflets measured $8\,^7/_{16}$ x $5\,^3/_8$ inches when folded to produce a four page leaflet of that size. Five leaflets were placed inside each other, and bundles about four inches thick were secured by a stout rubber band located some two inches from one of the narrow ends. The secured end of the bundle was fed into the flarechute first so that on emerging into the slipstream the loose end was presented to the full force causing the bundle to separate and scatter immediately. The brown paper parcels were about thirty or so pounds in weight and measured something like 26" x 17" x 12" containing eighteen, perhaps twenty-four bundles. There were, understandably, local variations which developed with changing circumstances, particularly when mixed loads of bombs and leaflets were carried.

'With the dawn we found ourselves above cloud cover. At about 06.40 hours, not having had any external check on our dead reckoning, and believing ourselves to be well clear of enemy territory, I broke wireless silence and obtained, in quick succession from three of our own DF stations bearings, which when plotted, placed us close to Dieppe. Being anxious about our fuel state we decided to take a look and on breaking cloud we found ourselves over water with Dieppe behind us. The pilot decided to land on a small aerodrome which seemed to be inactive but it was the only one we could see. On final approach we thought it judicious to unload the guns in the ventral turret. This was my responsibility and I had barely got the turret to the locked up position when we touched down. Looking rearwards through the small window slits in the fuselage I saw a blue clad figure being thrown off the leading edge of the port tailplane. Apparently this gallant French sentry had thrown himself onto the tailplane in an attempt to arrest our landing speed.

Although somewhat foolhardy, he was fortunately unhurt, and by the time we came to rest with the nose almost in the boundary hedge, he was some distance away strolling nonchalantly with his rifle in the slung position.

'Refuelling from small cans was a lengthy business even with the help of about a dozen French Air Force personnel who had arrived at the scene on bicycles from the nearby town. We were on the ground for three hours and thirty-five minutes being airborne again by 10.30 hours. Due to atmospheric phenomena affecting wireless transmissions I was unable to contact Driffield until we were halfway home. We arrived at base at 12.55 hours after a combined flight of nine hours and twenty minutes. Thus ended our first operational flight'.

Of the ten No.4 Group aircraft involved in operations that night, three from No.51 Squadron failed to take-off from Rheims due to engine trouble. The others carried out the operation successfully and returned safely except Whitley K8940 of 51 Squadron which force-landed on the beach at Cherbourg owing to fuel shortage.

Sergeant Bill Jacobs photographed whilst serving as an instructor at 19 OTU in July 1940. 'The thing in my hands is a Whitley Direction Finding Loop which we had specially mounted for classroom instruction. With this as a teaching aid we taught student operators to take bearings and how to sense the true from the reciprocal. *W. Jacobs*

The first production Whitley Mk.V N1345. *Real Photographs*

During that Monday, the first full day of war, there had been considerable daylight activity by the Blenheims and Wellingtons of Nos. 2 and 3 Groups. They had been despatched to attack German warships lying at anchor in the Shillig Roads and the Jade Estuary. Forced down by low cloud the Blenheims and Wellingtons suffered heavy losses at the hands of the warships lethal light flak. Only superficial damage was caused to the German ships and the loss of five Blenheims and two Wellingtons for so little return bode ill for the future of British daylight bombing.

For the next ten nights the leaflet operations continued with Whitleys from No.4 Group nightly visiting the ports and towns of north western Germany and the Ruhr. No.77 Squadron despatched their first 'Nickel' on the night of 5th September followed by 10 Squadron the following night when two Whitley Mk.IVs were sent to Cuxhaven and Wilhelmshaven. The pattern for these early operations was for individual crews to make their own way to a separate target, leaflets would be dropped and, cloud cover permitting, a general reconnaissance would be carried out. Although the first week of operations proved largely uneventful two aircraft failed to return from a Nickel/reconnaissance raid to the Ruhr. No.102 Squadron had despatched six Whitleys to the Ruhr on the night of 8th September and Squadron Leader Murray in K8950 'H' had to make a forced landing in Germany due to engine trouble. The whole crew was captured. Whitley K8985 'J', skippered by Flying Officer Horrigan, strayed into neutral Belgian airspace on the return flight from the Ruhr and was intercepted by a Belgian Air Force Fairey Fox and was forced to land at Nivelles airfield. Flying Officer Horrigan and crew were interned along with their Whitley.

The leaflet operations continued until the 14th September when the War Cabinet, sensitive to criticism, suspended operations. Critics claimed that while the Poles were bleeding to death at the hands of the invading Germans the only positive help being given by Britain was to bombard the German population with paper. Despite the fact that the results from 'Nickel' missions was unimpressive the training value of those early sorties was considerable. The benefits brought about by improved navigational techniques and intelligence gathering were to prove of great value as the bombing offensive developed in the future. The leaflet operations served the needs of reconnaissance and training as well as propaganda and before the end of September the War Cabinet withdrew its ban.

Operations recommenced on the night of 24th September with two Whitley IVs from 10 Squadron raiding Cuxhaven. Both aircraft became lost on the return flight due to faulty reception of the DF bearings which should have brought them onto a heading for the base at Dishforth. When the pilots realised that they were flying parallel to the coast instead of over it they ignored the DF bear-

ings and turned onto a new course that brought them back onto a correct heading. One aircraft returned to Dishforth, the other to Leconfield, but both with fuel tanks almost dry.

Unreliable DF bearings were to cause numerous navigational problems on those early flights. In the Whitley it was the responsibility of the wireless operator to obtain regular bearings via the Direction Finding Loop as a means of checking dead reckoning navigation. Wireless operators, besides providing the communications link, were the only navigational aid to the navigator's dead reckoning which was seriously affected by unreliable wind forecasts over Europe and the inability to see in the dark.

Faulty DF bearings again dogged No.10 Squadron on the night of 30th September when Hamburg and Bremen were the targets. Whitley Mk.IV K9027, skippered by Flight Sergeant Cattel, ran out of fuel and crashed near Bolton after being misled by DF bearings which caused the aircraft to fly over Scotland before the mistake was realised. Fortunately there were no casualties but Flight Sergeant Cattel's Whitley was severely damaged.

By the end of the month No.4 Group had received its first Whitley Mk.Vs when 78 Squadron handed over ten aircraft to 77 Squadron, who thus became the first operational unit to receive the type.

October 1939 got off to an historic start for No.4 Group when No.10 Squadron sent four of its Whitleys to Berlin on the night of the 1st, thus becoming the first RAF aircraft to fly over the city in wartime. In severe weather conditions, and harassed by the Berlin searchlight and gun defences, three of the Whitley crews claimed to have dropped their leaflets on Berlin. The fourth aircraft, K9018 (Flight Lieutenant Allsop), was unable to reach the German capital and scattered its leaflets over neutral Denmark. Unfortunately the last message received from Flight Lieutenant Allsop gave his aircraft's position as approximately 180 miles from St Abbs Head. The cold dark North Sea had claimed the first of many victims from 4 Group.

At the beginning of October the number of squadrons available for operations with No.4 Group was reduced from five to four when 58 Squadron went to Boscome Down on loan to No.15 Group, Coastal Command. No.58's Whitleys were employed on escorting convoys and flying anti-submarine patrols and were away from Yorkshire until January 1940.

Meanwhile, on 11th October, the commander of No.4 Group, Air Vice-Marshal Coningham, had reported to Bomber Command Headquarters on the problem of target location at night. 'The real constant battle', he wrote, 'is with the weather ... The constant struggle at night is to get light onto the target', and he foresaw 'a never ending struggle to circumvent the law that we cannot see in the dark'. Enemy opposition, Coningham had reported, was for the moment negligible, the principal threat to his Whitley crews was

from the weather. Early operations had shown that the night bomber aircraft and crews were ill-equipped for the conditions that they now had to face.

Icing, in the severe weather conditions of late 1939, was the greatest problem and potentially disastrous. On many occasions the Whitleys became so heavily coated in ice that it became impossible to maintain height: ailerons, elevators and rudders would jam up causing loss of control. Sometimes ice formed inside the cockpit and instruments would freeze. On many occasions oxygen systems failed too.

Frostbite was a constant hazard as the primitive heating systems proved altogether inadequate. Many flights would be accompanied by the strange light of 'St Elmo's Fire' playing around propellers, wing tips, gun turrets and cockpits.

Everything possible was done to ensure accurate weather forecasting before an operation but all too frequently crews ran into unexpected severe weather. On some occasions operations were carried out in the face of known or expected bad weather as happened on the night of 27/28th October 1939.

A detachment of Whitleys from No.51 Squadron had been standing by for three days at the French airfield of Villeneuve (codename *Sister*) awaiting suitable weather. On the afternoon of the 27th the forecast for the planned target areas of Munich, Stuttgart and Frankfurt was not encouraging. Rain, hail and sleet showers, risk of thunder, cloud 7 to 9/10ths, low base 1,000 feet, but 500 feet in showers, heavy icing anticipated in shower clouds up to 12,000 feet. Better conditions expected over base on return. Perhaps impatience with the delay of three days in getting operations started was the reason for the order being given for the nights task, a Nickel-reconnaissance, to be carried out, despite the prospect of severe conditions.

Five Whitley Mk.IIIs took-off at ten minute intervals from 17.40 hours with the promise of moderately improved weather en route. Soon after take-off Squadron Leader Marvin in K8981 'A-Apple' was forced to return to base owing to severe icing. The other aircraft pressed on through towering snow clouds and steadily worsening conditions. K8980 'E-Easy', piloted by Sergeant Cotton, successfully reached the objective, Stuttgart, but lack of oxygen caused the navigator and the wireless operator to become violently sick whilst unloading the leaflets. But it was on the return journey that problems really began for Sergeant Cotton and his crew. Heavy icing of the control surfaces made handling extremely difficult and with outside temperature of -30 degrees Centigrade the airspeed indicator froze up and became inoperative. Visibility became impaired as ice formed on the cockpit windscreen and on the front turret. Huge chunks of ice were thrown off the airscrews and smashed violently against the side of the fuselage. Nevertheless after six hours of blind flying Sergeant Cotton

An early edition of the 'Clouds Observer', special Austrian edition. An example of the type of propaganda leaflets dropped by the Whitleys of 4 Group during the winter of 1939-40. *W. Jacobs*

Sergeant Bowles and crew in 'N-Nuts' had similar difficulty with a frozen ventral turret that refused to budge, this time after the leaflets had been dropped. Worse was to follow as near the Franco-German frontier the cylinder head blew off the starboard engine. As the Whitley lost height the port engine began to fail and Sergeant Bowles was left with no choice but to give the order to abandon the aircraft.

The whole crew successfully escaped from the doomed Whitley with the exception of Sergeant Griffin, the rear gunner. Ignorant of the abandon aircraft order because of a faulty intercom point, Griffin remained with the bomber and miraculously survived the resulting crash. Emerging from the wreckage dazed and injured Griffin was amazed to discover that there was no sign of his fellow crew members. Making his way with some difficulty to a nearby French village Griffin was surprised to see the sight of familiar faces in the shape of his crew taking refreshments in a local café.

A significant event for the future of No.4 Group occurred on the 25th October 1939 with the flight of the Halifax bomber prototype at RAF Bicester.

The origins of the Halifax can be traced back to Air Ministry specification P13/36, issued in September 1936, which called for an all-metal monoplane powered by two Rolls-Royce Vulture engines. Development contracts were issued to a number of companies including Handley Page who eventually were awarded a contract in April 1937. Design work commenced immediately but problems with the Vulture engines, then still under development, resulted in a major re-think of the design. Expected delays with the Vultures led to their replacement with four Rolls-Royce Merlin engines. The use of four engines was dictated by the non-availability of any powerplant which could match the power of the twin Vultures. The revised design received the designation HP.57, eventually to be named Halifax.

Construction of the first prototype commenced at the Handley Page plant at Cricklewood in January 1938 and by the autumn of 1939 was complete. Transported in sections to RAF Bicester the new bomber was assembled under strict security and readied for flight testing. On the 25th October L7244 took to the air for the first time with Major J. L. Cordes, Handley Page chief test pilot, at the controls. Much development work was to follow the initial flight of the Halifax and it would be over a year before it entered squadron service.

returned 'E-Easy' safely to base.

Flight Sergeant Wynton in K9008 'J-Johnnie' was not so fortunate, the Whitley being coated in ice almost from the start. During the approach to the target, Frankfurt, the vacuum pump on the port engine became unserviceable. Further problems occurred after the leaflets had been released. The ventral 'dustbin' turret, which had been lowered for the dropping of the leaflets, became stuck two-thirds of the way down. The turret was eventually released but not before one of the crew members, Sergeant Hide, had collapsed from lack of oxygen and exhaustion. Hide had barely recovered when he had to take over the controls of the aircraft as the pilot had fainted. Meanwhile, severe icing had made the aircraft unstable and, as Sergeant Hide struggled to control the ice laden Whitley, the situation became critical when the starboard engine burst into flames. In an instant the aircraft went into a steep dive. Fortunately the pilot recovered in time, and together with Sergeant Hide, brought the aircraft out of its dive and onto an even keel. So much height had been lost, however, that it became impossible to prevent the aircraft from crashing. Only by desperate coaxing did the pilots manage to avoid a belt of trees and crash land in a clearing inside French territory.

Of the other two Whitleys detailed to drop their leaflets on Munich, K8989 'M-Mother' (Flying Officer Budden) and K8984 'N-Nuts' (Sergeant Bowles), only the former carried out the mission and returned to base, but not without problems. 'M-Mother's' ventral turret refused to be lowered to ease the task of leaflet dropping, resulting in a long and laborious effort for the dispatchers. During the return flight Flying Officer Budden suffered from sickness and the whole crew became affected by the intense cold and lack of oxygen.

Chapter Three

Security Patrols

With the coming of winter the scale of bombing operations was seriously curtailed. The Whitley navigators depended almost entirely on clear conditions to find their way to and from their targets. As had been discovered on earlier missions, navigational errors had resulted in aircraft failing to reach their targets or becoming hopelessly lost. The only aids to navigation at this time were from directional radio and the astro sextant, both requiring calm and clear weather conditions to operate accurately. Hardly the conditions to be expected over north western Europe during the winter months.

During November 1939 the 'Nickel' sorties continued, albeit on a much reduced scale. On the 24th, detachments from No.4 Group proceeded to Kinloss where they were to stand by to attack the German pocket battleship *Deutschland*. It was thought that the German raider might attempt to return to its base via Norwegian waters. Each of the Whitleys were to be armed with semi-armour piercing bombs. However, the detachment returned to Yorkshire, early in December, without having been called into action.

On 27th November six Whitleys carried out a 'Nickel' mission to the Wilhelmshaven/Heligoland area. The weather rapidly deteriorated during the course of the raid and a severe storm developed. Heavy icing was experienced with temperatures as low as -40 degrees centigrade at 20,000 feet. Squadron Leader Macdonald of No.102 Squadron, in Whitley N1380 'R', was forced to abandon the mission after his aircraft was struck by lightning, temporarily blinding his navigator. Another Whitley from 102, N1377 skippered by New Zealander Pilot Officer Gray, was severely damaged in the storm and lost much of its upper wing surfaces. Despite the damage, Pilot Officer Gray managed to return safely to Bircham Newton. The pilot and his navigator, Sgt Lofty Long - another New Zealander - were each awarded a DFC as a result.

With Poland crushed, the Germans now concentrated their efforts in the west. While preparations were made for the coming battle with the Allied armies the Luftwaffe confined its activities to mine-laying around Britain's coasts and general reconnaissance of the French frontier. The mine-laying was carried out by Heinkel 115 floatplanes from their bases on Sylt, Borkum and Norderney. The Heinkels, by dropping their deadly magnetic mines in the shipping lanes, had caused heavy losses and major disruption to British coastal traffic; so much so that the Admiralty requested that Bomber Command initiate security patrols over the mine-layers bases in an effort to prevent them taking off.

The patrols commenced on the night of 12th December with Whitleys from Nos. 77 and 102 Squadrons patrolling over the bases on Sylt, Borkum and Norderney. Some activity was reported, with lights on the water. Bombs were dropped on the lights but it was not possible to determine whether any hits were achieved. The next day, aircraft from No.51 Squadron joined in the patrols covering the Sylt/Borkum area. Flight Lieutenant Baskerville, in Whitley K9045, took off at 13.00 hours from Linton-on-Ouse in clear conditions, one of five Whitleys from the squadron operating that day against the seaplane bases. Half way across the North Sea keen eyes spotted a submarine on the surface. After receiving no reply to his light signal challenge, Flight Lieutenant Baskerville promptly attacked the submarine with 250lb bombs. The bombs missed the target, which was fortunate, as it was later discovered that the submarine was British.

Whilst taking part in the security patrols, crews were under strict orders to bomb only targets that were sufficiently clear of land to avoid causing civilian casualties. Sylt was the exception as there was no civilian population on the island. The real purpose of these operations was not appreciated by the crews at the time who, not surprisingly, thought them a waste of time.

On 18th December, in bright moonlight and clear visibility, nine Whitleys visited the Borkum/Sylt area. Again bombs were dropped on lights observed on the water. Earlier that day, Wellingtons from No.3 Group, had been involved in a disastrous clash with German fighters over the Jade Estuary. Twenty-four Wellingtons were despatched to attack warships in the Schillig Roads, Wilhelmshaven and the Jade Estuary despite the fact that heavy losses had already been sustained in earlier missions to this area – five Wellingtons had been lost on 14th December when they ran into a patrol of German fighters.

The resulting debacle was a major victory for the German fighters and in turn was to lead a complete reappraisal of daylight bombing operations by Bomber Command.

Alerted by two new experimental *Freya* radar detection stations on Heligoland and Wangerooge, the German defences were able to shoot down twelve of the Wellingtons. Only hours after the raid a worried Air Ministry ordered a temporary halt to armed reconnaissance missions over the Heligoland Bight. The heavy losses from these early, shallow penetration daylight raids made it clear that if they were to continue, Bomber Command faced a heavy sacrifice of aircraft and crews.

Meanwhile the Whitleys of No.4 Group continued their regular patrols of the seaplane bases and sweeps of the North Sea searching for surface vessels and submarines. These operations continued on a limited scale into the new year.

January 1940 heralded in one of the harshest winters in living memory with heavy snowfalls and leaden overcast skies that lasted well into February. Bomber Command's operations came to a standstill with airfields and aircraft under a blanket of snow. This was well into the period of the so called 'Phoney War' with little warlike activity going on on either side. The all embracing whiteness, holding everything in suspended animation, only added to the unreality.

Early in the month No.4 Group had carried on with its patrols over the seaplane bases in addition to occasional Nickel/reconnaissance flights to the Ruhr, even reaching as far as Prague and Vienna on the 12th January. That was to be virtually the last operation flown for nearly six weeks as by then the weather had closed in.

An attempt was made to mount a leaflet operation on the 26th January. At Driffield, the day had dawned bright and sunny with several inches of newly fallen snow on the aerodrome. Soon it seemed that everyone on the station was gathered outside the hangars. Then in line abreast about twenty-five yards wide, rank upon rank of airmen proceeded to tramp across the field to flatten and compress the snow to form a runway. The plan was for two Whitleys from No.102 Squadron to fly to Villeneuve, where they were to rendezvous with other aircraft from No.4 Group, and carry out a 'Nickel' operation against Prague, Vienna and Munich. It transpired that only two other Whitleys, both from No.77 Squadron, were able to reach Villeneuve and join with the two aircraft from 102.

Bill Jacobs was wireless operator with one of the 102 Squadron Whitleys awaiting clear conditions at Villeneuve. This was N1380 'R-Robert', skipper Squadron Leader J. C. Macdonald ('B' Flight commander).

Above: **Pilot Officer Gray's damaged Whitley Mk.V N1377 with extensive upper wing surface damage caused during a severe storm encountered on a recce/'Nickel' mission to Wilhelmshaven, 27th November 1939. For their feat, in bringing the damaged aircraft safely back home to Bircham Newton, Pilot Officer Gray and his navigator Sergeant Long** were both awarded the DFC. *IWM, C48*

Below: **Two views of a Whitley Mk.V of 78 Squadron at Linton-on-Ouse, early 1940. No.78 Squadron was the first unit to receive the Mk.V, in September 1939. This example is sporting Type A fuselage roundels.** *D. Webb*

'Our intended stay at Villeneuve was to be three days but weather conditions in that now legendary winter of 1940 virtually froze us to the ground and it was the 22nd February before we were able to do what we came for. Our task was to drop leaflets on Vienna and carry out a reconnaissance of Munich; take-off 22.30 hours. The two aircraft from 77 Squadron would be going to Prague and Pilsen to drop their 'Nickels'. I shall never forget the effect of our pre-flight meal in a corrugated iron shed on the aerodrome with its stove glowing red half way up the chimney pipe. A meal of canned stew of a brand we had not previously sampled. I doubt if any of us had ever experienced such raging thirst as was to attend us throughout that long flight.

'In quite good conditions we were able to pinpoint our route to Vienna which we found clear and not only bathed in moonlight, with its famous *Danube* and other features clearly visible, but also brightly illuminated for our special pleasure. We leisurely dropped our leaflets and turned westwards for Munich about 220 miles and slightly south of our outbound track. The weather, however, began to deteriorate and we found the Bavarian capital totally obscured by towering cumulonimbus. Our mission was to reconnoitre this city and report and, since we could see nothing but clouds, we decided to go down and have a look. In the next few minutes we were to sample, for the first time, what must surely be among the most terrifying of wartime night flying experiences. Whilst still in the towering cloud tops, trying to find a hole, we were subjected to considerable turbulence and buffeting. Loud detonations and flashes in the clouds about us led us to believe that we were in an electrical storm. However, closer flashes and smoke puffs with, by now, diffused searchlight beams confirmed our arrival over our target, Munich.

'Down we went through that piece of hell and somehow we managed to get safely below the cloud and heavy flak. The probing searchlights failed to locate us as we stooged around. Satisfied that we had had a good look at Munich and its defences we thought it propitious to leave the scene and get home to report. So heading west again we began our climb through those clouds back to smoother moonlit sky above. In the cloud tops again our watchful eyes caught a glint of something shining in the broken moonlight just off the port wing tip and three voices yelled in concert, 'Balloon Cable'. How many we had not seen we shall never know but looking upwards we could see those ghastly shapes above and before us. 'Mac' sat there like a block of granite and we thanked God for that moon by which we were able to judge angles and pick our way through those deadly cables'.

During the bad weather period, at the beginning of 1940, the Air Staff were given the chance to reappraise strategy for Bomber Command. Air Vice Marshal Coningham's report to HQ Bomber Command, on 11th

Flight Lieutenant Tomlin and crew and their Whitley Mk.V N1387 'L' of No.77 Squadron pictured at Villeneuve. On the night of 15/16th March 1940, Flight Lieutenant Tomlin and crew landed by mistake in Germany whilst returning from a 'Nickel' sortie to Warsaw. *IWM, C1011*

October 1939, had highlighted the problems of target location at night. Coningham's crews had reported that during their nocturnal leaflet/reconnaissance missions over the towns of north-western Germany, their ability to see a target depended, ultimately, on the state of the moon and weather; if the target was blacked out or self illuminating; upon the aircraft's height or the amount of interference from searchlights. In moonlight, features, such as lakes and rivers, were self-illuminating. Railway lines were visible under certain conditions, and towns were visible from 3,000 to 4,000 feet but not individual buildings. On moonless nights only crews fly-

ing at low-level could distinguish betweeen land and water. Under these conditions the only visible pinpoints at substantial height were lights from marshalling yards and the glow from blast furnaces.

As a direct result of Coningham's findings, No.4 Group were instructed to carry out reconnaissance of the Ruhr marshalling yards as a primary task to find whether these targets could be bombed at night. It was thought these vulnerable links in the enemy's communication system might become priority targets in the near future, particularly if the Germans were to mount an offensive against the Low Countries.

One proposal by Coningham in his report was, however, rejected. The No.4 Group Commander had suggested that an invisible target could be bombed successfully by timing a bomber's run in to the target from a visible pinpoint in the area. 'There is no reason why the bombing should not be as accurate as if the target itself was visible', Coningham had argued. The Air Ministry, conscious of the

dangers of civilian casualties and possible retaliation by the Germans, did not accept Coningham's 'offset bombing' method.

Further instructions were issued to No.4 Group in February 1940 to investigate rivers, canals and cooling towers in the Ruhr area. It was not until the weather had improved, however, that the necessary operations could be mounted. On the night of 26th February three Whitleys from No.102 Squadron carried out a reconnaissance of the marshalling yards and industrial complexes in the Rheine, Bielefeld, Bonn and Wesel areas. Crews reported identification of cooling towers and illuminated marshalling yards at heights between 4,000 and 9,000 feet. The river Rhine in the Ruhr area around Duisburg was clearly visible.

As a further aid to identification of ground features, flares were dropped by aircraft on night reconnaissance missions. This method of target identification was used by Whitleys from Nos. 10 and 51 Squadrons in a series of sorties to Berlin at the end of February and beginning of March. The flares used were the standard four and a half inch parachute flare which, when dropped from the flare chute of the Whitley, ignited at a predetermined height above the target. The despatching of the flares was no easy task in the narrow confines of the Whitley fuselage as the following description of the process by Bill Jacobs of 102 Squadron testifies:

'Flare despatching was a most unpleasant task particularly in flak conditions. In the darkened fuselage space between the centre-section petrol tank located above the short access passage to the cockpit, and the tail turret, was located the flarechute. The flares were held in stowages on either side of the fuselage and were not so much heavy as cumbersome in confined spaces, being some four and a half to five feet in length. The flarechute had a removeable extension not unlike a coal scuttle, at the top of which was a pulley which held a length of thin steel cable with a hook at the leading end to take the loop of the flare cord. As the flare left the chute the steel cable ran off the pulley to its full length and then the flare cord was pulled out of its retaining pocket, its end striking the fuse as it left the main body of the flare. The height at which the flare ignited was determined by a calibrated fuse-setting ring and this had to be set whilst the flare was in the chute and before removal of the safety pin. At the top of the flarechute extension was a handle which held the flare ready for release. It was easy enough when placing the flare, tail-fin first, in the chute to let the lot go whilst holding the flare with one hand and trying to close the retaining handle with the other, all in the feeble light of a hand torch. Add to this the effect of evasive action, the noise of exploding shells and the stench of burnt cordite as front and rear gunners tried to put out the searchlights, and one begins to get some idea of what it was like to take station at the flarechute.

'Periods spent at the flarechute always seemed to be agonisingly lengthy and it was easy to become quite exasperated as the aircraft circled back around each flare in an attempt to identify ground features, a difficult enough task even in the best conditions of night visibilty'.

At the beginning of March the Wellingtons of 3 Group and the Hampdens of 5 Group joined with the Whitleys in night reconnaissance flights over Germany. Leaflet dropping was no longer the primary task, the need now was to gather information of potential targets and their visibility at night. Slowly but surely Bomber Command was becoming a night force.

March also saw the first 'Nickel' operations to Poland. Two aircraft from 77 Squadron visited Poznan on the 7th and Warsaw received its quota of 'Nickels', courtesy of 77 Squadron, on the night of the 10th. The residents of the Polish capital again had their sleep disturbed on the night of the 15th, again it was Whitleys from 77 Squadron, two aircraft distributing 6,000,000 leaflets.

The difficulties of navigating to such distant targets and returning safely were highlighted by an unusual incident which occurred on the night of the 15/16th March and involved one of the No.77 Squadron Whitleys returning from Warsaw. Flight Lieutenant Tomlin and crew in N1387 'L-London' having returned safely across Germany were forced to land, due to bad weather, in what was thought to be French territory. However, a few words exchanged with local 'German' peasants sent the startled Whitley crew darting back to their aircraft for a hurried take-off, just as German troops on bicycles arrived on the scene. 'L-London' arrived at the forward French airfield of Villeneuve with fuel tanks almost dry but the crew were none the worse for their close shave.

On 16th March German bombers attacked the Fleet anchorage at Scapa Flow and stray bombs fell on the island of Hoy killing one civilian. Retaliation was called for and three days later, on the night of 19th March, Bomber Command was instructed to carry out its first bombing attack of the war against a land target; the seaplane base at Hornum on the island of Sylt.

Thirty Whitleys from No.4 Group were detailed for the raid, all crews being selected for their experience and knowledge of the target area. Four hours were allotted for the No.4 Group attack to be followed by two hours for the rest of the force, comprising twenty Hampdens from No.5 Group. Typical of the bomb loads that night were those carried by the Whitleys from 10 Squadron which consisted of seven aircraft with two 500 lb and two 250 lb general purpose bombs, and one aircraft with four 250 lb general purpose bombs and two containers of incendiaries. The raid was to be led by Squadron Leader J. C. Macdonald of No.102 Squadron in Whitley N1380 'R-Robert'. Macdonald's wireless operator, Bill Jacobs sums up the crews feelings about their first bombing operation against a land target:

'Now we were to drop bombs deliberately for the first time on German soil, and spirits were high. By the time we were in the locker room dressing for the raid, tension was being released with much noise, ribald comment and song – 'Any Old Iron' – somehow seemed to fit the occasion'.

In clear moonlit conditions Squadron Leader Macdonald was first on the target, and after releasing flares to assist target identification, he commenced his bombing run. It was at that moment that the defences came to life with snaking arcs of multi-coloured light flak and occasional bursts of the 'Flaming Onions' - wads of wire linked phosphorus, which exploded uncomfortably close. There was also much searchlight activity but Macdonald successfully released his bombs and brought 'R-Robert' through unscathed.

Wing Commander Bill Staton, the burly C.O. of No.10 Squadron, had meanwhile arrived early at the target area and had decided, much to the dismay of his crew, to

circle and watch the other aircraft bomb. At forty-two, Bill Staton - known to his crews as 'King Kong'- was fitter than most men half his age. He had flown Bristol Fighters with the Royal Flying Corps in the First World War and had won the Military Cross. Absolutely fearless, this larger than life character thought that the war was tremendously exciting and had been put on for his benefit. After so many boring leaflet raids he couldn't wait to get into the air and have a real crack at the Germans. Ignoring the hosing flak and weaving searchlights, Staton flew his Whitley calmly back and forth across the target, fascinated by the spectacle below. Eventually, much to the relief of his crew, Staton ordered the bombs to be dropped and headed for home.

One Whitley was not so fortunate and would become the only loss of the night. Flying Officer Birch in K9043 of 51 Squadron had been attacked earlier by a floatplane but fortunately was able to evade his opponent. It is possible that this same floatplane shot down Whitley N1405 (Flight Lieutenant J. Baskerville) also of 51 Squadron. Flight Lieutenant Baskerville was the unfortunate pilot who attacked the British submarine in the North Sea in December 1939. No trace of his Whitley or crew were ever found.

Of the thirty Whitleys that took part in the raid, twenty-six claimed to have attacked the target, one failed to locate the target, one returned early with engine trouble and one aircraft failed to return. All the bomb-aimers claimed to have clearly seen the target and as far as they were concerned their bombs had found their mark. Many hits were reported on hangars, slipways and living quarters and a huge fire was seen to be raging as the last aircraft left the target. However, photographic evidence from reconnaissance Blenheims, taken on the 6th April, indicated that no damage had been inflicted on the target. All the buildings and installations at Hornum remained outwardly intact. Surely the Germans had not been able to effect repairs in such a short time. Inevitably the conclusion was drawn that crews had been far too over-optimistic in their assessment of their efforts. The Bomber Command report on the operation concluded that, 'the operation does not confirm that, as a general rule, the average crew can identify targets at night, even under the best conditions, nor does it prove that the average crew can bomb industrial or other enemy targets at night'.

Meanwhile back in Yorkshire, No.10 Squadron and their extrovert commander Bill Staton were basking in their newly won fame. The press had been invited to Dishforth and on the following day headlines in the *Daily Mirror* told of 'Crack 'Em' Staton, leader of the first bombing raid on Germany and first of the Dishforth-based Whitleys on target. Over at Driffield the crews of 102 and 77 Squadrons were not impressed by this outrageous 'line shoot' particularly as it had been a Driffield Whitley that had in fact led the attack. Not to be outdone a hastily prepared 'Nickel' raid was carried out on Dishforth by a Whitley from No.77 Squadron dropping leaflets offering, 'Congratulations to Crack 'Em and Co from an admiring Driffield'. In addition a 'raiding party' of officers from Driffield sabotaged the mess at Dishforth with suitable inscribed greetings hidden behind pictures and under carpets. Retaliation was swift when a few days later No.10 Squadron returned the compliment showering Driffield with neatly printed toilet paper.

The frivolous mood was not to last, however, as on the 28th March news was received that of two No.77 Squadron Whitleys missing from a 'Nickel' raid to the Ruhr the night before, one had been reported shot down over Holland. On its return journey from the Ruhr Whitley N1357 (Flying Officer Geach), had unsuspectingly strayed into neutral Dutch territory, and at 07.00 hours, had been shot down by a Dutch fighter. The Observer, Sergeant Miller, was killed when he jumped from the aircraft at sixty feet and his parachute failed to open. The remainder of the crew were safe, interned in Holland.

On the 7th April No.4 Group Headquarters, which had been based at Linton-on-Ouse since June 1937, moved to the palatial surroundings of Heslington Hall, an Elizabethan mansion in the village of Heslington a few miles from the city of York. Squadron Leader Vernon Noble was No.4 Group public relations officer from 1940 to 1943 and was based at Heslington Hall.

'The Air Ministry had set up a Directorate of Public Relations, staffed by officers who were experienced journalists. Their job was to live and fly with the crews and write their stories, as well as providing a daily operations bulletin for Air Ministry News Service.

'I was recruited on the strength of my features writing for a national newspaper and as an author of magazine short stories. The Air Ministry had taken over this lovely old house at Heslington with its oak-panelled rooms and corridors, coats of arms on walls and ceilings looking incongruously down on uniformed men and women, and with boxtrees clipped in the shapes of chessmen on the lawns at the rear. I was allocated a small room on the top floor, overlooking a statue of Diana the Huntress in the forecourt, and across the corridor was the office of the Air Officer Commanding, Air Vice-Marshal Arthur Coningham.

An example of the leaflet, printed on toilet paper, dropped by crews from 10 Squadron on Driffield in retaliation for a similar 'Nickel' raid by the Dishforth squadrons. *I. M. Lucas*

Whitley Mk.V N1380 'R' of No.102 Squadron, April 1940. Piloted by Squadron Leader J. C. Macdonald, this was the first RAF aircraft to drop bombs on German soil. The occasion was the raid on the German seaplane bases at Hornum on the island of Sylt on the night of 19th March 1940. This particular illustration is believed to be a ground 'shot' that has been retouched. *Real Photographs*

Fie Fie ! Oh Driffield,
You didn't have to tell us,
Honours lie easily on our heads,
You must be frightfully jealous.

But then you came in rather late,
Still—it must be galling,
To have your thunder stolen away,
We sympathise—It's appalling.

Rumours reach us of your navigation,
Spread by that lying jade ;
Of your "Drivers" hitting the wrong constellation,
Over Hunland—where a landing was made.

And there are tales of indiscriminate bombing,
On mackerel in the Great North Sea,
But we're nice and accept all these stories
With a large pinch of S.Y.L.T.

But we're BIG and we wish you the best of luck,
And when your next job is "on,"
Remember we'll always help you out.
Lots of love—10 and 51.

Heslington Hall as it was in wartime. This beautiful old house just outside York was used as the headquarters of No.4 Group from April 1940 to April 1947. Today, Heslington Hall forms part of York University. *G. Clapperton*

Driffield groundcrew load 'Nickels', packets of propaganda leaflets, into No.102 Squadron Whitley Mk.V 'P-Peter', April 1940. *IWM, C912*

Opposite: Whitley Mk.V N1357 'KN-H' of No.77 Squadron. Returning from the Ruhr, on the night of 28th March 1940, N1357 was shot down by a Dutch fighter. *IWM, C966*

A 102 Squadron Whitley Mk.V comes into land at Driffield early 1940. *IWM, C914*

Another Whitley Mk.V of 102 prepares to leave Driffield on an air test, whilst in the background, groundcrews are busy preparing other aircraft for the night's work. *IWM, C923*

'The Hall was formerly the home of the Deramore family, and the heir to the title, the Hon Stephen de Yarburgh-Bateson, was an operations officer posted to his own residence, working in what was once the drawing room. Now it was 'furnished' with tables and telephones and boards on the wall on which were chalked the identification letters and numbers of each aircraft in the squadrons which were taking part in the night's attack, their time of departure, estimated time over the target, diversions if any, and the time of return – if they were lucky. Stephen Bateson, as we knew him (he became Lord Deramore after the war) pointed out to me the coincidence of one of the family mottoes, *Nocte Volamus* - 'We fly by night' - with bats wings on the crest.

'Here at the headquarters worked the administrative officers for the Group, the specialists in gunnery, navigation, engineering and the like, each with his own office and closely linked with the airfields, and the intelligence officers had their own large room. The Hall was the scene of ceaseless activity, day and night, peopled by men and WAAFs who seemed to get little opportunity for rest and yet never lost their cheerfulness. Certainly my own WAAF driver (I had a rota of them) had to be inexhaustible, ready to rush me off to an airfield at a minutes notice to interview crews. In the darkness of night before dawn it was astonishing how she could find her way through unmarked roads and lanes of the Yorkshire countryside to remote airfields'.

Two days after the new No.4 Group HQ became operational, moves of a more sinister kind were taking place off the coast of Norway. On the morning of 9th April, with a speed and efficiency that took everyone by surprise the German invasion of Scandinavia began.

Chapter Four

Norway

As far back as January 1940 Hitler had ordered plans to be drawn up for a possible intervention in Norway. Code-named *Weserubung* (Exercise *Weser*) the plan was designed to forestall any attempt by the British to seize the important Norwegian ports and airfields thus enabling them to seal off the entire North Sea from Scapa Flow to Stavanger. Early intelligence had warned of German preparations but warnings to the Norwegian government were ignored.

Surprised and caught off balance by the swiftness of the German move the Allies reaction to it was both late and disorganised and by the evening of the 9th April all the key Norwegian ports were in German hands. Attempts to intervene by the Royal Navy were thwarted by the Luftwaffe who quickly began to concentrate their forces at the newly captured airfields of Stavanger, Vaernes and Fornebu - enabling the Germans to mount crippling attacks on the units of the Home Fleet. With an Allied landing to capture Narvik planned to take place on the 15th it became imperative that the Luftwaffe bases should be put out of action at the earliest possible moment, and consequently Bomber Command was instructed to mount attacks against the important airfields, in particular Stavanger-Sola which commanded the approaches to Bergen, Trondheim and Narvik.

No.4 Group was called into action initially on the night of 11th April when, together with Hampdens of 5 Group, an attack was launched against a concentration of shipping in the Skagerrak and although, what looked like an ammunition ship was seen to explode, bad weather generally hampered the operation. A Whitley from No.77 Squadron, N1347 (Pilot Officer Saddington) failed to return from the raid.

It was against the vital airfields that all efforts were now concentrated and on the night of 15th Stavanger-Sola was attacked. Twelve Whitleys from No.10 and No.102 Squadrons, operating from Kinloss, carried out the raid. Seven aircraft claimed to have attacked the target which was heavily defended by concentrations of light flak, the streams of red, yellow and white tracer rounds coming at the attacking Whitleys horizontally from the surrounding high ground. Five aircraft returned early either with technical trouble or because of severe weather.

The following night the airfields at Oslo/Fornebu and Vaernes near Trondheim were the targets for the Whitleys of Nos. 10, 51 and 77 Squadrons. Wing Commander Staton from 10 Squadron in Whitley K9036, together with two aircraft from 51 Squadron, attempted a reconnaissance/bombing mission to the Oslo area, including the airfield at Fornebu. Unfortunately all three aircraft experienced severe icing and had to abandon the operation. Meanwhile three Whitleys from No.77 Squadron, led by Squadron Leader Hastings, were detailed to attack Vaernes airfield, west of Trondheim. Ivon Pacey, on his first operation that night, was rear gunner with Squadron Leader Hastings' crew in Whitley N1387 'L-London'.

'I had only just joined the squadron, having come from No.78, 4 Group's reserve unit, and this was to be my first operational flight. Squadron Leader Hastings always made up his own crew from the new arrivals prior to their being assigned to permanent crews. I was assigned to his crew as tail-end Charlie and would be flying with the rank of AC1 (Aircraftman 1st Class), later all NCO aircrew were made up to Sergeant. At this time the Air Gunner's insignia was a brass winged bullet, worn on the upper arm although later this was to be replaced with the half-brevet worn above the left upper pocket.

'Hastings was one of the 'old school', cool as a cucumber, resolute and a stickler for carrying out everything according to the book.

'Take-off was at 15.30 hours and we were to proceed to Kinloss to refuel and then on to our objective the German-held airfield at Vaernes. However, thick cloud over Trondheim made it impossible for us to locate the target, in those days positive identification of a target before bombing was the order of the day, so the skipper had no choice but to abandon the mission. So I settled myself down for the long flight home and remembering the Horlicks tablets and Kit-Kats provided for the journey, made myself a passable meal. After several hours with nothing but the steady drone from the twin Merlins for comfort I was beginning to feel rather lonely as I peered out through the perspex at the cold blackness of the night sky. Suddenly I was startled by the voice of the skipper on the intercom, 'Hello Pacey, a bit of bad news I'm afraid, we have 10/10ths cloud over Kinloss and there is not enough fuel to go elsewhere, sorry this is your first op but you will have to bale out, I'll tell you when to go, you know the drill, best of luck'. 'Are we over land?' I enquired. 'Yes, but we are in thick cloud', replied the skipper.

'Hell, I thought, isn't this a bit of alright, I may have practised the parachute drill out of a Whitley whilst it was on the deck in a hangar but this was for real. I heard the pilot tell the Observer to go out then it came, 'OK Pacey away you go'. Must remember the drill – place guns in fully lowered position, remove intercom and oxygen leads, slide out of turret, close and secure turret doors, take parachute from stowage point at the starboard side of the fuselage, fasten to harness by the two self-locking hooks on chest, open top hatch above head, stand on seat and ease out of hatch – watch out for slipstream, sit on top of fuselage, ease yourself past tailplane •to turret dome, stand on turret dome, grasp rip-cord handle, jump, count to three then pull rip-cord. The sudden violent jerk told me the parachute had opened and I was floating in cotton wool clouds. For some reason I seemed to be floating upwards instead of down, I thought I was not heavy enough for the 'chute and started bouncing in the harness to put things right. Much to my relief I soon realised, as I became used to the dark, that I was indeed descending and apart from heavy showers of snow swirling about me everything seemed to be functioning correctly.

'After what seemed an eternity and without any warning I hit the ground. Fortunately thick cushioning snow broke my fall but I still managed to twist my ankle painfully on landing. It was almost 05.00 and still dark and as I had no idea where I was I decided not to move but wrapped the 'chute around me and wait for daylight. When it came I found that I had come down in the mountains. In the distance I spotted a small shack at the base of a hill and as I headed towards it I could see a welcoming wisp of smoke coming from the chimney stack. It turned out to be a shepherd's mountain retreat and after a brief exchange I was able to convince a graggy looking Scottish shepherd that I was not a German parachutist but a weary English airman. 'Enough said, have a wee dram' says the Scot, 'and I'll take you to my Laird'.

'Well, taking me to his Laird involved a five mile hike through the valleys, but on arrival I was made most welcome and scotch pancakes with hot coffee were soon on the scene. A 'phone call to the nearest aerodrome was made and then I was conducted to the local police station in the village of Boat of Garten, not far from Aviemore, there to be reunited with my Wireless Operator'.

A Whitley Mk.V of No.102 Squadron (possibly
N1386) takes-off from Driffield in April 1940.
IWM, C916

The eighth production Whitley Mk.V, N1352,
photographed in August 1939. As KN-B of
No.77 Squadron, skipper Pilot Officer Hall,
was forced to ditch N1352 off Trondheim on
the night of 18/19th April 1940.
Real Photographs

Ivon Pacey's aircraft had come down near
Grantown-on-Spey, Squadron Leader Hastings having stayed with the Whitley and performed a perfect crash landing. The other
members of the crew were safe with only the
Observer suffering a broken leg from his
parachute descent. Whitley N1387, however,
was wrecked.

Until April 1940 no Whitley crew had managed to survive the ordeal of ditching their
aircraft in the sea. To carry out a successful
crash landing of an aircraft at sea, even in
relatively calm, daylight conditions, required
a high degree of skill, not to mention luck, on
the part of the pilot. To ditch an aircraft at
night in unfriendly, storm tossed seas was
extremely hazardous, particularly if the aircraft had suffered damage.

The design of the Armstrong Whitworth
Whitley did not exactly lend itself to making a
successful ditching at sea. The large frontal
area of the Tiger radial engines on the early
models and the bulky Galley radiators of the
Merlin-engined variants had a disturbing
tendency, when the aircraft struck the sea, to
cause the Whitley to 'nose in' even in moderate sea conditions. This would result in either
the aircraft sinking rapidly nose first or, the
front section quickly filling with water giving
the crew little chance of escape. The pos-

itioning and relatively few number of
emergency exits in the Whitley made rapid
escape difficult for crew members huddled
together at their ditching stations. The pilot
could make use of the outward opening hatch
in the roof of the cockpit, that is provided he
had time to free himself from his harness in a
cabin rapidly filling with water. Otherwise he
had to use the main entrance door situated
on the port side of the fuselage. This door was
the main escape route for the other members
of the crew who previously would have been
positioned at their ditching stations behind
the main bulkhead. This centre section door
opened outwards and upwards and unless it
was jettisoned before ditching it would be
extremely difficult to open with the aircraft in
the sea. It was not until later in the war that
revised instructions were issued to crews
that on ditching the Whitley the second pilot

should open the centre section door and
make sure it was jettisoned before the aircraft
hit the sea. This was to be accomplished by
hacking at the door fastenings with the fire
axe, provided that there was time. The other
exit points in an emergency were positioned
at the extreme front and rear of the fuselage,
the former a lower escape hatch under the
bomb aiming position and useless in the
event of an aircraft in the sea, and the latter a
small escape hatch in the roof of the rear
fuselage directly behind the rear turret and a
long way from the centre section ditching station.

On the night of 18/19th April, Flying Officer
Ray Chance was second pilot in Whitley Mk.V
N1352 'B-Baker', one of three aircraft from
No.77 Squadron detailed to attack shipping in
Trondheim Fjord and carry out a reconnais-
sance of the airfield at Vaernes. The crew of

'B-Baker' were destined to become the first Whitley crew to escape from their ditched aircraft.

'The plan was that we flew to Kinloss to refuel and bomb up and then onto Trondheim. I was with a scratch crew that night. Due to illness two crews were joined together, so I was among strangers. The skipper was Pilot Officer Hall, recently commissioned having served with No.77 Squadron as a sergeant pilot. Pilot Officer Hall handled the take-off then I took over. Whitleys flew with two pilots in those days, both trained as Navigators.

'Take-off was at 1935 hours and all went well until some thirty miles from Trondheim when the starboard engine began to give trouble and almost immediately stopped dead. I could see flames glowing in the dead engine and as we began to lose height rapidly Pilot Officer Hall insisted that he took over control of the aircraft. This was really exasperating for me, particularly in this situation, as I had been an instructor at Abingdon teaching pilots how to fly Whitleys on one engine. I had no choice but to vacate the pilots seat to Pilot Officer Hall who, although was junior in rank compared with myself, was the captain of the aircraft. I left him in the cockpit and went back to organise the rest of the crew for ditching. We had two non-swimmers in the crew so I told them to stick near me as I was a strong swimmer. I took off my Irving jacket and put on my 'Mae West' life jacket. We then threw out everything to lighten the aircraft but it was to no avail as we kept losing height.

'I had never heard of anyone surviving a Whitley ditching and I thought it might have been because the main exit door, situated half way down the fuselage, was hinged at the top to open outwards. It could happen that when the aircraft was in the sea, water pressure would prevent the door from being opened from the inside. There was one thought in my mind, I must get that door open, so I reached for the fire axe and chopped the door away and it flew off into the darkness.

'As we came down through 10,000 feet I took up a position at the open door and gave a running commentary as cheerfully as I could. Meanwhile the Wireless Operator, Leading Aircraftman O'Brien, continued to send out a *May Day* distress signal all the way down until I told him to take up his ditching station just before we went into the sea. Then it happened. I could just make out the wave crests in the darkness when from an estimated 500 feet the aircraft went into a near vertical dive and smacked into the sea. It was then that everything went black. I was flung from half way down the fuselage into the cockpit area and knocked unconscious. The aircraft had burst into flames on impact and when I came round the top half of the fuselage was blazing fiercely and the lower half was rapidly filling with water. As I began to gather my senses I could see flames from the burning petrol on the surface of the sea showing through the open fuselage door. Unaware of my injuries (I had sustained a broken ankle and suffered a hairline fracture of the skull) I crawled towards the open door where I saw two of the chaps clinging desperately to the tailplane. Nobody had gone for the dinghy which was stowed in the rear of the fuselage so I reached for the dinghy parcel and threw it towards the blackness near the tail. The water was on fire from the spreading petrol so I dived under and popped up clear of the flames. I then reached for the dinghy parcel and released the pull string that automatically inflated the dinghy. I helped the two chaps who were clinging onto the tail into the dinghy while a third emerged from the darkness from the other side of the aircraft.

'At this time there seemed to be no sign of the pilot. With three of the crew safely in the dinghy I noticed to my dismay that the wind was blowing us into the burning petrol near the aircraft. I seized the rope on the side of the dinghy and swam on my back with one arm and one leg. I nearly fainted at this stage but the rest of the crew told me later that I never stopped swimming. By pulling on the dinghy I was just able to keep us from the flames.

'After about ten minutes the aircraft burnt out and the last we saw of it was when the tail turret disappeared beneath the waves. The others then tried to pull me in the dinghy but without success as my foot had become entangled in the ropes underneath and everyone was so exhausted and beginning to feel the effects of the numbing cold. Apparently the dinghy had inflated upside down in the confusion. I waited about fifteen minutes until I had somewhat recovered from the effects of my swim and then dived under and successfully released my foot. The others then hauled me into the dinghy whereupon I collapsed exhausted.

'It was then that we heard Pilot Officer Hall calling for help. It was a nightmare but there was nothing we could do. We were all by then so desperately exhausted and suffering from exposure. His voice grew weaker and weaker. Once I tried to go over the side and swim to the sound of his voice but when I tried to move I fell back into the dinghy helpless. The sound of his calls became fainter and then after about thirty minutes we heard no more. It haunts me to this day that I could not save him.

'After about five hours, it must have been 02.00 hours, we heard the sound of engines and I looked up thinking it must be one of our aircraft going back. Then someone pointed to a darker shape in the water about 100 yards from us. I thought it was a U-boat. We shouted 'Are you British'. A searchlight then came on us!'

The ship was the destroyer HMS *Basilisk*, later to be sunk at Dunkirk. The First Officer, told Ray Chance later that the *Basilisk* had entered a Norwegian minefield in pursuit of a submarine and had mistaken the airmen's dinghy for a mine and were about to shoot at it when they heard calls for help. The other members of 'B-Baker's' crew that night were Sergeant Tindall (Observer Bomb-aimer), Leading Aircraftman O'Brien (Wireless Operator), Aircraftman Douglas (Tail gunner). The body of the pilot, Pilot Officer Hall was later found washed up at Lerwick on 29th April.

As the situation in Norway deteriorated Bomber Command was asked to step up its attacks on the enemy airfields. On 20th April twelve Whitleys from Nos. 10, 51 and 58 Squadrons attacked Stavanger-Sola airfield in the face of heavy and sustained anti-aircraft fire. On the night of 22nd April No.51 Squadron sent six aircraft to the Danish airfield of Aalborg, one of the main assembly points for German transport aircraft ferrying supplies to Norway. Again the Whitleys were met by heavy anti-aircraft fire and one aircraft, K9043 (Flying Officer Birch) was shot down.

Losses on these airfield attacks, although not heavy, nonetheless did not justify the negligible results obtained. To reach their distant objectives the aircraft of Bomber Command were forced to operate at their maximum range and the small bomb loads carried meant damage inflicted was minimal. To knock out a target such as an airfield required a huge weight of bombs to crater runways and destroy aircraft and installations. Bomber Command just did not possess the necessary capability in 1940 and the most that could be achieved with the force available was to cause temporary disruption.

By the end of April the Norwegian situation had become so critical that the Allies had decided to abandon Central Norway and concentrate all available forces against Narvik, thereby securing the blocking of the German iron ore supply route. By 3rd May the Franco-British forces at Namsos and Andalsnes had been evacuated. Direct support by Bomber Command of the ground forces was out of the question because of the distance involved. The end of April saw the last attacks mounted against the airfields.

Twenty-four Whitleys struck at Stavanger-Sola and Fornebu on the night of the 30th. No.58 Squadron lost one aircraft and another from 51 Squadron, K9039 (Pilot Officer Cotton), ran out of fuel on the return journey and crashed at Burnside Fell, Yorkshire, killing two and injuring three of the crew. Three of the attacking force all from No.10 Squadron, were forced to return early when it was discovered that the armourers had left the safety pins in their bombs. The next night twelve Whitleys from Nos. 10, 77 and 102 Squadrons attacked the same airfields and in clear conditions crews reported seeing sticks of bombs bursting across hangars and amongst dispersed aircraft.

The tragic situation in Norway in the first week of May 1940, and the final moves leading to the complete occupation of that country, were rapidly overtaken by events of a more dramatic nature taking place in the Low Countries.

Chapter Five

The Storm Breaks

In October 1939 plans had been prepared in the event of a decisive German breakthrough in the west for Bomber Command to carry out a massive daylight assault on the Ruhr. Known as the 'Ruhr Plan' this attack on Germany's vital industrial heartland was designed to inflict a crushing, if not fatal, blow against German morale. The French High Command, however, showed little enthusiasm for the British plan. Imbued with a defensive outlook on the war, the French regarded the use of heavy bombers for anything less than the support of the ground forces as a diversion and waste of effort. They argued that Bomber Command would be much better employed attacking German troop columns, military communications and airfields. In addition the French were fearful of German reprisal raids against their own vulnerable industrial regions.

Partly because of the French objections, plus the risk of heavy casualties – perhaps as high as 50% of the attacking force, the – 'Ruhr Plan' was dropped in favour of a more flexible strategy. This was to include attacks on oil plants as well as communications. The 'Ruhr Plan' would only be resorted to in the most dire of emergencies.

When the Germans launched their attack on the Low Countries on 10th May 1940, units of the RAF's Advanced Air Striking Force, equipped with their vulnerable Fairey Battle light bombers, were the first to go into action, attacking advancing German columns passing through Luxembourg. The Battles suffered fearful casualties when they ran into a storm of anti-aircraft fire. Meanwhile in London the new Prime Minister, Winston Churchill, found one of his first tasks was to face demands for the immediate employment of the RAF's heavy bomber squadrons to stem the tide in France and the Low Countries. As the War Cabinet hesitated the situation on the Continent became more grim by the hour. Eventually, after repeated requests for help from the commander of the RAF in France, Air Marshal Barratt, Bomber Command was instructed to join in the battle. On the night of 10th May, Waalhaven airfield was attacked by thirty-six Wellingtons. On the same night, nine Whitleys from No.77 and No.102 Squadrons bombed lines of communication on the routes of the German advance through southern Holland. The Whitley's targets included road and rail junctions at Geldern, Goch, Aldekerk, Rees and Wesel. These proved very difficult targets to locate and considerable time was spent in the target area pin-pointing by the light of flares before bombing.

The following night Bomber Command made history by launching its first large scale attack against the German mainland when seventeen Whitleys from Nos. 51, 58, 77 and 102 Squadrons joined eighteen Hampdens in bombing road and rail communications near Mönchengladbach. Two Hampdens and one Whitley from No.77 Squadron, N1366 (Pilot Officer Parrott), failed to return. German reinforcements passing through Mönchengladbach were again the target on the night of 14th May when five Whitleys from 102 Squadron and seven from No.77 attacked crowded road and rail junctions from as low as 4,000 feet. Crews from 77 Squadron reported many hits on crossroads choked with vehicles whilst near the railway running through the town large fires were started. Altogether the Whitleys dropped twenty-six 500 lb and forty 250 lb bombs. All the raiders returned safely. Earlier, on the afternoon of that same day, German Heinkel He 111 bombers from Kampfgeschwader 54 attacked Rotterdam, destroying large areas of the old city and inflicting heavy casualties on the civilian population.

The Germans were now indulging in indiscriminate bombing and as result civilians were being killed and made homeless. Reluctantly Bomber Command was authorised to attack targets east of the Rhine as a direct reprisal for the Rotterdam bombing. On the night of 15th May 1940 ninety-nine Wellingtons, Whitleys and Hampdens from Nos. 3, 4 and 5 Groups struck at targets in the Ruhr and immediately west of the Rhine. The strategic air offensive had begun.

Targets for that night included oil plants, steelworks, rail junctions, marshalling yards, autobahns and airfields. No.4 Group dispatched thirty Whitleys - nine each from Nos. 51 and 58 Squadrons and twelve from No.10. Their targets included oil plants at Wanne-Eickel and Gelsenkirchen, marshalling yards at Schwerte, an electricity station at Reisholz and blast furnaces and rail centres at Düsseldorf. In the hazy conditions many crews had difficulty finding their objectives, consequently, only a small proportion of the force claimed to have attacked their allotted targets.

Whatever hopes held by the War Cabinet that attacks by Bomber Command would halt the German advance were soon dispelled. On 13th May the Germans broke through at Sedan and on the 15th the Dutch surrendered. Paul Reynaud, the French Prime Minister, awoke Winston Churchill with an early telephone call on the morning of the 15th declaring, 'we have been defeated'.

The Germans swept into France and there was little that Bomber Command could do to stem the avalanche. Attacks by the heavy bombers continued on the 16th, 17th, 18th and 19th May but they were unco-ordinated and haphazard. Marshalling yards at Aachen and Maastricht were the targets for the Whitleys of 4 Group on the night of the 16th and oil plants at Bremen were bombed on the 17th. During this attack, carried out by nineteen Whitleys from Nos. 10 and 51 Squadrons, four aircraft from No.10 circled the area firing green Very lights to attract the rest of the force. This was one of the earliest attempts at target marking and a harbinger of things to come.

Oil refineries were again the targets on 18th May, this time at Hannover, and from an attacking force of nineteen Whitleys one each from 51 and 77 Squadrons failed to return. Flight Lieutenant Raphael and crew flew Whitley Mk.V N1388, one of seven aircraft from No.77 Squadron which took off that night for Hannover. The night was clear except for a slight haze near the ground. When some sixty miles from the Dutch coast and flying at 9,000 feet Raphael's Whitley was attacked by a Messerschmitt Bf 110 nightfighter firing a lethal combination of cannon and machine gun fire. The effect was devastating on the unarmoured bomber and almost immediately one of the Whitley's engines burst into flames. As the Bf 110 passed over the doomed bomber's tail the rear gunner, Aircraftman Parkes, directed a well aimed burst of fire from his four Brownings into the belly of the night-fighter. The enemy aircraft was seen to burst into flames and dive into the sea. Meanwhile Flight Lieutenant Raphael, despite suffering from bullet wounds, successfully brought the disabled Whitley down onto the sea and the crew were able to get safely into their dinghy. After four hours they were picked up by a destroyer and landed at Yarmouth. Aircraftman Parkes success that night was the first confirmed 'kill' by a No.4 Group gunner.

The German's oil industry, particularly their synthetic oil producing plants, were high priority targets. The synthetic oil plant at Gelsenkirchen-Buer was attacked by six aircraft from Nos. 102 and 77 Squadrons on the night of 19th May. It was to prove an

unlucky night for No.102 with two out of four of their number failing to return: N1417 'B' (Flying Officer Logman) and N1376 'O' (Flight Sergeant Hall) falling to the Ruhr defences.

With the situation in France now desperate, the heavy bombers were redirected to try to stem the tide of the German advance. The important road bridges across the River Oise at Catillon, Hannapes and Mont-d'Origny, on the line of the enemy thrust towards Arras, were attacked by twenty-four Whitleys on the night of the 20th. Crews from 10 Squadron reported direct hits on the bridge at Mont-d'Origny. Two Whitleys failed to return. The following night No.4 Group mounted its greatest effort to date when thirty-eight Whitleys were despatched to attack rail junctions and marshalling yards at Julich and Euskirchen. A Whitley Mk.V from No.10 Squadron, P4955 (Pilot Officer Cattell), was attacked by four single-engined fighters at 5,000 feet over Julich railway station. The enemy aircraft attacked from astern and came to within 400 yards. In all seven attacks were made but remarkably no damage or casualties were sustained. Thirty-two crews reported successful attacks that night with two aircraft failing to return, one each from Nos. 51 and 102 Squadrons. Pilot Officer Wormersley and crew of 102 Squadron's N1528 'E', successfully bailed out near Metz and were reported safe.

During the battle for France the Air Staff were under pressure to justify Bomber Command's duel strategy in support of the land forces. On the one hand encouraging reports were being received from Germany about the effects of the strategic attacks on the Ruhr (these reports later proved to be untrue). On the other hand the French High Command were appealing for total and immediate air support for their beleaguered forces. To the French the attacks on Ruhr industry were irrelevant when the need was to halt the Germans in France. But the Air Staff were not to be deflected from what they saw as the best way to help the land battle. Consequently, for the remaining weeks of the battle of France, Bomber Command continued to divide its efforts by attacking Ruhr industrial/oil and communications and French road/rail bridges and junctions.

Briefing, 1940 style, Linton-on-Ouse. No.58 Squadron crews listen intently. *IWM, CH219*

'Many hands make light work!' 250 lb GP bombs about to be hoisted into the bay of a Whitley Mk.V of No.58 Squadron. Armourers are using hand winches to hoist the bombs whilst helping hands steady the load into position. Note open bomb doors of wing bomb cells. *IWM, CH224*

'Steady as they go!' No.58 Squadron armourers bombing up a Whitley Mk.V at Linton-on-Ouse. *IWM, CH227*

Whitley Mk.V's of No.102 Squadron at Driffield. Nearest the camera is N1421 'C-Charlie'. *IWM, C921*

Silvan surroundings for 58 Squadron Whitley Mk.V N1426 'O' at Linton-on-Ouse, June 1940, as she patiently awaits her load of bombs.

N1426 came to grief whilst on a cross country flight when serving with 19 OTU in July 1941. *IWM, CH223*

No.4 Group's contribution to this effort was to attack road and rail bridges and road junctions at Hirson, Givet, Aulnoye and Bapaume on the nights of 22nd, 23rd and 25th May. In addition industrial/oil plants and rail traffic at Leverkusen, Duisberg, Mannheim and Essen were attacked on the 24th and 25th. In four days 114 sorties were flown for the loss of one aircraft, but bombing results proved to be poor. The French targets, river crossings and road junctions, were almost impossible to bomb accurately at night. The Ruhr targets were even more difficult to bomb shrouded as they almost inevitably were in industrial haze.

On the night of 27th May the Ruhr marshalling yards were the target for thirty-six Whitleys from No.4 Group. On the way to the target Pilot Officer Warren of 10 Squadron, flying in Whitley P4952, ran into a severe magnetic storm whilst crossing the North Sea. After struggling for some time to control the aircraft in the storm the pilot asked the Navigator, Sergeant Donaldson, for a course to their secondary target, Flushing airfield in Holland. They were by now hopelessly behind schedule due to the buffeting they had received in the storm. Turning onto their new heading the crew commenced a search of the sea below for a pinpoint. At last they saw the Rhine Estuary below and soon after, the flarepath of Flushing airfield. They successfully dropped their bombs on the target, the airfield runway, and headed back to Dishforth. It was not until first light, when they arrived over Liverpool instead of Dishforth, that they discovered to their horror that their compass had been thrown out of true by the storm. They had mistaken the Thames Estuary for the Rhine and had neatly laid a stick of bombs across the Fighter Command airfield at Bassingbourn in Cambridgeshire. Fortunately there were no casualties or damage. However, Pilot Officer Warren was demoted to second pilot and known to the rest of 10 Squadron from then on as 'Baron von Warren'.

May 1940 had been a costly month for Bomber Command. 2,419 sorties had been flown at a cost of seventy aircraft missing. No.4 Group had flown 350 sorties since 10th May and had lost eleven Whitleys. The last casualty of the month was the unlucky Flying Officer Geach of No.77 Squadron, shot down over France on the night of the 28th. Geach had been the pilot of the Whitley shot down by a Dutch fighter exactly two months earlier over then neutral Holland.

Meanwhile the German advance continued. On 28th May the Belgian army surrendered. By that date the Germans had reached the Channel coast and had split the allied armies in two. The British Expeditionary Force was being squeezed in the Dunkirk pocket and Operation *Dynamo*, the evacuation from Dunkirk – was under way. The Air Staff were still confident at the beginning of June, despite the desperate situation in France, of continuing effective long range bombing of industrial targets in Germany. At the beginning of the month the new AOC-in-C Bomber Command, Air Marshal C. F. A. Portal, was directed to continue the support of the land battle but the primary aim would be attacks on Germany's oil resources. It was believed at the time that if 300,000 tons or more of the enemy's oil stocks could be destroyed by August then they would be placed in a serious position. At the same time, anticipating the inevitable defeat of France and the commencement of aerial operations against Britain, the Air Staff directed that on moonless nights aircraft plants and their associated industries should be attacked.

The beginning of June 1940 saw No.4 Group better equipped to face the coming offensive. Although still operating with the original five squadrons, plus one in reserve, with which it had commenced hostilities in September 1939, the Group was by now using the improved Whitley Mk.V, the old Mk.IIIs and IVs having been transferred to the new Operational Training Units which had been formed in April 1940. The Bomber OTUs were formed to cope with the large number of aircrews required for the expansion of Bomber Command. These training units would eventually expand into large formations equipped with first line aircraft and, if the need arose, could become fully operational. Initially there were eight OTUs serving Bomber Command. No.10 Operational Training Unit, based at Abingdon, supplied crews to No.4 Group and was formed from Nos.97 and 166 Group Pool Squadrons. The unit's early equipment was Whitley Mk.IIs, IIIs, IVs and Avro Ansons.

No.4 Group's contribution to Bomber Command's campaign against the German oil industry, the so called 'Oil Plan', was to mount a series of attacks on oil targets in the Ruhr in early June. Bill Jacobs of 102 Squadron took part in these early visits to 'Happy Valley' as the Ruhr was soon to be called.

'In the first few days of June quite a large intake of new boys arrived and we began to feel somewhat overcrowded with bods; among them was a dapper Pilot Officer by the name of Cheshire. Those of us who had been with the Squadron before the outbreak of war had no notion that these new faces, when they were properly settled in, would soon replace us.

'First operation in June was on the 3rd in Whitley N1471. Raid FDM466: oil storage tanks at Essen. Take-off 21.00; duration 6 hours 45 minutes. Our route out took us over Rotterdam which we had seen burning only a few weeks earlier. At briefing we were assured that as we would not be lower than 10,000 feet and still climbing over that unfortunate city, we would be quite safe from ground defences as they could not possibly have anything there heavy enough to reach us. It transpired that as we approached the Dutch coast we could see the flak up ahead of us. And what a reception we received as we flew over Rotterdam. The first shot was right in front of our nose and spot on height, followed immediately by at least a dozen more close about us. I should also add that we were being firmly held by searchlights. Down went the nose in a steep dive to throw them off aim and we eventually got out of it with our height advantage lost.

'We managed to regain most of the lost height by the time we reached Essen. The night sky above the city was lit by probing searchlights, flares, exploding flak and those 'Flaming Onions' which seemed to twist their way heavenwards so lazily until, at closer quarters, they looked enormous as the whole string of them passed with a mighty sound of rushing air. Although horizontal visibility was good the vertical was affected by industrial haze and I was called upon to add some of our own flares to the illuminations. I was no sooner at the flarechute than we were held fast in a cone of searchlights which seemed to snap onto us instantaneously and we were immediately under concentrated fire. I could hear shrapnel peppering us as the nose went down and we started to weave all over the sky. Eventually we evaded the searchlights and resumed our search for the target. I dropped the first flare from about 5,000 feet but it produced nothing in the way of positive identification and I was asked for another. The releasing technique for flare dropping from the chute was to pull the release handle with the right hand at the same time giving the flare a push down with the left hand. I called out over the intercom 'Flare gone' and we started a wide turn to starboard. 'Where the hell's that bloody flare' came the pilot's call over the intercom. With the next flare already cradled in my arms I looked down the chute and saw to my horror that it was jammed across the mouth of the chute. I had not imparted sufficient impetus and the slipstream catching the tail fins had forced them back far enough to cause the nose of the flare to jam across the mouth of the chute. This situation posed great danger. If the magnesium charge in the flare ignited then the resulting explosion would at least cause serious structural damage and, most likely, fire. It had to be cleared and I asked the pilot for speed variations and erratic movement but it was to no avail.

'By removing the chute extension and taking care not to further extend the cable attached to the fuse cord, I reached down into the chute with my left arm and found I could just touch the rounded cap covering the fusesetting mechanism. I could not move it even by using my torch as an extension of my arm. Somehow I had to get hold of it and pull it back up the chute. My greatest worry was the possibility of the flare igniting in the chute and it seemed wise, therefore, to try to unhook the fuse cord from the cable. I removed my parachute harness, slipped the Mae West and Sidcot suit from my shoulders and took off my jacket. Now, with a bit of wriggling, I was able to get my shoulder further into the top of the chute and get a better grasp on the flare cap. I found the hook at the end of the wire, released the cord, and then I knew I was fairly safe. Somehow in sheer desperation I found sufficient strength in my overworked left arm to pull the flare back up the chute at least part way. I had thoughts of saving it but could not raise it more than a few inches, but enough to push it clear. All this had happened in less time than it has taken to describe in writing and the rest of the crew, being otherwise occupied whilst waiting for the flare, were quite oblivious to what was going on in the mid-fuselage.

'I quickly had the chute together again and this time successfully sent a flare on its way. The bomb-aimer was able to identify the target and during our first run we were the target for some rather inaccurate flak. Our second run was attended by more intense gunfire and we had to do a bit of weaving after releasing the last of our bombs. Back at base in the grey light of dawn we found that we had suffered quite a bit of flak damage. One shell had passed through the port aileron leaving a ragged hole about sixteen inches across and, presumably, had exploded above us, a good job that one wasn't instantaneous. A fairly large piece of shrapnel was also found in the casing of a flare in its stowage adjacent to the flarechute - only inches from where my head had been'.

Also operating that night was Whitley P4963 of No.10 Squadron (Flight Lieutenant Phillips), one of twenty-four aircraft from No.4 Group detailed to attack oil plants at

Homburg on the western bank of the Rhine. The Whitley developed engine trouble soon after bombing and was forced to make the return journey on one engine. Losing height all the time Phillips managed to coax the crippled aircraft as far as England only to crash at Battisford, Suffolk, whilst attempting to land at Wattisham airfield. The tail gunner, Pilot Officer Field died in the crash, Flying Officer Bagshaw and Sergeant Donald were injured. The Homburg oil plants had been attacked the previous night by Whitleys from Nos. 10 and 51 Squadrons. Squadron Leader Bickford of 10 Squadron had acted as a 'Pathfinder' aircraft on this raid by remaining in the target area continuously dropping flares to provide illumination for following aircraft. This proved hazardous as Bickford's Whitley became the target for Homburg's considerable anti-aircraft defences. In the process his aircraft was badly shot up, the rear gunner Aircraftman Cornforth being severely wounded.

This was not the first occasion that rudimentary 'Pathfinding' techniques had been employed by the Whitleys of No.4 Group. The firing of Very lights and the dropping of flares had been used to locate targets and to mark aiming points on earlier raids. These initial attempts to improve bombing accuracy were organised at squadron level, as Squadron Leader Mahaddie (later Group Captain T. G. Mahaddie DSO, DFC, AFC of Pathfinder fame) recalls the early experiments conducted by No.77 Squadron in June 1940.

The following extract is from Pathfinders at War by Chaz Bowyer, published by Ian Alllan Limited, 1977.

'Flying Officer 'Jimmy' Marks (later Wing Commander J. H. Marks) got a few of us together and suggested that we made a time-and-distance run from the seemingly ever-lasting fires of Rotterdam to the target – a large concentration of troops, some thirty-five miles away. It was a relatively easy business to navigate from Spurn Head to the Dutch coast since the glow of Rotterdam could be seen about 100 miles away. Marks suggested that after a careful time/distance run from the centre we would all drop a flare and at the same time fire a red Very light.

Whitley Mk.V's of No.58 Squadron await their crews. Ground staff make a few last minute adjustments in this late afternoon scene at Linton-on-Ouse in June 1940. In the foreground is N1460 'R-Robert'. Flying Officer McInnes and crew took this aircraft to Turin on the night of 11th June 1940 – one of ten No.4 Group crews who were able to reach their target – the Fiat Engine works. McInnes and crew failed to return in 'R-Robert' from the Ruhr just a week later. *IWM, CH222*

The interesting thing about this – in my experience the very first co-ordinated attempt to find a target – was that despite assurance of all the enthusiasts to the scheme, one Pilot Officer Leonard Cheshire included, that the run was made with great care, not one of the dozen or more taking part in this quite un-official effort claimed to have seen one of the other's flares or Very lights. This occasion was really under ideal conditions, from an easily-defined start point and with no oppos-ition. An afterthought, but one which may be taken as a portent of the future, was that Marks was not deterred by this initial failure and he then selected crews for his next exper-iment and reduced the numbers to the four best navigators in the squadron.

'Please remember that the navigator at this period was also the second pilot. I considered mine was as good as any on the station – he was included. On this occasion the timed run was made with a stopwatch, all compasses had been re-swung and the ASI recalibrated. At the end of the run from Rotterdam, and within a five second period, four flares and four Very lights were visible in a radius of approximately three miles and one flare had pinpointed the target – a large, distinctly shaped wood concealing troops and armour. At once more flares were identifying the target area and a fair concentration of bombs directed at the aimimg point. This was con-firmed by the immediate reaction from the ground. The time it should be recalled, was June 1940'.

As the last remnants of the BEF were being evacuated from the beaches of Dunkirk and the fast disintegrating French army strove to hold back the tidal wave of the German advance, the Italian dictator, Mussolini, con-sidered that the time was right to move in for his share of the spoils. A possible Italian declaration of war had been anticipated by the allies and plans had been prepared for joint Anglo-French operations against Italy. Preparations for Bomber Command to carry out attacks on Italian targets from French bases were well advanced when Italy declared war as from midnight on 10th June 1940.

Operations from French bases by Welling-tons of Nos. 99 and 149 Squadrons, planned for the night of the 11th June, ran into unex-pected complications when local French authorities refused to allow the British bombers to leave. The French were fearful of Italian retaliation and the force commander was left with no choice but to abandon the raid. In anticipation of possible French opposition to the RAF using bases in southern France, the AOC-in-C Bomber Command had ordered the Whitleys of No.4 Group to pre-pare for a mission to Italy on the night of the 11th. The raid, an attack on the Fiat works at Turin, would involve a refuelling stop in the Channel Islands and the carriage of a minimum bomb load to enable the Whitleys to reach their distant target. The round trip

from the Channel Islands to Turin is approxi-mately 1,100 miles and with the Alps to negotiate, the Whitley crews and their air-craft would be stressed to the limit.

On a glorious summer afternoon the Whit-leys began to arrive at the airports of Jersey and Guernsey and after one or two dummy runs, as pilots struggled to land on the short runways, all thirty-six aircraft arrived safely and were immediately prepared for the night's work. Nos. 10, 51 and 58 Squadrons were to fly from Guernsey airport and Nos.77 and 102 from Jersey. The primary target would be the Fiat aero-engine and motor works in Turin, with the Ansaldo factories in Genoa as alternative.

Over France the No.4 Group force ran into severe electrical storms and above 10,000 feet the icing was severe. Bill Jacobs of 102 Squadron vividly remembers that night:

'About two and half hours out from Jersey and climbing to clear the Alps, we entered cloud and soon encountered severe turbu-lence. Electrical disturbance was quite the worst any of us had ever experienced and the noise in my headphones was unbearable. Fearing for my wireless equipment led me to disconnect the aerials and in so doing I suf-fered some superficial burns to the fingers of my right hand. It became agonizingly cold and we soon felt the depth of its penetration'.

Another Whitley, that of Squadron Leader Hanafin of 10 Squadron, was also struggling to get above the cloud and icing. Hanafin managed to work his aircraft up to 12,000 feet but no higher because of the weight of icing forming on his Whitley. The aircraft's trailing aerial was then struck by lightning, severely burning the hands of the wireless operator. Squadron Leader Hanafin was left with no choice but to abandon the mission. Other crews were coming to the same conclusion. Bill Jacobs again:

'The cloud seemed solid and without top as we struggled laboriously for height. We now heard ominous bumps as of something strik-ing the aircraft and soon deduced that ice was being flung off the propellers. The skipper asked me to shine the Aldis lamp along the leading edges of the wings and we could see the ice building up, despite the action of the pulsating de-icer boots. The ice formed with great rapidity and soon we could see it build-ing up thickly over the leading edges and we began to wallow very badly. We descended rapidly as low as we dared but there was no improvement in our condition which was now one of extreme hazard. We were obvi-ously not going to make it this trip and reluc-tantly decided to abort'.

Ivon Pacey, rear gunner with a Whitley from No.77 Squadron, recalls how his aircraft was beaten by the severe conditions:

'We just had to get more height to clear the Alps but our poor old Whitley was not up to the task. Ice was constantly building upon the wings and control surfaces and the cockpit windows and turrets became heavily coated. The anti-icing Glycol just could not cope and

eventually 'boiled over' issuing out great clouds of steam in the sub-zero tempera-tures. There was no way we were going to get over the Alps so the mission was aborted. After jettisoning our bomb load we still needed to throw out all non-essential equip-ment, including the fuselage door, to enable us to get above the weather'.

Of the thirty-six aircraft that had taken off only ten attacked the primary target and two more – both from No.51 Squadron – bombed the alternative. The others found the storms and severe icing over the Alps too much of a strain for their lumbering Whitleys. One of the aircraft that did manage to reach the target that night was N1460 'R-Robert' (Flying Officer McInnes) of 58 Squadron. 'R-Robert' was the only aircraft from No.58 Squadron which was able to negotiate the barrier of the Alps out of six Whitleys despatched. McInnes arrived at the target at 02.20 hours to dis-cover that the Turin black out was poor and the Italian anti-aircraft defences wild and inaccurate. His bomb load, consisting of four 500 lb and six 250 lb bombs, fell on the corner of the aero-engine sheds at the south end of the Fiat works. Other bombs were seen to burst on the railway track alongside the fac-tory. The Italian gunners misjudged the height of the attacking Whitleys as most of their shells were seen to burst as much as 5,000 feet above the British aircraft. One Whitley, however, failed to return, N1367 (Sergeant Songest) from 77 Squadron. The Turin raid, although far from a success, had been yet another 'first' for 4 Group. It had also demonstrated what the heavy bombers of the RAF were capable of and was a portent of what the enemy would face in the near future.

With the battle for France lost, Bomber Command's efforts were now to be directed against targets whose destruction would have the greatest effect on the forthcoming German air offensive on Britain. Priority targets were to be aircraft plants and depots. In addition attacks on river, canal and railway systems in the Ruhr were to be increased. When the opportunity presented itself oil plants were to be attacked, but only as a sec-ondary task. Among targets attacked by No.4 Group during the period from 14th to the 18th June were barges and tugs on the Rhine be-tween Mannheim and Bingen, marshalling yards at Schwerte, and oil plants at Gelsen-kirchen, Frankfurt and Castrop-Rauxel. The Focke-Wulf aircraft factory at Bremen was bombed on the nights of 25th and 30th and aluminium factories in the Ruhr were attacked on the 23rd and 25th June.

At the beginning of the war, German defence against nocturnal air attack was dependent on flak and searchlights. The limitations of the Luftwaffe's anti-aircraft defences soon be-came obvious however when the RAF commenced its nightly attacks on German industrial targets in May 1940, and so with typical skill and energy the Germans had, by early June, formed the basis of a night-fighter force. By July the first night-fighter unit,

Above: 'L-London' takes off from Linton-on-Ouse, 1940. This Whitley Mk.V of No.58 Squadron wears the conspicuous Type A1 fuselage roundels and light grey codes common to aircraft of Bomber Command in 1940. *IWM, CH257*

Below: Crews of No.58 Squadron get dressed before boarding their Whitley, probably prior to an air-test. The aircrew clothing in this June 1940 photograph includes Irvin jackets, 'Para-suits' and Sidcot suits. *IWM, CH235*

Nachtjagdgeschwader 1, had been set up equipped with Bf 110s, Ju 88s and Bf 109s. Early tactics involved close co-operation with the searchlights – so called illuminated night-fighting. The first success for the Luftwaffe, using this method of attack, occurred on the night of 9th July 1940 when Ofw Förster of Nachtjagdgeschwader 1 shot down a Whitley from No.10 Squadron near Heligoland. The Whitley had been part of a force of five aircraft from No.10 Squadron despatched to attack Kiel. The last message from the pilot, Flight Lieutenant Ffrench-Mullen, was received at 01.45 hours stating that he was abandoning the mission. The crew of Whitley N1496 were later reported as POWs. The raid on Kiel was one of a series of attacks against ports and naval bases carried out in response to a directive issued on 4th July 1940. This called for operations to be mounted against ports containing concentrations of shipping which intelligence estimated were being prepared for the invasion of Britain. These targets were considered 'a first priority' along with objectives in the aircraft industry.

No.4 Group received a boost early in July when No.78 Squadron at Dishforth became fully operational. The Squadron's first operation of the war was flown on the night of 19th July when four Whitleys attacked the Ruhr marshalling yards. Squadron Leader Wildey, 'A' Flight Commander, bombed the primary target the marshalling yards at Recklinghausen whilst the other three aircraft attacked alternative targets; Sergeant Monkhouse, the Munster rail yards; Flying Officer Eno, the Gelsenkirchen-Buer oil plant and Pilot Officer Denny, a marshalling yard forty miles north of the primary. All four aircraft returned safely.

No.4 Group Bomber Command, July 1940

Sqn	Equipment	Airfield
10	Whitley V	Leeming
51	Whitley V	Dishforth
58	Whitley V	Linton-on-Ouse
77	Whitley V	Driffield
78	Whitley V	Dishforth
102	Whitley V	Driffield

'They're on their way!' 'E-Easy' of 58 Squadron tucks its wheels in as it bids farewell to Linton, June 1940. *IWM, CH244*

Instrument panel of a Whitley Mk.V of No.78 Squadron 1940. Prominent in this view is the open door to the bomb aiming position in the nose. *D. Webb*

Opposite, bottom: **Crew members of 'A' Flight, No.78 Squadron, July 1940, who took part in the squadron's first operation on the night of 19th July 1940 – an attack on the marshalling yards at Gelsenkirchen and Recklinghausen. Left to right back row: (first three unknown), Flying Officer Robinson, Pilot Officer Denny, Sergeant Roberts. Front row: Sergeant Heyworth, Squadron Leader Wildey ('A' Flight commander), Pilot Officer Webb.** *D. Webb*

No.78 Squadron was in action the following night, this time, the aircraft assembly plants at Wenzendorf and Wismar were the targets. Squadron Leader Whitworth in P5001 joined other Whitleys from No.4 Group in the attack on the airfield at the Wenzendorf plant. Whitworth, believing that he had successfully bombed the target returned to base only to discover that his bombs were still in their racks. A blown fuse in the electrical system of his Whitley had cut all current off from the bomb releasing gear. Unhappily there was more bad news for No.78 Squadron on the night of 21st July when Sergeant Monkhouse and crew failed to return from a raid on the important marshalling yards at Soest. Four other Whitleys from the Squadron successfully bombed the rail yards while two others from No.51 Squadron raided the marshalling yards at Hamm. Three days later No.10 Squadron sent five Whitleys to strike at naval and merchant shipping targets at Hamburg, including the new battleship *Bismarck*, then known to be fitting out at the Blohm & Voss yards. Unfortunately 10/10ths cloud over the target, extending from 3,000 to 18,000 feet, prevented a successful attack. Only one aircraft, Sergeant Green in N1497, managed to bomb through thick cloud, the others returned with their bomb loads.

Top: **Pilot Officer J.R. Denny and crew of 78 Squadron in front of their Whitley Mk.V, N1486, July 1940. Left to right: Sgt Roberts, wireless operator; Pilot Officer Webb, rear gunner; Pilot Officer Denny, pilot; Sgt Wilson, 2nd pilot; Sgt Walker, observer.** *D. Webb*

A Whitley Mk.V of No.51 Squadron about to receive its load of 250lb bombs at Dishforth in July 1940: note the ubiquitous Fordson tractor. Also of interest is the black finish on the prop blades, washed off by anti-icing fluid and the recently applied matt black paint on the fuselage sides – a common feature on Whitleys from the summer of 1940. In the background in another Mk.V, this one belonging to 78 Squadron, who shared Dishforth with No.51. *W. Baguley*

With the coming of August the Luftwaffe's aerial assault on Britain was intensified and Fighter Command was now facing its sternest test to date. Bomber Command, under pressure to assist the struggle by attacking aircraft factories and airfields, was forced to accept diversions from the main effort during these crucial weeks. The Ministry of Economic Warfare, an influential government department set up to analyse the effect of strategic bombing on the German economy, had long been recommending the possibility of destroying German crops and forests by means of a special incendiary device. In June they were predicting that the harvest prospects in Europe would be very poor and would be as much as 25% below normal.

Early August, it was suggested, would be the best time to carry out such attacks. Experiments had been carried out with a new American invented incendiary pellet – code named *Razzle*, which consisted of two strips of celluloid between which was sandwiched a small piece of phosphorus. Stored in water filled containers to prevent ignition from contact with the air, they were designed to be scattered over crops and forests via a special chute attached to the underside of an attacking bomber. It was considered that the resulting crop and forest fires would have a serious material and psychological effect on nearby German industrial and military activity. Ivon Pacey of No.77 Squadron recalls his first encounter with 'Razzle':

'During the summer of 1940 our crew were instructed to fly to RAE Farnborough. On arrival we were taken out to the middle of the airfield where we were later joined by 'Boffins' in white coats carrying containers. Inside each container, immersed in water, were the strangest of objects, about six inches long and closely resembling those little bugle things that as kids we used to blow into, producing the same effect as a comb and tissue. There the resemblance ended, however, as sandwiched between the upper and lower sections was a phosphorus wadding, that

whilst submerged in water was quite safe, but once exposed to the air (as demonstrated by the Boffins) would, after a short time, ignite. We were informed that a special chute would be fitted to our aircraft down which we would pour these wonders of modern science over the enemy's harvest. Garden type sprayers were also to be provided to squirt water down the chutes to unstick any reluctant Razzles'.

The first occasion that 'Razzle' was used on operations by No.4 Group was on the night of 11th August. The target that night was an oil plant at Gelsenkirchen, with additional 'Razzling' of forest areas near Cologne. Over at Leeming during briefing of the crews of No.10 Squadron, the commanding officer, Wing Commander Bufton, gave a demonstration of how to use 'Razzle' pellets. Bomb loads for the Leeming Whitleys included two 500 lb and four 250 lb general purpose bombs, 50% delayed timing; two containers of 4 lb incendiaries and fifty tins of 'Razzle' pellets to each aircraft. Although on this occasion the 'Razzles' were successfully despatched, the results of this and further attacks were poor and future plans to use the device were abandoned. This was not before a number of aircraft were damaged by 'Razzles' sticking to the fuselage or jamming in the specially designed chutes as Ivon Pacey recalls.

'Over the target, down went the chute and we began to tip out the containers. All went well until we came to the last container. Whilst pouring the contents down the chute the slipstream somehow managed to catch a number of these little wonders and promptly blew them back into the aircraft. One can imagine the almighty scramble that occurred as we endeavoured to get rid of the devilish little devices as quickly as possible'.

Meanwhile the Luftwaffe's aerial assault was reaching new heights of ferocity. On 15th August the Germans flew 1,786 sorties and no effort was spared in the attempt to smother Fighter Command's defences. Faulty intelligence had led the Luftwaffe to believe that the North Eastern flank of Britain was largely devoid of fighter cover. It was for this reason that a large scale attack was launched against Newcastle and Sunderland on 15th August, by Luftflotte 5 from bases in Scandinavia. A separate force, Junkers Ju 88 bombers of Kampfgeschwader 30 flying from Aalborg in Denmark, were to attack the 4 Group station at Driffield. Harried all the way from Flamborough Head by Spitfires and Hurricanes from Leconfield, the seventeen strong force struck Driffield shortly after 13.00 hours. Despite spirited and accurate anti-aircraft fire from Driffield's defence batteries, the enemy force were not prevented from carrying out a devastating attack which caused widespread damage. Several Whitleys from Nos. 77 and 102 Squadrons were destroyed, one aircraft exploding so violently that it wrecked two others. Four hangars were hit and many other buildings destroyed. In all twelve Whitleys were destroyed and thirteen personel killed. In the opinion of driver Dougie Fulbrook the death toll might well have been higher if the raid had come earlier.

'As luck would have it the air raid alarm sounded as most of the station were having their mid-day meal break. If the Germans had come earlier they would have caught us cold as there was considerable activity in the area where most of the bombs fell. As it was they arrived over the airfield before many people had time to take cover'.

Driffield was so badly damaged that the station was out of action for the rest of the year. By the end of August 102 Squadron had moved to Leeming and No.77 to Linton-on-Ouse.

August saw further attacks against Italian targets by the Whitleys. This time Abingdon was used as a refuelling stop. Milan and Turin were raided on the 13th and 15th, the Caproni works and Pirelli tyre factory in Milan on the 18th, and an electrical equipment works, also in Milan, on the 24th. During the Turin raid on the 13th August, a Whitley from No.10 Squadron, P4965 (Pilot Officer Parsons), was attacked and severely damaged by an Italian fighter. Parsons managed to fly the aircraft most of the way back on one engine but was forced to ditch in the sea off Hythe. Unfortunately Parsons and his second pilot were lost.

On the night of 24th August the first bombs fell on central London and the same night Birmingham, Bristol and Liverpool were attacked. The War Cabinet's immediate reaction was that Berlin should be bombed in retaliation. Churchill was adament that the Germans should get as good as they were giving. As a result of this a force of eighty-one aircraft from Nos. 3, 4 and 5 Groups were briefed to attack a variety of industrial and military targets within the Berlin central area on the night of 25th August. Sergeant Jock Hill was a wireless operator with 78 Squadron and had only just joined that unit having come direct from 10 OTU at Abingdon. The Berlin raid was to be his first operational trip.

'My pilot on the Berlin raid was Flight Lieutenant Patterson, a fellow Scot, who was killed later in the war. As was the custom in those days the rear gunner was, in fact, the second wireless operator, and my first trip was in the rear turret with short spells on the wireless to gain experience. The Wireless Operators were vital members of the crews as there was no radar and all bearing fixes and controlled landings (known as ZZ landings) were obtained and controlled by the operator. About noon on that August day I recall someone whispering in my ear 'It's the Big City tonight'. This meant nothing to me, as was obvious to my informant, so he enlightened me by saying 'Berlin, you clot'. I can't say that I was any more apprehensive than I had been before receiving this advance warning. As far as I was concerned enemy territory was enemy territory, whether it was Cologne or Wilhelmshaven or anywhere else in the Third Reich.

'In the afternoon we positioned our aircraft at Topcliffe, one of the sophisticated bomber airfields planned before the war but not quite completed. However, its runways were ready and, as Dishforth was a grass airfield at that time, and to avoid congestion with No.51 Squadron, it was decided to make use of Topcliffe. So across to Topcliffe we proceeded on a glorious August evening with the Yorkshire countryside quite golden in the glow of an autumnal sunset. The trip took nine hours and forty minutes but whether we ever got to Berlin I cannot say, because on ETA the whole area was obscured by thick cloud. In those early days we were briefed to bring our bombs back if we did not locate the target. However, we were authorised to bomb an alternative target, provided we could identify it as being a military one. Not unnaturally, few aircraft brought the bombs home. We found a lighted airfield and down went ours.

'Shortly after this raid the Squadron was visited by Lord Trenchard who was, of course, delighted that some twenty-two years later, the aim of his Independent Air Force in 1918 had been fulfilled. We were paraded before him, informally in the hangar, and he called us his 'Berlin Boys' and seemed to suggest that we were on the way to winning the war by ourselves'.

The Berlin mission had been hampered by

thick cloud – 9/10ths down to 2,000 feet – and only twenty-nine crews claimed to have bombed the target. Of the other fifty-two, twenty-seven claimed to have reached the target area but could not see their aiming point so returned with their loads. Eighteen selected alternative targets and the remaining seven aborted. Five Hampdens failed to return but all the No.4 Group contingent returned safely. Bomb damage to Berlin was negligible with most of the bombs falling in unpopulated areas on the outskirts of the city. The main effects of the raid, however, were psychological. The fact that British bombers had penetrated as far as Berlin was a personal humiliation for Hermann Göring, commander of the Luftwaffe. He had boasted that no enemy plane would ever fly over the Reich. The population of the German Capital were deeply shocked and the German press ran headlines condemning this 'Cowardly British Attack' designed to 'massacre the population of Berlin'. The effect on the morale of the Germans seemed to support the view that the will of the population could be broken by indiscriminate air attack. An analysis of raids on Germany, and the Luftwaffe's attacks on London, had shown that the life of the community could be seriously dislocated if its sources of power, gas, water and electricity supplies were destroyed. These then were the strong arguments that were being put forward by a lobby that included the Prime Minister, who wanted to see widespread bombing of German towns.

For the time being, however, Bomber Command was being directed to attack specific industrial and military targets and the Air Staff were still confident in the ability of the bombers to not only find but successfully attack such targets. On 26th August, the day after the Berlin attack, the Whitleys visited Italy. The Magnetti Marelli magneto works at Sesto San-Giovanni, in Milan, providing the target for 10 Squadron, whilst No.77 went to the Fiat works at Turin. No.10 Squadron despatched six aircraft of which four successfully bombed the primary in Milan. One aircraft, P4990 (Sergeant Howard), failed to return. The Italians later claimed to have shot down an aircraft at Valera, near Varese, and not far from the secondary target for that night, the Sesto Calende airframe factory. Milan and Turin were again the targets for No.4 Group squadrons on 1st September along with the BMW aero-engine plant at Munich.

The long distance flights to the Italian targets tested the endurance of the Whitleys and their crews to the limit. Vast amounts of precious fuel would be consumed in the struggle to get above the Alps and pilots needed to keep a wary eye on their fuel gauges on the return leg of their journey. On many occasions there was just not enough fuel left in the tanks to reach home as happened to Squadron Leader Bartlett and Flight Sergeant Moore – both of 58 Squadron – on the night of 2nd September. That night No.58 had despatched five Whitleys to attack a power station at Genoa. Fuel tanks were topped up at Honington in Suffolk on the outward leg but even so Squadron Leader Bartlett, in N1427 'K', was forced to ditch on the return journey due to lack of fuel. Bartlett's Whitley came down off Margate and all five crew members were able to reach the shore in their dinghy. Flight Sergeant Moore brought his fuel-starved Whitley, N1459 'A', down into the sea off Aldeburgh where the crew were picked up by a ship from a nearby convoy.

On 3rd September 1940, the first anniversary of the war, No.10 Squadron marked the event in suitable fashion by raiding Berlin. The primary target that night was a transformer station in the Friedrichsfelde district with an aircraft component factory at Spandau as an alternate. One aircraft dropped its load, consisting of two 500 lb and six 250 lb bombs, on the transformer station from 7,500 feet. Another Whitley hit a gas works in Danzigerstrasse, causing a large fire with enormous quantities of smoke. More embarrassment for Göring came on 4th September, this time in the shape of Whitleys from No.51 Squadron. Six aircraft were despatched to the German capital, four attacked the Bewag power station and two bombed the Deutsch Industrie works at Spandau. In addition to their standard bomb load of two 500 lb and six 250 lb general purpose bombs, each of the No.51 Squadron Whitleys carried twenty-five tins of 'Razzles'. These were to be distributed over suitable forest areas on the outward journey.

The intensity of the Luftwaffe's attacks on Britain in September brought a clamour for more retaliation, and as a result, Berlin was to feature prominently in the list of targets attacked in that month. On eleven nights during September substantial raids were mounted by RAF Bomber Command against specified targets in Berlin, culminating in a heavy blow on the night of the 23rd. That night a 129 - strong force of Whitleys, Wellingtons and Hampdens were sent against Berlin and 112 claimed successful attacks. A fine night for No.4 Group, which saw seventeen tons of bombs dropped, was marred by a take-off accident at Linton-on-Ouse. Sergeant Cornish of No.58 Squadron ran into difficulties seconds after taking off for Berlin and his Whitley, N1470 'J', lost flying speed and height and crashed. In the resulting fire three members of the crew, including Sergeant Cornish, were killed.

Also receiving considerable attention in September 1940 were the large numbers of invasion barges and shipping massed in the north German ports and the captured harbours of Belgium, Holland and France. Ostend was attacked by Whitleys on the nights of the 8th and 15th and Antwerp heavily bombed on the 14th. During the latter raid, by Whitleys from Nos. 10, 51 and 78 Squadrons, considerable damage was inflicted on transports: five steamers were hit, one barge sunk, two cranes destroyed, an ammunition train blown up and several sheds left burning.

The following day the great aerial battle was fought over London and Southern England. The resulting defeat of the Luftwaffe marked the turning point in the Battle of Britain.

With his invasion armada in considerable disarray, due in no small part to the efforts of Bomber Command, Hitler was left with no choice but to abandon Operation *Sealion* – the invasion of Britain.

Above: **A Whitley Mk.V of 58 Squadron about to receive its bomb load at Linton-on-Ouse, sometime in 1940. On the left trolley is a 2,000lb bomb whilst on the right armourers prepare the carrier on a bulky 1,000 pounder.** *W. Baguley*

Below: **Sergeant Wilson and crew in front of their No. 78 Squadron Whitley, Autumn 1940. Left to right: Sergeant Astle, rear gunner; Sergeant Clarke, navigator; Sergeant Wilson, pilot; Sergeant Tarrent, wireless operator; Pilot Officer Glover, 2nd pilot.** *D. Webb*

Chapter Six

Enter the Halifax

With the approach of winter it was realised that Bomber Command's efforts to mount a decisive offensive would depend very much on the weather conditions. Precision bombing of specified targets would become more difficult as the weather deteriorated. In an effort to maximise results Bomber Command was instructed to carry out concentrated attacks on objectives in large towns and centres of industry with the primary aim of causing very heavy material destruction. This would have the effect of demonstrating to the enemy the power and severity of air bombardment and the hardship and dislocation which would result from it. The next few months would see developing the trend towards area bombing.

Berlin was still very much the primary target and during the months of October and November 1940 the city was attacked whenever conditions were favourable. No.4 Group squadrons visited Berlin on 7th October with 51 Squadron attacking the Air Ministry and War Office and No.78 the BMW works. Other locations bombed that night by the Whitleys included the Fokker factory in Amsterdam and an oil plant in Gelsenkirchen. During the latter raid a 58 Squadron Whitley, T4137 'K' (Pilot Officer Hadley), suffered engine failure when leaving the target. After struggling home on one engine Pilot Officer Hadley's Whitley burst into flames and crashed at Bircham Newton killing the entire crew.

Whenever weather conditions and moonlight were favourable the opportunity was taken to make precision attacks on oil plants. Among the oil plants raided by the Whitleys in mid-October were the Wesserling oil plant near Cologne, the Leuna oil plant at Merseburg and the synthetic oil plant at Politz. Also bombed during October were the Italian targets and, although little material damage was done, these attacks had an adverse effect on Italian morale. During one such raid on Milan, on the night of 20th October, Sergeant Wally Lashbrook (later Squadron Leader), pilot of a No.51 Squadron Whitley, had a close encounter with the Milan flak:

'There was little or no heating in our Whitleys in those days so on operations I wore an inner lining, leather trousers and jacket over my battledress. We arrived over Milan and reduced height rapidly after coming under a pretty heavy barrage of flak. Almost at once there was a very near burst just as we released our bombs. As we climbed away

from the target I suddenly felt a wetness around the top of my thigh and the pain started and it soon became pretty intense. I rapidly came to the conclusion that the dampness was blood and that I must have been hit by shrapnel. Having climbed back to some 8,000 feet, and being clear of the flak, I handed over the controls to my second pilot so as I could inspect my wounds. After struggling to remove the various layers of clothing, and with the aid of a torch, I was able to examine the damage more closely. The top of my thigh was found to be very inflamed but the skin did not seem to be broken, so much relieved, and with the pain fading, I returned to the controls. We landed at Manston some 8½ hours after take-off and only then did I discover that my painful "shrapnel wound" had been caused by a cigarette lighter fuel capsule bursting in my pocket'.

During the autumn of 1940 German night fighters commenced intruder operations against Bomber Command airfields in East Anglia, Lincolnshire and Yorkshire. The Luftwaffe's radio monitoring service was able to determine from Bomber Command's radio tuning transmissions, the number and location of bombers preparing to take off. Night fighters would then intercept the bombers at their most vulnerable moment, as they took off. One of the first interceptions, involving an aircraft from No.4 Group, occurred on the night of 20th October. Pilot Officer Brown of 58 Squadron had just taken off from Linton-on-Ouse, along with ten other Whitleys, for an attack on the Skoda works at Pilsen. Brown's Whitley, T4171 'O', was intercepted by a Junkers Ju 88C-5 of the newly formed night intruder Gruppe 1/NJG2, piloted by Hptm Karl Hulshoff, kapitan of the 3rd Staffel. The Whitley crashed near Thornaby and four of the crew were killed. Another Whitley fell victim to the intruders four nights later. This time a Whitley of 102 Squadron, P5073 'D' (Pilot Officer Davies), had just left Tholthorpe for Berlin when it was shot down in flames again by a Junkers Ju 88C-5 of NJG2. In the resulting crash Pilot Officer Murfitt and Sergeant Scoular were killed and Pilot Officer Davies, Pilot Officer Lee and Sergeant Wilson severely injured. For the time being bomber crews were not able to feel safe even over their own bases.

Clear conditions in the last week of October 1940 made it possible for a series of attacks to be mounted by 4 Group squadrons against oil refineries and synthetic oil plants.

Targets included plants at Magdeburg, Reizholz, Stettin, Hamburg and Merseburg.

November's operations commenced with raids on Italian targets on the 2nd and 5th. The latter raid, on the Fiat motor works in Turin, was carried out by Whitleys of Nos.77 and 78 Squadrons. Pilot Officer Miller and crew of No.77 Squadron were the only members of the squadron to successfully bomb the target. On the return journey Miller was forced to ditch his aircraft in the North Sea due to fuel shortage. Whitley T4151 'M' came down eight miles east of North Shields and all the crew were later picked up by a steamer.

It was back to oil targets again on the following night; this time the synthetic oil plants at Merseburg and Hamburg were visited by Whitleys from Nos. 10, 77, 78 and 102 Squadrons. Flying Officer Lawson of 102 Squadron in T4135 'S' was forced to return early due to bad icing of the aircraft's airspeed indicator. Lawson's Whitley, with bombs still on board, crashed at Linton-on-Ouse on return and was severely damaged. Pilot Officer Cheshire in P5005 'N', also of 102 Squadron, was unable to locate the primary target, the Leuna oil plant at Merseburg, so bombed a road junction at Pretzsch.

Pilot Officer G. L. Cheshire, (later Group Captain Cheshire, VC) had joined No.102 Squadron in June 1940 with fourteen hours night and 380 hours day flying experience behind him. A shy 23-year old, he was a new boy amongst hardened old hands and he had much to learn. Cheshire's biographer, Russell Braddon, wrote of those early days in *Cheshire VC*, the following extract being reproduced by kind permission of Unwin Hyman, an imprint of HarperCollins Publishers Limited:

'In his first days on the squadron, however, nothing impinged on his mind except that he seemed totally unfamiliar with everything that was now supposed to be his workaday life. Everything was new, and everything had to be learnt and there was much to learn. What speed to fly at, engine revolutions, boost, bomb-loads, guns, turrets, bomb selector switches, bomb-sights, petrol cocks, engine pressure, crew drill, how to unhook a dinghy, navigation and wireless procedure, evasive action, ack-ack and searchlights'.

And in Cheshire's own words: 'There was a maze of details running through my mind. Couldn't seem to sort them out. I'd figured you more or less got into your plane, took-off, dropped your bombs, came back and that was that. I seemed to be learning!'.

He learned fast and by the winter of 1940 he was already an experienced pilot in command of his own aircraft.

On the night of 12th November 1940 Pilot Officer Cheshire was pilot of a Whitley Mk.V, P5005 'N', part of a force despatched to attack an oil refinery at Wesserling near Cologne. Due to an intercom defect Cheshire had failed to receive instructions from his navigator, Sergeant Roberts, and had missed the target by some twelve miles. In the meantime, cloud had completely obscured the primary, and it was decided to bomb the alternative target – Cologne marshalling yards. As Cheshire approached the target his aircraft was suddenly hit by a succession of violent explosions. A further extract from Russell Braddon's *Cheshire VC,* by kind permission of Unwin Hyman / HarperCollins Publishers Limited:

'Then came the explosion. A vicious flash and a roar in front of him, leaving him blind. Another crash and a horrifying glare of light from the rear. The plane bucketed and lurched and then careered groundwards. Cheshire's thoughts were chaotic. "I'm blinded . . . no, it's only the flash . . . I feel sick . . . We'll have to bale out. Always wanted to try a jump. Not this way, though. Don't want to jump at all now. Anyway – where the hell is my 'chute? . . . No more letters from mother . . . What a foul smell. Can't breathe. Oxygen mask, that's the thing".

'Frantically he tore off his gloves, found the press-stud of the mask and clipped it on. Glorious clean oxygen. Then, unconsciously, the training of a captain asserted itself.

"Have you dropped the bombs yet?" he demanded. The words surprised him. He hadn't thought them - they had just come. No answer. Yes, there was. A faint "I've been hit. I've been hit".

'He remembered that awful flash behind him. They must all be dead or dying. The plane wallowed downwards; but he could see well enough to check his altimeter. 5,000 feet it read. Strange – he thought they would have lost more height. He fought with sluggish controls and a reluctant machine. Gradually they levelled out – and the long Jewish snouts resumed their even roar of defiance. "Good old engines," he thought lovingly, "they never let you down".

'A grotesque, blood-streaming figure appeared beside him. He could not recognise it and had no desire to look at it again to try and do so. The bloody apparition stood there a moment apparently bemused. Then it looked back down the fuselage and screamed: "Fire, the tank's on fire".

"Well, put it out," snapped his voice. Again that subconscious ability to command. It astounded him and, in doing so, brought him entirely to his senses. He was the captain of a wrecked, blazing bomber. He would fly it - nothing else mattered. And the bleeding figure, jolted by the peremptory orders of a seemingly unmoved skipper, promptly vanished to put out the fire near the petrol tank!

'Cheshire wriggled in discomfort as his uniform stuck to him moistly. His back was sweating with the heat of the flames to the rear. He looked behind him and saw thick, oily smoke and red gashes of fire. More shells from the ground, their explosions deafening now because the perspex hatch over his head was torn and the noise, like the wind, came roaring in. A rattle of splinters through the fuselage. Desmond appeared. "Can you keep

Whitley Mk.V T4273 of 102 Squadron, pictured after a mishap at Topcliffe late in 1940. Note the extended black finish on the fuselage sides ending in a wavy line – typical camouflage features of the period as more and more black paint was used on Whitleys in a bid to beat the searchlights. *RAF Museum, P016005*

Opposite: **Pilot Officer Leonard Cheshire's damaged Whitley V, P5005 'N', showing damage to the fuselage caused by an exploding flare over Cologne on the night of 12th/13th November 1940.** *IWM, CH6374*

her in the air?" he asked. "What do you think?".

'That was all Desmond wanted to know. He returned and, with Taffy, deliberately crawled under the petrol tank and, fighting from the middle of the fire, put it out. They left their parachutes behind them to do so. Half the plane's fuselage had vanished. The fire had been caused by a fragment of shell which exploded the first flare as Davey leant over it and just before it had dropped. Although in flames from head to foot himself, Davey had still thrown out the second flare so that it could not ignite and blow the bomber to bits.'

Although Cheshire's Whitley was severely damaged – there was a gaping hole in the side of the fuselage (see photo) – he was able to successfully drop his bombs in the marshalling yards. Despite losing all the maps in the fire he was able to navigate by sheer guesswork and make a successful landfall on the English coast.

For his exploits Pilot Officer Cheshire was awarded the DSO. The citation read: 'Showing great coolness Pilot Officer Cheshire regained control of his aircraft, which had lost considerable height and was being subjected to intense anti-aircraft fire, and although the explosions had blown out a large part of the fuselage and caused other damage he managed to regain height ... Although the aircraft was only partially answering the controls Pilot Officer Cheshire succeeded in returning to his aerodrome.' Cheshire's wireless operator, Sergeant Davidson, received the DFM.

The German attack on Coventry on the night of 14/15th November 1940 was an ominous portent of what was in store for the citizens of Britain and Germany. The widespread and seemingly indiscriminate destruction and the heavy loss of life was to lead to a hardening of attitudes in the British War Cabinet. On the same night that the Luftwaffe were setting fire to the centre of Coventry, Bomber Command squadrons were raiding Berlin. The attack on the German capital, carried out by fifty Hampdens, Wellingtons and Whitleys, was to prove a costly night for the bombers. Twenty-two Whitleys from Nos.58, 77 and 102 Squadrons were despatched from 4 Group of which fourteen claimed successful attacks.

Losses, however, were the heaviest sustained so far by Bomber Command in one night with ten aircraft failing to return. From 4 Group No.58 Squadron lost three and Nos. 77 and 102 lost one each. In addition, a 77 Squadron Whitley, T4172 'R' (Sergeant Bizley), came down in the North Sea on return due to lack of fuel. The ditched Whitley stayed afloat and drifted in on the tide and was beached near Hornsea.

On the following two nights Hamburg was raided, Bomber Command despatching 67 and 130 aircraft respectively over the two nights. In the first attack, carried out in two separate waves, heavy damage was caused to the Blöhm and Voss shipyards and an oil refinery. Hamburg records state that sixty-eight fires were started and twenty-six people were killed and 1,625 made homeless. The second attack, on the 16th, was spoilt by bad weather over the target. All the No.4 Group aircraft returned safely from both operations except a Whitley from 58 Squadron which suffered a collapsed undercarriage on landing at Topcliffe.

The problem of fuel shortage on raids to Italian targets caused losses for No.4 Group the following week. Five aircraft were lost when they ran short of fuel on return from an attack on the Royal Arsenal at Turin on the night of 23rd November. Two aircraft from 77 Squadron were lost. T4169 'F' (Pilot Officer Rees) struck high tension cables and force-landed west of Laxfield, near Halesworth, Suffolk. The crew were uninjured but the aircraft was wrecked. T4160 'L' (Pilot Officer Bagnell), ditched in the sea off Dover and four members of the crew were lost when the dinghy only half inflated and drifted away from the aircraft. No.102 lost three aircraft. P5012 'C' (Sergeant Pearce) force-landed near Tangmere and was wrecked. P5074 'Q' (Sergeant Rix), the crew abandoned the aircraft four miles north of Midhurst, Sussex. T4216 'F' (Flying Officer Young) ditched in the sea off Start Point and two of the crew were injured.

A significant event for No.4 Group in the month of November 1940 was the formation of the first Halifax squadron in Bomber command. Just a year had passed since the first Halifax prototype, after making its initial

flight at RAF Bicester in October 1939, had been flown to the experimental establishment at Boscombe Down to complete the test programme. On the 17th August 1940 the second prototype, L7245, made its first flight at Radlett airfield. This machine, unlike the first prototype, was fully equipped with turrets (albeit mock-ups) and was close to the production series. On 11th September 1940, L7245 was flown to Boscombe Down to undergo an extensive series of tests. It was joined four weeks later by the first production Halifax B.Mk.I, L9485. Apart from a number of minor modifications the Halifax was declared ready to enter service. No.35 Squadron, reconstituted under the command of Wing Commander R. W. P. Collings on 5th November 1940, was chosen as the first unit in Bomber Command to receive the new bomber. At this time crews with experience of four-engined bombers were few and far between but the task of No.35 Squadron was made easier as the initial crews were all operationally experienced airmen.

After first being attached to the A&AEE at Boscombe Down the Squadron moved to Leeming on 20th November and became part of No.4 Group. The pace of training with the new aircraft was slow initially, due to the shortage of aircraft, and it was to be March 1941 before the Halifax was ready for operations.

Meanwhile Bomber Command was about to adopt tactics similar to those already successfully employed by the Luftwaffe in their night blitz of Britain's cities. The Germans had made use of a leading 'Pathfinder' formation to illuminate a target with incendiary bombs. Following waves of bombers would then converge on the now clearly marked target to add their bombs to the conflagration. The Luftwaffe had used this method of attack during November and December 1940 with devastating results against Coventry, Birmingham, Bristol and Southampton.

The German town of Mannheim was selected as the target for the first of Bomber Command's 'area' attacks. The aim of the raid was to cause as much damage as possible to the centre of Mannheim. Authorisation for the raid, codenamed *Abigail Rachel*, was given on 13th December, and the attack was scheduled

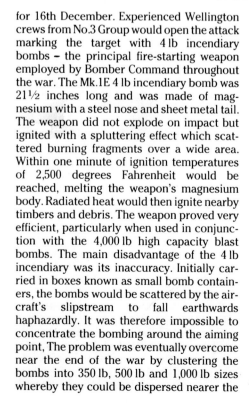

for 16th December. Experienced Wellington crews from No.3 Group would open the attack marking the target with 4 lb incendiary bombs – the principal fire-starting weapon employed by Bomber Command throughout the war. The Mk.1E 4 lb incendiary bomb was 21½ inches long and was made of magnesium with a steel nose and sheet metal tail. The weapon did not explode on impact but ignited with a spluttering effect which scattered burning fragments over a wide area. Within one minute of ignition temperatures of 2,500 degrees Fahrenheit would be reached, melting the weapon's magnesium body. Radiated heat would then ignite nearby timbers and debris. The weapon proved very efficient, particularly when used in conjunction with the 4,000 lb high capacity blast bombs. The main disadvantage of the 4 lb incendiary was its inaccuracy. Initially carried in boxes known as small bomb containers, the bombs would be scattered by the aircraft's slipstream to fall earthwards haphazardly. It was therefore impossible to concentrate the bombing around the aiming point, The problem was eventually overcome near the end of the war by clustering the bombs into 350 lb, 500 lb and 1,000 lb sizes whereby they could be dispersed nearer the

aiming point. In the meantime, however, Bomber Command had to make do with the present less efficient method of delivery.

The Mannheim attack was made in bright moonlight and in clear weather. The force consisted of 134 aircraft, including thirty-five Whitleys from No.4 Group, and was the largest force despatched by Bomber Command to a single target so far. Results, however, were largely disappointing, with much of the bombing by the main force being scattered. This was due to the inaccuracy of the 'Pathfinder' Wellingtons incendiary bombing, which failed to mark the centre of Mannheim. Thirty-three Whitley crews claimed to have bombed the target successfully, reporting that the whole central area of the town was burning. The AOC-in-C Bomber Command, Sir Richard Peirse sent a rather premature congratulatory signal to the groups on a highly successful operation. Later, photographic reconnaissance revealed that, although considerable damage had been inflicted on Mannheim, the vast majority of bomb loads had fallen outside the central area. The inference was that many crews who had bombed what they thought was the target were in fact in some cases many miles from the target.

OPERATION COLOSSUS

Late in 1940 plans were prepared, after much prompting from the Prime Minister Winston Churchill, to form an experimental British Paratroop force. The experiment, if it proved to be a success, could result in the formation of an airborne capability for the British Army for future use in the invasion of Europe. The formation and training of this new force, known as 'X' Troop No.11 SAS Battalion, was to lead to one of the most unusual operations carried out by No.4 Group.

By January 1941 'X' Troop, composed entirely of volunteers, was ready and eager for action. A target to try out this experimental force had, as yet, to be decided on. A strike at Nazi occupied Europe was rejected as this would have been suicidal. Italy, however, looked the most attractive target for both military and political reasons. Mussolini's main forces were, at this time, fully occupied fighting in Albania, so an operation by a small force, although risky, could strike a useful blow at Italian morale.

Possible targets in Italy had been examined with a view to future bombing and it was suggested that the huge aqueduct spanning the River Tragino in the province of Campagna might warrant some attention. The aqueduct, part of an elaborate system built in the 1930s, carried the main water supply for the province of Apulia – and to Brindisi, Bari and Foggia where there were dockyards and factories. Bombing of the aqueduct had been ruled out as the mountainous terrain was far too dangerous. But not so for a small commando strike; consequently in January 1941 preparations for Operation *Colossus*, the Tragino Aqueduct raid were set in motion.

Bomber Command was asked to supply aircraft and crews for the operation. The Whitley could be easily adapted for paratroop dropping as the floor of the fuselage was already framed and stressed for the 'dustbin' lower gun turret – removed from the Mark V versions then in squadron service. This circular hatch would be fitted with doors to make a suitable exit for paratroops.

The operation would be carried out by four selected crews from each of Nos.51 and 78 Squadrons under the command of Wing Commander 'Willie' Tait. The plan was to drop the parachutists on the north side of the aqueduct whereupon sappers would place explosives against one of the pillars. Two of the Whitleys, meanwhile, would carry out a diversionary bombing raid on nearby railway marshalling yards at Foggia. After the mission was completed the commandos were to make their way on foot in small groups a distance of fifty miles to the west coast. The submarine HMS *Triumph* was under orders to rendezvous with the commandos on the night of 15/16th February for the evacuation at the mouth of the River *Sele*. Eight Whitleys were required for the operation which was planned to be launched from Malta on 10th February,

weather permitting. Squadron Leader Wally Lashbrook was one of the crew members selected from 51 Squadron:

'The operation was carried out by four selected crews from each of the two Whitley squadrons stationed at Dishforth - 51 and 78. I was priviledged to be selected as captain of one of the crews involved. Captains of aircraft were allotted crew members and attached to RAF Ringway on 15th January 1941 to undergo a course in parachute dropping. The dropping practice was carried out initially in Whitley Mk.II aircraft; drops being made from 300 feet. I flew Whitley Mk.II K7220 under dropping instruction before becoming proficient enough to practice in the aircraft I was to fly on the operation. This was a Whitley Mk.V T4165.

'The dropping load for the operation was to comprise six paratroops and six containers of explosives or stores to each aircraft. Each container had a different coloured parachute, thus making its contents quickly recognised. The Whitleys were also fitted with autopilots and auxiliary fuel tanks mounted in the bomb bays'.

On 3rd February 1941 Wing Commander Tait flew into RAF Mildenhall with his Whitley force. The thirty-nine members of 'X' Troop arrived that same day by road under conditions of absolute secrecy. Warrant Officer Albon, a wireless operator with one of the No.78 Squadron crews, that of Pilot Officer Wotherspoon in T4167, recalls his crew's welcoming reception at Mildenhall.

'The day we flew into Mildenhall from Ringway the locals were expecting the imminent arrival of an enemy raider that had been making regular attacks on the station. When we broke cloud above the airfield we were met with anti-aircraft fire from the defences. The mistake was quickly rectified and no damage was done but the operation had not got off to the best of starts'.

Neither the parachutists nor the bomber crews were told of the target for their mission as complete secrecy was the order of the day. All the participating aircrew were issued with service revolvers and told to wear them at all times. This was because their ultimate destination, Malta, was under threat of invasion. This was to lead to some awkward questions being asked by inquisitive personnel at Mildenhall and as a result relations between aircrew in the mess were strained.

On 7th February Admiral Sir Roger Keyes, Chief of Combined Operations and the man responsible for commando training, arrived to give the men an official send-off. 'X' Troop and the Whitley crews were assembled in one of the hangars. Wally Lashbrook recalls the occasion.

'The Admiral shook hands with each man and chatted briefly. It was obvious to all of us that his face was extermely grave. When he came to me the Admiral seemed puzzled to have a sergeant pilot introduced to him as captain of an aircraft when most of the remainder of the crew were officers'.

That night the eight Whitleys took off for Malta. The aircraft were routed over France, down the Rhone Valley and over the Mediterranean Sea, west of Corsica and Sardinia to a point on the northern coast of Tunisia; south over Tunisia to a position inland from Sfax then due east to a DR point south of Malta, then north to the island. At dawn on 8th February they arrived at Luqa airfield and were immediately told they could not land until bomb craters from the previous night's bombing raid had been filled in. Needless to say after nearly eleven hours in the air the Whitley pilots decided to risk landing between the craters, and amazingly this was accomplished without any mishaps.

Operation *Colossus* could not begin at once as bad weather prevented photographic reconnaissance of the target area. In the meantime crews were briefed and the aircraft prepared for the expected take-off date of 10th February.

On the evening of the 10th the members of 'X' Troop were gathered together to be told by their Commanding Officer, Major T. A. G. Pritchard, the object of their mission. The full party of thirty-five parachutists allocated to the six carrier aircraft included three Italian interpreters. Wally Lashbrook remembers:

'The weather conditions that night were perfect, a cold dry night with plenty of moonlight. We carried out a thirty minute air test before take off which was scheduled for dusk. Finally airborne we formed up into two loose formations led by Wing Commander Tait and were soon flying at 10,000 feet over Mount Etna bound for the Italian coast south of Salerno. In addition to our load of commandos and their equipment we also carried two 250 lb bombs as an extra present for the Italians. The two Whitleys detailed to bomb the marshalling yards at Foggia, some thirty miles from the aqueduct, left us to make their own way to their target.

'The flight to within a few miles of the target was carried out at around 9,000 feet. Wing Commander Tait led the first formation, I maintained the port beam position. It was a beautiful moonlit night and we were at our dropping height of 300 feet just before reaching the valley, more or less line astern. I saw the leader overshooting the turning point to the dropping zone and turned in before him. Before despatching the paras we reduced speed to just over 100 knots and lowered flaps. The rear gunner, Flight Lieutenant Williams, reported over the intercom that we were on target and the troopers and their containers were on their way down. During this time we were heading directly towards Mount Vulture. I recall opening up the throttle while carrying out a climbing turn to port and we just managed to scrape over the side of the valley.

'Our next task was to select a suitable target for our 250 pounders. After circling over the town of Calitri I decided there was no justification or satisfaction in bombing such a sleepy looking town so I followed a railway line to a junction and dropped our bombs on a station. We returned back to Luqa after seven hours in the air to learn that all but one of our aircraft had returned safely'.

The missing Whitley was T4167 (Pilot Officer Wotherspoon), one of the two aircraft detailed for the diversionary raid on Foggia. Warrant Officer Albon, Wotherspoon's wireless operator, recalls what happened.

'We were forced to abandon our aircraft due to engine trouble, baling out south of Naples. I landed inside an army barracks and was captured at once. The rest of the crew were caught within a few hours'. Pilot Officer Wotherspoon and crew were unaware at the time that their unfortunate demise was to result in the cancellation of the rendezvous of 'X' Troop with the submarine HMS *Triumph*.

Their Whitley had come down in the same general area arranged for the departure of the parachutists. Fears that Italian police and troops searching for the crew would compromise the pick-up, led to the cancellation of the submarine's sailing orders.

Meanwhile at the aqueduct, 'X' Troop had run into problems. Five of the Whitleys had dropped their parachutists bang on target but the sixth aircraft had spent forty-five minutes circling the area, apparently lost, before dropping its cargo into the next valley. Unfortunately included with this party were some of the sappers and their explosives. In addition, icing had caused the bomb racks on one of the Whitleys to jam robbing the force of more valuable explosives. Consequently there was not enough explosives to destroy the aqueduct. Nevertheless the commandos succeeded in placing the available charges at one end of the aqueduct and the resulting explosion caused considerable damage. Unaware that there would be no submarine to pick them up the members of 'X' Troop made their way to the rendezvous point. The following day the whole party were captured and conveyed in triumph by their captors to the prison in Naples. There they were joined by the unfortunate members of the Whitley crew and spent the rest of the war as POWs.

The months of January and February 1941 saw the number of major raids by Bomber Command reduced to a minimum. The main reason for the reduction in scale of operations was that Bomber Command was struggling to maintain an adequate force. Losses, an acute shortage of crews and production difficulties – particularly with the new types of aircraft – had all combined to reduce the number of aircraft available for maximum strength night operations. Even so the Air Staff were confident in the ability of the Bomber Force, despite evidence to the contrary, to carry out successful attacks particularly on oil targets. Latest reports indicated that Germany's oil position would become critical by the spring of 1941. Consequently on 15th January Bomber Command was directed to concentrate its attacks on the German synthetic oil industry.

Meanwhile in No.4 Group the Halifax training programme was gathering pace. No.35 Squadron, now based at Linton-on-Ouse, had four of the new Halifaxes on strength by the first weeks of January 1941. There had been a setback on 13th January when one of the new aircraft, L9487, crashed in flames whilst on a measured climb and consumption test. The pilot, Flying Officer Henry, and his entire crew were killed. Undaunted by this sad event the squadron continued to work up for operations.

On 10th March No.35 Squadron were ordered out on their first operation with the new bomber. Seven aircraft were detailed to attack the docks at Le Havre. Before take off a message was received from the AOC-in-C Bomber Command which read:

Whitley Mk.V T4261 'S' was presented to 102 Squadron by the Governor and people of Ceylon, hence the inscription on the nose. The photograph was probably taken at Topcliffe during the early months of 1941. 'S-Sugar' was later lost on operations. *IWM, CH2052*

'Good wishes to No.35 Squadron and the heavyweights on the opening of their Halifax operations tonight. I hope the full weight of the squadron's blows will soon be felt further afield'.

First off that night, in perfect weather conditions, was Wing Commander Collings in L9486 'B' at 19.00 hours. Collings located the target successfully and dropped his bomb load consisting of twelve 500 lb semi-armour piercing bombs from 13,000 feet. Through a break in the cloud he reported seeing his bombs bursting along the edge of the main dock area. Second off was Flight Lieutenant Bradley in L9496 'N' at 19.05 hours. Bradley was unable to bomb Le Havre because of thick cloud. Cloud also prevented an attack on the secondary target Boulogne so Dieppe was selected and bombed from 13,000 feet but no result was observed. Third off was Squadron Leader Gilchrist in L9489 'F' at 19.08 hours. Gilchrist located the target and bombed from 11,800 feet but no result was observed due to thickening cloud. Unfortunately, on the return flight, Gilchrist's Halifax was mistaken for an enemy aircraft and shot down by a British fighter at Normandy, Surrey. Squadron Leader Gilchrist and his flight engineer Sergeant Aedy managed to escape by parachute but the rest of the crew, Pilot Officer Arnold, Sergeant Lucas, Sergeant Broadhurst and Pilot Officer Cooper were all killed. Fourth off was Flying Officer Warren in L9493 'G' at 19.12 hours. Warren successfully attacked the primary from 11,000 feet but his Halifax was damaged by shrapnel from a near miss. The port inner engine was damaged and had to be shut down and hydraulic failure caused the port undercarriage leg to come down. Despite these difficulties the aircraft returned safely to base. Fifth off was Pilot Officer Hilary in L9490 'L' at 19.15 hours. Hilary bombed Le Havre from 10,000 feet through thick cloud and no results were observed. Last off was Flight Lieutenant Lane in L9488 'M'. Lane was unable to bomb the primary target because of cloud. Shortage of fuel prevented an attack on the secondary so the bombs were jettisoned in the Channel on return. The seventh Halifax, that of Pilot

Officer Murray, was unable to take off due to hydraulic failure.

The following night No.35 Squadron was in action again this time sending three of their new Halifaxes to attack the Blöhm and Voss U-boat yards at Hamburg. Also taking part in the raid were contingents of Whitleys, Hampdens, Wellingtons and Manchesters. Off Nordeney, Flight Lieutenant Lane's Halifax was attacked by a twin-engined fighter. After making four attacks the fighter was driven off, leaving the Halifax none the worse for the encounter. U-boat slipways, office blocks and warehouses were damaged in Hamburg. That same night Berlin came under attack from a force of seventy-two aircraft which included fourteen Whitleys. Bombing, however, was scattered with only minor damage being inflicted mainly in the southern districts of the city. Returning early with engine trouble, T4140 'H' (Pilot Officer Malim), of 102 Squadron, overshot Bircham Newton airfield and crashed. In the ensuing fire Malim and Flying Officer Cubitt were killed. News received later at Topcliffe, that Flight Lieutenant Long and crew were missing, completed an unhappy night for No.102.

Bomber Command's operations in March 1941 should have seen all efforts directed to attacks on oil targets. But the combination of bad weather and fresh instructions from the Air Staff – calling for attacks on U-boat yards and their associated industries – meant that the campaign against oil never really got under way. German U-boats and Focke-Wulf Condor long-range bombers were now taking a heavy toll of Allied shipping in the North Atlantic. Bomber Command was instructed to shift emphasis in an attempt to destroy this menacing new threat. During March, No.4 Group Whitleys joined in attacks on the U-boat yards at Kiel, Bremen and Wilhelmsha-

ven and the bases at Lorient. In addition Brest harbour, where the German battlecruisers *Scharnhorst* and *Gneisenau* were sheltering, was raided on the night of 30th March.

By early April sufficient progress had been made to allow the formation of another Halifax squadron. On the 12th, orders were received to prepare for the formation of the new squadron, No.76, to be commanded by Wing Commander S. O. Bufton. Crews from 10 Squadron were to form the nucleus of the new squadron, initially as 'C' Flight of No.35. Three days later the Halifaxes were back in action this time joining in an attack on Kiel. Sergeant Wally Lashbrook had joined 35 Squadron from No.51 in early March and was taking part in his first Halifax operation that night.

'My first Halifax raid, in L9493 'G', was a bit of a disaster. We arrived over the target and successfully delivered our load on the Kiel U-boat yards. Unfortunately whilst over the target we were hit by shrapnel in the hydraulic lines. In those days there were no uplocks fitted so the undercarriage and flaps promptly descended under their respective accumulator pressure. With flying speed drastically reduced we struggled home. On arrival at Linton-on-Ouse we were prevented from landing by the presence of an enemy intruder in the circuit. Whilst circling the darkened airfield, awaiting the signal to land, both starboard engines suddenly failed due to lack of fuel. The flight engineer then attempted to switch tanks but unfortunately in doing so he mistakenly cut off the fuel supply to the port engines which promptly shut down. I ordered the crew to crash stations as we glided in for a crash landing. We ran across the corner of a field and collided with a tree which tore off the port wing, the aircraft finally breaking apart against a hedge!'

Fortunately only the navigator and the tail gunner were slightly injured in the crash, Wally Lashbrook and the rest of the crew suffering only a severe shaking. The Halifaxes, meanwhile, were withdrawn from operations for two months whilst modifications were carried out to the hydraulic system to prevent the persistent undercarriage hydraulic failure.

Chapter Seven

New Squadrons

In addition to the expansion of Halifax-equipped squadrons within No.4 Group, the spring of 1941 saw the arrival of two new units equipped with Wellingtons. The first to arrive was 104 Squadron which formed at Driffield on 1st April equipped with Wellington Mk.IIs. No.104 Squadron was followed on 23rd April by 405 (Vancouver) Squadron - the first Canadian bomber squadron to form overseas; also with Mk.IIs.

The Whitley units, meanwhile, were in the thick of the action and bearing the brunt of the losses. On the night of 17th April, twenty-eight Whitleys took part in a 118 aircraft attack on Berlin. Five of the eight aircraft lost that night were No.4 Group Whitleys. Sergeant Stanley McNeill (later Squadron Leader) was a navigator in a Whitley from No.58 Squadron that took part in the Berlin raid:

'The Berlin trip was only our sixth operation. Damaged by flak over the target we struggled back over the North Sea, leaking glycol from the port engine. The damaged engine eventually overheated and had to be shut down. As we lost height the starboard engine caught fire and we had to come down in the sea. We managed to get into the dinghy and spent the next seventy-two hours huddled together trying to keep warm. We were eventually picked up but all of us were in a pretty bad way'.

Many new faces began to arrive at the squadrons by the spring of 1941 as increasing losses on operations began to take their toll of the experienced old hands. What was it like for a newcomer, fresh from an Operational Training Unit? Sergeant Phillip Brett was an air gunner with 102 Squadron and in March 1941 he had just arrived from an OTU. Reporting to the Squadron Adjutant at Topcliffe,

along with thirty-five other new hopefuls, he recalls his apprehension:

'We had all just passed out from our final OTU and I wondered as we stood there what strange mixture of feelings we must all be experiencing. Some were vainly boastful of the things they were about to do, others just quietly thoughtful, but all of us - each and every one - realising that at long last this was it. This was the day we had all been preparing for during the last twelve months or so. We were beginning to wonder if all our extensive training had really fitted us properly for the tremendous task ahead.

'Standing there we were all forced to realise with horrible suddenness that war, even during our training, had only been front page headlines; something impersonal and far away; something to be discussed in the mess.

'It was the notice board that did it – that all-too-official looking, somewhat insignificant notice board over the Adjutant's desk. A mere piece of wood and rows of names – names of squadron aircrew, neatly arranged in alphabetical order, and against many – far too many, a neat strip had been inserted with that horribly significant word . . . missing . . . missing . . . missing. Even the entrance to our crew room greeted us with the large glaringly decorative inscription, "Abandon hope all ye who enter here". Then as we passed through its doorway we found, not abandoned hope, but all the wonderful comradeship and unconquerable spirit of youth with simply a job of work to be done.

'I can remember even now the feeling of absolute awe with which we regarded some of the older members of the squadron, and the feeling of almost reverence with which we surveyed the non-committal entries in their log books - Hamburg, Bremen, Essen, Berlin, Wilhelmshaven and scores of others. They were a fine crowd, the real solid backbone of our whole Empire, they made us feel humbly proud that we ourselves were now just some of the boys.

'Then came the morning we saw our names posted on the "Ops Tonight" notice board in the crew room. The wording itself was quite insignificant, and merely stated that the following crews were detailed for operations tonight, 30th April 1941. Aircraft 'Y', Captain Squadron Leader Burnett, Navigator Pilot Officer Williams, Wireless Operator Sergeant Morton, Rear Gunner Sergeant Brett. My goodness how that last name seemed to

stand out on the list. My mind was a turmoil as I went out to the aircraft to check over the rear turret and ensure that all four guns were in tip-top condition. All the time a sickly uneasy feeling persisted inside of me. I have since tried to analyse it, but without much success because it seemed to be such a mixture of excitement, apprehension, uncertainty, and above all, fear, of what was then "the unknown".

'The early afternoon saw us airborne for a short but very thorough air test, during which time all our aircraft equipment was tested for any last-minute snags. With this over we returned to the crew room for a check of our personal equipment, before proceeding to briefing.

'I don't really know why but I felt extremely proud and confident as I entered the briefing room, and this feeling of pride and confidence grew as the thoroughness of our briefing was unfolded. The very simple words – "Gentlemen, your target for tonight is Kiel" opened the proceedings, and then one after another the various specialist officers covered their particular aspects of the operation. I was amazed, and a little frightened perhaps, at our vast knowledge of the German flak positions and their strength, and the location of searchlights, and above all the uncanny knowledge we possessed of the intricacies of German defence against our bombers.

'Then with briefing over we returned to the mess for the most trying part of all operations – waiting for take-off. We only had a few hours to spare, but oh how long those hours seemed. Most of us played cards or listened to the radio, while some just sat around idly discussing either the pending operation or the relative merits of their many girl friends in Harrogate.

'However, the time eventually came round for us to have our pre-operational meal, consisting of fried egg and baked beans, which always produced unpleasant results in the crowded atmosphere of a bomber, and then to the crew room for the distribution of our flying rations and the last minute scramble. Our rations were always very acceptable as they usually consisted of chocolate, Horlicks tablets, biscuits, barley sugar or clear gums together with the inevitable packet of chewing gum.

'My gosh, what a job it is dressing for an operational flight – sweaters, flying suits, thick woollen gloves and scarves and other odd items of clothing until one assumes

Wellington Mk.II Z8345 of 104 Squadron flies over the peaceful Yorkshire countryside. No.104 was one of two Wellington-equipped units to form in 4 Group in April 1941 – the other being 405 (RCAF) Squadron. Both units were based at Driffield. *C. E. Brown, RAF Museum, 5909-12*

Halifax Mk.1 and crew of 76 Squadron, Middleton St. George, Summer 1941. No.76 Squadron was the second Halifax unit to form within 4 Group in May 1941 *IWM, CH3396*

gigantic proportions. Then came the trickiest job of the lot when the whole assortment is forced into a bundle by fastening on a parachute harness, after which everyone walks around in a semi-sitting down position. After all the convulsions needed to don this cumbersome attire, I was perspiring freely, and I helped this along considerably when I tried to dash around picking up the rest of my gear – parachute, helmet and goggles, thermos flask, torch and rations. Then with these clutched in my arms I staggered outside and climbed aboard the lorry that was to take us out to our aircraft. This last short journey brought to me a repetition of that horrible sickly feeling in my stomach. I found myself listening with very little interest to the good natured joking that was going on between different crews, wondering all the time what the hell was so funny about the whole business. All the laughing enthusiasm there was, to take on bets as to which aircraft would be the first one back. The tremendous roars of laughter which accompanied sarcastic remarks about particular pilots ropey take-offs and landings, and the general feeling that everything connected with the operation was so damned funny. Oh yes, I was very, very green and inexperienced and little realised then that this was just another of those safety valves that became part of one's nature in operational flying. Anyhow, I took an extremely dim view of the whole business and was very relieved when that short bumpy ride was over.

'Having carefully stowed away my parachute and the rest of my gear, I adjusted my helmet and plugged in to the inter-communication telephone in time for the Captain's check call. My next job was to load the four Brownings, and although I had done this dozens of times before, I found that on this occasion I was all

fingers and thumbs, and I was bathed in perspiration by the time they were all loaded.

'Very soon then we were lumbering around the perimeter track, and with a "green" from the control caravan, I felt that exciting surge of power from our Merlin engines and we were soon hurtling across the drome and into the air for my first operational take-off. I spent the next few minutes making myself as comfortable as possible in the confined space of my rear turret, and looked out in time to see the friendly lights of our 'drome disappearing into the darkness. Then came the awful realisation that I was alone – perched in my small turret for the next eight or ten hours – completely out of touch with the rest of the world, and even out of touch with the rest of the crew apart from the conversation that reached me over the inter-com. It is surprising how comfortless such a position is, and on this my first trip, it seemed even more comfortless and remote. I found myself longing to see one of my fellow crew – everything seemed so weird and unreal, and that feeling of complete detachment was one of the worst I have ever experienced.

'We were well on our course by this time, passing over Flamborough Head, and out over the North Sea, and I was beginning to feel extremely cold. I soon warmed myself up, however, with a spot of hot coffee from my flask, and dived into my packet of biscuits for a short private tea party.

'My first glimpse of German flak, both heavy and light, came as we were passing to the north of the Frisian Islands and also near Borkum. To my amazement, instead of appearing as terrifying as I had imagined, it looked so much like a Crystal Palace firework display gone haywire. I found it both interesting and amusing.

No.78 Squadron crews gather outside the crew room to await the transports: Middleton St George, Spring 1941 *D. Webb*

Sergeants Simpson and Beaton have a quick smoke and chat before the crew bus arrives: 78 Squadron Middleton St George, May 1941. *D. Webb*

'We crossed the rest of the North Sea without incident and were soon approaching Meldorf Bay, our first landfall on the enemy coast. Here we found that visibility was getting bad, and before long we were flying over a layer of complete cloud. Unfortunately, things were exactly the same in the target area, and although we dropped several flares and searched for almost an hour, we could see absolutely nothing to give us a pin-point on the target. We could see large concentrations of searchlights and flak below us under the cloud, and although it was a regrettable descision, we flew over the thickest concentration of searchlights and dropped our bombs right across. We must have hit something good because I saw some vivid explosions after our bombs had gone off. The excitement was spoiled, however, by the clouds blanketing out everything below us and somewhat reluctantly we turned and set course for home.

'The journey back across the North Sea was long and wearisome but at last we caught a glimpse of breakers on the good old English coast – a most cheerful sight that did wonders for my tired condition. It wasn't long before we were once more parked in our dispersal. I staggered out of our aircraft dirty, cold and unbelievably tired, but so very thankful that after seven hours in the air, my first bombing raid on Germany was over'.

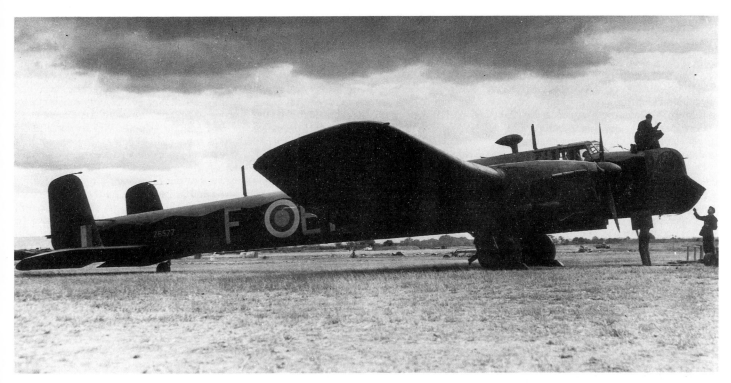

Whitley Mk.V Z6577 'F-Freddie' of 78 Squadron receives some attention from ground crews at Middleton St George, Spring 1941. 'F-Freddie's skipper at this time was Sgt Harry Drummond, later Wing Commander and CO of 1658 HCU at Riccall. *G. Lawrence*

No.4 Group Bomber Command, May 1941

Sqn	Equipment	Airfield
10	Whitley V	Leeming
35	Halifax I	Linton-on-Ouse
51	Whitley V	Dishforth
58	Whitley V	Linton-on-Ouse
76 (non-op)	Halifax I	Linton-on-Ouse
77	Whitley V	Topcliffe
78	Whitley V	Middleton-st-George
102	Whitley V	Topcliffe
104	Wellington II	Driffield
405 (non-op)	Wellington II	Driffield

The bombing offensive reached a new height of intensity on the night of 8th May 1941 when 364 sorties were flown against Hamburg and Bremen. It was the largest number of aircraft despatched by Bomber Command in a single night. No.4 Group were detailed to attack Bremen, sending seventy-eight Whitleys and six Wellingtons to bomb shipyards and city targets. The Wellingtons were Mk.IIs from the newly formed No.104 Squadron, making their operational debut. Four of the Squadron's aircraft reached Bremen and carried out successful attacks. One aircraft, skippered by Sergeant Doherty, bombed Wilhelmshaven and the Wellington of Sergeant Stiles did not bomb owing to the rear turret door being jammed.

No.104 Squadron were out again the following night with Squadron Leader Beare, 104's temporary CO, leading six aircraft to Ludwigshafen in Wellington W5432 'H'. The raid caused heavy damage and casualties to the city, 1,399 people being made homeless. The AOC No.4 Group sent the following message to 104 Squadron:

'At Group we are full of admiration for the work done by all units, for my part I particularly wish to thank all concerned in bringing No.104 Squadron's first two operations to a very highly successful conclusion. Well done'.

As part of their preparations for the invasion of Russia the Germans executed a number of heavy air attacks against Britain during May 1941. These raids, part of an elaborate deception plan to cloak the movement of Luftwaffe squadrons to the east, culminated in a heavy attack on London on 10th May. Two nights later three Ju 88s struck at Linton-on-Ouse in the early hours of 12th May. The attack lasted for approximately half an hour during which time incendiaries started fires in the hangar roofs. Prompt action by fire fighting teams prevented serious damage and, apart from holes in the hangar roofs, only two Halifaxes were slightly damaged. The station commander, Group Captain F. F. Garraway, was killed conducting fire fighting operations; three other airmen were killed and ten injured.

A period of unsettled weather at the end of May prevented a sustained effort being mounted from 4 Group. However, Cologne, Kiel and Düsseldorf were all attacked during this period with moderate results. Dortmund was raided by thirty-seven Whitleys on the night of 8th June, but industrial haze prevented accurate bombing. Low clouds over the North Yorkshire moors caused two Whitleys, one each from Nos. 51 and 78 squadrons, to crash with the loss of both crews as they searched for their bases on return from Dortmund.

Schwerte marshalling yards were the target for eighty No.4 Group Whitleys on the night of 12th June as Bomber Command made a concerted effort to disrupt the important rail centres east of the Ruhr. Taking part in the operation that night were four Wellington Mk.IIs of No.405 (RCAF) Squadron, the RCAF's first bombing mission of the war. Ground haze prevented a successful attack, only forty-one aircraft bombing the primary target. Three Whitleys failed to return. A Whitley from No.10 Squadron, Z6721 (Pilot Officer Littlewood), ran into difficulties and had to ditch in the North Sea when its engines began giving trouble on the outward flight. Near the Dutch coast the port engine overheated and lost power. Upon reaching the Dutch coast Littlewood decided to turn back and jettison the bombs in the sea. Soon after turning back the port engine completely failed but the pilot was able to bring the aircraft down onto the sea and the crew managed to get into the dinghy. At 06.00 hours an unidentified aircraft circled the dinghy and then made off. An hour later two Heinkel He IIIs appeared and whilst one of the German aircraft circled the dinghy, the other went back towards the English coast and chivalrously directed an RAF rescue launch onto the scene, the crews being rescued at 07.35 hours.

Also operating for the first time were the Halifaxes of No.76 Squadron, the second Halifax squadron, flying from their new base at Middleton St George which they had occupied since 4th June. The target for the

Halifaxes was the chemical works at Huls. Detailed for the raid were eight Halifaxes from No.35, three from 76 and seven Stirlings from 7 Squadron. The attack was largely unsuccessful due to poor visibility with only one of the Halifaxes from 35 Squadron reporting an attack on the primary. Of the contingent from 76 Squadron only one crew (Pilot Officer Richards), was able to bomb a useful target and that was Essen. The other two aircraft returned early with engine trouble.

On the night of 16th June, No.4 Group despatched thirty-nine Whitleys, sixteen Wellingtons and three Halifaxes to Cologne. Again only scattered damage was caused to the target. No.405 (RCAF) Squadron suffered its first loss that night when one of its Wellingtons, W5522 (Sergeant McGregor), came down in the sea off the Dutch coast with the loss of the entire crew. Two Whitleys also failed to return from the raid. One aircraft from 10 Squadron, (Sergeant Baston), falling victim to a Junkers Ju 88 intruder from NJG.1. Intruders struck again two nights later and again a 10 Squadron Whitley was the victim, Sergeant Bradford and crew in Z6671, failing to return from an attack on Bremen.

At this early stage of the war, German night fighters did not carry airborne interception radar, but a new control procedure, known as *Himmelbett* (translated as 'Four-poster Bed'), enabled ground controllers to vector the night fighters to within 400 yards of a victim. At this stage the pilot was able to see the glow of the bombers exhaust and would be able to carry out a visual attack. The *Himmelbett* system relied on two types of ground radar systems working in conjunction. The *Freya* equipment gave early warning of the approach of a bomber and then two *Wurzburg* radars plotted the target and the selected night fighter for a ground controlled interception. What became known as the 'Kammhuber Line' – named after the General of Night Fighters, Josef Kammhuber – was established in 1941 and was a series of *Himmelbett* sectors located at first in the immediate approaches to the Ruhr but by March 1941 had been extended to the Danish border.

The introduction of the Kammhuber line air defence system resulted in a steady increase in Bomber Command losses during the spring and summer of 1941 culminating in the heaviest night loss of the war so far on the night of 27th June. During that night an attack by seventy-three Wellingtons and thirty-eight Whitleys was attempted against Bremen. The raiders encountered early, severe storm conditions with heavy icing with the result that many crews failed to reach the target. More significant were the numerous reports of intense night fighter activity, heavy flak and large numbers of searchlights working in cones and co-operating with the flak and fighters. It turned out to be a disastrous night for No.4 Group with eleven Whitleys lost, four each from Nos.10 and 102 and three from 77 Squadron. In addition three Wellingtons failed to return.

Throughout June 1941, 'Circus' operations – as daylight attacks by Bomber Command with strong fighter escorts were known – had been attempted with moderate results. The majority of these attacks had been carried out by Blenheims of No.2 Group with heavy escorts of Spitfires. Now with the introduction of the new heavy bombers, including the Halifax, with their greatly increased defensive armament, thoughts began to turn to attempting limited penetration, unescorted, daylight missions. The first daylight test for the Halifaxes was attempted on 30th June when six aircraft from No.35 Squadron, led by Squadron Leader K. B. Tait, raided Kiel. In excellent visibility a successful attack was made on the dock area, two flights of three aircraft bombing from 17,000 and 18,000 feet respectively. Coming through the heavy and accurate flak defences both formations came under attack from a flight of Bf 110 fighters. In the ensuing fight one fighter was seen to go down in flames followed by Flight Lieutenant Robinson's Halifax, L9499 'Q'. The raiders managed to fight their way out of the difficult situation but not before Flying Officer Owen's Halifax, L9501 'Y' had been badly shot-up, with the loss of one of the beam gunners, Sergeant Simpson. For his leadership of the raid Squadron Leader K. B. Tait was awarded the DSO and Flying Officer Owen received a DFC. Results appeared to show that daylight bombing may yet prove a success.

There was a shift of emphasis to the bomber offensive at the beginning of July 1941 with the issuing of a new directive. The danger at sea had receded for the time being, and with German attentions firmly focused in Russia, it was possible for Bomber Command to return to the offensive against Germany. All efforts were now to be directed against the enemy's transportation system, particularly railway centres and inland waterways. Primary targets suitable for attack on clear moonlit nights included rail centres at Hamm, Osnabruck, Soest, Schwerte, Cologne, Dusseldorf and the internal rail-water trans-shipment port at Duisburg-Ruhrort (the largest inland port in Europe). All these targets were situated in congested industrial areas and the directive stressed the importance of incidental damage to surrounding areas and its effect on the civil population, in particular the morale of the industrial workers. Secondary targets, when weather conditions were unsuitable over primary targets, included Hannover, Bremen, Hamburg, Frankfurt, Mannheim and Stuttgart.

No.4 Group began July with attacks on Cologne, Bremen, Essen and on the night of the 4th, the German battlecruisers which were sheltering in Brest harbour. An all No.4 Group attack three nights later, by fifty-four Whitleys and eighteen Wellingtons, on the railway yards at Osnabruck ushered in the new bombing phase. Damage to the target, however, was slight and three Whitleys were lost. On the night of the 8th July, Nos 35 and 76 Squadrons sent their Halifaxes to the Leuna

oil plant at Merseburg. That same night Whitleys from Nos. 10, 58 and 78 Squadrons raided marshalling yards at Hamm. One No.78 Squadron Whitley, T4209 'Q', (Sergeant McQuitty), was damaged by flak over the target. With his starboard engine dead and pitot head shot away McQuitty set course for home. Just after crossing the Dutch coast near Texel, the crippled Whitley came under attack from a Bf 110 fighter. There followed a five minute inconclusive duel after which the enemy aircraft was seen to dive away. With his aircraft rapidly losing height McQuitty struggled in vain to reach the English coast. With just nine miles to go, and down to only 400 feet, the remaining engine cut out and the Whitley dived into the sea. The crew were able to get into the dinghy but unfortunately it had been damaged in the crash and immediately began to sink. The Observer, Sergeant Haffenden, by a superhuman effort swam the nine miles to the English coast and survived. Sadly the rest of the crew were lost.

Encouraged by the results of recent shallow penetration daylight operations, Bomber Command again turned its attentions to the three German warships - *Scharnhorst*, *Gneisenau* and *Prinz Eugen* sheltering in Brest harbour.

Originally it had been planned to strike at all three ships in daylight with a combined force of heavy and medium bombers heavily escorted by Spitfires. At the last minute, however, the plan had to be changed as the *Scharnhorst* was moved to a new berth at La Rochelle, some two hundred miles further south. The plan now called for two separate attacks. The first was to be carried out by a force of one hundred aircraft – mainly Wellingtons, and including nine each from Nos. 104 and 405 Squadrons – on the *Gneisenau* and *Prinz Eugen* at Brest. Three squadrons of Spitfires fitted with long range fuel tanks were to provide the escort. The second attack would be by fifteen unescorted Halifaxes from Nos.35 and 76 Squadrons on the *Scharnhorst* at La Rochelle.

The raid on Brest went ahead on schedule on 24th July in clear conditions. Eighteen Hampdens, escorted by the Spitfires, opened the attack by decoying many of the defending German fighters away from the main force of seventy-nine Wellingtons. Nevertheless, many fighters broke through the escorts and reached the main force and, together with an intense and accurate flak barrage, succeeded in shooting down ten of the Wellingtons and two Hampdens. Several crews from No.104 Squadron reported seeing Pilot Officer Nicholl's Wellington, W5436 'E', taking violent evasive action whilst boxed in by intense, heavy flak. Later the same aircraft came under attack from three single-engined fighters and was seen to fall in flames. Meanwhile Squadron Leader Budden's Wellington, W5583 'P' of No.104 Squadron, came under attack from an enemy aircraft without warning as it left the target area. Badly shot-up, the port engine was dead and with hydraulics,

Rear gunner, Sergeant Kilminster of 58 Squadron poses by the turret of his Whitley Mk.V in the warm sunshine at Linton-on-Ouse, Summer 1941. He is wearing a flight Jerkin over his service dress which incorporates an integral parachute harness fitted with snap-hooks. In an emergency he would clip the 'D' rings of his parachute onto the two snap-hooks. *R. Kilminster*

With an impressive scoreboard showing 36 ops completed, Whitley Mk.V T4131 'W' of No.78 Squadron displays its well weathered Night Black undersurfaces. T4131, like many other Whitleys that survived operations, ended its days at an operational training unit. It was eventually wrecked in a landing accident. *RAF Museum, 5909-1*

Whitley Mk.V of 58 Squadron, Linton-on-Ouse, Summer 1941. The lead from the aircraft's nose is to a trolley accumulator used to provide starting boost. *R. Kilminster*

Smoke screens successfully cloak the *Prinz Eugen* during an attack on Brest, on the night of 4th July 1941. The strike photograph of Flight Lieutenant Petley of 77 Squadron was taken from 11,000 feet. *S. Pickles*

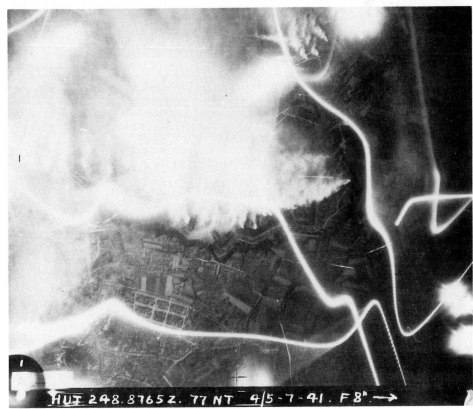

Above: **Flying Officer G.L. Cheshire DSO, DFC, 35 Squadron, with his air and groundcrew in front of their Halifax *Offenbach*, Linton-on-Ouse, Summer 1941.** *RAF Museum via MAP*

Below: **A Wellington Mk.II of No.405 (RCAF) Squadron is just about to lift off from the runway at Pocklington, in the Summer of 1941.** *RCAF*

flaps and undercarriage damaged, Budden was able to escape his attacker by diving to sea level, eventually crash landing at Exeter. Two crew members were badly injured during the fighter attack, Sergeant Ebrill later died of his wounds whilst the rear gunner, Sergeant Armstrong was to spend many months in hospital; his injuries included five bullet wounds in the chest and a cannon shell through the knee.

Meanwhile, the fifteen unescorted Halifaxes were about to receive an equally hostile reception over La Rochelle. As the Halifaxes formed up to attack, having flown at low level for most of the way to the target to avoid detection, they were met by a heavy concentration of flak and a large force of fighters. Two Halifaxes were lost before the target was reached, as the fighters swept through the tightly packed formation, raking the Halifaxes with cannon and machine gun fire. Despite the attentions of the fighters, the bombers were able to reach the target and carry out a concentrated attack, bombs being seen to burst across the dock area where the *Scharnhorst* was berthed. Three more Halifaxes were lost as the raiders left the target area. The rest of the formation all received damage to some extent but five direct hits had been obtained on the *Scharnhorst,* causing severe damage. That night the battlecruiser was moved to Brest. The raid had been successful in putting the *Scharnhorst* out of action but it had also shown that the heavy bombers still faced the prospect of severe losses if similar operations were attempted again.

On 25th July 1941, Air Vice-Marshal Arthur Coningham, after two years service in command of No.4 Group, moved on to take command of the Desert Air Force. He was replaced on 26th July by Air Vice-Marshal C. R. Carr, a tough New Zealander who was to prove a worthy successor.

Charles Roderick Carr was born in the town of Feilding, Wellington, North Island, New Zealand on 31st August 1891. He served in the New Zealand army during the First World War, before transferring to the RNAS and then to the new RAF. His distinguished pre-war career included a spell as Chief of Air Staff in Lithuania in 1920. He took part in Shackleton's Antarctic Expedition in 1921-22, and in 1927 flew on the RAF's first long distance, non-stop flight from England to the Persian Gulf. Flying in a much modified Hawker Horsley, he completed the 3,400 miles in 35 hours. In 1939, at the outbreak of war, Carr was in France with the Advanced Air Striking Force. He then moved on to become AOC RAF Northern Ireland in 1940, the post he held until his appointment as AOC No.4 Group in 1941.

The new AOC No.4 Group, Air Vice-Marshal C.R. Carr, pictured in his office at Heslington Hall. *J. Harding*

Chapter Eight

The Mounting Cost

As July gave way to August, Bomber Command began to intensify its attacks on inland German targets: Cologne, Berlin, Hamburg and Frankfurt all featuring in the target lists at this time. As the effort increased in intensity so the losses mounted.

On the night of 12th August No.4 Group's squadrons were involved in a heavy raid on Berlin. Bad weather prevented many aircraft from reaching their allotted targets centred around the Air Ministry buildings in the Alexander Platz. The defences claimed two Wellingtons from No.104 Squadron and two Halifaxes from No.76. One of the No.104 crews lost was that of Squadron Leader Budden in Wellington Mk.II W5461 'R'. Budden's crew had earlier survived being badly shot up over Brest three weeks before. However, their luck had finally run out and they were to spend the rest of the war as POWs. Also captured that night were five members of Flight Lieutenant Christopher Cheshire's 76 Squadron crew. Cheshire's Halifax had been shot down near Bremen and apart from the front and rear gunners all the crew escaped by parachute. To complete an unhappy night for the Group three aircraft crashed on return, including Sergeant McHale's Halifax of No.76 Squadron, the entire crew dying in the resulting fire.

Two nights later railway centres at Magdeburg, Brunswick and Hannover were attacked. Fourteen aircraft were lost including six from No.4 Group. Three of those lost were from 102 Squadron. Sergeant Philip Brett was a wireless operator with Sergeant Bill Wilson's crew and their Whitley, Z6798, was one of the many aircraft that returned with some kind of damage that night:

'We slipped through the coastal defences quite easily noticing as we did so, that the searchlights seemed to be particularly effective. Then we started to climb as high as we could, ready to cross the formidable belt of searchlights with which the Huns had covered all approaches to the Ruhr. We had reached about 18,500 feet before we found the edge of the searchlight belt below us. Bill put the nose down slightly and opened out the throttles to speed us on our way through the danger area, which at the best of times would take us about twenty or twenty-five minutes to clear. We were completely mystified on this occasion by the fact that we were immediately caught and held in the revealing glare of several searchlights, and even more mystified to find that as we proceeded on our way, the Huns seemed to have

not the slightest difficulty in picking up our aircraft. It was horribly uncanny to see the searchlights come into operation and swing on to us right away. We began to wonder what new equipment the enemy were using to give them such amazing accuracy.

'We were just discussing this phenomenon when there was a terrific explosion on the port wing just outside my cabin window. Nick, our rear gunner, reported "enemy aircraft coming up astern and attacking". Yes he was attacking alright. I could have told him that, and I wondered at the same time how much of our port wing had been shot away by his first burst of fire. Nick then reported that he was coming in again, so I put my parachute handy, and opened the door into the fuselage ready for a quick exit if necessary. I then sat down at my radio and sent out a message to base to let them know that we were being attacked. By this time Jerry was about 500 yards astern and coming in fast, and as he got within range of our guns, Bill held our aircraft steady and told Nick to give him hell. Nick, bless him, carried out these instructions to the letter and let loose a stream of fire which put his port engine out of action and sent him diving down to become lost in the clouds below us. We didn't see any more of him, thank goodness, and afterwards claimed one Bf 110 damaged, believed destroyed.

'This hectic episode over we returned to sanity once again and settled down to our real job of bombing Hannover, which we did with very little opposition. Returning once more across the searchlight belt we once again found the searchlights picking us up with no trouble at all and although we got through with no more fighters after us we did, however, collect a few nasty flak holes. Then, when we were approaching the enemy coast, and I happened to be looking down the flare chute in the fuselage, I noticed that we had our downward identification lights on below the aircraft, and of course, they had been on for the whole trip. Well, I ask you! No wonder the searchlights had been able to pick us up so easily, and no wonder we had been shot up by a Jerry fighter.

'We must have collected a few flak holes in our petrol tanks, because as we were approaching base, we noticed that our petrol gauges were registering zero, and sure enough as we landed and taxied across the 'drome, both engines spluttered and fizzled out.

'Clambering out of the aircraft, we found

our port wing in a terrible state from cannon shells and machine gun fire from the fighter. Our poor old Whitley was indeed a sorry sight - the ground crew expressing wonder at the fact that our port wing had not crumpled with such severe damage.'

Two visits to Cologne rail yards on the 16th and 18th August produced meagre bombing results and more heavy losses for No.4 Group. A total of thirteen Whitleys and one Wellington were lost to the Group over the two nights. These were indeed difficult days for RAF Bomber Command who stood to be put out of business by these serious losses. A further blow came in August when the Butt Report became available.

The Butt Report was an independent detailed analysis of bombing photographs taken on night raids in June and July 1941. Its findings indicated that the majority of the bomber force were failing to find their targets. Only one fifth were able to drop their bombs within five miles of their appointed target.

As a result of the Butt Report steps were immediately taken to hasten the development of electronic aids designed to improve bombing accuracy. In addition the bomber force, despite its failings, was to be expanded. By the beginning of September 1941 plans were prepared for the expansion of Bomber Command to a first line strength of 4,000 aircraft.

Meanwhile, the longer dark nights of autumn and winter allowed Bomber Command to try deeper penetration raids into Germany. Berlin, Frankfurt, Stettin and the city of Turin in northern Italy were attacked in September with good bombing results claimed.

After a period of bad weather over the northern bases at the beginning of October 1941, operations by No.4 Group got under way again with raids against Essen on the 10th and Nuremburg on the 12th. Bombing on the Nuremburg operation was widely scattered with some bombs falling as far away as sixty-five miles from Nuremburg. Such were the difficulties of target location on such long distance flights to inland targets.

The met forecast for the night of 7/8th November 1941 indicated clouds building up over Germany, with the chance of thunderstorms, hail and severe icing. Despite the unfavourable forecast a long projected maximum effort raid on Berlin was approved. Also being attacked that night were the cities of Cologne and Mannheim and the total of 392

Halifax Mk.1 series II L9530 'L' of 76 Squadron at Middleton-St-George in July/August 1941. Normally the mount of Flight Lieutenant Christopher Cheshire – brother of Leonard Cheshire (serving with No.35 Squadron) – 'L' was lost attacking Berlin on 12/13th August 1941. Except for the front and rear gunners, all the crew escaped by parachute and were made prisoners of war, including Flight Lieutenant Cheshire. *IWM, CH3393*

aircraft despatched represented the greatest effort by Bomber Command to date.

On that night the crews found the weather conditions much worse than had been forecast. Many decided to attack alternative targets than risk the severe icing that they would face if they tried to reach Berlin. Of those who chose to go for Berlin many succumbed to the effects of icing or had to ditch because they had used up too much fuel trying to climb above the cloud.

The night's operations were a disaster with a total of thirty-seven aircraft (9.4 per cent) lost. No.4 Group, who were targetted against Berlin and Essen, lost twelve aircraft including nine Whitleys. The Berlin raid of 7th

November 1941 was the last major raid on the city until January 1943. As a direct result of 7th November, and the unhappy period it climaxed, the War Cabinet directed that the scale of operations through the winter months was to be severely reduced while the future policy of Bomber Command and its offensive were debated.

The rest of the month of November was a quiet period for the squadrons of No.4 Group as bad weather brought operations almost to a standstill.

Missions got under way again on the last night of the month with a raid on shipyard and city targets in Hamburg. With a full moon and no cloud, bombing conditions were perfect, it was also perfect weather for the defences.

Forty-six aircraft were despatched from No.4 Group including contingents from Nos.35 and 76 Squadrons operating with a number of their newly arrived Halifax Mk.IIs.

The Mk.II Halifaxes had been delivered in October and they differed from the Mk.Is in having 1,280-hp Merlin XX engines and a Boulton Paul two-gun dorsal turret.

Sergeant Philip Brett of No.102 Squadron remembers that night and the hot reception

he and his crew faced over Hamburg:

'It certainly was a grand sight, with perfect visibility, a clear sky and a full moon, we shouldn't have any trouble in finding the target.

'Very soon we were flying to the north of the Frisian Islands, all of which we could see quite clearly, and as usual they were sending up their terrific welcoming barrage of light and heavy flak and clusters of searchlights.

'Approaching Meldorf Bay and the mouth of the river, we were able to see the whole coastline stretched out for miles, and we took the opportunity of checking our position to set course for our final run to the target.

'We flew down to the town on the east side of the river, and then circled to pick up our actual target. About three miles away we could see this clearly in the moonlight, but in between the sky was absolutely torn assunder with unbelievable concentrations of heavy flak, and filled with countless hundreds of searchlights. Immediately we came within range we were caught and held by about twenty searchlights and were met with a colossal barrage of heavy flak. Our poor old kite was literally bumping and bouncing about in the sky with the terrific explosions'.

Halifax Mk.1 series I L9503 'P' of 35 Squadron flew on many of this squadron's early operations including the first daylight attack by Halifaxes on Kiel on 30th June. It was lost attacking Hamburg on the 15th September 1941. *IWM, CH17539*

Wellington Mk.II W5461 'R' of 104 Squadron. Skippered by Squadron Leader Buddon W5461 was one of four aircraft from 4 Group that failed to return from Berlin 12/13th August. To complete an unhappy night three more crashed on return. *C. E. Brown, RAF Museum*

Whitley Z6954 of 77 Squadron returned with its starboard tailplane shot away, Autumn 1941. *D. Dean*

Flight Sergeant Larry Donnelly, wireless operator with Sergeant Harwood's 76 Squadron Halifax, recalls his crew's 'narrow squeak' that night as they ran the gauntlet of the Hamburg defences:

'We made our first run at 17,000 feet and we were coned by searchlights. During the violent evasive action that followed the aircraft stalled and it took the combined efforts of both pilots to pull the aircraft out of the ensuing dive.

Top: **Whitley Mk.V Z6575 of 58 Squadron at Linton-on-Ouse. This Whitley flew many operations with No.58 in the Summer and Autumn of 1941. It was lost attacking Hamburg on the night of 30th November 1941 with Sgt McKay and crew.** *R. Kilminster*

Above: **No.10 Squadron Whitley Mk.V in flight, late 1941. 'K' Z9226 shows off its soot black finish, dull red serial numbers and grey codes. Also of interest is the white areas of the fin**

flash and roundel darkened with grey wash, a camouflage measure designed to tone down the bright markings. *RAF Museum, P019764*

Below: **Two Halifax Mk.II series I's of 10 Squadron in close formation over Yorkshire. Note the bulbous Boulton Paul C dorsal turret fitted to R9376 'D-Donald'.** *IWM, CH4433*

Top left, page 65: **A 35 Squadron Halifax turning over Brest, 18th Dec 1941.** *H. Mennell*

'We recovered at 10,000 feet and commenced another run but we were picked up again by the searchlights and the flak was coming up thick and fast, you could smell the cordite from the bursts and the aircraft lurched as the explosions got nearer. Again we took violent evasive action but we were unable to escape from the flak and searchlights. By this time we were diving through 5,000 feet, so we dropped the bombs and continued down to ground level. The searchlights and flak followed us all the way down but we screamed over the roof tops and headed for home going like a bat out of hell.

'During de-briefing we heard another crew captained by Pilot Officer Hank Iveson, (later Group Captain Iveson), reporting that they had seen searchlights shining horizontally over the target - we were able to substantiate their report!'

The Hamburg defences were particularly aggressive that night, shooting down thirteen bombers. Eight of the victims were from No.4 Group including four from No.58 Squadron.

On 7th December 1941 the Japanese struck at Pearl Harbor and many other places in the Pacific and South East Asia. The war was now truly a global affair. These were indeed dark days for the Allies, and with the loss of HMS *Prince of Wales* and HMS *Repulse* to Japanese aircraft, Britain's hopes of defending her possessions in South East Asia had been struck a severe blow.

It now became even more imperative to cripple the heavy units of the German Navy sheltering in Brest harbour as soon as possible, lest they take advantage of the Allies weakened situation. Consequently, early in December 1941, Bomber Command was directed to prepare plans to strike at the German battlecruisers in daylight.

During December 1941, Stirlings of No.3 Group had been using a new radio bombing aid – TR3098, code named 'Trinity' – and the forerunner of the device which would be developed into 'Oboe'. The new device was used operationally for the first time by Stirlings from Nos. 7 and 15 Squadrons against the warships in Brest on 7th December. The targets were once again Bomber Command's old opponents 'Salmon and Gluckstein', the *Scharnhorst* and *Gneisenau*. This attack and further raids, mounted on the 11th and 12th December, were not successful. It was therefore decided to mount a heavy day raid, using Halifaxes, Stirlings and Manchesters, to try once and for all to cripple the battlecruisers before they escaped onto the convoy routes to harass Allied shipping.

Intensive daylight formation flying practice now became the order of the day for the Halifax squadrons earmarked for the raid: Nos. 10, 35 and 76. No.10 Squadron would be using their new Halifax Mk.IIs having just converted from Whitleys.

A force of forty-seven bombers would take part in the operation planned for 18th December. From No.4 Group six Halifaxes from each of Nos. 10, 35 and 76 Squadrons,

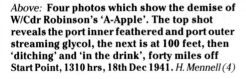

Above: **Four photos which show the demise of W/Cdr Robinson's 'A-Apple'. The top shot reveals the port inner feathered and port outer streaming glycol, the next is at 100 feet, then 'ditching' and 'in the drink', forty miles off Start Point, 1310 hrs, 18th Dec 1941.** *H. Mennell (4)*

Upper Right: **Two 35 Squadron Halifaxes over Brest, 18th December 1941. Smoke can be seen rising (top left) from the *Scharnhörst* and *Gneisenau*.** *IWM, C2228*

Above right: **'Bombs gone!' Wing Commander Robinson's Halifax Mk.II V9978 'A-Apple' drops its bombs over Brest.** *H. Mennell*

from No.3 Group eighteen Stirlings and from No.5 Group eleven Manchesters. Fighter cover was to be provided by Spitfires with long range fuel tanks.

The plan, coded named *Veracity 1*, was for the No.4 Group contingent to rendezvous over Linton-on-Ouse before proceeding to a point off Lundy Island were they would join up with the Stirlings and Manchesters. The fighter escort would sweep ahead and attempt to lure the German fighters away as the bombers made their run in to the target.

Shortly after 10.00 hours on 18th December six Halifaxes from No.35 Squadron joined up with eleven others from Nos. 10 and 76 over Linton. The 4 Group force had earlier been reduced to seventeen aircraft when Wing Commander Tuck from No.10 Squadron was forced to return his Halifax, L9619, to Leeming with a jammed starboard undercarriage. The rest of the formation set course for Lundy Island for the rendezvous with the other bombers, timed for 11.20 hours.

The formation was further reduced before the rendezvous point was reached when one of the Halifaxes from 76 Squadron, (Squadron Leader Packe), had to head for Boscombe Down with a badly mis-firing engine. Meanwhile the Stirlings had arrived early over Lundy Island so they tracked out westward before turning south just in time to meet the incoming Halifax formation which tucked in behind them, followed in turn by the Manchesters.

In a clear, sunny, cloudless sky the mixed formation, in neat vics, approached the French coast. Up ahead the bombers could see the Spitfires already mixing it with the Luftwaffe.

At approximately 12.30 hours the Stirlings began attacking from the south-east through a heavy and concentrated flak barrage. German fighters, which had managed to avoid the Spitfire escorts, ignored the intense anti-aircraft fire and swarmed around the bombers. The Stirlings lost two of their number at this stage but were rewarded with the sight of their bombs bursting across the twin docks housing the warships.

Leading the Halifax force, and close in behind the Stirlings, was Wing Commander Basil Vernon Robinson of No.35 Squadron in Halifax V9978 'A-Apple'. Basil Robinson, 'Robbie' to his crews, was a pre-war pilot born in Gateshead. He had led a distinguished career in the RAF to-date having been awarded the DFC in July 1941 whilst completing a tour of operations with No.78 Squadron. Up in the front turret of 'A-Apple' wireless operator Sergeant Harold Mennell had a grandstand view of the attack:

'The Stirlings were first on the target followed by us with the Manchesters close in behind. Bombing height was 16,000 feet in order to provide maximum penetration of the four 2,000 lb and two 500 lb armour piercing bombs with which we were armed.

'We approached Brest in 'V' formation, changing to line astern for the bombing run. Our fighter escort kept the enemy fighters away from us, but the flak was very accurate, the first shell bursting dead on height and just ahead of us so that we flew through its smoke.

'We had a hang-up of one of our 2,000 pounders and 'Robbie' decided to come in again but from the landward side this time. It was during this second run that we received a near miss which put out the two port engines, one catching fire and the other suffering damage to the glycol cooling system. The extinguishers put out the fire in the port inner, but as one of the airscrews would not feather, we had to lose height to maintain flying speed, having the two starboard engines working'.

Wing Commander Robinson's aircraft was not the only Halifax to sustain damage from the withering flak barrage. Pilot Officer Hank Iveson of 76 Squadron received a near miss that sent a piece of shrapnel into the cockpit of his Halifax, narrowly missing his second pilot, Pilot Officer Perry. A Halifax from 35 Squadron was hit by flak and lost two engines but was able to limp away to eventually reach Boscombe Down.

The bombing appeared to have been successful with sticks of bombs seen to burst in and around the dock area. With the attack completed, the bombers put their noses down and headed away out across the Channel. It was now that many of the bombers became separated and fell prey to fighters. The Halifaxes, Stirlings and Manchesters, in ones, twos and threes, were tempting targets for the Messerschmitts, several of which had come down from the dog fights above to latch onto individual bombers. Two Stirlings and a Manchester were sent cartwheeling into the sea as the running fight continued above the wave tops.

A fine shot of an ex-78 Squadron Whitley V. Z6640 is shown whilst serving with No.1484 Target Towing Flight based at Driffield. As 'R-Robert' this Whitley completed 29 operations with 78 Squadron, its final raid before 'retirement', was against Emden on the night of 10th January 1942, skippered by Sergeant Stevens.

Meanwhile Wing Commander Robinson was struggling to maintain height with only two good engines. Sergeant Harold Mennell was preparing for the worst:

'As we lost height, two other aircraft from our squadron formated on us and followed us down, the second pilot of one taking photographs. Apart from Wing Commander Robinson we had all taken up our ditching positions, between the main spar or behind the rear spar, bracing ourselves against them.

'I imagined that when we hit the water we would slide along the surface but that did not happen. The crash turned out to be more violent and we came to a very abrupt halt with a wall of water sweeping through the fuselage. In fact Flight Lieutenant Rivaz, our tail gunner, sustained a broken bone in his foot from the force of the impact.

Halifax Mk.II series I, L9619 of No.10 Squadron. Abandoned by her crew on return from St. Nazaire on the night of 15/16th February 1942, L9619 crashed into high ground near Keld, North Yorkshire.
IWM, CH4435

'The dinghy inflated all right but was ruptured by the trailing edge of the mainplane so we had to make a hasty repair with the wooden stoppers provided in the dinghy. We were able to step off the mainplane straight into the dinghy all except 'Robbie' who insisted on going back into the aircraft to look for his pipe - he normally flew on operations with his unlit pipe poking from the side of his oxygen mask. We were very anxious to see him do this as we expected the aircraft to sink at any moment, but in fact it stayed afloat for another twenty minutes.

'As we sat calmly in our dinghy 'F-Freddie' from our Squadron was circling us and radioing our position. After about two hours we were approached by what appeared to be two high speed Air Sea Rescue launches, but after circling us they indicated that another vessel would be coming to collect us, and they shot off at high speed.

'As it got later and the sun went down we became more and more anxious, until finally we saw the masts of a ship appear on the horizon, and soon we were rescued by a large Royal Navy torpedo boat.

'The following day we returned to Yorkshire by train to be met at York by half the Squadron on the platform singing 'Wingo's in the drink'. We must have been a peculiar

looking group, being dressed in a variety of clothing, having gratefully given away all our flying gear to our rescuers. I must admit I was a little disappointed to find that there was no 'survivors leave' and that we were on standby for another daylight on Brest'.

Wing Commander Robinson's successful ditching of his Halifax had been a notable event. Not only did it demonstrate Robinson's skill and courage as a pilot but it was also the first time that a Halifax had ditched. Basil Robinson would later receive the award of a DSO.

Back from the raid the squadrons were disappointed to hear that no serious damage had been inflicted on the *Scharnhorst* or *Gneisenau*. Congratulations from the C-in-C Bomber Command 'on a very successful and gallant action', did little to compensate for the loss of four Stirlings, one Halifax and one Manchester.

The failure of Operation *Veracity I* to cripple the German warships meant that they would have to try again. Operation *Veracity II* was planned for 30th December, but unfavourable weather conditions over the No.3 and 5 Group bases meant that the Halifax component – again comprising of eighteen aircraft from Nos. 10, 35 and 76 Squadrons – would attack unassisted. Fighter

escort was to be provided by Spitfires who would cover the attack and the withdrawal of the bombers.

The Halifax force, reduced to sixteen aircraft by technical malfunctions, ran into well-alerted German defences as they approached Brest. Two Halifaxes were shot down in the run in to the target and a third, an aircraft from No.10 Squadron, was so badly shot up by flak that it was unable to maintain formation and was pounced upon by a fighter. Badly damaged with both inboard engines out of action, Flight Sergeant Whyte managed to ditch his Halifax off Lizard Point and the entire crew were rescued.

Again bombing results were disappointing and three aircraft and two crews had been lost. In addition most of the Halifaxes had suffered considerable flak damage.

The year of 1942 was to be a make or break year for Bomber Command. Supporters of the RAF's night bombing offensive would have to confound the critics. Fortunately their cause would be helped by a number of significant events during the year, not least of all being the appointment of Air Marshal Harris as Commander in Chief of Bomber Command in February.

Meanwhile in No.4 Group, the turn of the year saw the squadrons re-equipping with Halifaxes at a gathering pace. The faithful old Whitleys, which had served with such distinction since 1937, were to be finally retired from Bomber Command in the spring of 1942.

February 1942 saw the formation of a new squadron within No.4 Group when on the 14th of the month, No.158 Squadron was re-formed as a bomber squadron at Driffield from the home echelon of 104 Squadron. No.104 had been operating in a much reduced capacity since October 1941 as the main body of the Squadron had moved to Malta. As a result of the changes 104 was re-numbered 158. The Squadron continued to operate with Wellington Mk.IIs until their replacement with Halifaxes in June 1942.

No.4 Group Bomber Command, February 1942

Sqn	Equipment	Airfield
10	Halifax II	Leeming
35	Halifax II	Linton-on-Ouse
51	Whitley V	Dishforth
58	Whitley V	Linton-on-Ouse
76	Halifax II	Middleton-St-George
77	Whitley V	Leeming
78	Whitley V	Croft
102	Whitley V / Halifax II	Dalton
158	Wellington II	Driffield
405 (RCAF)	Wellington II	Pocklington

Almost exactly a year since Whitley bombers were successfully involved in Operation *Colossus*, the attack by parachutists on the Tragino aqueduct in Italy, No.4 Group were asked to supply aircraft and crews for another commando style operation. Operation *Biting*, the code name for the Bruneval raid, was planned for late February 1942 and was to be a combined operation involving parachutists dropping from twelve Whitleys of No.51 Squadron, led by its CO, Wing Commander P. C. Pickard.

The aim of the raid was to land parachutists near to a German radar station on the French Channel coast at Bruneval near Le Havre. The commandos were to capture the radar station and return, via a small naval flotilla, with sample components of the radio location equipment of the *Wurzburg* radar. British scientists were most anxious to study this secret German radar which could enable flak gunners to engage unseen aircraft.

The operation took place in bright moonlight on the night of 27th February and was an outstanding success and the captured radar equipment disclosed many secrets to waiting British scientists.

Above: **The Duke of Kent chats with Sgt Gardiner of 35 Squadron, at Linton-on-Ouse, January 1942. Also present is the AOC 4 Group, Air Vice-Marshal Carr, and (far right) Linton's CO, Group Captain John Whitley.** *H. Mennell*

Below: **Sergeant Gardiner introduces his crew to the Duke of Kent, on the same occasion.** *H. Mennell*

Chapter Nine

Twilight of the Whitleys

When Bomber Command came under the leadership of Air Marshal Arthur T. Harris, on 22nd February 1942, its squadrons had just come through one of their most humiliating experiences. On 12th February the German battlecruisers *Scharnhorst, Gneisenau* and the *Prinz Eugen,* making use of bad weather and low cloud, slipped through the Straits of Dover and escaped to the safety of German ports. Although Bomber Command attempted to mount strikes on the warships most of the bombers were unable to locate the enemy in poor conditions.

The failure to sink the warships was a serious blow to British pride. As far as Bomber Command was concerned the escape of the German warships, although a humiliation, was not all doom and despondency. The fact that the warships could now be penned up in northern Germany meant that Bomber Command would be free to resume uninterrupted bombing attacks on German cities.

Bomber Command received the 'green light' to resume the offensive at full effort with the issuing of a new directive on 14th February 1942. Until further notice Bomber Command's primary objective 'should now be focused on the morale of the enemy civil population and in particular of the industrial workers' (Bomber Command Directive 14th February 1942, Appendix 8: *The Strategic Air Offensive Against Germany 1939-45*: HMSO, 1961). The directive contained a list of targets most suitable for attack by area bombing, in particular those situated within range of 'Gee', the new radio aid which it was hoped would improve bombing accuracy. Gee was a position fixing system which relied on pulses being received in an aircraft from three ground stations situated in England.

The principal limitation of Gee was its range, which was approximately 400 miles, and its susceptibility to jamming by the Germans. To make the best use of the limited number of Gee-equipped aircraft, (some 150 aircraft had been fitted with the aid by mid-March 1942, including the Halifax squadrons of No. 4 Group) a new bombing technique was devised known as 'Shaker'. This involved splitting the bombing force into three sections: the illuminators, the target markers and the followers. The illuminators, all Gee-equipped aircraft, would arrive over the target first, dropping bundles of flares at ten second intervals and then bombing with high explosive. The result would be that the position of the target would be indicated by long

lanes of flares; these would guide the target markers to the scene who would then commence dropping their maximum loads of incendiary bombs. This would cause a concentrated area of fire which would be clearly visible to the followers with their loads of high explosive.

As a preliminary to the Gee - assisted raids a full scale trial was attempted to ascertain whether the flares would be successful in illuminating the target. The trial was carried out on the night of 3-4th March 1942 and the target was the Renault factory at Billancourt near Paris. The raid was an outstanding success with almost every building in the plant damaged and 40% of the Renault machine tools destroyed. Unfortunately, French civilian casualties were high, 367 being killed and a further 341 injured. This had been due to the close proximity of the Renault workers housing blocks to the factory.

No. 4 Group's contribution to the attack was modest due to the fact that the Halifax squadrons were screened from operations to allow the fitting of Gee equipment. In addition two of the original Whitley-equipped squadrons, Nos. 78 and 102, were in the process of working up with their new Halifaxes and were not ready for operations. Nevertheless, twenty Halifaxes, sixteen Wellingtons and twenty-three Whitleys from the Group were part of the 235 strong force sent to Billancourt – representing the greatest number of RAF bombers despatched to one single target so far.

Squadron Leader Thompson, of 10 Squadron, carried out a perfect attack from 1,000 feet and reported seeing his two 4,000 lb bombs burst right on the target causing buildings to collapse inwards. Squadron Leader Lane of 158 Squadron reported seeing many fires burning in the target area, accompanied by flashes from 4,000 lb bombs.

The first occasion that the Shaker bombing technique was used operationally was on the night of 8th March when 211 aircraft attacked the giant Krupps complex in Essen. Success however was limited, in spite of the use of Gee, with industrial haze preventing accurate bombing. On the following night thick haze again spoilt bombing accuracy as 187 aircraft re-visited Essen. Two crashes involving No. 4 Group aircraft on this night claimed the lives of twelve airmen. All seven crew members were lost when a No. 35 Squadron Halifax came down in the sea thirty miles off Mablethorpe and there was only one survivor

when Flight Lieutenant Duff's 158 Squadron Wellington crashed at Driffield on return.

An attack on Cologne, the fourth raid in the present Gee series, on the night of 13th March produced better results. The leading fifty Gee-equipped aircraft successfully marked the target and almost half of the 135 strong force dropped their bombs within five miles of the incendiary marked area. During the same night two No. 4 Group Whitleys were involved in disastrous crashes as they landed from a minor operation to Boulogne. At Leeming a 77 Squadron Whitley stalled in the darkness whilst on approach and crashed in a ball of fire killing the entire crew. Just over an hour later at Croft, Pilot Officer Ferris of 78 Squadron, was making his fifth attempt to land his Whitley, Z9389, when the aircraft stalled, hit the runway and exploded. Only two of the crew were rescued from the blazing inferno.

Later in the month, on the night of the 27th, thirty-five Whitleys, from Nos. 51, 58 and 77 Squadrons, took part in a raid on the French port of St. Nazaire. The raid was in support of an attempted commando raid to destroy the dry dock gates. 10/10ths cloud and severe icing conditions prevented accurate bombing and the majority of the force jettisoned their bombs in the Channel. Flight Sergeant Gray from No. 58 Squadron was forced to ditch in the sea on return, the entire crew being picked up by a minesweeper. Three other Whitley crews, two from 51 and one from 77, were not so fortunate. Bad visibility over Yorkshire caused all three aircraft to become lost on return. As the pilots struggled to find their way home in the murk all three aircraft crashed into high ground miles from their bases.

The following night seventeen Wellingtons from Nos. 158 and 405 Squadrons joined the main force of 234 aircraft, mostly carrying incendiaries, for a massive attack on the medieval port of Lubeck. In this highly successful attack large areas of the Altstadt were laid waste. The narrow streets and old timbered buildings centred around the aiming point proving particularly vulnerable to the effects of a highly concentrated incendiary attack. Crews from No. 405 Squadron reported seeing huge fires visible over 100 miles from the target.

At the end of March 1942 the three operational Halifax squadrons, Nos. 10, 35 and 76, sent detachments to Scotland to attack the German battleship *Tirpitz* sheltering in

Above and left: **Whitley Mk.V Z6580 of 58 Squadron at Linton-on-Ouse, March 1942. 'A-Apple' was normally the mount of Pilot Officer Pestridge and is shown having completed 54 operations. Note the 'Devil in the Moon' nose art with bomb log and claim for one night fighter. Also of interest are the dispersed Halifaxes of 35 Squadron in the background, just in front of Aldwark Woods.** *G. Lawrence*

Right: **A contemporary German drawing of one of the special 1,000lb spherical mines used by Halifaxes in their attacks on the German Battleship *Tirpitz*. It was hoped that these mines, by exploding underneath the ship, would rupture the underhull.**
Drawing courtesy of Flypast Magazine

Norway at Asen Fjord near Trondheim. Earlier attacks by the Halifaxes in January had been frustrated by bad weather. Operating from the airfields at Tain, Kinloss and Lossiemouth the thirty-four strong Halifax force would be trying to sink the giant battleship with an unusual weapon as Sergeant Harold Mennell, wireless operator with Squadron Leader Wilding's No. 35 Squadron crew, recalls:

'The Norway operations were a little unusual inasmuch as they were low-level attacks carrying a kind of 'football' shaped bomb cum depth charge. We had to follow Trondheim Fjord at low-level approaching the *Tirpitz* at the end of Asen Fjord. The battleship was moored under an overhanging cliff face. At the last moment we had to climb steeply away after releasing the bombs so that they would be thrown at the cliff face and roll down under the ship to explode in an area without armour plating'.

The 'football' shaped bombs were in fact 1,000 lb spherical mines. Each of the twenty-two aircraft from Nos. 10 and 35 Squadrons would be carrying four of these weapons which were designed to roll down the sloping sides of the fjord whereupon hydrostatic fuses would explode the mines in the shallow

water underneath the battleship. The task of the other twelve aircraft from No. 76 Squadron would be to neutralise the considerable flak and searchlight batteries deployed to protect the *Tirpitz*. This was to be accomplished with 4,000 lb blast bombs and 500 lb high explosives.

The target lay at the extreme range of the Halifax and poor weather severely hampered the operation, which took place on 30th March. By the time the No. 4 Group force reached Norway 10/10ths cloud and fog foiled all attempts to locate the *Tirpitz*. After remaining in the area as long as fuel reserves would allow, the Halifaxes either jettisoned their bombs in the sea or onto the enemy defences. Unfortunately the operation was to prove costly as six Halifaxes failed to return. It is almost certain that the long flight, at the limit of Halifax endurance, together with the severe weather conditions, were the reasons for the losses.

Further attacks on the *Tirpitz* were planned and the Halifax squadrons waited another five days in Scotland in anticipation of better weather. After a frustrating period of waiting, with no improvement in the forecast, the detachments returned to their bases in England.

April was to prove an eventful month for No. 4 Group with much coming and going of squadrons and aircraft. The month also saw the withdrawal of the faithful old Whitleys from operations with Bomber Command. Of the three Whitley squadrons within the Group, No. 58 transferred to Coastal Command on 7th April and Nos. 51 and 77 Squadrons flew their last Whitley sorties on 29th April (an attack on Ostend docks) before moving on loan to Coastal Command early in May. Simultaneously the re-equipment of the Group's squadrons with Halifaxes continued apace. Two more squadrons, Nos. 78 and 102, became operational during April and No. 405 was screened from operations on the 18th to prepare for the replacement of their Wellingtons with Halifax Mk.IIs.

Meanwhile the new AOC-in-C Bomber Command was determined to maintain the momentum of attacks on Germany. During April 1942 he despatched large raids to Cologne, Essen, Hamburg and Dortmund. It was during an attack on Essen, on the night of 10th April, that Sergeant Harwood and Pilot Officer Renaut, both of 76 Squadron, dropped the first 8,000 lb bombs on Germany. Sergeant Harwood was the first to attack the target, the

Krupps works, from 17,000 feet. The huge 8,000 lb bomb was too bulky to be accommodated in the bomb bay of the Halifax and it was necessary to fly with the bomb bay doors partly open. A canvas strip was used to cover one end of the open bay to reduce drag.

April's attacks culminated in a devastating series of raids on the Baltic port of Rostock, commencing on the night of 23rd April. Again using the same formula of a high percentage of incendiary bombs - so successfully used against Lubeck in March - nearly two thirds of the city was destroyed. 204 people were killed and there is no doubt that the casualties would have been much higher had not the mass of the population evacuated the city after the first raid.

TO AN ABSENT FRIEND

Take down his coat,
Pack up his things -
The scribbled note,
The tunic with wings;
The books, cricket pads and bat,
And his beloved misshapen hat.

Auction his car,
Attend to his debts,
And then there are
His several pets -
The Tortoise, Collie dog and Bird
Whose cheerful chirp is now unheard.

No more kissing
Or popsies thrilled;
He's reported 'Missing,
Believed killed'.
He had no ribbons, won no fame,
We'll toast his memory just the same.

*Squadron Leader Vernon Noble,
No. 4 Group, 1942.*

Above: **The German Battleship *Tirpitz* lies at anchor in *Asen* Fjord, Norway. Note the torpedo net booms and camouflage protection.** *IWM, C2356A*

Above right: **A Halifax crew of 35 Squadron check their route before taking-off from Linton-on-Ouse.** *via W. Baguley*

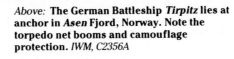

An improvement in the weather at the end of April made it possible for No. 4 Group to renew its personal battle with the *Tirpitz*. Thirty-two Halifaxes from Nos. 10, 35 and 76 Squadrons once more flew to their advanced bases in Scotland in preparation for the strike at the ship, planned to take place on the 27th. Similar tactics were to be employed as on previous attacks. Aircraft from Nos. 10 and 35 Squadron were to attack the ship with the special mines whilst those from No. 76, plus a contingent of Lancasters from No. 5 Group, struck at the defences. Pilot Officer Ian Hewitt was wireless operator with Pilot Officer Don McIntyre's No. 35 Squadron Halifax W1048 'S-Sugar', and this is his account of the attack, being an extract from an article in the October 1982 issue of *Flypast* magazine, and reproduced with their kind permission:

'Our Group Commander, Air Vice-Marshal Carr, turned up at the station together with his Senior Air Staff Officer. There was thus an abundance of brass to see that we all knew what we were supposed to be about. The key to the raid was going to be the weather. The raid was to be at night but in moonlight, and there had to be no cloud which had caused the March raid to be abortive. A special Norwegian Met expert had therefore been brought up to forecast the weather conditions.

'Being trained land crews and having now no radar equipment – our Gee sets were removed as we would be out of range of the stations – the idea when routeing us, was to fly over as much land as possible. Our route lay first over the Orkneys and then over the Shetlands before turning for the Norwegian coast.

'Each day all we had to do was to wait upon the Norwegian weather expert to tell us whether we were to go that night or not. Although cold, the weather was bright and sunny and we managed to make the trip into the nearest town (Forres). Isolated stations like Kinloss had to make the best of their own resources for entertainment and there at the time, I saw about the best camp show of the whole war.

'Anyway we were not there to enjoy ourselves and as the weather on the night of 27th April was seemingly correct for the attack, at 20.30 hours on that evening, we set off. Early after take off, I made the first of a number of careless mistakes that might well have cost me my life. I had decided – quite wrongly as subsequently proved by other airmen – that attacking at mast height would give us no chance to bale out. I had therefore removed my parachute harness which I had wrapped round my feet as one could feel the cold in those early Halifaxes.

'The trip over the Orkneys and Shetlands was uneventful enough. We would be flying at about 4,000 feet and in those latitudes, it was still light enough to see the land. On reflection, we might have routed a bit too near the naval anchorage at Scapa Flow for comfort, but presumably the fleet had been warned and in any case, we would have our IFF (friendly aircraft identification) switched on. By the time we had passed Herma Ness at the northern most tip of the Shetlands we would be approaching nearly half way to Trondheim. It would thus be a matter of steering something like 040 degrees for four to five hundred miles - or about three hours flying.

We would not have much to go on over the sea, but the forecast winds with which we had been provided to calculate our courses, must have been fairly accurate. Anyway, we hit the Norwegian coast more or less on time. I do not think that I had any particular sense of foreboding, but the rocks sticking out of the water reminded me of so many dead men's skulls.

'Finding the actual entrance to Trondheim Fjord cannot have caused us much concern, certainly not enough to remember and as I recall matters, it was then bright moonlight. We arrived some few minutes before we were due to attack and as our time was synchronised to fit in with other aircraft from our squadron and also particularly those dropping the 4,000 pounders, we had to orbit round at the fjord entrance waiting our proper time to attack. We were then flying at about 2,000 feet. We must have been attacking towards the end of those from our squadron, as shortly after arrival, we had a very good view of the light flak hose piping up and then down as the aircraft came in from 2,000 feet to mast height. It was the heaviest concentration of light flak that I had ever seen and to us in waiting, it was hard to see how an aircraft could live through it.

'However, it was soon our turn to chance our luck and off we went. We had a target map of the Asen Fjord area, but the main thing in a situation such as this was to point the aircraft towards where the *Tirpitz* was supposed to

be and get the thing down to 250 feet just as quickly as possible. I was in the nose, charged with releasing the mines. It seemed as though we had scarcely begun when we found we were flying in thick smoke. As a form of protection, the Germans had fired smoke pots. We had been warned of this hazard, but meeting it on a target run was a somewhat different experience. We would be flying below the tops of the sides of the fjord and the whole experience was very unpleasant. Blinded as we were by the smoke there was nothing for it but to release our mines, hoping perhaps that very good fortune would intervene at a time when any skill we possessed was availing us nothing.

'Don MacIntyre began to pull up the nose and the next moment there was a very loud bang. It seemed to me to be the starboard outer which had been hit and had caught fire, a fairly useful glare was lighting up the cockpit. Somehow or other Don kept control of the aircraft and we managed to clear the cliff tops of the fjord. The next thing to decide was what to do. We had been briefed if damaged to make for Sweden. There was some discussion about our chances, but Don quite wisely ruled that the aircraft would blow itself and the lot of us up sometime before Sweden could be reached.

'We were lucky enough then to see a stretch of lake before us, namely Lake Hoklingen. We could not be certain whether the lake was frozen over or not, but in any case a

No.76 Squadron crew of Halifax Mk.II R9487 'X', April 1942. Left to right: Sergeant Dickie Moule, rear gunner; Pilot Officer Bobbie Fairclough, navigator; Sergeant Phil Wheldan, engineer; Sergeant Keith Lloyd-Jones RAAF, pilot; Sergeant Jock Wilson, mid upper gunner; Pilot Officer Bill Culmsee, 2nd pilot; Sergeant Jock Batchelor, wireless operator. All except Bobbie Fairclough were killed when 'X-Xray' was shot down by flak over Essen on the night of 12th April 1942. *L. Donnelly*

belly landing seemed to be the most sensible option. Prior to the landing, I had come back from the nose in order to secure myself. However, whilst I was making up my mind what to do, the aircraft hit the ice with just enough force to make me loose my balance. Until running out of momentum, the aircraft skated across the ice at a seemingly enormous speed.

'When the aircraft came to rest, we all hurried to make good our escape in case of an explosion. I had selected escape by one of the top hatches. I duly made my exit and then ran along the port wing from which I jumped off to join the others. I fear however, I had not reckoned that ice which would bear the weight of chaps would not bear the weight of chaps augmented by a few feet of gravity. Anyway, I jumped clean through the ice and could only be fished out with difficulty, albeit not without some laughter on the part of the others.

Halifax 'S' Sugar, W1048 of No.35 Squadron, comes to the surface of Lake _Hoklingen_, still in remarkably good condition after 31 years under water. 'S' Sugar is now on display in unrestored state, at the RAF Museum, Hendon.
RAF Museum, W1048

'As to the rest of us, poor old Vic Stevens, our flight engineer, was found to have hurt his foot. However, he remained very cheerful and could manage with a bit of support. The problem was to get away from the aircraft which appeared to be burning itself into the lake. We were not more than four or five miles away from the _Tirpitz_ and there was still an awful lot of noise coming from that direction. Also the ice seemed to be cracking. One or two of our own aircraft were seen overhead turning for home, and perhaps more than anything else, this brought us sharply to the realisation that we had a bit to do before we would be getting home'.

Pilot Officer Don MacIntyre's crew were lucky. Apart from the injured Vic Stevens, who had to be left behind to become a POW, the rest of the crew managed to avoid capture, and with the help of a Norwegian farmer, were able to reach Sweden where they were interned, eventually to be returned to Eng-

The late Air Vice-Marshal Don Bennett CB, CBE, DSO, joined 4 Group in December 1941 when he was appointed commander of 77 Squadron. In April 1942 he took command of 10 Squadron and three months later he was appointed to command the new Pathfinder Force. Writing in 1981, Don Bennett paid this tribute to No.4 Group: 'No.4 Group's contribution to the great bomber offensive was steady and consistent. It was not punctuated by any public relations exercises nor any "gong" hunting. The personnel of 4 Group both in the air and on the ground did a dangerous and highly important job throughout the years of the offensive. Their results were outstanding'. _Chaz Bowyer Collection_

land. As for their Halifax, 'S-Sugar', she sank through the ice of Lake Hoklingen and came to rest in ninety feet of water, there to remain until June 1973 when she was raised by an RAF recovery team. Today 'S-Sugar' is on display at the RAF Museum, sadly still in the dilapidated condition in which she emerged from Lake Hoklingen. Hopefully one day she will be restored to her former glory.

Three other Halifaxes were shot down by the murderous flak over the _Tirpitz_ that night, another from 35 Squadron – Flight Lieutenant Pooles in W1020 'K', and two from No.10 Squadron including that flown by No.10's new CO, the late Wing Commander Don Bennett — later Air Vice Marshal Don Bennett, wartime leader of No.8 (PFF) Group. Bennett's Halifax, W1041 'B', had been repeatedly hit by flak as he ran into the target. His tail gunner was wounded and his starboard wing was a mass of flames but he pressed home his attack and then remained at the controls of his doomed aircraft whilst the rest of his crew baled out. With his crew safely away Bennett then made his escape, and not before time because he almost immediately plunged into deep snow. Joining up with his wireless operator, he made his way to Sweden and within a month had returned to resume command of No.10 Squadron.

For all their courageous efforts the giant battleship still remained very much afloat, and with the weather still favourable the crews of Nos. 10, 35 and 76 Squadrons would

have to try again. A repeat attack was mounted the following night, this time the Halifax force reduced to twenty-four aircraft. Again they were met with a withering flak barrage and a blanketing smoke screen. Almost every aircraft sustained damage, and once again unlucky No. 35 Squadron lost two aircraft. The *Tirpitz* was undamaged.

With the recent successes at Lubeck and Rostock behind him, Air Marshal Harris set about planning a dramatic demonstration of the power of the bomber force. Harris envisaged a master stroke that would demonstrate to the critics of the bomber offensive what a properly equipped and expanded force could achieve. Harris had in mind a 1,000 bomber raid.

To raise the required 1,000 bombers, Harris planned not only to employ his entire front line strength, of just over 400 aircraft, but also to draw on bombers from his Operational Training Units - the latter would be flown by instructors and crews in the final stages of training. With the backing of the Prime Minister and the Chief of the Air Staff, the scheme quickly gathered momentum and by the end of May, Operation *Millenium*, the first 1,000 bomber raid, was on. The choice of target was narrowed down to Hamburg or Cologne, the final choice being dependent on the weather.

At noon 30th May, Harris, after studying the latest weather reports, ruled out an attack on the first choice target Hamburg and selected Cologne, conditions being more favourable in the Rheinland area and also on the return leg. The plan of attack envisaged a ninety minute assault, the first fifteen minutes of which would be allocated to all aircraft of Nos. 1 and 3 Groups equipped with Gee. The last fifteen minutes would be devoted to an attack by the heavy bombers of Nos. 4 and 5 Groups. In between the two fifteen minute periods would come the main body of the force. All aircraft taking part were to carry the maximum load of incendiaries. Nos. 1 and 3 Groups were given an aiming point in the centre of the Old City; Nos. 4 and 92 OTU Groups were given an aiming point about a mile to the north of this and Nos. 5 and 91 OTU Groups a point, a mile to the south. The bombing, if successful, would cut a swathe of destruction from north to south through the heart of Cologne.

Crews of 35 Squadron have a tea break from a YMCA tea van, Linton-on-Ouse, Summer 1942. *via W. Baguley*

Halifax Mk.II, W7671 'W' of 76 Squadron, operating in the Middle East, July 1942. Note the freshly applied desert camouflage scheme of Middle Stone and Dark Earth with Night Black under surfaces. *MAP*

Halifax Mk.II, W7676 of No.35 Squadron, May 1942. 'P-Peter' had a long career with this squadron but was eventually lost on a raid against Nuremburg on 28/29th August 1942. *Real Photographs*

Opposite page: see caption on page 76

No. 4 Group's contribution to the raid was as follows'

The Cologne Raid 30th/31st May 1942
No.4 Group Raid Statistics

Sqn	Det'd	Took off	Early Ret.	Attck Prim.	Missing
10	22 Hals	21	4	15	1
35	22 Hals	21	1	20	-
76	21 Hals	21	2	19	-
78	22 Hals	22	1	20	-
102	20 Hals	19	3	16	-
405 (RCAF)	19 Hals	14	1	10	1
1652 CU	13 Hals	12	2	9	1
158	9 Wells	9	4	3	2
1502 BAT Flt 1484 TT Flt HQ 4 Group	9 Whits	7	4	2	1
Total:	157	146	22	114	6

Of the 130 Halifaxes that took part in the raid, twelve were from No. 1652 Conversion Unit based at Marston Moor near York. No. 1652 had been formed in January 1942 from No. 28 and No. 107 Halifax conversion flights. The role of the conversion units was to mould crews together on the Halifax bomber in preparation for their posting to an operational squadron. Also operating for the first time with their new Halifaxes were the Canadians of No. 405 (RCAF) Squadron. Another unit – No. 158 Squadron – although in the process of converting from Wellingtons to Halifaxes and officially stood down from operations, managed to supply nine Wellingtons for the raid.

Just before 00.47 hours on the morning of 31st May the first bombs fell on Cologne. Of a total of 1,047 bombers that were despatched to the target approximately 898 bombed the primary. The result was devastating. 1,445 tons of bombs, mainly incendiaries,

destroyed over 600 acres of Cologne's built-up area. Approximately 250 factories, including metal works, rubber works, blast furnaces, chemical works, an oil storage plant and many other manufacturing establishments were destroyed or severely damaged. Among the many public buildings totally destroyed were nine hospitals, seventeen churches, sixteen schools, four university buildings, four hotels, two cinemas and six department stores. 50% of the City's power supply was put out of action and gas and water supplies were badly disrupted. German records listed 486 killed, 5,027 injured and over 59,000 made homeless. The raid had indeed been a stunning blow.

Bomber Command's losses were high but much lighter than had been anticipated. Forty-one aircraft failed to return. Within the third wave attack, which included the Halifaxes from 4 Group, the losses had been light, only 1.9%, as opposed to 4.8% and 4.1% for the first and second waves. The reason for the low loss rate among the third wave was due to the fact that by the time this wave arrived over Cologne – some seventy-five minutes into the attack – the defences had been overwhelmed. In addition the flak guns were ordered to cease fire during this stage to give the nightfighters a chance to engage the bombers. This tactic, however, appears to have failed.

The following night, with the weather still favourable and the 'Thousand Force' still assembled, Air Marshal Harris took the opportunity to launch another massive attack, this time against Essen. A force of 956 bombers was despatched, including 138 aircraft from No. 4 Group. The results, however, were disappointing. Cloud and inevitable 'Essen Haze' caused few crews to assert with any confidence that they had attacked the

target. Daylight reconnaissance revealed little damage in Essen. Thirty-six aircraft failed to return including nine Halifaxes. No.10 Squadron were badly hit with the loss of three of their Halifaxes. One of the Squadron's crews, that of Pilot Officer Senior, came down in the sea off the Dutch coast but were rescued with the loss of one of their number.

After the Essen raid the Thousand Force was temporarily disbanded. Nevertheless, Harris was convinced by the success of his tactics and he proposed another Thousand raid during the end of the June moon period. On the night of 25th June, 1,067 aircraft, including a contribution from Coastal Command, took off to attack Bremen. Once again a gamble had been taken on the weather. A reconnaissance over the target prior to the attack reported cloud, but it was reckoned this would clear by Z hour. In the event, it did not, and very few crews saw the target. Damage was caused to the Focke-Wulf plant and shipyards and warehouses in the dock area were hit, but nowhere was there damage on the scale of the Cologne raid. Losses were heavy, forty-eight bombers failing to return. Included in that number were six Halifaxes, four from unlucky No. 102 Squadron. No. 4 Group was now fully equipped with Halifaxes and the Bremen raid was the first operation in which all seven of the Group's Halifax squadrons had taken part. It was also the last Thousand raid mounted by Bomber Command until 1944.

The City of Bremen, however, was not to have any respite. Two substantial raids on 27th and 29th June and another on 2nd July caused further damage to areas hit during the Thousand raid. No. 4 Group Halifaxes flew a total of 108 sorties over the three days and lost six aircraft, five of these were from No. 405 (RCAF) Squadron.

At the end of June 1942 the situation in the Middle East had become critical. With the fall of Tobruk the British 8th Army were struggling to hold Rommel's advance to the Suez Canal. Urgent calls went out for reinforcements for the Allied air forces supporting the 8th Army. It was agreed to send two detachments of Halifaxes as soon as possible and early in July, sixteen aircraft from each of Nos. 10 and 76 Squadrons were ordered to proceed to Aqir in Palestine. Operation *Barefaced*, as the detachment to the Middle East was called, was meant to last for only sixteen days. The squadrons were told that they would be used to bomb the Italian Fleet. The reaction of the crews to their imminent move to the Middle East was less than enthusiastic as Sergeant Matthew Holiday, flight engineer with No. 10 Squadron recalls:

'Wing Commander Bennett had said "Special mission to bomb the Italian Fleet in Taranto harbour, sixteen days only, take your best blue, leave everything else behind. Unfortunately, I am not able to go with you, I have been ordered to stay behind". That sixteen days stretched to eight months. When Air Marshal Tedder met us at Fayid and asked us if we had any questions, one flight engineer asked, "When are we going home?" This summed up the feelings of most of the crews. It might seem a bit petty when one remembers what others out there had to put up with, but the point was that all the lads thought it was a shabby way to build up the Desert Air Force. Also, quite a number of the aircrew were almost at the end of their first tour, and one or two of the ground staff NCOs had only just, returned from overseas'.

The diversion of two Halifax squadrons to the Middle East further reduced the strength of No. 4 Group, already denuded by the recent transfer of No. 58 and the loan of 51 and 77 Squadrons to Coastal Command. The home echelon's of 10 and 76 Squadrons remained behind in England to operate, albeit in much reduced capacity, for the next six months.

On the credit side a new squadron, No. 425 Alouette (RCAF), formed in the Group in June.

W7710 *The Ruhr Valley Express* of 405 (RCAF) Squadron took part in the Squadron's first Halifax operation, the 1,000 bomber raid on Cologne, 30th May 1942. W7710 was lost on the 2nd October 1942, attacking Flensburg.
Royal Canadian Air Force

Halifax Mk.II series 1, W1245 'B' of 78 Squadron was one of four Halifaxes from the squadron that were lost on a raid to Mainz on the night of 11/12th August 1942. Skipper of 'B-Baker' that night was Pilot Officer Kingston.
IWM, CH8034

Page 75: **A mixed load of 1,000lb General Purpose bombs and 'cans' of incendiaries arrive at 'Q-Queenie's dispersal, 405 (RCAF) Squadron, Pocklington, early Summer 1942. W7703 'Q' was lost over Bremen on the night of 27th June 1942 with its regular crew skippered by Flight Sergeant Field.**
IWM, CH6594

No. 425 was the fifth Canadian bomber squadron to form overseas and was unique for the organisation order designated it 'French Canadian'. The Squadron was formed at Dishforth on 25th June 1942 under the command of Wing Commander J. M. W. St. Pierre and was equipped with Wellington Mk.IIIs. However, it would be October before the Squadron became operational.

Meanwhile, during the midsummer months, the squadrons of Bomber Command were despatched on attacks to German targets whenever weather and moon conditions were favourable. Shallow penetration raids were all that were possible during the short summer nights. On 13th July the first of a series of attacks was launched on the important inland port of Duisburg. Six nights later the Vulkan submarine building yards at Vegesack, situated on the River *Weser* some thirty miles from its North Sea estuary, came under attack from a force of ninety-nine bombers, including forty from No.4 Group. Cloud cover prevented a visual attack so the main force bombed by Gee. However, results were poor with no reports of any damage to the U-boat yard. Three Halifaxes failed to return.

Over the next six days three more attacks were mounted against Duisburg but without much success as cloudy conditions and poor marking by the Gee-equipped marker aircraft, caused the bombing to be scattered. On his return from Duisburg, in the early hours of 24th July, Flight Sergeant Albright of No. 405 Squadron, couldn't prevent his Halifax, W7769 'K' crashing into the school at Pocklington. All eight crew members, including the second pilot, Pilot Officer Strong, were killed.

There were better results on the night of 26th July when seventy-three Halifaxes joined a 403 aircraft maximum effort to Hamburg, where extensive damage was caused to mainly residential districts. The cost in missing aircraft, however, was heavy: twenty-nine aircraft failed to return, eight from No. 4 Group.

Chapter Ten

Problems with the Halifax

The first half of 1942 had seen Bomber Command making steady if unspectacular progress. Apart from the Thousand raid on Cologne, bombing accuracy and concentration still left much to be desired. If better results were to be achieved more accurate methods of target finding and marking would be required. The idea of a specially trained force, whose brief would be to find and mark accurately the target, had been proposed early in 1942. Even with the backing of the Air Staff it was to be the middle of the year before the machinery for the creation of the special force was set in motion.

On 15th August 1942 the 'Pathfinder Force', as the new group was called, came into being. With its HQ at Wyton in Huntingdonshire, the new force consisted initially of five squadrons, one from each of the operational groups of Bomber Command. No. 4 Group's contribution to the new force was in the form of the Halifaxes of No. 35 Squadron who left Linton-on-Ouse for their new base at Graveley, Huntingdonshire, on 16th August. Another link with No. 4 Group was to be the new commander of the Pathfinders, Group Captain D. C. T. Bennett, former CO of Nos. 77 and 10 Squadrons.

No.4 Group Bomber Command, August 1942

Sqn	Equipment	Airfield
10	Halifax II	Melbourne
76	Halifax II	Middleton-St-George
78	Halifax II	Middleton-St-George
102	Halifax II	Pocklington
158	Halifax II	East Moor
405 (RCAF)	Halifax II	Topcliffe
419 (RCAF)	Wellington III	Topcliffe
420 (RCAF)	Wellington III	Skipton-on-Swale
425 (RCAF)	Wellington III	Dishforth

Note: Squadrons 419, 420 and 425 were non-operational at this time.

The autumn and winter months saw many new squadrons form within No. 4 Group. The majority were Canadian earmarked for the formation of No. 6 (RCAF) Group, which was planned to be established in January 1943. No.6 Group, almost entirely funded by the Canadian government, would be occupying the most northerly bases in Yorkshire and Durham.

Meanwhile, a review of the performance of the Halifax on operations had shown that the past eighteen months – the period since its introduction – had been far from trouble free.

The Halifax squadrons had suffered from a continuous series of unexplained crashes in which the aircraft had got into an inverted dive. Attempts at Boscombe Down to simulate the conditions under which the crashes had occurred failed to produce the desired effect. Finally, after a prolonged and worrying period of testing it was ascertained that the trouble was from rudder stalling. Under certain conditions the triangular fin stalled and turbulent air passing through the gap between fin and rudder locked the latter hard over. During the autumn of 1942, modifications to all Halifax tail assemblies were carried out in an effort to cure the rudder stall problem. This necessitated a reduction in the scale of involvement of the Halifax squadrons in operations during this period.

The rudder stall problem was not the only reason for the apparent disappointing performance of the Halifax. The aircraft had always been slightly underpowered, and the appreciable increases in loaded weight now began to tell. A programme of divesting the Halifax of many of its most characteristic features was now initiated to reverse the trend towards high losses which had grown alarmingly during 1942. The programme involved taking a standard Halifax Mk.II and stripping it of all non-essential equipment. This involved the removal of the front powered turret and its replacement with a metal fairing, known as a 'Z' fairing. Also removed was the drag producing mid-upper turret, together with exhaust shrouds, fuel jettison pipes and radio mast. Together with other weight saving measures the Halifax performance was dramatically improved, gaining some 16 mph in top speed and improving range and handling quality. The modified aircraft were known as Halifax Mk.II Series I Specials and they began to reach the squadrons of 4 Group in the late autumn of 1942, in time to take part in the deeper penetration raids of the longer, darker nights.

During August and September 1942 the first Pathfinder led raids were carried out with mixed results. Familiar problems began to manifest themselves as the Pathfinders struggled to master the technique of accurate target marking. The attack on Saarbrucken on the night of 1st September, when the main force bombed the town of Saarlouis, some thirteen miles from Saarbrucken, due to the inaccurate marking by the Pathfinder Force, was typical of the early raids.

During September No. 4 Group squadrons, now fully operational after completion of the

modifications to the tailplanes of their Halifaxes, took part in main force attacks to Bremen, Duisburg, Frankfurt, Düsseldorf, Wilhelmshaven and Essen. During the attack on Düsseldorf on 10th September the Pathfinders successfully marked the target with 'Pink Pansies', modified 4,000 lb blast bombs converted into super incendiaries for target marking. Damage to Düsseldorf was widespread and many thousands were bombed out. During the raid a Halifax from No. 405 Squadron was coned by searchlights and badly shot up. The pilot, Sergeant Webb, managed to regain control in spite of losing the propeller from his port outer engine after being hit by flak. During the confusion the rear and mid-upper gunners had baled out. Despite the damage, Sergeant Webb managed to return to Pocklington but crashed into a parked Wellington and in the ensuing blaze Sergeant Brennan, the wireless operator, was killed. The Pilot was lucky to escape injury that night but the 'grim reaper' was not to be denied as less than two weeks later, Webb and his entire crew were lost, along with four others from No. 4 Group, whilst attacking the U-boat base at Flensburg. This raid, carried out by twenty-eight Halifaxes, without marking from the Pathfinders, was not a success. Only sixteen crews reported bombing the target and the loss of five Halifaxes testified to the growing prowess of the enemy's defences.

There was worse to come a week later when on the night of 1st October a repeat attack on Flensburg, this time by twenty-seven Halifaxes, was attempted. The result was a disaster. Twelve aircraft were lost, nearly half the force. Intense and very accurate flak fire coupled with numerous searchlight batteries seem to have been the cause of the carnage. No. 10 Squadron were particularly badly hit by the disaster. Of five trainee crews despatched only one, (Sergeant Allen), returned to base, a grim foretaste of what was in store for many crews in the coming months.

During October 1942 No. 4 Group commenced the first of many mining sorties. Mining operations, code named *Gardening*, were an important part of the continuous battle to disrupt enemy coastal shipping. Favourite mining areas were off the French ports of Lorient, St Nazaire, Brest and Ostend and off Texel and the Frisian Islands. As well as sinking and damaging enemy shipping, Gardening was useful for initiating trainee crews to the rigours of operational flying.

The Flensburg Raid 1st/2nd October 1942
No.4 Group Raid Statistics

Sqn	Took-off	Early Return	Attacked Primary	Missing
10	5	-	1	4
76	3	-	2	1
78	8	1	5	2
102	3	-	1	2
405	8	2	3	3
Totals:	27	3	12	12

Two of No. 4 Group's Canadian squadrons, Nos. 420 and 425, flew their first operational missions on the night of 5th October when they took part in a main force attack on Aachen. No. 425 (Alouette) Squadron sent eight of their Wellington Mk.IIIs of which four bombed Aachen. One Wellington, X3843 'G', failed to return. Bad weather on the outward flight probably caused Sergeant O'Driscoll's aircraft to crash at Finchingfield, Essex, with the loss of the entire crew.

On the night of 15th October, 10 Squadron, only just recovering from the loss of four crews on the Flensburg mission two weeks before, received more sad news when their CO, Wing Commander Wildie, failed to return from Cologne. Also lost with Wildie's crew were No. 10's station navigation officer and gunnery leader.

At the end of October there began a series of attacks on Italian targets timed to coincide with the Eighth Army's offensive in North Africa and the Allied landings in Morocco and Algeria. It was hoped that by raiding the Italian cities the Axis air strength would be drawn away from North Africa. Genoa was raided on the night of 23rd October by a force of aircraft from Nos. 3 and 4 Groups. Thick cloud cover, however, prevented a successful attack. On his return from Genoa, Wing Commander Bruce Bintley of No. 102 Squadron, landed his Halifax at Holme-on-Spalding Moor with a burst tyre. The airfield was shrouded in fog at the time, and as Bintley's aircraft was about to leave the main runway, another Halifax from the Squadron, (Flight Sergeant Berry), struck it a glancing blow. The nose of Bintley's Halifax was ripped off by the impact,

Berry's aircraft ending up some one hundred yards further down the runway, minus its undercarriage. Sadly Wing Commander Bintley and his wireless operator were killed, a tragic loss to the Squadron.

The city centre and the Fiat motor factory were the aiming points in Turin as medium strength raids were mounted on the 18th and 20th November. Heavy damage was caused to the centre of Turin on both occasions. On the night of 28th November Turin was again the target for the main force, made up of some 228 aircraft. A Halifax from No. 78 Squadron, (Canadian Sergeant Spragg), ran into difficulties on its way to Turin, as mid-upper gunner Sergeant Evans recalls:

'As we climbed for height to clear the Alps we began to ice up badly. After staggering almost to a standstill the skipper called to us to abandon the aircraft. Being a fairly green crew I suppose panic stations took over. For myself, I remember being tangled up by intercom and oxygen leads, chute harness and Lord knows what else. For what seemed minutes, it was probably only a matter of a few seconds, I just couldn't get myself free. By the time I fell out of my turret, in an undignified heap on the fuselage floor, the aircraft was falling away. I must have struck my head on the turret step as I fell out of the turret for I was unconscious for a few moments.

'When I came to I knew that the aircraft was still in the air but I thought everyone must have baled out. I therefore put my head in my hands and waited for the crash. When it didn't come I looked up and saw the light from a torch winking in the darkness of the forward fuselage. By the time I had got to my feet the bomb aimer, Sergeant Simmonite, had reached me and proceeded to help me into the rest position. He then explained that the pilot had managed to regain control of the aircraft and had cancelled the abandon aircraft signal. I had been in such a mess that my intercom lead had become disconnected and I never heard the skipper's call. Unfortunately our rear-gunner, Pilot Officer Wilbey, had been very quick off the mark and had jumped out of the aircraft. We heard later that he had landed in France and reached Spain safely some time later'.

No.4 Group Bomber Command, 31st December 1942

Sqn	Equipment	Airfield
10	Halifax II	Melbourne
51	Halifax II	Snaith
76	Halifax II	Linton-on-Ouse
77	Halifax II	Elvington
78	Halifax II	Linton-on-Ouse
102	Halifax II	Pocklington
158	Halifax II	Rufforth
196 *	Wellington X	Leconfield
408 (RCAF) *	Halifax II	Leeming
419 (RCAF) *	Halifax II	Middleton-St-George
420 (RCAF)	Wellington III	Middleton-St-George
424 (RCAF) *	Wellington III	Topcliffe
425 (RCAF)	Wellington III	Dishforth
426 (RCAF) *	Wellington III	Dishforth
427 (RCAF)	Wellington III	Croft
428 (RCAF) *	Wellington III/X	Dalton
429 (RCAF) *	Wellington III	East Moor
431 (RCAF) *	Wellington X	Burn
466 (RAAF) *	Wellington X	Leconfield

These Squadrons were non-operational at this time.

Bad weather throughout December 1942 caused a reduction in the scale of major operations. Attacks by the main force on Frankfurt, on the night of the 2nd, and Mannheim four nights later, were frustrated by thick cloud cover. On both occasions the Pathfinders were unable to locate the target. The week was an unhappy one for No. 102; the Squadron was to lose three crews over Frankfurt, two on the Mannheim mission and one failed to return from a mining sortie to the Frisian Islands on the 8th.

In addition to the Canadian squadrons, two new units equipped with Wellington Mk.Xs formed in No. 4 Group at the end of 1942. They were No. 466 (RAAF) Squadron, which formed at Driffield on 15th October under the command of Squadron Leader R. E. Bailey, and No. 196 which formed at the same base on 7th November. Both units, however, were to remain at Driffield for only a short time as the station was due to close at the end of the year for reconstruction work. During December, both squadrons moved to Leconfield.

The scene at Holme-on-Spalding Moor following the collision of two Halifaxes of 102 Squadron as they landed in thick fog on return **from Genoa on 24th October 1942. In the foreground is Wing Commander Bruce Bintley's Halifax, DT512 'Q', minus its nose** **section, whilst some one hundred yards further down the runway is Flight Sergeant Berry's aircraft, W1181 'D'.**

Chapter Eleven

The Battle of the Ruhr

'This is not the end. It is not even the beginning of the end. But it is, perhaps, the end of the beginning'. Winston Churchill's immortal words, spoken after the victory at El Alamein, appropriately describe the tide of events which heralded in the new year of 1943. The first month of 1943 saw the German armies facing a series of fatal disasters which, in the long term, would cost Germany the war. At Stalingrad the Red Army had encircled and annihilated Field Marshal Paulas's 6th Army, comprising some 300,000 men. In North Africa, Rommel's Afrika Korps had crumpled in the face of Montgomery's victory at El Alamein. Although, for the enslaved peoples of Europe there was still much bloodshed and pain to come, the tide of Nazi conquest had finally turned.

At the beginning of 1943 RAF Bomber Command was still the only force which could engage the very heart of the enemy. Although, in the autumn of 1942, the United States Army Air Force had commenced daylight raids on targets in France and Belgium, it would be some time before the B-17s and B-24s would seriously threaten targets deep into Germany. The coming months would see the American theories on unescorted, daylight precision bombing put to the test. RAF Bomber Command meanwhile, were about to see their own theories come to fruition. The Command's improving operational capacity and increasing strength meant that the strategic air offensive could now threaten Germany's capacity to wage war. The directive issued to Bomber Command by the combined Chiefs of Staff after their meeting at Casablanca on 21st January 1943, indicated the direction in which the RAF and USAAF joint offensive was to follow. What became known as the 'Casablanca Directive' (Bomber Command Directive 21st January 1943, Appendix 8: The Strategic Air Offensive Against Germany) stated that: 'Your primary object will be the progressive destruction and dislocation of the German military, industrial and economic system, and the undermining of the morale of the German people to a point where their capacity for armed resistance is fatally weakened.' For Bomber Command at the beginning of 1943, area bombing was seen as the best and only means of achieving the enemy's downfall.

A whole new range of electronic aids were introduced to Bomber Command during 1943 that were to revolutionize the night offensive.

The first of these was called 'Oboe' which was a blind bombing system in which an aircraft was controlled by two ground stations in England. The ground stations transmitted pulses and then received them back from the aircraft. As a result the ground stations were able to calculate the aircraft's exact position, and were able to determine when it would reach the target. A signal would then be sent to the aircraft to release its bombs at the precise moment it passed over the target. The small number of Oboe - equipped aircraft that could be used at any one time meant that the device was best employed by marker aircraft with the Pathfinder Force.

The second new electronic aid was 'H2S', a radar map-reading device which could be used for navigation as well as a means of blind bombing. The H2S scanner produced a map on a cathode ray tube display of a 360 degree arc of the ground below the equipped aircraft. The operator was able to differentiate between water and land and between built-up areas and open countryside. Because H2S was not dependent on ground transmitters it was potentially superior to Oboe and the existing Gee systems.

During 1942, the Germans had not been slow to counter the ever growing threat posed by the RAF's night bomber offensive. During the year the German *Himmelbett* night fighter defences were considerably strengthened. More and more of the fighters began to carry the *Lichtenstein* airborne radar and with this new device the defences began to take an increasing toll of the bombers. By the beginning of 1943 the Luftwaffe's night fighter defences, directly facing Bomber Command's onslaught, numbered some 363 aircraft. Included in this number were many of the formidable new 'G' versions of the Messerschmitt Bf 110, three-seat night fighters. These were equipped with either FuG 202 Lichtenstein BC or FuG 212 Lichtenstein C-1 radars and powerful twin 20mm cannon. These weapons were particularly lethal against the lightly armoured Lancasters, Halifaxes and Stirlings of Bomber Command. On average, five hits were enough to bring down a bomber, particular if the fuel tanks were hit.

By January 1943, the Kammhuber Line – the areas covered by Himmelbett fighter control sectors – stretched from Troyes, eighty miles south-east of Paris, to the northern tip of Denmark, and extended in depth from the coast to 100-150 miles inland. This area

covered the low countries, the vital Ruhr sector, Westphalia, the Hanover-Hamburg area, and the whole of Denmark. Only by flying several hundred miles north or south of this defensive sector would the RAF bombers avoid crossing the network of night fighter traps.

To make interception of individual bombers as difficult as possible for the defences Bomber Command planners made every effort to pass the bomber stream through the Kammhuber Line as quickly as possible, thus overwhelming the system. By the early months of 1943, instead as before a question of hours, it was now taking between thirty and forty minutes for a compact bomber stream to cross the Kammhuber Line.

Meanwhile in No. 4 Group, the squadrons began to receive more of the modified Halifax Mk.II Series 1 Specials. Initially the modifications were carried out on existing aircraft at unit level, but at the turn of the year brand new Halifax Mk.II Series 1 Specials began leaving the production lines. To meet the demands of Bomber Command an intensive production programme for the Halifax bomber was now in full swing. Early contracts for the large scale construction of the Halifax quickly exceeded the production capacity of the Handley Page factories at Cricklewood and Radlett. The 'Halifax Group' of companies was therefore set-up to handle the manufacture of the aircraft. The Group consisted of the English Electric Company, Rootes Securities Ltd at Speke, the Fairey Aviation Co Ltd at Stockport and the London Aircraft Production Group. The latter consisted of five firms: Chrysler Motors, Duplex Bodies and Motors, Express Motor and Body Works, Park Royal Coachworks and the London Passenger Transport Board. In addition to the 'Halifax Group' a special Halifax repair depot had been established at Rawcliffe airfield, York. The Rawcliffe Depot was designed to serve the bases of Nos. 4 and 6 Groups with repair and servicing facilities. At its peak of production, the Halifax Group would eventually employ almost 51,000 people, and one Halifax would leave the production lines every working hour.

Bomber Command, with its new accession of strength, was ready to demonstrate its power over Germany. However, at the turn of the year, the U-boat menace was again threatening to become a decisive factor. During the months of November and December 1942 the Allies had lost over 200 merchant

ships to the U-boats - amounting to well over one million tons. As a result of the worsening situation in the Atlantic, Bomber Command was instructed to postpone its offensive against Germany until the U-boat threat had been contained. From 14th January 1943 area bombing attacks by the heavy bombers of RAF Bomber Command were to be mounted against the U-boat bases at Lorient, St Nazaire, Brest and La Pallice. Air Chief Marshal Harris had many reservations about the new campaign, particularly as he was aware that the Germans had constructed huge concrete bomb proof shelters to house their U-boats. This would mean that the new offensive would be largely ineffective.

Attacks on the U-boat bases commenced on the night of 14th January when 122 aircraft of the main force struck at Lorient. The same target was attacked the following night, this time by 157 aircraft including four Wellingtons from No. 466 (RAAF) Squadron, participating in their first operational bombing mission. Three of the Wellingtons were able to attack the primary target and one returned early. Damage to the town of Lorient was widespread and a number of French civilians were killed. The U-boat bases remained largely undamaged.

Berlin came under attack for the first time since 1941 when six Halifaxes from No. 4 Group joined in a 201 aircraft assault on the German capital on the night of 16th January. A diversion from the campaign against the U-boats, the Berlin attack was disappointing with cloud and haze causing the bombing to be scattered. However, the bombers arrived over Berlin just as the sirens were sounding and many people were killed before they had time to take cover. During the course of the raid the huge Deutschlandhalle – that night staging an annual circus event with nearly 10,000 spectators – was destroyed by incendiaries.

Top: **W/Cdr G.B. Warner, DFC, AFC, (third from left) CO of 78 Squadron, with his crew, in front of their Halifax Mk.II series 1 (Special) W7930 'W', 14th January 1943.** *T. Slater, CH8901*

Above: **'One of our aircraft is missing!' The crew of a Halifax lie beside the twisted wreck of their aircraft, shot down over Hamburg on the night of 3rd February 1943.** *IWM, HU25782*

Below: **No.196 Squadron photographed at Leconfield, Spring 1943. The squadron flew its first operational mission on the night of 4th February 1943 when eight Wellingtons bombed Lorient.** *R. Williamson*

Fortunately a major disaster was avoided as air raid police were able to evacuate the hall before it burned down. All the aircraft from No. 4 Group returned safely.

Bombing was again scattered as a repeat attack on Berlin was mounted the following night. The same route was used as on the previous nights attack, and as a result the night fighters were able to intercept the bomber stream early and shoot down twenty-three bombers. Sixteen Halifaxes from No. 4 Group took part in the raid and two crews – Captain Bjorn Naess (RNAF) and Sergeant Gold, both from No. 76 Squadron – failed to return. Captain Naess was one of a large contingent of Norwegian airmen serving with 76 at this time.

During a major mining operation, carried out by over seventy aircraft off the Frisian Islands (code name, *Nectarines*), on the evening of 21st January, No. 4 Group lost two Halifaxes and two Wellingtons. One of the

Wellingtons lost was from No. 429 'Bison' (RCAF) Squadron, one of three taking part in that Squadron's first operational mission. In addition a Halifax from 51 Squadron, piloted by Pilot Officer Getliffe, became lost on return and crashed into a hill near Hebden Bridge, Yorkshire. Two members of the crew died in the crash.

The U-boat bases at Lorient were again under attack from No. 4 Group Halifaxes on the night of 23rd January and by Wellingtons from Nos. 429 and 466 Squadrons on the 26th. There were no losses to the Group from either of these operations. On the following night Halifaxes from Nos. 51, 76, 78 and 102 Squadrons took part in a main force attack on Düsseldorf. This was the first occasion that Oboe Mosquitos carried out ground marking using 250 lb marker bombs. These marker bombs were designed to burst just above the ground and scatter clusters of coloured flares

that burnt at or near the target. Bombing was highly concentrated and there was widespread damage, particularly in the southern part of Düsseldorf. Halifaxes from No. 51 Squadron were carrying two 1,000 lb bombs and 900 4 lb incendiaries to each aircraft on that night. One of the Squadron's crews, that of Warrant Officer Weakley, failed to return.

During February, apart from raids early in the month to Hamburg, Cologne and Turin, the U-boat bases at Lorient were the focus for much of Bomber Command's effort. The port was raided on four nights during February, the last attack taking place on the 16th. During the series of attacks on Lorient Bomber Command had flown 1,853 sorties and dropped nearly 4,000 tons of bombs. The town and port area of Lorient was devastated by the bombing but the important U-boat base, safe under the protection of its bombproof, concrete roof, was virtually undamaged.

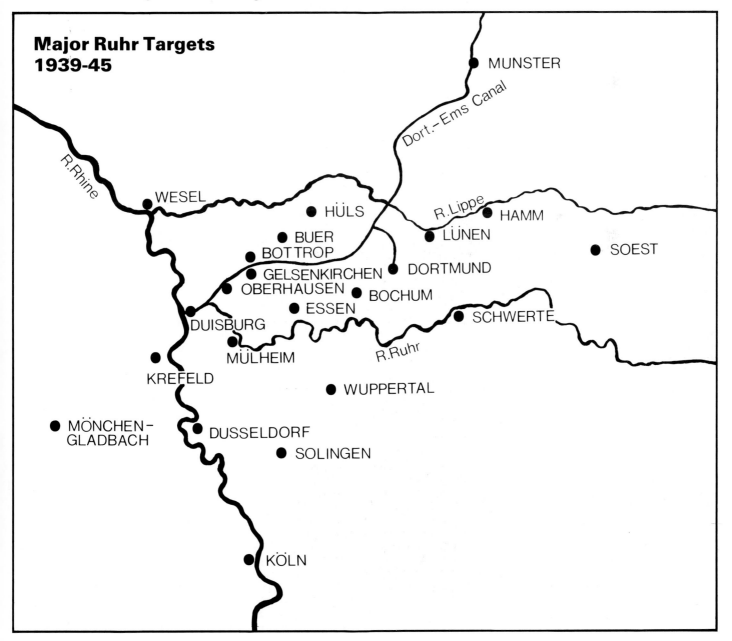

Major Ruhr Targets 1939-45

THE REAPER

The aircraft droning up above,
The aircrew dozing in it.
Can all become a tangled wreck,
In less than half a minute.

'But how?' you ask, and well you may,
You who stay on the ground.
The answer to the question is
The Reaper is around.

He plods the lonely skies at night,
His black beard dangling low.
His beatled eyebrows, long thin nose,
His eyes a fiery glow.

Then suddenly he stops, he laughs,
An ugly sinful laugh,
And swings his scythe along the skies
As though 'twere cutting chaff.

He hurries where his victim drones,
'A Halifax!' he cries.
'I'd sooner prang a Halifax
Than anything that flies'.

He creeps behind, his scythe aloft,
His evil lips drawn tight.
And with a cry of 'Die you dogs!'
He'll swish with all his might.

So readers take this warning,
Look out, and search the skies.
Remember, perhaps it's your turn next
To hear the Reaper's cries.

*By Sergeant Steer,
a Halifax air gunner who failed to return.*

By early March 1943 the U-boat danger had receded and, although limited attacks on the submarine bases would continue until April, Bomber Command was now to turn its attention back onto Germany. The successful trials with the Oboe system meant, that by the beginning of March 1943, all was ready for its introduction as a method of target marking for the Main Force.

Lying comfortably within range of Oboe was the world's greatest concentration of industrial power, the Ruhr. Fed by immense, natural deposits of bituminous coal, the Ruhr region was the heartland of the Reich's industrial base. Steel mills, iron works, chemical plants, oil refineries and coal mines situated in over a hundred cities and towns made up this vast complex. The area was criss-crossed by an extensive network of railways and inland waterways with access to the River Rhine and the North Sea via the giant inland port of Duisburg. At the very heart of this vital area was the city of Essen with the giant Krupps' works at its centre. Krupps was the largest individual armament and engineering plant in Germany and excelled in the manufacture of tanks, naval and other heavy guns, torpedo tubes, bombs, armour plate, armoured cars and rolling stock.

Founded in the late 19th Century, Krupps of Essen became a byword for quality and efficiency, and at the outbreak of the Second World War its reputation was known the world over. The firm had developed into a vast complex of factories, blast furnaces and assembly shops which dominated Essen and the whole of the Ruhr. The Krupps works, and most of the towns of the Ruhr region, had been subjected to numerous attacks by RAF Bomber Command since 1940 without suffering any serious damage. The natural smoke screen, caused by many thousands of belching factory chimneys, meant that there was a permanent haze over the area making accurate target identification impossible. In addition, the Ruhr was blessed with the most formidable defence system of any target in Germany. Numerous flak and searchlight batteries protected the approaches to the area and a ring of night fighter airfields surrounding the region meant that any incursion by a bomber would be a hazardous undertaking. It was no wonder that bomber crews had christened the area 'Happy Valley'.

With the introduction of Oboe it was now hoped that for the first time accurate bombing of this prime target could be achieved. The period, which was to become known as 'The Battle of the Ruhr', commenced on the night of 5th March 1943 with an attack on Essen. The battle was to last for five months and of forty-five attacks mounted by the Main Force during this period, twenty-five were against targets in the Ruhr, including raids on Essen, Duisburg, Dortmund, Bochum, Düsseldorf, Krefeld, Mulheim, Wuppertal, Gelsenkirchen and Cologne. In addition, Bomber Command would also range far and wide during this period attacking targets which included Berlin, Nuremburg, Stettin and the Italian cities, but always the emphasis would be on reducing the Ruhr.

The importance of the Essen attack was brought home to the crews by a special note on the operational order, the form 'B', sent to all groups and stations before the raid. As well as the normal instructions detailing timing, bomb loads etc, there was a note to crews which stated: 'The method of placing TI markers for this operation is a new and very accurate one and it must be impressed on crews that they should make every effort to concentrate their bombing on the TI markers. If this is done, this most important target will be entirely destroyed. Crews are to be warned of the necessity for carrying on after dropping their bombs, before turning left, so as to avoid the usual error of undershooting'.

The plan for the attack was as follows. Zero hour was to be 21.00 hrs when eight Oboe - equipped Mosquitos, from No. 109 Squadron, would drop a salvo of red target indicator bombs on the aiming point, the Krupps works. Backers-up, twenty-two heavy bombers from the Pathfinder Force, would then arrive between 21.02 and 21.38, and drop green TIs on the Oboe marked reds. It was hoped either the red or green TIs would be

visible to the main force throughout the raid which was to be compressed into forty minutes following zero hour. The main force attack was divided into three overlapping waves. The first wave, consisting of Halifaxes of Nos. 4 and 6 Groups, was to attack between zero plus two minutes and zero plus twenty minutes. The second wave, comprised of Wellingtons and Stirlings, was to attack between zero plus fifteen and zero plus twenty-five minutes and the third wave, made up of Lancasters, between zero plus twenty and zero plus forty minutes. Bomb loads were to be in the proportion of two thirds incediaries to one third high explosive.

The resulting attack was by far the most successful yet delivered against Essen. The Mosquito marker aircraft dropped their red target indicators just two minutes before zero hour, and within eight minutes fires had taken hold in the target area. By the time the Halifaxes of the first wave had left the target, the bombing was seen to be well concentrated with the whole area covered with fire and smoke. Damage was severe and widespread, at least fifty-three separate shops of the Krupps works sustaining heavy damage, while thirteen of the main buildings were virtually destroyed. Several smaller factories were partly gutted, together with the gasworks, the power station and the municipal tram depot, the last named being the main source of transport in the town. 450 acres of residential and commercial property were devastated and nearly 500 people were killed.

**The Essen Raid 5/6th March 1943
No.4 Group Raid Statistics**

Sqn	Took-off	Early Return	Attacked Primary	Missing
10	14	2	12	-
51	11	-	11	-
76	12	2	9	1
78	12	2	9	1
102	12	-	12	-
158	6	-	6	-
196	10	-	10	-
429	7*	1	5	-
431	3	-	3	-
466	12	-	11	1

**Minelaying Operations in the Frisian Islands
5/6th March 1943**

77	2	-	2	-
102	1	-	1	-
431	4	2	1	-

* One aircraft, Wellington BJ775, crashed on take-off.

Losses were suprisingly low, with fourteen aircraft failing to return, including one each from Nos. 76, 78 and 466 Squadrons. One Halifax crew had a lucky escape over the target. Flying Officer Garforth of 51 Squadron had just bombed Essen when his Halifax, W7772, was hit by what was thought to be flak. On return to Snaith, investigations revealed a 4 lb incendiary bomb wedged between two petrol tanks. Garforth's Halifax had

been hit by a bomb from another aircraft passing overhead, a not uncommon occurence over a crowded target area. The bomb had pierced one wing and come to rest between tanks full of high octane petrol. When the bomb was carefully removed, it was found to be very unstable, requiring only a slight blow to ignite it.

The Oboe marking technique had proved on outstanding success but many targets lay far beyond the range of Oboe. For these targets reliance would have to be placed on the skill of the Pathfinders to find and accurately mark the target, aided by H2S. The limitations of this method of target marking soon became apparent during a main force attack on Nuremburg, on the night of 8th March. The target was marked by a combination of H2S and visual means, but because of ground haze, both marking and bombing became spread over ten miles. The main force, as in the previous raid to Essen, was split into three waves led by 4 Group Halifaxes. Because of the dispersed marking, the majority of bomb loads fell in the suburbs of Nuremburg instead of in the centre of the city.

It was back to Essen four nights later, and again the Oboe marking technique was very successful. Krupps factory complex was again the centre of the main bombing area and severe damage was caused to the already badly hit area. Losses were higher than the 5th March raid, twenty-three aircraft missing from a force of 457. A maximum effort of Halifaxes and Wellingtons from No. 4 Group produced good bombing results, but seven

Flight Lieutenant A.P. Dowse and crew pictured in front of their 78 Squadron Halifax, JB784 'S-Sugar' at Linton-on-Ouse. Left to right: F/O A.N. Orr; Sgt A.W. Hoare; Sgt T. Slater; F/Lt A.P. Dowse; Sgt P. Langsford (RNZAF); Sgt J. Kershaw; Sgt H.E. Thompson. *T. Slater*

Halifaxes were lost including three from No. 102 Squadron.

At the end of March Berlin was the target for two 300-plus raids by the main force. The first attack was on the night of 27th March. Flight Lieutenant Dowse and crew of No. 78 Squadron, strayed off track that night and ran into difficulties, as Sergeant Phil Langsford, Dowse's wireless operator from New Zealand recalls:

'As I remember, in the early stages of the flight all went well. However, we came unstuck near Bremen, soon after crossing the coast. We were flying at our maximum height of 19,000 feet over a layer of 10/10ths cloud, which was several thousand feet beneath us. Presumably, through a navigational error, we flew into the Bremen defences because, all of a sudden, we were being bracketed by predicted flak. The German fire was very accurate and our aircraft was filled with cordite fumes from the nearby flak bursts. Our skipper did a marvellous job by throwing the Halifax all over the sky and eventually we managed to shake off the flak but not before a nearby burst sheared off one of the blades from the port inner propeller. The dismembered blade promptly struck the fuselage forward of the

bomb bay and smashed its way into the cabin, not far from my position below the pilot. The aircraft immediately went out of control, due to the disabled motor, and we lost several thousand feet as the skipper struggled to regain control. But not before he had ordered us to abandon the aircraft, (fortunately he cancelled the instruction in time, having regained control).

'Our bombs had been jettisoned during this episode as we now headed, hopefully, in a direction which would take us back to Linton-on-Ouse. Meanwhile, our navigator had lost all his instruments, both compasses were u/s and the astrodome had been hacked off by a shell splinter, just like the top off a boiled egg. In addition, my wireless was on the blink, but with the help of the navigator, who held the internals of the set while I carried out the necessary repairs, I was able to get it working again. I then was able to call up for what was known as a QDM (magnetic course to steer with zero wind in degrees and time). This entailed contacting three widely spaced D/F stations in England, who took bearings on my signal and then transmitted our position back to us. Whoever the operators were, they did a magnificent job. Bearings were written down and handed to the navigator who in turn eventually got us safely back home.

Flight Lieutenant Dowse and crew had luck with them that night, but it did not last. They were fated to 'get the chop' on the night of 16th April during a trip to the Skoda works at Pilsen. Sergeant Phil Langsford spent the rest of the war as a guest of the Germans.

Two nights later it was another 'Maximum Effort' to Berlin. No. 4 Group sent its Halifaxes to the German capital, whilst the Group's Wellington units, Nos. 196, 429, 431 and 466, took part in an all Wellington raid on the Ruhr town of Bochum. Weather conditions, however, spoilt both attacks, with severe icing causing many aircraft to make early returns. From No. 4 Group, five Halifaxes and three Wellingtons were lost. The diary entry for 29th March, by Sergeant Tom Wingham – bomb-aimer with Sergeant Hewlett's No. 102 Squadron crew – sums up a frustrating night for many crews of Bomber Command:

'Occlusion over bases. Take-off delayed. Using oldest aircraft in Squadron (HR663) unable to climb above cloud level – flew at 16,000 feet, iced up. Bombs jettisoned near Flensburg and returned to base. Upon landing two engines u/s. One cannister of 4 lb incendiary bombs jammed in bomb bay doors (port wing). Other crews returning from Berlin suffered from navigational errors due to 90 knot wind changing direction by 100. Squadron Navigation Officer calling for D/F fix found himself over Zuider Zee when he reckoned to be over Thames Estuary'.

To add to an unhappy night at Pocklington, Flight Sergeant Comrie and crew all died when their Halifax, JB848, crashed one minute after take off for Berlin.

The first major attack of April was on the night of the 3rd when 348 aircraft went to Essen. 113 Halifaxes, the majority from No. 4 Group, took part in another successful strike at this important target. In the surprisingly clear conditions over the Ruhr, the bombers were able to bomb accurately the well placed target markers of the Pathfinders. Also enjoying the clear weather were the German night fighters who managed to shoot down twenty-one of the bomber force, including seven from No. 4 Group. A 51 Squadron Halifax, DT686, skippered by Flying Officer Johnstone, was intercepted by a Junkers Ju 88 night fighter when just twenty miles from the target. The enemy aircraft attacked without warning raking the Halifax from nose to tail on its first pass. Five members of Flying Officer Johnstone's crew were injured by cannon and machine gun fire, and the Gee and wireless sets blew up and caught fire. Only by violent corkscrewing did the pilot manage to throw off his attacker and make his escape. Nursing his crippled bomber all the way, Johnstone was able to return safely back to Snaith, where he was immediately recommended for a DFC.

Attacks on Kiel, Duisburg and Frankfurt followed in quick succession during the first week of April 1943. The Frankfurt attack, on the night of the 10th, was a complete failure. Thick cloud cover over the target prevented any of the 502 aircraft of the main force from making an accurate attack. As Flight Lieutenant Renolds, pilot of a Wellington Mk.X from No. 466 (RAAF) Squadron, was leaving the cloud covered target his Wellington was in collision with an unidentified aircraft. Flight Sergeant Joe Camm, Renold's rear gunner, recalls the incident:

'As we left the target area we collided with another aircraft, fighter or bomber, we will never know. The point of impact was just below my turret and I was lucky not to have been crushed to death. As it was we had one or two anxious moments until the skipper regained control. On return we examined the damage to our Wellington, and its a wonder how we ever got home. The tailplane was pushed back and the rear fuselage was almost severed.'

No. 4 Group lost two Halifaxes and two Wellingtons that night on the Frankfurt mission. One of the two Halifaxes missing was from 76 Squadron, skipper Flight Lieutenant Hull. His aircraft was intercepted by a night fighter over Belgium and shot down. Flying as second pilot with Flight Lieutenant Hull's crew was Group Captain (later Air Marshal Sir John) Whitley, popular station commander at Linton-on-Ouse. Jock Hill, Group Captain Leonard Cheshire's former wireless operator, recalls the sadness of the crews of Nos. 76 and 78 Squadrons at the loss of Linton's station commander:

'John Whitley's failure to return caused dismay among all ranks. This dismay was not lessened by the fact that someone had to inform Mrs Whitley, who as the CO's wife, was permitted to live on the station. I cannot remember who performed this unhappy task, but I know that she took the news extremely bravely. Fortunately the Squadron Commanders were Wing Commander Smith of No. 76 and Wing Commander Warner of No. 78, consequently the morale of the aircrew remained high.

'Weeks passed with everyone hoping for news that their old CO was a POW, but no such news was forthcoming and gradually hopes faded. All hope had gone when one day a stranger appeared in the ante-room of the Officers Mess at Linton, dressed in civilian clothes. No one paid any attention until, after a considerable length of time, the stranger blurted out, "Good God! Doesn't anyone here know me?" It seemed that no one did, until somebody, suddenly shouted, "Bloody Hell! It's Group Captain Whitley!". And it was. Anticipating that he might one day have to bale out, and being able to speak fluent French, he had always taken with him a black beret and other items designed to disguise himself as a French workman. Together with three other members of his crew who had survived the crash he had made contact with the French underground and escaped to England via Spain'.

A week after the attack on Frankfurt, a major assault on the Skoda armament works at Pilsen in Czechoslovakia was carried out by 327 bombers of the main force, that included almost a hundred No. 4 Group Halifaxes. The raid, on the night of the 16th April, was another disappointment. The Pathfinders mistook a large lunatic asylum, situated some seven miles from the Skoda plant, as their aiming point. As a result only six crews brought back photos that showed bombs had fallen within three miles of the objective. The raid had taken place by the light of a full moon which enabled the night fighters to stay in visual contact with the bomber stream. Fifteen Halifaxes from No. 4 Group were lost, including five from No. 51 Squadron and three each from Nos. 76 and 78. Squadron Leader Wally Lashbrook had only recently joined 102 Squadron at Pocklington as 'C' Flight Commander. He had in fact only been with the Squadron for seven days and the Pilsen raid was his second trip, having safely come through a raid on Stuttgart two nights earlier:

'Looking back it seems incredible that I only had seven days on the station. I had spent the previous eighteen months at No. 28 Conversion Unit having completed one tour, and I was glad to be back in an operational squadron again. My crew were given special responsibilities on future raids. Our job was to make an extra circuit of the target after the Halifax waves had passed through and take photographs of the bombing.

'Our target that night was the Skoda works at Pilsen, and after bombing we circled to come in again to take our photographs. This proved a bit more 'dicey' than on our last trip to Stuttgart. This time the Lancasters of the second wave had closed up on our Halifax wave, and consequently they were above us as we flew over the target. However, after one or two near misses from Lancaster bombs and German flak, we completed our task and were on our way home.

'Flying just above a layer of stratus, we got as far as the Franco-Belgian border. It was a beautiful clear night and as we came out of the cloud cover I realised that we were particularly vulnerable to fighter attack. In fact, as we entered the clearer air I saw somebody else getting the chop someway off on the port side. I warned our gunners to keep a sharp look out for fighters, and as I finished speaking it happened! A stream of tracer fire struck the underneath of our fuselage, the port wing and cockpit. I immediately threw the aircraft into a steep turn to port; the direction from which the attack came. I called up the crew to see if anyone had been hurt and received no reply from the rear turret. Sergeant Neil, the mid-upper gunner reported that he was wounded. Meanwhile, the port wing by now was well alight and I could not get any response from the port throttles. The night fighter must have been satisfied that we were finished, one attack had been sufficient. My attempts to get the aircraft out of a steadily increasing dive proved negative. At about 6,000 feet I ordered the crew to bale out. I remember seeing the navigator, bomb-aimer and wireless operator going through the front hatch as I remained at the controls. The flight engineer, Flight Sergeant Knight, came up to me and yelled that the root of the port wing was a blazing mess. He said that the rear gunner had been hit in the chest and the mid-upper in the thigh, the latter had been pushed out through the rear door. I told Knight to clip on my parachute for me and then get out quick. This he did, by which time we were down to 3,000 feet. I decided I had better go myself, and as I let go of the control column, the aircraft turned over and went into a spin. I made two unsuccessful attempts to get through the hatch, each time I was thrown back in. The third attempt proved successful and I came out like a cork from a champagne bottle. Suddenly I was out and dangling from my 'chute. As I was deciding which cord to pull to stop my swing, I hit the ground hard on my backside. The aircraft, meanwhile, had come down and crashed about 100 yards from me and was blazing furiously.'

Squadron Leader Wally Lashbrook had come down in Belgium. He later crossed into France and was able to contact members of the French Resistance who gave him shelter. Later, and after a number of narrow escapes, he was re-united with his bomb-aimer, Flying Officer Alf Martin, in Paris. Together with an American B-17 crewman, the three airmen escaped to Spain. Nine weeks after being shot down they returned to England, grateful to the many brave French men and women who helped them on their way. Sadly many were later to be executed for assisting Allied airmen.

Two other members of Lashbrook's crew were able to avoid capture and return to England. They were, navigator Flying Officer Bolton and wireless operator Sergeant Lanes. The flight engineer, Flight Sergeant Knight and the mid-upper gunner, Sergeant Neil, were captured. Pilot Officer Williams, the rear gunner – hit by fire from the night fighter, died in the crash.

The date is 3rd April 1943 and Linton-on-Ouse armourers are busy preparing incendiary canisters and 500lb HE bombs before loading into W7805 'M-Mother', Halifax Mk.II series 1 (Special) of 76 Squadron. That night Flight Sergeant Howarth and crew took 'M' to Essen but they did not return. *IWM, CH9137*

Flight Lieutenant Renolds (fourth from left) with other members 466 (RAAF) Squadron, Leconfield, April 1943. Far left is F/Sgt Joe Camm, Renold's rear gunner who narrowly escaped death when their Wellington was in collision with an unidentified aircraft on the night of 10th April 1943. *J. Camm*

Officers of 102 Squadron pictured outside their 'rustic' Officers' Mess at Pocklington in April 1943. Front row, left to right: Flying Officer Hinchcliffe, Flight Lieutenant Milne, Wing Commander Marchbank , Wing Commander Coventry, Squadron Leader Marshall, Flying Officer McDonald and Flying Officer Bolton. Back row: the tallest airman is Flying Officer Alf Martin who, together with Flying Officer Bolton baled out of Squadron Leader Wally Lashbrook's Halifax over Belgium on the night of April 16/17th 1943. The other airmen on the back row are unidentified. *K. Bolton*

After the disappointment of the Pilsen raid there followed a highly successful attack on another long distance target. This was against Stettin, on 20th April. Situated on the Baltic coast of Northern Germany, and some 600 miles from England, Stettin was to be attacked by using an unusual outward and inward flight. The bombers were to fly at low level (under 700 feet) across Denmark and the Baltic and then climb to 14,000 feet to bomb. The return leg was again to be at low level. Sergeant George Honey was detached from No. 1663 Conversion Unit and that night was flying as second pilot with a crew from 51 Squadron:

'The raid was routed across Denmark at low-level and in the moonlight it was possible to see cottages and on occasions, people standing in lighted doorways and at windows waving. Height was gained over the Baltic for bombing and lost again on the return.'

The great danger of a low-level approach flight was flak. In addition to land-based flak sites, flak ships were positioned on likely seaward approach routes used by the bombers. Bristling with light and heavy anti-aircraft guns and radar, the flak ships could strike without warning against an unsuspecting bomber. Several bombers were lost that night on the outward flight across Denmark and the Baltic.

'I touched the skipper's arm and pointed across the port wing where, in the distance, three or four coned searchlights appeared, conically groping the sky. Then a 'firefly', appeared, caught in their midst, followed by a dozen pinpoints of exploding flak. The 'firefly' then turned into a deep red flamer and tumbled earthwards. That would be one bomber less for Stettin, bad luck so early on in the raid'. (Sergeant 'Dave' Davis, No. 76 Squadron).

Over the target, the Pathfinder marking was highly successful and of 304 crews who claimed to have attacked the primary, 256 dropped their bombs within three miles of the aiming point. Over 100 acres of the centre of Stettin was destroyed, including many important industrial premises.

It was back to the Ruhr at the end of April, with heavy raids on Duisburg on the 26th, and Essen on the last day of the month. On 4th May the town of Dortmund suffered its first attack of the war when nearly 600 bombers of the main force (apart from the two 1,000 raids this was the largest attack of the war so far by Bomber Command), struck at the central and northern sections of the town. Substantial damage was caused to the town centre and dock area, and some forty-five acres of the main industrial area were gutted. Warrant Officer Peter Stead, a pilot with No. 196 Squadron, recalls in his diary his impressions of the scene of the stricken town of Dortmund:

'I flew at 20,000 feet, weaving very gently to upset any attempt by the defences at predicting us. I also had the engines of my Wellington, HE178 'D', desynchronised to make

the wurr-wurr noise, as was my usual practice.

'By the time we reached the turning point the attack had begun and we could see a great many searchlights in the target area. These were operating in cones of 20 - 30 and the aircraft caught were having a hot time from the flak. In addition to the predicted flak there was a very heavy curtain barrage being maintained over the target.

'As we ran in we saw a Pathfinder being engaged very fiercely over the target, and after a little while he blew up. Not a very pleasant sight to see as one is running in. We could tell he was a Pathfinder when the candles he was carrying exploded'.

From April 1943 two new Halifax variants began to arrive at the squadrons of No. 4 Group. A shortage of the standard Messier undercarriage units resulted in Dowty levered, suspension undercarriages being introduced onto a number of Halifax production lines. The result was the Halifax Mk.V Series 1 (Special). Identical in every respect to the Mk.II's, except for the slender looking Dowty undercarriage units, the Mk.Vs were supplied to No. 6 (RCAF) Group and to No. 76 Squadron.

Also coming off the production lines in the spring of 1943 was the Halifax Mk.II Series 1A. This new mark of Halifax included many of the improvements that had been recommended in the earlier review of the aircraft's performance. A new streamlined turretless nose, ending in a transparent fairing fitted with a Vickers 'K' gun, was introduced. This gave more space for the navigator and bomb-aimer. In addition, a compact Boulton Paul four gun dorsal turret was fitted as standard. As a result of the general clean-up, the Halifax Mk.II Series 1As had a 10% edge in performance over the basic Mk.IIs and Vs.

No.4 Group Bomber Command, April 1943

Sqn	Equipment	Airfield
10	Halifax II	Melbourne
51	Halifax II	Snaith
76	Halifax V	Linton-on-Ouse
77	Halifax II	Elvington
78	Halifax II	Linton-on-Ouse
102	Halifax II	Pocklington
158	Halifax II	Lissett
196	Wellington X	Leconfield
431 (RCAF)	Wellington X	Burn
466 (RAAF)	Wellington X	Leconfield

May was to see the heaviest blows yet against the Ruhr towns. During the month the main force struck at Duisburg, Bochum, Dortmund (twice), Düsseldorf, Essen and Wuppertal. On the night of the 12th the huge August Thyssen steel making plants in the Meiderich district of Duisburg were badly damaged. In addition, Duisburg-Meiderich station, and its adjacent rail yards, were wrecked. This success, however, had been bought at some considerable cost; the formidable Ruhr defences accounting for thirty-four bombers, including four crews from No. 51 Squadron. These were sad

days at Snaith. Since the commencement of the Battle of the Ruhr, No. 51 had lost sixteen crews in ten weeks of operations. The chances of a crew completing a tour during this recent run of bad fortune, were indeed slim. The following night the Bochum defences claimed two more victims from No. 51. The same night Sergeant Beveridge of 10 Squadron was flying at 18,000 feet on his way to Bochum. In the vicinity of the Rhine, near Dusseldorf, his Halifax, 'D-Donald', was suddenly held by searchlights and immediately bracketed by accurate flak fire. A near miss caused the rudders of the Halifax to overbalance and the aircraft overturned and plunged 10,000 feet before Beveridge was able to regain control. The mid-upper gunner, meanwhile, thinking that the aircraft was doomed, baled out. The searchlights once more latched onto 'D-Donald' but by jettisoning the bomb load, Beveridge was able to make good his escape. On the return flight over Holland, the rear gunner, Sergeant Compton, sighted two Ju 88 night fighters about to attack. The German pilots then commenced a series of attacks on the Halifax, singly and in pairs from both port and starboard. However, accurate fire from the rear-gunner kept the attackers at bay, and after seven inconclusive assaults the Halifax made its escape and returned safely to Melbourne.

After a break due to bad weather, operations recommenced on the night of 23rd May with another attack on Dortmund. Accurate Pathfinder marking, in clear conditions, resulted in a highly devastating attack. A No. 102 Squadron Halifax, JB894 'X- X-ray' (Sergeant Dave Hewlett), had just added its load of two 1,000 lb bombs and a large quantity of incendiaries to the conflagration that was about to overwhelm Dortmund. Sergeant Tom Wingham was 'X- X-ray's bomb-aimer:

'We had just closed the bomb doors, being among the first to bomb, and right on the aiming point. Suddenly a flak shell exploded nearby and shrapnel cut-in the fire extinguishers on three of our engines. We immediately lost power and started falling rapidly. The intercom became fuzzy as a voice called out, "What's happening – what's wrong Dave?" Pilot: "Who's that?" Rear gunner: "It's me, Andy". Pilot: "Prepare to bale out". I turned around from the bombing position in the nose and sat by the forward hatch and clipped on my parachute. I was then surprised to see a pair of white stocking feet doing a dance in the second pilot's position. Apparently Andy Reilly, our rear-gunner, had shot out of his turret, leaving his boots jammed in the turret, and had scrambled through the fuselage to Dave Hewlett at the controls, and was shouting at him:

'I don't believe it, this can't happen to us, it can't be true'.

'In the event it didn't happen, the engines picked up again. Andy was only expressing what we all felt, being shot down only happens to other crews, not us. I doubt whether any of us would have baled out. I for one, did not fancy baling out over the Ruhr and suspected that anyone who did was likely to be lynched on arrival.'

A split second delay in leaving an aircraft in trouble could mean the difference between life and death. A pilot of a Wellington of No. 431 (RCAF) Squadron decided to make a quick exit when his aircraft was hit by flak soon after leaving Dortmund on the night of the 23rd. There appears to have been some confusion as to whether a bale-out order had been given, certainly the rest of the crew remained with the aircraft, and the bomb-aimer, Sergeant Sloan, took over the controls. He was able to bring the damaged Wellington safely back to England, despite having never flown an aircraft before. Sergeant Sloan was awarded a CGM and posted to a pilot's training course.

That night the Dortmund defences claimed eleven Halifaxes of No. 4 Group. No. 51 Squadron lost another four crews, and three were lost from No. 78.

At the end of May, Bomber Command carried out its most effective area attack to date when 719 aircraft were sent against the Barmen district of Wuppertal. The attack, which took place on the night of 29th/30th May, was remarkably successful with the majority of the main force dropping their bomb loads within three miles of the aiming point. Over 90% of the built-up area of Barmen was devastated and 118,000 people were bombed out. Around the centre of the town there developed an enormous area of fire that proved impossible to extinguish. Roads blocked by rubble prevented Wuppertal's inadequate fire-fighting units from reaching the seat of the fire. Eventually, with the help of units from neighbouring Ruhr towns, the fires were brought under control, but not before some of the town's largest factories, 211 industrial premises and nearly 4,000 houses were destroyed. Bomber Command lost thirty-three aircraft, including eight from No. 4 Group. Twenty-two of the bombers had fallen to night fighters.

Halifax Mk.II series 1 (Special) BB324 'X' of 10 Squadron undergoing single-engined handling tests, April 1943. 'X-Xray' failed to return from Mulheim on the night of 22nd June 1943, with Sgt Pinkerton at the controls. *via W. Day*

Air Chief Marshal 'Bomber' Harris chats to Air Commodore 'Gus' Walker (later Air Chief Marshal Sir Augustus Walker) during a visit to Pocklington on 8th May 1943. At 30, Walker was the youngest Air Commodore in the RAF. Whilst commanding RAF Syerston in 1942, he had lost his right arm when a blazing Lancaster had exploded as he was attempting to rescue its crew. From March 1943 he had been in command of No.42 Base, which included the stations of Pocklington, Melbourne and Elvington. Also accompanying Harris on his visit is the AOC No.4 Group, Air Vice-Marshal Carr (centre).

Reconnaissance photograph of Duisburg-Ruhrort taken early in 1943. Clearly visible is the heavy river traffic in and around the docks area. Duisburg is the largest inland European port and its location at the confluence of the Rhine, the Ruhr and the Herne-Rhine Canal make it a key access point for the Ruhr industrial region. Top centre of the photograph can be seen the huge Thyssen steel making factory complex with areas of previous bomb damage. *IWM, C2354*

Crew of a 196 Squadron Wellington Mk.X pictured at Leconfield May 1943. Left to right: Warrant Officer Mellor, pilot; Flight Sergeant Webb, bomb aimer; Warrant Officer Quick, navigator; Flight Sergeant Allison, rear gunner; Flight Sergeant Williamson, wireless operator. Wellington HE980 failed to return from Cologne 3rd July 1943. *R. Williamson*

At this stage of the Battle of the Ruhr Bomber Command was losing between thirty and forty bombers per operation. It was also clear from intelligence reports that the majority of these losses were to night fighters. Just how helpless a bomber was, when picked up by a night fighter, can be judged from the following account of a night fighter interception that took place on the night of 12th June 1943. That night a massive attack was launched against Düsseldorf and involved 783 aircraft of the main force.

In the early hours of 12th June, night fighter ace Hauptman Eckart-Wilhelm von Bonin, and his radio-man, Oberfeldwebel Johrden, were patrolling in their Messerschmitt Bf 110G in Sector 6B near Liege. They had taken-off from their base at St Trond airfield, home of II/NG1, at 00.35, and so far it had been an uneventful patrol. Suddenly, at 01.39, von Bonin was directed onto a contact that was being tracked by a *Wurzburg* ground radar station. One minute later he spotted the *Kurier* (the target aircraft) directly below him

and flying at approximately 18,000 feet. The bomber was clearly silhouetted against the searchlight lit cloud base. Von Bonin immediately lost height, so as to be in a position to carry out a classic attack – from directly behind and slightly below the bomber. Closing to within 100 metres of the target, von Bonin was able to identify the bomber as a Halifax. He opened fire, aiming between the starboard engines, and directing his fire at the bomber's vulnerable fuel tanks. Flames immediately began to stream back from the wing tanks and the starboard inner engine and fuselage began to burn. The doomed Halifax quickly lost height and then went into a vertical dive. Trailing a banner of fire, it was seen to crash twelve kilometres north of Liege at 01.47. During the attack, which had lasted no more than three minutes, there had been no defensive fire from the Halifax and its pilot had not carried out any evasive action. Hauptman von Bonin had carried out a text book interception and added another 'kill' to his tally. Von Bonin was to

survive the war with thirty-nine victories to his credit.

Hauptman von Bonin's victim that night was Halifax Mk.II JD168 'T-Tommy', of No. 77 Squadron, on its return trip having just bombed Düsseldorf. Sergeant Alfred Endicott and his crew were on their second operation of their first tour. All seven managed to bale out of 'T-Tommy', but the rear gunner, Sergeant Walter Hammond, severely wounded in the night fighter attack, was found to be dead on landing. Sergeant Les Blanchard was 'T-Tommy's' bomb-aimer. He remembers that the time on target was approximately midnight and there was heavy defences and many shell bursts in their vicinity. The target was identified and the bombs dropped successfully.

'My "Bombs Gone!" call on the intercom was accompanied by the sudden lift of the aircraft which signified that it had shed its lethal load. The navigator announced the course to steer for home and the pilot acknowledged and re-set his compass.

Crew of 102 Squadron Halifax JB894 'X-Xray' in May 1943. Back row, left to right: Sergeant E. Holliday, flight engineer; Sergeant D. J. Hewlett, pilot; Sergeant Blackallar, navigator; Flight Sergeant N.A. Beale, wireless operator. Front row: Sergeant A. Reilly, rear gunner; Sergeant S.T. Wingham, bomb aimer; Sergeant J. Nightingale, wireless operator; Sergeant D.W.V. Hall, mid-upper gunner. *T. Wingham*

Halifaxes of 158 Squadron on their way to Düsseldorf, 25th May 1943. Leadng the way is Squadron Leader Elliot in HR734 'P', followed by Sergeant Pope in HR719 'M' with, in the distance, Sergeant Clarke's HR735 'N'. Within just six weeks of this photograph being taken, all three Halifaxes had been lost on operations. *IWM, CH10244*

'From my position, lying prone in the nose of the Halifax, I noted a tremendous concentration of bursting anti-aircraft shells ahead. I felt the pilot alter course slightly to steer around the bursts. Suddenly the flak stopped and the searchlights came on. That was the usual sign that night fighters were operating in the vicinity, and sure enough a few minutes later, I saw tracer bullets on the starboard side.

Flying officer W. G. W. 'Bill' Warren and crew, in Halifax Mk.II series 1 (Special) JB781 'W' lift off from the runway at Elvington on their way to Cologne, 28th June 1943, on the first operation of their successful 77 Squadron tour. Of interest in this photograph is the Boulton Paul four gun mid-upper turret, then being introduced on to Halifaxes, and the 'Monica' tail warning aerial protruding from the rear of the aircraft just below the tail turret. *W. Plunkett*

A 77 Squadron Halifax about to take off for Düsseldorf on 11th June 1943. At the extreme left of the photograph, next to the airman with the Aldis lamp, is Wing Commander Lowe, the CO of No.77. *W. Plunkett*

Flight Lieutenant Bond and crew of 158 Squadron at Lissett on completion of their first tour of ops, June 1943. Behind is HR751 'J-Jane' with 25 ops recorded on her bomb log. 'Jane' went on to complete 34 operations before being shot down by Hamburg flak on the night of 2/3rd August 1943. *IWM, CH10799*

Someone shouted that there were three fighters attacking us, but I personally saw two, both Messerschmitt 109s. (The German combat report indicates that only one night fighter was involved in the attack, and that was Hauptman von Bonin's Bf 110G-4). They were flying slightly above and on the quarter beam. I saw tracer bullets entering the starboard inner engine and at the same time heard the rear gunner call on the intercom, "I think I've been hit". That cry of his is something that will ring in my ears for ever. He was fatally wounded. He was only eighteen, a Londoner, Walter Hammond, a sergeant like myself.

'The enemy fire was concentrated on the starboard side of our Halifax and the starboard inner engine caught fire. This rapidly spread to the wing and the wing fuel tanks. I saw a long sheet of flame enveloping the wing and spreading back along the fuselage. We had dropped from about 18,000 feet to 15,000 feet. The pilot calmly gave the "Prepare to abandon aircraft" order and a few seconds later told us to leave.

Top: **Sgt Les Blanchard, 21 year old bomb aimer of No.77 Squadron.** *L. Blanchard*

Halifaxes of No.102 Squadron taxi onto the main runway at Pocklington in preparation for take off to Le Creusot, 19th June 1943. First off is 102's CO, Wing Commander Coventry, in JD144 'Q-Queenie'; take off time 21.47 hours. Close behind and next off at 21.48, is Flight Lieutenant Hartley in W7920 'D-Dog'. *IWM*

A 'green' from the control caravan sends Sergeant Dargavel and crew, in 102 'Squadrons' DT743 'O-Orange' off to Le Creusot from Pocklington, 19th June 1943. *IWM, CH16331*

'There was no mad rush for the escape hatch. Fear, I think, had been numbed by shock. We went about it quickly, but as though we were doing the normal drill. There was initial difficulty in lifting the hatch, perhaps because by this time we were in a fairly steep dive. The navigator was first to go, then the wireless operator, and I was third. I rolled forward, as we had been taught, into space. I can remember turning over and over, because I saw a sequence of darkness, a burning Halifax, darkness and flames. All the time I had my hand on the ripcord handle. When I was well clear I pulled it and the parachute opened. I looked around and saw the burning aircraft going down. At the time I didn't know if the rest of the crew had got out safely, although in fact they all baled out'.

Halifax 'T-Tommy' crashed into a row of cottages in the Belgian village of Oupeye, demolishing one house and badly damaging six others. There was a large explosion, possibly caused by a hung-up bomb, which killed five Belgians. (The site of the crash has been turned into a memorial by former members of the Belgian resistance movement. In 1950, Sergeant Les Blanchard – together with two other survivors from the crash and the dead rear gunner's mother – returned to the site and each were presented with an engraved ring, made from metal of the crashed Halifax).

Of the six surviving members of the crew of 'T-Tommy' only Sergeant Les Blanchard and mid-upper gunner Sergeant Dennis Burrows were to avoid immediate capture. Both received help from the local Belgian resistance and were eventually reunited in the house of a member of the underground in Liege.

They eventually reached Paris, but were betrayed to the Gestapo and arrested. For ten days they were kept in solitary confinement on starvation rations, and constantly interrogated. They were able to convince the Gestapo that they were genuine RAF men and not spies or saboteurs, and were handed over to the Luftwaffe. Les Blanchard was sent, initially, to Stalag Luft I at Barth on the Baltic coast. He was then transferred to Stalag Luft VI, the main POW camp for Air Force NCOs, at Heydekrug close to the Lithuanian frontier. After several more moves, including a spell at the notorious Fallingbostal camp, he was able to reach the safety of the advancing Allied armies.

Another Halifax crew that fell victim to a night fighter, on the night of 11th/12th June, was that of Sergeant Wilson of No. 76 Squadron. The Düsseldorf raid was the Wilson crews's first trip. They were shot down by a Messerschmitt Bf 110G-4 flown by Oberleuntnant Barte of NG1. Only the navigator, Sergeant John Lobban, was able to escape from the violently spinning Halifax. The rest of the crew died in the crash which occurred near Bladel, Holland.

Although the attack on Düsseldorf had been highly successful, the city sustaining very severe damage, the cost to Bomber Command was high. Thirty-eight bombers were lost, eleven from No. 4 Group. One of the last aircraft to be shot down was a Halifax from No. 51 Squadron. Flight Sergeant Collins and crew were returning across the North Sea in the early hours of 12th June and no doubt the crew of Halifax DT742 were beginning to wind down after the last few, anxious hours spent over enemy territory. Suddenly, when just ten miles off the Norfolk coast, they came under fire from a convoy and, despite Collins firing the recognition colours of the day, their Halifax continued taking hits and eventually crashed in the sea off Sheringham. Sergeant Spreckly, Collins' wireless operator, was killed. The rest of the crew were later rescued by a trawler.

The following night the night fighters were again very active within the bomber stream during an attack on Bochum. A bomber crew's chances of survival were slim if attacked by a night fighter. If that night fighter had an experienced pilot at the controls then the odds would indeed by very heavily weighted in the enemy's favour. Occasionally, if a bomber crew were alert, and if luck was with them, they would be able to give a good account of themselves. On the night of 12th/13th June, the Luftwaffe did not have everything their own way.

At 01.58 Flying Officer Ernie Herrald of No. 51 Squadron was flying his Halifax, HR834 'V-Victor', at 18,000 feet on route for Bochum. Suddenly in the moonlight, a single-engined fighter was spotted approaching from astern. The enemy fighter appears to have been unaware of the presence of the Halifax because the fighter's navigation lights were lit. Herrald immediately took evasive action by putting the Halifax into a diving turn to port as the rear gunner opened fire on the fighter. The German pilot, now fully alerted to the presence of the Halifax, started to follow Herrald's manouvre. The fire from the rear gunner, however, had been very accurate and the fighter began to lose speed and was seen to dive away trailing flames and smoke. There was then a mid-air explosion and the enemy fighter fell to the ground in pieces.

A crew from 158 Squadron had lady luck on their side on the return leg from Bochum. As they approached the German-Dutch border they were set upon by two Messerschmitt Bf 110s. During the encounter the guns of the rear turret jammed. One cannon shell from a night fighter came in through the port side of the rear fuselage and glanced off the control rods before passing between the legs of the pilot, Sergeant Robinson. The same shell struck the bomb aimer, Sergeant Dunning, a glancing blow before bursting through the perspex nose. Despite only having the mid-upper turret in action, Sergeant Robinson and crew were able to shake off their attackers by skillful use of the corkscrew manoeuvre and accurate fire from Sergeant Cuthbert, the mid-upper gunner.

Sergeant Ken Hewson, skipper of 'U-Uncle' of No. 76 Squadron had just crossed the Dutch coast at 16,500 feet on the return leg from Bochum when his rear gunner, Sergeant Dave Davis, shouted over the intercom, 'Corkscrew skipper!' The pilot flung the Halifax into a steep dive to port, just in time to avoid a burst of cannon fire from a Junkers Ju 88 night fighter. As the enemy fighter followed Ken Hewson's corkscrew manoeuvre, and then broke off port quarter up, the rear gunner was presented with a brief view of his underside. From a range of 200 yards Sergeant Davis sent a stream of tracers into the upturned belly of the Ju 88. The stricken fighter turned sharply to port and fell in a steep dive, where it was seen to strike the sea and was enveloped in flames. The enemy fighter continued to burn for some time as the triumphant bomber crew returned home.

On the night of 19th June there was a break from attacks on the Ruhr when 290 aircraft were sent to bomb the Schneider armaments factory at Le Creusot in France. Two incidents at No. 4 Group airfields on that day, marred the start of what was a reasonably successful operation. At Snaith, home of No. 51 Squadron, there was the usual mid-day activity in the bomb dump when 'ops are on', as the armourers sweated to prepare the bomb loads for the waiting Halifaxes. Many of the 'Erks' had worked on through their lunch,

probably only snatching a quick cuppa and a'wad', as they laboured over their dangerous and exhausting work. Suddenly, at 13.30 hours, there appears to have been an explosion in one of the fusing sheds. Large quantities of incendiaries caught fire, which in turn set off many of the high explosive bombs which were in the process of being fused. Huge explosions rocked the base for the next three and a half hours as all personnel were forced to take cover. Despite the chaos and damage, bombs were transported from Holme-on-Spalding Moor and fourteen aircraft were bombed up in time for the mission to Le Creusot. Eighteen airmen were killed in the disaster.

The other incident occurred over at Elvington. Sergeant Holledge and crew had just taken-off for Le Creusot when their Halifax, JB863 'V-Victor', swung as it left the runway. Despite efforts by the pilot to gain altitude, 'V-Victor' refused to climb and crashed near Heslington village, not far from No. 4 Group HQ at Heslington Hall. The entire crew of 'V-Victor' was killed.

Two nights later, on the 21st June, Krefeld, situated on the west bank of the Rhine and on the edge of the Ruhr industrial region, was subjected to a particularly accurate and concentrated attack. The whole centre of the town was burnt out as an area of fire became established which proved very difficult to extinguish. Sergeant George Honey (latter day Senior Vice-President of the Pathfinder Association) was skipper of Halifax JD206 'T-Tommy' of No. 102 Squadron. 'T-Tommy' was a new Halifax and Sergeant Honey and crew were taking it on its second operation. The Krefeld operation was the crew's sixth trip of their first tour.

While crossing the Dutch coast, flying at 19,000 feet, they were hit by flak and the Halifax was severely damaged. Three engines and the hydraulics were put out of action, the coolant tanks holed and after the bombs were jettisoned, the bomb doors could not be closed. Height was lost rapidly and at 16,000 feet Sergeant Honey decided to ditch the aircraft. He instructed his wireless operator to send out a distress signal, but the trailing aerial could not be reeled out and the range obtained on the fixed aerial was insufficient for reception. Meanwhile the Halifax was approaching sea level about eighteen to twenty miles WNW of Overflakee, at a speed of about 120 mph. A full moon and fifteen miles visibility favoured the ditching, although the wind was blowing 15 - 20 mph across a slight swell. In the circumstances Sergeant Honey decided it was preferable to land up-moon rather than into wind. This was performed very successfully at 85 mph, with full boost on the starboard outer engine - the only one serviceable. The first impact with the water was gentle and the final impact only slight. The Halifax stayed afloat for thirty minutes and the crew were able to get safely into the dinghy. The ditching had been seen by other returning bombers, subsequently two ASR Walruses were despatched and succeeded in picking up the entire crew some eighteen hours after ditching.

Mulheim, Wuppertal, Gelsenkirchen and Cologne suffered very heavy attacks during the last week of June 1943 as the Battle of the Ruhr drew to a close. The Cologne attack, on the night of the 28th, was that city's heaviest raid of the war. Damage was widespread and casualties the highest suffered so far by a German city. 4,377 killed and 10,000 injured. Sergeant Cameron and crew, in Halifax HR837, 'F-Freddy', of 158 Squadron, had just released their bombs over Cologne on that night when they came under attack from a night fighter. One cannon shell from the fighter, identified as a Ju 88, struck the fuselage on the starboard side, forward of the mid-upper gunner's position, and left a large hole in the side of the aircraft. Sergeant Cameron was able to shake off the fighter but almost immediately his aircraft was hit by a 1,000 lb bomb from another aircraft. The bomb struck 'F-Freddy' near the mid-upper turret and passed through the fuselage and port wing. Sergeant Young, 'F-Freddy's' mid-upper gunner, was only slightly injured but his turret was severely damaged. Sergeant Cameron's Halifax returned to Lisset with a huge hole in the fuselage.

Cologne received two further heavy blows within a week at the beginning of July. The series of highly destructive attacks on the city resulted in 350,000 people being bombed out.

Air Commodore Gus Walker, (second left) discusses the previous night's raid on Le Creusot with Squadron Leader Marshall, (extreme left) and Wing Commander Coventry (second right), Pocklington, 20th June 1943. *IWM, CH10335*

Some of Flying Officer Ernie Herrald's crew sitting on *Auld Reekie*, their 51 Squadron Halifax Mk.II series 1A HR834 'MH-V', at Snaith, 13th June 1943. Left to right: Sergeant Bill Higgs, engineer; Flying Officer Stan Gibbon, wireless operator; Sergeant Arthur Kell, bomb aimer; Sergeant Dick Sibley, rear gunner. *W.H. Higgs*

No.77 Squadron crew of Halifax Mk.II series 1 (Special) JD110 are all smiles at Elvington, June 1943. On return from Mulheim, on the night of 22nd June, their Halifax, already badly damaged by flak, was intercepted by a Me 110 over the North Sea. Despite the damaged condition of the Halifax, the rear gunner, Sergeant Speeday, was able to shoot down the fighter. Left to right: Sergeant French, wireless operator; Sergeant Muffett, mid-upper gunner; Flying Officer Simpson, navigator; Sergeant Mathers, pilot (from Sydney, Australia); Sergeant Gough, engineer; Sergeant Goldsborough, bomb aimer; Sergeant Speeday, rear gunner. *IWM, CH10479*

Gelsenkirchen and Aachen were attacked early in July as the Battle of the Ruhr finally came to an end. The Battle had cost No. 4 Group over 200 aircraft in the eighteen week campaign. Before moving on to the next phase of the night offensive, 4 Group aircraft took part in an all-Halifax attack on the Peugeot motor factory in the Montbeliard suburb of the French town of Sochaux. Led by thirty-one Halifaxes from the Pathfinders the 134-strong force of Halifaxes from No. 4 Group attacked the Peugeot plant on the night of 15th/16th July. Unfortunately the marking by the Pathfinder Halifaxes was inaccurate, consequently the vast majority of the No. 4 Group bomb loads fell in the town of Sochaux, with disastrous results: 123 French civilians were killed and 336 injured. The Peugeot plant suffered only minor damage and production was not affected. A Halifax crew from No. 78 Squadron had a narrow escape very early on in the Montbeliard mission. Flying Officer Carver and crew had just taxied their Halifax, DT771 'D-Dog', onto No. 3 runway at Breighton in preparation for take-off to Montbeliard. 'D-Dog' was an old Halifax that was not renowned for its reliability, and the Carver crew were not exactly overjoyed at being chosen to fly in her. Things started to go wrong soon after the final preparations for take off had been made, as Flying Officer Gerry Carver recalls.

Below: **A hive of activity around 'V-Victor's dispersal at Elvington 1943. One 'erk' appears to be repainting DT643's serial number. That and the slight variation in the camouflage pattern suggests DT643 may have only recently received a new tail section.** *IWM, CH10591*

Flight Lieutenant Storey (back row, third from left) and 102 Squadron crew manage a few nervous smiles for the camera before setting off for another trip. Their Halifax, 'G-George', a Mk.II series 1 (special), was subscribed by the people of Ceylon and shows 40 operations completed. Note the two pigeon carriers in the foreground. The practice of carrying pigeons on operations, in case crews ditched or crashed, was abandoned at the end of 1943. *J. Mitchell*

'We trundled on our way down the main runway and into the gathering dusk. At the half way point, with approximately 1,000 yards of runway to go and having assumed a tail-up flying position, I noticed with some trepidation that the airspeed indicator gauge still registered zero. We were now in a very critical situation that called for an instant go or no-go decision.

'Having first established that the airspeed indicator was not just stuck, by giving it a sharp rap, my decision was made. I closed the throttles, applied the brakes and full flap. Unfortunately 'D-Dog' didn't respond. The momentum of such a heavily laden aircraft defied the braking action. We rumbled on, overshooting the end of the runway, the 150 yard overshoot area, through a hedge, across a country lane, finally coming to rest in a potato field.

Fortunately, the emergency drill eliminated any risk of fire and no injuries were sustained, we had been lucky. Much good humoured micky taking resulted, the spot where 'D-Dog' came to rest becoming known as 'Gerry's potato patch dispersal.'

'It transpired that the cause of the unserviceable airspeed indicator gauge was the air pressure pipe leading from the pitot head to the ASI on the instrument panel. Somehow the pipe had become bent restricting the flow of air.'

Sergeant Cameron and crew pose in the hole left by a 'friendly' 1,000lb bomb which hit their Halifax 'F-Freddie', HR837 of 158 Squadron, over Cologne on 28th June 1943. Left to right, back row: Sgt Young, mid-upper gunner; Sgt Cameron, pilot; Sgt Hulme, flight engineer; Sgt Lane, navigator. Front: Sgt Hardwick, wireless operator; F/Sgt Young, rear gunner. *IWM, CE82*

Thousands of roofless buildings are a testimony to the two highly destructive raids on Cologne on 28th June and 3rd July 1943. During the two attacks, 300,000 people were bombed out, 5,000 were killed and 11,000 injured. Top right is the famous Cologne Cathedral, which suffered only slight damage during the raids.

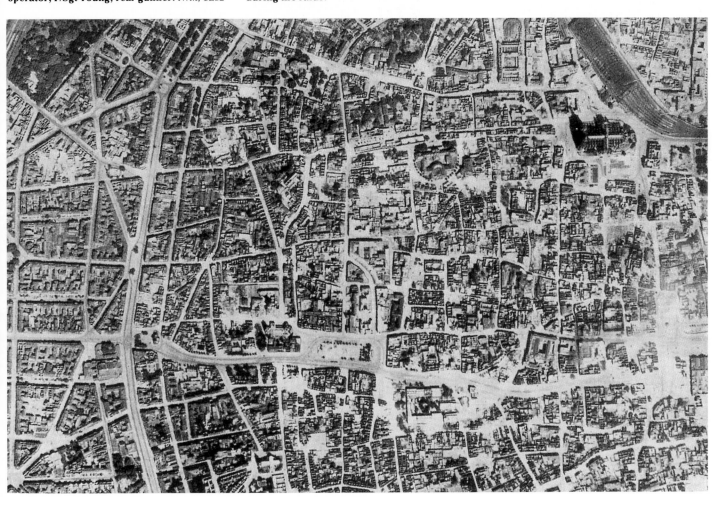

Above: **The pilot of Halifax JB911 'X' of 77 Squadron, demonstrates some hair raising low level flying at Elvington, July 1943. Note the ground crew bicycles, dispersal hut made** from tarpaulin and oddments of corrugated sheeting. JB911 was passed to 1658 HCU and was struck off charge in November 1946. *IWM, CH10593/4*

Halifax Mk.III series 1A JD206 'T-Tommy' of No.102 Squadron at Pocklington, June 1943. JD206 failed to return from operations to Krefeld on 22nd June 1943. *IWM, CH16776*

Chapter Twelve

The Battle of Hamburg

The Battle of the Ruhr ended in mid-July 1943. For the first time during the war German cities had suffered severe and widespread damage and heavy civilian casualties. Nearly all the centres of the leading towns of the Ruhr had been burnt out.

The cost to Bomber Command had been heavy, 872 bombers had been lost, 4.7% of the force despatched. Bomber Command's losses during the battle were at times – in the words of the official history – 'approaching perilously close to the unbearable'. The increasing success rate of the German night fighter force was threatening to put an end to the night bomber offensive, just when it seemed that the offensive was inflicting decisive damage on the enemy.

Despite the losses, Air Chief Marshal Harris was confident that the force under his command would overcome the difficulties and force the enemy to his knees. Bomber Command's night offensive was, for the next eight months, to become a war of attrition which has its parallel with the trench warfare of the First World War. Whilst his bombers were still very much involved in demolishing the Ruhr, Harris had already decided on his next move.

The north German city of Hamburg – Europe's largest port, had been largely ignored during the recent offensive. It was now to receive the full attention of Bomber Command in a series of attacks that were to prove the most destructive of the war.

For their attacks on Hamburg, the bombers were to use a new device which at a stroke would paralyse the German defences. This new device, called 'Window', consisted of strips of aluminium foil 27 cm long and 1.5 cm wide. When dispersed from an aircraft, the bundles of Window would break up into a large cloud of fluttering strips which would appear on the enemy's radar screens as a large aircraft. Window was cut to exactly half the *Wurzburg, Wurzburg-Reise and Lichtenstein* radar wavelengths. With one blow all German fire-control and air reporting systems were rendered useless. The whole *Himelbett* night fighting system was disrupted and it was impossible either to direct the night fighters or fire radar predicted flak barrages.

Window had been ready for use in April 1942 but fear that the Germans might also use the device prevented it being used earlier.

The city of Hamburg had been attacked on 98 previous occasions by Bomber Command, but had suffered only minor damage. As an important manufacturing centre the second city of Germany had always been high on the target lists. Hamburg's shipyards were particularly noted for the production of U-boats, and it was for these reasons that the city had been earmarked for destruction.

The first attack took place on the night of 24/25th July 1943 and was carried out by a force of 791 aircraft. No. 4 Group supplied the largest contingent which consisted of 158 Halifaxes and 17 Wellingtons. In clear conditions twenty H2S-equipped Pathfinders dropped yellow target indicators and strings of flares, designed to illuminate the target for the visual markers, who marked the aiming point with red target indicators. The aiming point was situated halfway between the southern end of the Binnen Alster lake and River Elbe, both features which would be visible on the H2S screens. The bombing by the main force was designed to take place over a period of fifty minutes, and during that period a fairly concentrated attack took place as the six waves of bombers swept in from the north west of the city. It was towards that direction that a substantial 'creep-back' developed as the main force crews began to dispose of their bomb loads early. Severe damage was caused in these districts of Hamburg, particularly in Altona, Eimsbuttel and Hoheluft. 2,284 tons of bombs had been dropped in what was a highly successful operation. Thanks to the effects of Window the Hamburg defences had been rendered ineffective. Only twelve bombers were lost including four Halifaxes from No. 4 Group.

Because their radar screens were blotted out by Window, the German night fighters were ordered to search for bombers visually in the Hamburg area, but they met with little success. Sergeant Fletcher and crew of No. 51 Squadron were attacked by a Dornier Do 217 night fighter near the Danish coast on the outward leg of their journey to Hamburg. Quick reactions from the rear gunner, however, proved decisive and the German fighter was seen to dive away on fire.

The following night Essen was the target. Large areas of the Krupps complex were left in ruins and the town suffered its most damaging raid so far. The torment of Hamburg, meanwhile, had continued with a daylight attack, on 25th July, by 123 B-17 Flying Fortresses of the US Army Air Force. The B-17s were targetted on the Blohm and Voss U-boat yards and the Klokner aero engine factory.

Large areas of the north western section of the city were still burning from the RAF raid of the previous night and by the time the B-17s arrived over Hamburg, smoke from the fires was obscuring the target areas, and as a result their bombing was largely ineffective.

For the citizens of Hamburg there was to be no respite. Air Chief Marshal Harris was determined to destroy the city before its defences had any chance of countering the effects of Window. On the night of 27/28th July he launched 787 bombers against the beleaguered city. On this occasion the bombers approach route was from the north east. The designated aiming point was again in the city centre but the Pathfinders, using H2S dropped their marker bombs two miles east of the correct position. The marking error, however, was not a serious one as there was still a large built-up area to the east of city centre for the main force to aim at. The first markers went down at 00.55 and five minutes later the main force arrived. The attack soon became highly concentrated as a huge area of fire began to develop in the Borgfelde and Hammerbrook districts, north east of the city centre. In this area, which was mainly residential in character, was witnessed the phenomenon of the 'Fire Storm' - a huge super heated area of fire where convection currents caused winds of up to 150 mph and temperatures of 1,000 degrees centigrade were exceeded.

The extent of the firestorm area measured approximately four square miles and at the height of the fire nearly 16,000 apartment blocks were burning. There was little chance of escape from this area. Those who chose to leave their shelters were either swept into the fire by the howling winds or gassed by the high levels of carbon monoxide poisoning. There were few survivors from the districts affected by the firestorm. 40,000 people were killed and approximately 1,200,000 fled Hamburg, leaving behind the shattered remains of a demoralised city.

Two nights later Harris's crews struck at Hamburg again. This time there was no repeat of the disastrous firestorm, nevertheless severe damage was inflicted on the Barmbeck district and in other areas already damaged by previous bombing. Despite the handicap of Window, the German defences had recovered enough to account for twenty-eight bombers, eight of these were No. 4 Group Halifaxes.

During the last raid of the series, on the night of 2nd August, thirty bombers failed to return. Many of those lost that night succumbed to severe icing as a large thunderstorm developed over Germany. The bad weather ruined any chance of the bombers repeating the successes of the previous raids. No. 4 Group's Strategic Air Staff Officer, Air Commodore W. A. D. Brooke had an eventful night when he flew to Hamburg with Squadron Leader Belton's Wellington crew of No. 466 (RAAF) Squadron. Sergeant Murry Roberts was Belton's navigator:

'One engine went u/s before we reached the target so we had to jettison our bombs and try to get back home. We had difficulties immediately in trying to control the aircraft on one engine. To counteract the tendency of the Wimpey to pull to one side, Squadron Leader Belton had to use all his strength on the rudder pedals. Unfortunately he had only short legs and it required the combined efforts of the skipper and Air Commodore Brooke (minus his flying boots) to control the rudder. Fortunately they were successful and we reached base safely.'

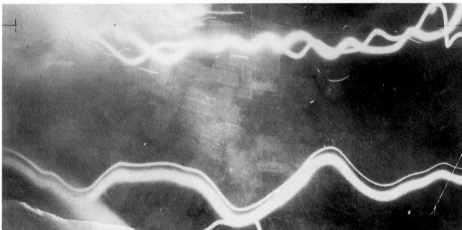

The bomb log of 158 Squadron's HR755 *Xpress Delivery*, shows 28 missions including two trips to the 'Big City' Berlin, (large bombs) and one mining sortie (a spade for 'gardening'). In front are Flight Lieutenant Brown RNZAF and crew on their first tour, July 1943. *IWM, CH10800*

A centre portion of Sergeant Falgate's strike photo of Hamburg, 24th July 1943, from Halifax 'Q-Queenie' of 76 Squadron. *W. Day*

No.76 Squadron Halifaxes await their crews on the peri-track at Holme-on-Spalding Moor, Summer 1943. *IWM, CH10227*

Another crew from No. 466 were able to reach Hamburg, despite the deteriorating weather conditions. Flight Lieutenant Morton's Wellington was in fact the last bomber over the target, releasing his bomb load at 02.55 hours.

Despite the anti-climax of the fourth raid in the series against Hamburg, Operation *Gomorrah* had been a great victory for the bombers. The highly successful introduction of Window had left the German defences largely impotent. Losses over the four nights were only eighty-seven aircraft. No. 4 Group flew 662 sorties and lost eighteen Halifaxes. No. 102 Squadron had suffered the heaviest losses with five crews missing. A break down of No. 4 Group's losses reveals the vulnerability of inexperienced crews in the early stages of their tours. Of the eighteen Halifax crews lost, two thirds had only completed five or less trips. Five crews were on their third trip and two were on their first operation.

Devastation at Krupps Works, Essen: Reconnaisance Mosaic taken after the raid of July 25th 1943 in which Krupps was to suffer its most damaging raid of the war. Key numbers indicate important sections of the plant damaged or destroyed in this or earlier attacks. *IWM - C3682A*

1. Wheel axle workshop
2. Sheds demolished.
3. Machine shop
4. Machine shop (heavy guns, loco wheels)
5. Machine shop (field gun carriages)
6. Diesel engine works (heavy and medium)
7. Probable engineering shop
8. Probable engineering shop
9. Machine shop (long range guns)
10. Repair shops (fuses)
11. Engineering or assembly shop
12. Open hearth and electric foundry
13. Smith and forge
14. Hydraulic presses shop
15. Finishing shop and generator
    for electric/furnace
16. Open hearth furnace shops and steel foundry
17. Open hearth furnace shops and steel foundry
18. Rolling mill (shell forging)
19. Steel foundry and rolling mill
20. Annealing shop
21. Small foundry
22. Forge and smithy shop
23. 75% of this area gutted by fire
24. Locomotive works
25. Machine shops
26. Probable engineering shops
27. Foundry, tyre and ball mill
28. Loco tenders and wagons
29. Probably armoured trains
30. Wagon shop (rolling stock and howitzers)
31. Proving ground
32. Machine shop (light field carriages)
33. Machine shop (small and medium guns)
34. Forge and rolling mill
35. Probably a finishing shop
36. Spring steel workshop
37. Wood storage and sawmills
38. Machine shop (shell turnery)
39. Foundries (shell turnery)
40. Workers billets

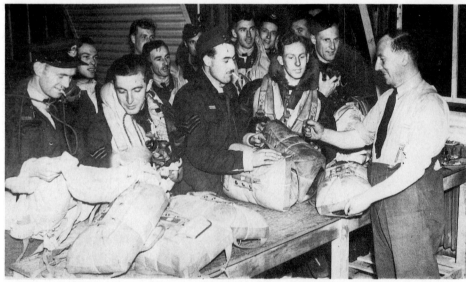

Devastation in Hamburg was enormous. Approximately 8,344 tons of high explosive and incendiary bombs had been dropped by the RAF in four attacks. The districts of Hammerbrook, Eilbek and Barmbek had suffered almost complete destruction. Nearly 600 industrial premises and 2,632 commercial premises had either been destroyed or severely damaged. But it was the residential areas which suffered most. 35,719 residential buildings were destroyed and some 5,666 damaged. Approximately 45,000 people were killed and 900,000 were made homeless. The triumph of the area bombing was complete.

With the success of Hamburg behind him, 'Bomber' Harris now set his sights on the prize target, Berlin. Harris calculated that if the Nazi capital was administered a strong dose of the 'Hamburg' medicine then surely the enemy would be ready to sue for peace. However, Harris would have to be patient and await the longer, darker nights of winter before unleashing his bombers on such a distant target as Berlin. In the meantime the month of August 1943 would see the bomber force taking full advantage of a spell of fine weather to attack a variety of targets which included Mannheim, Nuremburg and targets in Italy.

The attacks on Italian targets were designed to encourage the Italians to surrender. Milan was bombed on the night of 12th August, No. 4 Group providing 138 Halifaxes towards the main force of 504 bombers. During a successful attack the Alfa-Romeo motor works and the main railway station were severely damaged.

Operations Order 12th August 1943. Target: Milan No.77 Squadron, RAF Station Elvington

Acft	Captains	Route	Times	
	2nd phase		2nd	3rd
D	F/Lt Rowe		phase	phase
E	F/Lt Pritchard	Take-off	20.46	20.50
A^M	F/Sgt Clinch	Set course	21.16	21.22
G	P/O Munns	Selsey Bill	22.33	22.39
P	F/Lt Fitzgerald	Cabourg	23.04	23.10
M^+	F/Sgt Massie	North end of		
K	F/Sgt Daffey	Lake Bourget .	00.45	00.51
U	S/Ldr Wright	Target On	01.23	01.29
Y	Sgt Baxter	Target Off	01.29	01.35
O	F/Sgt Brannigan	4520N 0903E ..	01.32½	01.38½
R	Sgt Jones	South end of		
C	Sgt Chester	Lake Bourget .	02.24½	02.30½
Z	Sgt Hill	Cabourg	04.20½	04.26½
	3rd phase	Selsey Bill	04.52	04.58
V^RA	P/O Warren	Base	05.58	06.03
H	Sgt Brown			
X	Sgt Shefford			
N^M	Sgt Ellis	^M *Equipped with 'Mandrel' for*		
B	P/O Needham	*jamming German radar;*		
J	Sgt Gay	^+ *2nd Pilot;* ^RA *Raid Assessment.*		
L	F/Sgt Galletly			
T	Sgt Manson			

Bomb Load: Aircraft B, J, K, L & P carry 1x1000 lb GP Special; 5SBC (90x4 lb) with 6% 'X' type; 5SBC (8x30 lb).
All other aircraft carry 1x1000 lb GP (TD 0.025); 5SBC (90x4 lb) with 6% 'X' type; 5SBC (8x30 lb).

Opposite: **Ready to go! Sunset at Holme-on-Spalding Moor, 1943.** *IWM, CH10226*

Drawing parachutes at Holme-on-Spalding Moor, No.76 Squadron, 27th July 1943. *W. Day*

Crews await the transports at Holme-on-Spalding Moor. The date is the 27th July 1943 again and 76 Squadron is about to take part in the second raid of Operation *Gomorrah*, the destruction of Hamburg. *W. Day*

'All aboard . . . next stop Hamburg! No.76 Squadron crews about to leave for their aircraft, 27th July 1943. *W. Day*

Severe damage in the St Georg dockside area of Hamburg. This area was on the edge of the main fire storm, even so there are many thousands of roofless buildings and large areas of total destruction.

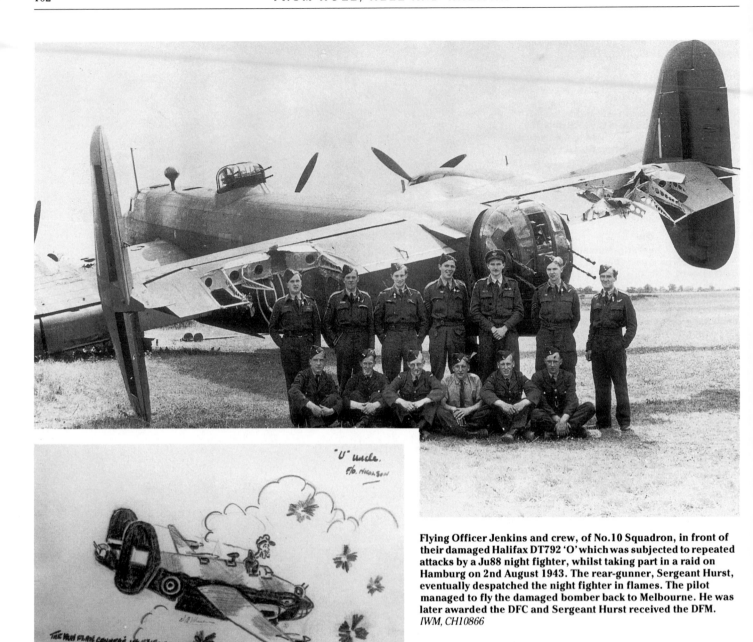

Flying Officer Jenkins and crew, of No.10 Squadron, in front of their damaged Halifax DT792 'O' which was subjected to repeated attacks by a Ju88 night fighter, whilst taking part in a raid on Hamburg on 2nd August 1943. The rear-gunner, Sergeant Hurst, eventually despatched the night fighter in flames. The pilot managed to fly the damaged bomber back to Melbourne. He was later awarded the DFC and Sergeant Hurst received the DFM.
IWM, CH10866

Cartoon by Flying Officer Nicholson of No.51 Squadron. The caption reads: 'the Hun flak gunners haven't got the range and the WOP is dropping window as he's never done before, and there's bags of silver paper lying on the floor. Press on, Press on!'

Ever since 1937 German scientists had been developing a liquid-fuelled rocket capable of carrying a high explosive warhead. Development work on the rocket, known as the A4, was being carried out at the Military Experimental Station at Peenemünde, a highly secret, purpose-built complex on Germany's Baltic coast, 125 miles north of Berlin.

Early in 1943, Hitler, despite his earlier scepticism of the project, began to see the potential of the rocket programme. Here at last was a weapon that could revenge the merciless Allied bombing and turn the tide of war back in Germany's favour. Peenemünde was awarded top priority, and by the summer of 1943 development was proceeding apace.

The Allies, meanwhile, were aware of the secret experimental work being carried out at Peenemünde. Regular photographic reconnaissance missions, during May and June 1943, had revealed the existence of the rockets. Further intelligence gathering disclosed the threat posed by the A4 rocket programme, and the War Cabinet decided that the RAF should attack the Peenemünde rocket establishment as soon as possible.

The raid took place on the night of 17th August 1943 in clear moonlight conditions. An attack on such a distant target in moonlight meant a high risk of heavy losses from night fighters. The fact that Bomber Command was willing to accept the risk indicates the high priority given to Peenemünde's destruction.

At briefing the crews were not told the true identity of the target or the kind of experimental work that was being carried out there, as Flight Sergeant Dai Pugh, pilot of No. 102 Squadron recalls:

'At the time we knew nothing about the V-2 rockets. At briefing we were told that Peenemünde was a Radio Location Site, and that is the entry in my pilot's log book. This was to be a precision raid and our target was to be the workers housing estate. The aim was to destroy the site and kill as many of the scientists and technicians as possible. I can tell you that we were none too pleased about flying all that way in moonlight.'

Halifax Mk.II series 1A HR952 'X-Xray' receives its load of 500lb general purpose bombs and cans of incendiaries at Snaith, August 1943. 'X-Xray' flew its first trip with 51 Squadron, a raid on Mannheim on 9th August 1943, skippered by Sergeant Carder. Later transferred to 10 Squadron, it was lost on a raid to Berlin, 29th January 1944.
via W. Baguley

Flying Officer James Keirl and crew had just completed a heavy conversion course at Riccall and on the morning of 17th August they arrived at their new squadron, No. 78 at Breighton. Keirl's rear gunner, Sergeant John Greet, takes up the story:

'Here we were, at our first operational squadron, and by heck we were nervous. Much to our surprise, Jim Keirl and myself discovered that we were on 'ops' that very night. Jim was to fly as second pilot with another crew and I as mid-upper gunner with Pilot Officer Ferguson. From that moment on I was both excited and nervous, it was indeed a surprise to be on operations so quickly after arriving at the squadron. During the afternoon, as we checked our equipment on our Halifax, we were all wondering what the target was going to be.

'At briefing we were told that the target was an experimental station on the Baltic coast. We were to attack from between 6,000 and 10,000 feet in the first wave. We were also told in no uncertain terms, that the attack had to be successful otherwise we would have to go again and again until the target was destroyed. You can imagine how I felt, a young lad just turned nineteen – I think I was the youngest member of the crew – flying on my first raid with a crew of complete strangers'.

The force despatched to attack Peenemünde comprised 324 Lancasters, 218 Halifaxes (145 from No. 4 Group) and 54 Stirlings. The bombing plan was an unusual one for a main force night attack in that there were three separate aiming points. No. 4 Group Halifaxes, together with Stirlings and Lancasters of 3 Group, were to open the main force attack by bombing the first aiming point, the workers housing estate. Lancasters of 1 Group were allocated the second aiming point, the production works, whilst aircraft of Nos. 5 and 6 Groups were to strike at the experimental works. The thinking behind the decision to destroy the workers housing estate was clear from the Bomber Command Operation Order which stated:

'All available Halifaxes are to attack the living and sleeping quarters in order to kill or incapacitate as many of the scientific and technical personnel as possible.'

For the first time Bomber Command would be employing a 'Master Bomber' to control the progress of a raid. The task of Group Captain John Searby was to fly back and forth across the target and ensure that both marking and bombing went according to plan.

The Peenemünde Raid 17/18th August 1943
No.4 Group Raid Statistics

Sqn	Took off	Early Return	Attacked Primary	Missing
10	18	1	15	1
51	24	-	24	-
76	20	-	20	-
77	21	1	19	1
78	21*	1	19	-
102	17	-	17	-
158	24	1	22	1

* One aircraft crashed soon after take off.

The raid was carried out on schedule and the attack destroyed large areas of the Peenemünde works. A diversionary Mosquito raid on Berlin successfully lured away the majority of the night fighters, with the result that the first and second waves of the raid received little interference. Unfortunately, by the time the third wave arrived the German night fighters had recovered from the ruse and had started to arrive over the target in force. They took a heavy toll of the third wave, comprised of the bombers of Nos. 5 and 6 Groups.

Before . . . Target for the Halifaxes of 4 Group:
the Peenemünde workers housing estate. *IWM, C3753*

. . . and After:
the Peenemünde workers housing estate, pictured after the raid. *IWM*

Below: 'U' Uncle, a Halifax Mk.II series 1 (Special) JD324, comes into land at Elvington, August 1943. 'U' Uncle was hit by flak over Peenemünde on the night of 17th August 1943, the bomb load exploded and Sergeant Shefford and his entire crew were killed. During the Summer of 1943, Halifaxes of 77 Squadron, bearing the code letter 'U', were to prove unlucky for their crews; 'Uncle's did not survive more than three or four trips before 'getting the chop'. *W. Plunkett*

Bottom: Flight Lieutenant 'Timber' Wood and crew of Halifax Mk.II series 1 (Special) JD119 'C' of No.10 Squadron, August 1943. Left to right: Pilot Officer Alan Redbond, Pilot Officer George Stevens RNZAF, Flight Lieutenant 'Timber' Wood, Flight Sergeant Bill Knott, Flight Sergeant 'Blondie' Palmer, Flight Sergeant Jock Denwette, Sergeant 'Paddy' O'Kill. On August 20th 1943 JD119 crashed whilst on a cross country flight with Flight Lieutenant Smith at the controls; five of the crew were killed. *W. Knott*

The German night fighters employed a form of freelance tactics for the first time. The introduction of Window had rendered the system of fighter control obsolete and as a result the night fighters were now instructed to hunt for their targets over or near the main bombing area. In addition several twin-engined night fighters were now equipped with twin, upward-firing 20 mm cannon in a so called *Schrage Musik* (Jazz Music) installation. These aircraft were able to attack an unsuspecting bomber from directly below, making use of tracerless ammunition fired from their upwards firing cannons. The only warning of attack that a bomber crew usually received was when their aircraft burst into flames, by which time it was too late to take evasive action. Two *Schrage Musik* equipped night fighters are known to have intercepted the bomber stream returning from Peenemünde and believed to have accounted for six of the forty bombers shot down.

Detail of the *Schrage Musik* installation of two 20mm cannons mounted against the rear bulkhead of the cockpit of the Messerschmitt Bf 110 night fighter. Its operational debut was on the night of 17th August 1943, during the attack on Peenemünde.

One that did not make it to Berlin. The wreckage of Halifax JD379 'M-Mother' of 77 Squadron which came down near Celle following an attack by a night fighter, 23rd/24th August 1943. No.4 Group lost 13 Halifaxes that night out of a total Bomber Command loss of 62 aircraft. Compare this with the photograph immediately below, which is captioned on the opposite page.

Chapter Thirteen

The Battle of Berlin

Shaken by the destruction wreaked in Hamburg and the Ruhr, the Nazi authorities began to warn that Berlin would be next on the RAF's list. Goebbels, in his capacity as Gauleiter of the Reich capital, ordered a partial evacuation of the city. By the end of August 1943, the city's defences were at a high state of readiness for the expected attack. It came as no surprise then to the Germans when Harris launched two massive attacks on Berlin at the end of August 1943. Although the Battle of Berlin did not officially commence until the middle of November 1943, the two attacks in August, and one early in September, were really the opening rounds in a ferocious contest that was to last until the end of March 1944. Harris's aim was 'to wreck Berlin from end to end' and force Germany to surrender early in 1944. But success for Bomber Command in the coming Battle was to prove elusive. The German night fighters had recovered from the setbacks of the summer and by the autumn of 1943 they had improved their tactics and equipment. Bomber Command was now to pay a high price for failure.

The first main force raid on Berlin in five months took place on the night of 23/24th August 1943. 335 Lancasters, 251 Halifaxes, 124 Stirlings and 9 Mosquitos took off on the long, seven hour journey to Berlin and back.

Opposite, centre: **Air and ground crew of Halifax Mk.II series 1 (Special) JD379, 'M-Mother' of No.77 Squadron, August 1943. Front row, third from left Flight Sergeant Bill Plunkett, navigator; fourth from left Sergeant Chas Brister, mid-upper gunner; fifth from left Flight Sergeant Alex Massie, pilot; seventh from left Sergeant Reg Croft, flight engineer. Back row, third from left Flying Officer 'Pip' Stiff, wireless operator; fifth from left Sergeant Bill Peers, bomb aimer; sixth from left Flying Officer Chas Rollings, rear-gunner. Alex Massie, Bill Peers and Chas Rollings were killed when 'M-Mother' was shot down on 23rd/ 24th August 1943 (see above). The other crew members survived as PoWs.** *W. Plunkett*

Warrant Officer Kennedy and crew of JD166 'G-George' of 10 Squadron, Melbourne, August 1943. Left to right: Sergeant Payne, engineer; Sergeant Round, mid-upper gunner; Sergeant Beard, rear gunner; Flying Officer Rath, navigator; Warrant Officer Kennedy, pilot; Flight Lieutenant Keenan (10 Squadron's 'flying' Adjutant who accompanied many crews on operations as an unofficial extra crew member); Pilot Officer Skinner, bomb-aimer; Sergeant Capstick, wireless operator. *M. Keenan*

The largest contribution was from 4 Group, who provided a maximum effort of 157 Halifaxes from its seven Halifax squadrons. The Group's last remaining Wellington-equipped unit, No. 466, sent sixteen of its aircraft on a mining operation off the Frisian Islands.

The German night fighters, meanwhile, were fully alerted to the possibility that Berlin was to be the main target. They began to concentrate their forces in and around the target area approximately one hour before the opening of the attack, set to commence at 23.45 hours. Already some of the bombers had fallen victim to the night fighters long before they reached Berlin. One 77 Squadron Halifax, JD379 'M' (Flight Sergeant Alex Massie), was late taking off from Elvington that night due to a glycol leak. Flight Sergeant Bill Plunkett was 'M-Mother's' navigator:

'As a result of the glycol leak we were late getting off, and we were way behind the rest of our wave. The early stages of our trip were uneventful except for the usual coastal flak as we crossed the Dutch coast. We were somewhere over the Lüneburg Heath, not far from the town of Celle, when we came under attack. Chas Brister, our mid-upper gunner, suddenly shouted a warning to the skipper to take evasive action as a Jerry fighter was approaching from the port quarter. I was surprised that the fighter didn't attack from that direction. Instead he slid below us, and the next thing we knew was that the port wing was on fire. I now know something that I did not know at the time. The German fighter was obviously equipped with 'Schrage Musik' – upward firing cannons. He had positioned himself directly below us, and whilst following the skipper's evasive action movements, had calmly pumped 20 mm cannon shells into our wing tanks.

'Alex Massie tried desperately to extinguish the flames by diving but it was hopeless. He then told us to abandon the aircraft. I managed to lift the hatch under my seat but was then thrown to the floor as the Halifax went into a violent spin. There I was, held fast by the 'G' forces, unable to move. I thought this is it, I've had it now!

'Something then made me make a last desperate effort. I heaved myself over to the edge of the hatch and forced myself, head first, through the opening. To my horror I discovered, that instead of falling clear of the aircraft, I was in fact being dragged down with it. One of my boots had become wedged in the opening and

I was stuck fast, suspended upside down below the doomed aircraft. Fortunately my foot came out of the boot and I fell clear of the blazing Halifax as it spiralled down. The next thing I remember is swinging first one way and then the other as I floated peacefully down on my parachute.'

Flight Sergeant Bill Plunkett was lucky that night to escape from his blazing aircraft. The brave pilot, who had remained at the controls of the Halifax to allow the other crew members to escape, paid the ultimate price, along with the bomb-aimer and rear gunner.

At the target, the Berlin flak defences restricted their fire to approximately 15,000 feet to allow the night fighters to attack any bombers illuminated by searchlights and fires. When the bombers arrived they were met by a host of single and twin-engine fighters co-operating very effectively with the searchlights. As a result Bomber Command suffered its highest loss of the war so far. Sixty-two aircraft failed to return, or 8.7 per cent of the force. Thirteen of those missing were from 4 Group, including five each from 78 and 158 Squadrons.

Fifteen airmen lost their lives in a spectacular crash between two 78 Squadron Halifaxes, on their return from Berlin. The sole survivor from both crews was rear gunner Sergeant John Greet. Forty-three years on, John Greet has only fleeting memories of what happened on that fateful morning:

'As I look back on those days I remember that most of the crews were delighted to be going to the "Big City". I do not recall a lot of detail about the raid other than the fact that we had a rough trip. I have visions of something terrific happening.

'The next thing I remember was when I woke up in the RAF Hospital at Rauceby some two to three weeks later. I was eventually told that I was the only survivor from a mid-air collision. Subsequently I have been able to piece together what actually happened.

'Our aircraft, Halifax JB874 'E', skipper Flying Officer Keirl, had suffered damage during the raid but we were able to return to Yorkshire safely. Because of bad weather over Breighton we were diverted to Leconfield. On arrival at Leconfield we were told to go to Hutton Cranswick, an airfield some five miles north of Leconfield. Shortly after, we collided with another Halifax from our squadron, BB373 'K' skipper Sergeant Bell. According to witnesses, there was a violent explosion and both aircraft crashed at Hull Bridge, one mile north-east of Beverley. There were no survivors from

Sergeant Bell's crew which included a second pilot, Flight Sergeant Gilbert, and an additional crew member. I was the only one to survive the impact but I was still in a pretty bad way when they pulled me from the wreckage.

'When I regained consciousness in hospital, I then began the long road back to mobility. My injuries were extensive and included several compound fractures of both legs, a fractured skull, a fractured jaw, lacerations of my face and numerous burns and other minor injuries. After four years in hospital and rehabilitation units, I finally reached an acceptable degree of mobility.

'Looking back, I realise how lucky I was to escape death, particularly as I would normally have been in the mid-upper turret, which was my usual crew position. For some reason the rear gunner, Sergeant Fred Roberts, was not happy in that position and asked me if I would change places with him. This I was quite happy to do.'

Much of the bombing of the 23/24th August raid fell outside of Berlin. This was due to the failure of the Pathfinders to identify the city centre. Nonetheless damage caused to the southern districts of the city was considerable and over 800 people were killed.

After a disappointing raid on Nuremburg, on the night of 27/28th August; which cost nine 4 Group Halifaxes out of thirty-three lost to Bomber Command, a dual attack was mounted three nights later against the neighbouring towns of Mönchengladbach and Rheydt. Heavy damage was inflicted on both towns in what was described as a highly successful attack. However a mid-air collision again caused tragedy amongst No. 4 Group aircraft on their return from Germany. Two Wellingtons from 466 (RAAF) Squadron collided in a spectacular explosion over Goole and both crews were lost. Returning to Snaith, and flying in the same area, was Halifax HR782 'V-Victor' of 51 Squadron. As it approached its base, 'V-Victor' collided with a Lancaster of a nearby Conversion Unit. Although severely damaged in the collision – the Halifax had several severe gashes in the port fuselage, the port fin was missing and the rear turret was pushed in – 'V-Victor's' pilot, Flying Officer Burchett, managed to make a successful crash landing at Snaith. None of the crew was seriously injured.

On the night of 31st August the bombers returned to Berlin. 622 aircraft were despatched, including a hundred Halifaxes from 4 Group. Records show that on this night there was a high percentage of early returns amongst the Halifax squadrons. Apart from the normal reasons given for aborting a mission, usually because of some technical malfunction, many crews complained that their aircraft would not climb to their designated height in the bomber stream. In addition, many reported their engines overheating as they struggled to gain height. It was not surprising that many crews decided to abort rather than wallow along several thousand feet below the rest of the stream, where they would be easy prey to night fighters and flak. It would appear

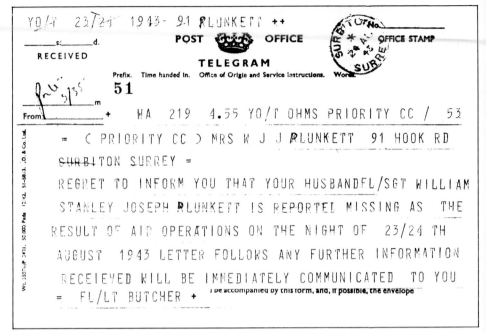

No. 77 Squadron,
Royal Air Force,
Elvington,
Near York.

24th August, 1943.

Reference:-
77S/317/473/P.1.

Dear Mrs Plunkett,

It is with regret that I have to confirm my telegram informing you that your husband, Flight Sergeant William Stanley Joseph Plunkett, is reported missing from operations.

Your husband was the Navigator of an aircraft that took off on an operational flight over enemy territory on the night of 23/24th August, 1943. The aircraft did not return.

It may be several weeks before definite news is received, but, without wishing to raise false hopes, I can tell you that a large number of aircrew members reported missing under similar circumstances ultimately prove to have made a successful parachute jump, and to be prisoners of war. I sincerely hope that this may be the case now.

Flight Sergeant Plunkett had been with the Squadron since May of this year, and had proved himself a keen and capable member of an operational crew. He will be very much missed here, especially amongst his fellow N.C.O's.

I am enclosing a list of the names and addresses of the next-of-kin of the other members of your husband's crew, in case you should care to get into touch with them.

Immediately I receive any information I shall, of course, get into touch with you. In the meantime, please do not hesitate to write to me if there is any way in which I may be of assistance to you.

Yours sincerely,

Wing Commander, Commanding,
No. 77 Squadron, R.A.F.

Mrs. W.S.J. Plunkett,
91, Hook Road,
Surbiton, Surrey.

Opposite: **Copies of the telegram received by Flight Sergeant Bill Plunkett's late wife, the day after he was shot down on the way to Berlin, also of the letter which followed shortly afterwards, from his Commanding Officer, Wing Commander Lowe.**

This Page: **After nearly four weeks of not knowing whether her husband was dead or alive, Mrs Plunkett's prayers are answered.**

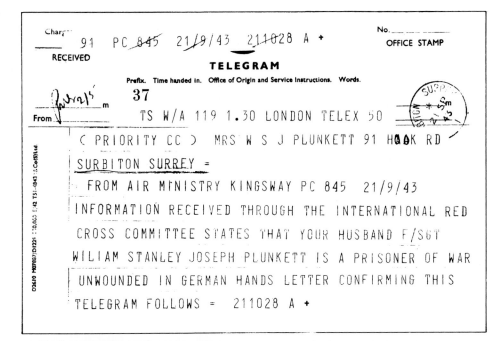

Halifax Mk.V DK193 'Y' of 76 Squadron was destroyed in a spectacular take-off accident at Holme-on-Spalding Moor on the 30th August 1943. Whilst taking off for a raid on Mönchengladbach a tyre burst caused DK193 to veer sharply off the runway. The undercarriage collapsed and the luckless Halifax caught fire. Fortunately, Flight Lieutenant Lemmon and crew were able to escape before the bomb load erupted. *via W. Baguley*

Halifax Mk.II series 1A's at their dispersals, Breighton, Autumn 1943. Note the variety of rudder styles, some with unmodified rudders, others with the later D-shaped types.
Guy Lawrence

Queue here for Berlin! No.78 Squadron crews wait for the transports at Breighton, 31st August 1943. For some of the men in this picture there would be no return trip: two crews from No.78 were fated not to return from Berlin that night, among 47 others from Bomber Command. *Guy Lawrence*

Wing Commander Guy Lawrence, CO of 78 Squadron, chats with his crew before departure to Berlin, 31st August 1943. In the background is their Halifax Mk.II series 1A JD173 'V-Victor', displaying a score of seven completed operations. 'Victor', went on to complete a total of twenty-three operations with No.78 before passing on to 1658 HCU. It was finally struck off charge in February 1945. *L. Broadhurst*

Aussie rear gunner Flight Sergeant J. M. Cunningham, an ex-insurance agent from Sydney, squeezes into the cramped rear turret of his 446 (RAAF) Squadron Wellington at Leconfield in August 1943. *J. M. Cunningham*

that freak atmospheric conditions, possibly caused by the recent spell of hot weather, was the reason for the problems with the Halifax engines.

The weather also caused problems over the target. An unexpected veer in the forecast wind below 20,000 feet, coupled with erratic timing of the early Pathfinder marking, spoilt what promised to be a telling blow on the German capital.

The official Bomber Command report records that the enemy made use of fighter flares for the first time that night. High flying twin-engined aircraft, some equipped with searchlights in the nose, flew back and forth across Berlin dropping lanes of powerful white flares to illuminate the bomber stream for the large number of single and twin-engined night fighters that had gathered over the target. The flares were designed to fall slowly by parachute and illuminate a large area over the clouds. The CO of 78 Squadron, Wing Commander Guy Lawrence, (now Sir Guy) was detailed to make a special reconnaissance report on the night's raid:

'The gunners reported enemy night fighters, some with lights and some without, from the moment we crossed the enemy coast.

'It was not until we got to the capital that I saw any of the new flares. About a dozen were dropped at a time. They fell very slowly from a great height, burning with a brilliant, bright light. They were coming down in parallel lines. My navigator, Flight Lieutenant Alan Dowden, counted forty flares coming down at one time, dropping more slowly than a leaf falls through the air. The scene over Berlin was like a series of flare-paths on an airfield with air fights going on in and around them. The night sky was alive with flares, shell bursts and the glare of searchlights.'

Flight Lieutenant Hunter in JD475 'Z', leads other Halifaxes of 78 Squadron to the start point at Breighton. The date is 31st August 1943, the target is the 'Big City', Berlin. Flight Lieutenant Hunter in 'Z-Zebra', failed to return from Mannheim on 5th September.
Guy Lawrence

The take-off period was the most hazardous time for a bomber crew, particularly if the aircraft was heavily laden with bombs and fuel. An engine failure at this critical moment could prove disastrous. This 77 Squadron, Elvington based Halifax Mk.II series 1 (Special), 'J-Jane', tucks its wheels in and is safely on its way, in the Summer of 1943.
W. Plunkett

This unidentified Halifax Mk.II series 1A of No.77 Squadron is seen departing from Elvington, 1943. *W. Plunkett*

Blazing apartment blocks in Berlin during one of the heavy night attacks of August 1943. *IWM, HU10604*

The 78 Squadron CO and his crew relax as they wait to be de-briefed after returning from Berlin, early on 1st September 1943. Seated at back, left to right: Sergeant Ferris, mid-upper gunner; Sergeant Hardcastle, rear gunner. Front, left to right: Flying Officer Kelt, bomb-aimer; Flight Sergeant Petrie, flight engineer; Flight Lieutenant Dowden, navigator; Wing Commander Lawrence, pilot; Sergeant Fawcett, wireless operator. *Guy Lawrence*

A Halifax from No. 158 Squadron, JD246 'R-Robert' (Sergeant Ward), was one of the early arrivals over Berlin. Sergeant Ron Thurston was the wireless operator on 'R'-Robert:

'We were on our twenty-first operation of our first tour so we were quite an experienced crew, even so we'd not seen anything like this before. We immediately came under attack from two fighters, and as the rear gunner traded shots with our attackers, the skipper flung the aircraft into a wild corkscrew. We were hit several times and the port inner engines began to burn, it was then that we started to go down very rapidly. The fire quickly spread to the fuselage as we spiralled down out of control. At first we found it hard to move due to the rapid descent, but eventually the navigator removed the escape hatch under his feet and baled out followed by the bomb-aimer. I followed, with the flight engineer's feet practically on my shoulders.'

Sergeant Ron Thurston along with three other members of the crew of 'R-Robert', were able to escape from the doomed bomber as it plunged into Berlin. Sadly the twenty year old pilot, and the mid-upper and rear gunners, were killed. The fight had not all been one sided, however, as one of the night fighters was seen to go down in flames.

That night over Berlin, the German defences took a heavy toll of the bombers. Forty-seven were shot down, two-thirds of that number by night fighters operating in the Berlin area. No. 4 Group lost eleven Halifaxes including four from 158 Squadron.

In the days that followed the newspapers in Britain carried optimistic headlines that read: 'Great Damage in Berlin' and 'New Defensive Tactics Fail'. Even the official Air Ministry communique was reassuring: 'Our bombers made another heavy attack on Berlin, when a great weight of high explosive and incendiary bombs was dropped in forty-five minutes. Broken cloud at low levels made it difficult to assess results, but large fires were seen and preliminary reports indicate that great damage was done. Many night fighters were active over the target and along the route, but failed to prevent a concentrated attack, and several of them were destroyed. Forty-seven bombers are missing.'

The reality was that Berlin had only received minor damage, much of the bombing again, as in the previous attack, falling well to the south of the city. The two recent attacks on the German capital had cost Bomber Command over 100 aircraft, and the Halifax squadrons had been particularly badly hit. Together with the less numerous Stirlings, they had borne the brunt of the losses. The final week of August 1943 had cost No. 4 Group alone thirty-eight Halifaxes lost on operations. Many began to question whether losses on this scale could be sustained.

Although these were difficult days, Air Chief Marshal Harris was not to be put off from his desire to see Berlin destroyed. In the meantime however, he decided to switch his bombers back to other targets in Germany.

The late Wing Commander Harry Drummond AFC, DFM. After a tour of ops on Whitleys and Halifaxes with 78 Squadron, Harry Drummond became an instructor. He served with various conversion flights within 4 Group before being appointed Flight Commander and finally OC No.1658 Heavy Conversion Unit and Deputy Station Commander at Riccall. *via W. Baguley*

Interrogation for 78 Squadron crews as others await their turn, following the raid on Berlin on 31st August / 1st September 1943. *G. Carver*

No. 78 Squadron crews enjoy their post-debriefing egg and bacon, upon return from the raid on Berlin. *G. Carver*

S/Ldr Dobson of 1658 Heavy Conversion Unit test flying a Halifax Mk.II series 1 on one engine. 1658 HCU was established at Riccall at the end of 1942. *W. Day*

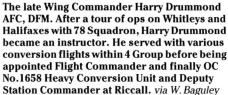

This next phase was to last for approximately ten weeks. Harris was prepared to wait until the longer, darker nights of winter made conditions more favourable for his bombers to have another crack at Berlin.

On the night of 5/6th September 1943, a double attack was launched against Mannheim and Ludwigshafen. 1,500 tons of high explosive and incendiaries were dropped by a force of 605 aircraft on these twin armament and chemical producing centres. Crews reported seeing huge fires, visible 180 miles away. By the end of what was a highly concentrated attack, a great pall of smoke, rising at times nearly four miles high, hung over the target. A German war correspondent broadcasting over the German radio from Mannheim stated:

'The British have pitilessly and without sense or aim during a night of rage and hatred, dropped their bomb loads on an old town. The smell of burning houses, of a fire which is spreading from roof to roof and street to street, fills the air. Black and impenetrable clouds of smoke cover the town and its collapsing buildings. This town has become a battle area.'

**DT807 'R-Rita', a Halifax Mk.II series 1
(Special) of 77 Squadron stands quietly in the
late Autumn sunshine whilst Elvington
farmers are busy haymaking. Rita's career
with No.77 started on 11th March 1943 with a
trip to Stuttgart and ended with Sergeant
Cracknell and crew who were lost on an
operation to Kassel on 3rd October.**
IWM, CH1059A

The defences were very active over Mannheim shooting down thirty-four bombers
including nine Halifaxes from 4 Group. No. 78
Squadron were able to send twenty-one aircraft that night. Two returned early with
engine trouble. The rest successfully bombed
the target but four crews failed to return.

The following night Munich suffered its
first major air raid in over six months when
257 Lancasters and 147 Halifaxes struck at
this distant target, deep into southern Germany. The Germans again made use of fighter
flares and crews reported these being dropped from a great height and extending to over
two miles in lanes across the city. As Flying
Officer Bob Atkinson and crew, of Halifax
JB921 'S', No. 102 Squadron, approached the
target about midnight, their aircraft was
attacked by three night fighters. They had the
satisfaction of fighting them off and seeing
one, a Junkers Ju 88, go down trailing smoke
and flames. Their jubilation did not last long,
as bomb-aimer Sergeant Hugh Moore remembers:

'We had just unloaded our bombs when I
heard a massive explosion. A burst of flak had
hit the starboard wing and the petrol tanks
had exploded in flames. The skipper put the
Halifax into a steep dive, hoping that this
would blow out the flames, but it didn't work.
The skipper then asked for a course to head
for Switzerland, hoping against hope that a
miracle would happen and that the flames
would go out, and we would at least reach
neutral territory. George Butcher, our
navigator, gave him a course to steer, but the
rear gunner called out, "the flames are
streaming past my turret, skipper!" They
were the last words I heard him speak.

'With the help of the navigator I released
the front escape hatch as the skipper calmly
gave the order to bale out. The navigator rolled out first and I followed close behind.

'I learned later that the flight engineer clipped on the pilot's parachute - his last act of
duty, for he was killed by another burst of flak
as he was descending to the escape hatch in
the nose. The pilot too, was hit, shrapnel
penetrating his parachute pack and entering
his stomach'.

By the time the pilot, Flying Officer Atkinson, got out, the Halifax's burning wing was
folding up in a mass of flames. For a moment
he thought that he was doomed, but a second
explosion blasted him from the aircraft.

Meanwhile, Sergeant Hugh Moore remembers counting five before he pulled the
parachute ripcord. He then became unconscious:

'I came to, still falling, with the blazing aircraft a dull red cross below me. I then hit the
ground and again passed out. When I
regained my senses I was being supported by

a middle-aged German and his teenage son in a back garden. They had already removed my parachute and harness. I asked them, in German, for a glass of water and one was given me. I had landed in the village of Penzberg, about fifteen miles from Munich. I was taken to a police station where I was handed over to the authorities.'

Sergeant Moore was taken to Munich airport, along with his navigator who had also been captured, and passed over to the Luftwaffe. He learned later that the pilot was in hospital with a broken leg and stomach wounds.

On the night of 8th September 1943 an incident occurred which serves to illustrate the dangers faced by instructors 'resting' between tours at Conversion Units. That night Flight Lieutenant Coverley, an instructor with 1658 HCU at Riccall, was detailed to take up a pupil on night dual instruction in Halifax Mk.II, V9989. Flight Lieutenant Coverley describes what happened:

'The perimeter track at Riccall ran very near parallel to the runway in use, and quite close to it. As we approached the holding point we were given a red as apparently a pupil on a cross country had lost an engine and was returning on three. While we waited I continued to brief the pilot from where I was sitting – on the right hand 'jump seat'. I watched the aircraft turn in for finals. He appeared to be rather low and coming straight for us which did not concern me as he may well have been allowing for drift which he would take-off at the last minute. However, it quickly became evident to me that he was finding difficulty in straightening up on the runway. I just had time to duck before his wheels took the props off our two inner engines. A couple of feet either way, or the tailwheel a bit lower, and I would not have been here to relate this story and my aircraft and the two or three lined up behind me would have made a spectacular blaze.

'I taxied back to dispersal on the outers and as far as I can remember the chap who caused the damage succeeded in overshooting and then landing safely. After this incident I was, quite frankly, glad to be going back on operations even though losses at that time were very heavy.'

No.4 Group Bomber Command, September 1943

Sqn	Equipment	Airfield
10	Halifax II	Melbourne
51	Halifax II	Snaith
76	Halifax V	Holme-on-Spalding Moor
77	Halifax II	Elvington
78	Halifax II	Breighton
102	Halifax II	Pocklington
158	Halifax II	Lissett
466 (RAAF)	Halifax III (non-op)	Leconfield

Note: 466 (RAAF) Squadron were converting to the Halifax III.

During the first weeks of September 1943 heavy raids were mounted, by large forces of mainly Halifaxes and Stirlings from Nos. 3, 4 and 6 Groups, against targets in France. On the night of 15/16th September the Dunlop rubber factory at Montlucon, forty-five miles north-west of Vichy, was badly damaged. Large fires were started in the target area and crews reported the strong smell of burning rubber even when they were at 12,000 feet. The following night railway communications between France and Italy were bombed. A force comprising 340 aircraft, including 100 Halifaxes from No. 4 Group, attacked marshalling yards at Modane, a small town in eastern France at the entrance of the famous tunnel under Mont Cenis.

A week later the bombers were back attacking Germany again. Hanover had escaped the attention of Bomber Command in recent months but on the night of 22/23rd September the first in a series of four heavy attacks was launched against the town.

Despite clear conditions adverse winds over the target caused the bombing to drift mainly to the south-east of the city centre. The night fighters were very active that night and twenty-six bombers were lost, including eight from 4 Group. Flight Lieutenant 'Taff' Jenkins and crew in Halifax HR924 'N' from 10 Squadron were attacked by a night fighter from below just as they were about to commence their run in to the target. Despite frantic evasive action by the pilot, the German fighter was able to rake the underside of the Halifax with his upwards firing cannons. Fortunately by successful use of the corkscrew manoeuvre they were able to shake off the night fighter but not before the Halifax suffered serious damage. The aircraft's hydraulic system had been shattered by cannon fire preventing the operation of the bomb doors and undercarriage. In addition, the H2S scanner had been shot away leaving a gaping hole in the fuselage floor.

Unable to drop their bomb load of a 4,000 lb cookie and incendiaries, Flight Lieutenant Jenkins decided the safest course was to remain with the bomber stream, with its protecting curtain of Window, and continue over the target and return with the main force. This they did, successfully avoiding the lanes of fighter flares that were being cascaded over the bombers route out of Hanover. On return to base the crew of HR924 were ordered to abandon the aircraft rather than attempt a crash landing with a 4,000 lb bomb aboard. The crew successfully baled out, despite being fired on by trigger happy army gunners, and the Halifax came down in the sea off Partrington, Yorkshire.

A Halifax crew from 158 Squadron had a narrow escape over Hanover five nights later. Again only skilful manouevring by the pilot made all the difference between life and death for the bomber crew. Flight Sergeant Grey and crew of Halifax HR858 'O-Orange' were attacked by a Ju 88 as they were going

The crews of P/O D. J. Hewlett (102 Sqn) and P/O Rank (77 Sqn) with ground crews, were seconded to the Intensive Flying Development Flight at Boscome Down, June to October 1943, for trials with prototype Halifax Mk.III R9534 and early production model HX227 (in photo).

Flight Lieutenant L. A. Carey (RNZAF) and crew chat with their 102 Squadron ground crew at Pocklington after returning from a raid on Frankfurt, 4th October 1943. It was the last 'op' of their tour – hence the smiles. Note the assortment of air and ground crew clothing. *S. Freeman*

into the target. The fighter was driven off by fire from the rear gunner and the Halifax was able to complete its bombing run. Flight Sergeant Les Harman, the rear gunner in 'O-Orange', describes what happened next:

'After we had bombed the target we were again attacked by a Ju 88, which might well have been the same fighter that had attacked us earlier. This time only one of my four Brownings would fire, and that soon broke down after firing only a few rounds. The skipper, meanwhile, began to throw the aircraft all over the sky in a desperate bid to shake off the fighter. At the same time I continued to give a running commentary on the direction of the fighter's attacks whilst as the same time frantically trying to un-jam my guns.

'The skipper did a superb job and we managed to avoid most of the cannon fire that was directed at us. Nevertheless we were hit by two particularly accurate bursts of fire which left the starboard wing, one engine and landing gear badly damaged. Despite the damage we finally lost the fighter and were able to return to England. We put down at Downham Market ending up at the side of the runway on the grass.'

Kassel, Frankfurt and Hanover were all raided by Halifaxes of 4 Group in the first week of October 1943. Returning from an attack on Kassel, on the night of 3rd October, Halifax JD467 'V-Victor' of No. 102 Squadron began to experience engine trouble. The pilot, Flight Sergeant McPhail, feathered the port inner propeller, the engine having suffered flak damage over the target. Later, as they crossed the Yorkshire coast, the crew of 'V-Victor' suddenly felt a terrific vibration coming from the port inner engine. The vibration continued to get worse, the engine eventually ripping itself free from its mountings to fall away from the aircraft, striking the port outer propeller blades as it did so. Fortunately the pilot was able to maintain control and land safely at Pocklington. Flight Sergeant McPhail was awarded an immediate DFM.

Two superb shots of Halifax Mk.II series 1A, LW235 'B' of 78 Squadron, late Autumn 1943. This particular aircraft was to be destroyed in a crash on 20th October 1943 whilst serving with 1666 HCU. *G. Carver (upper) and L. Broadhurst (lower)*

The following night Frankfurt was subjected to a heavy and accurate attack by over 400 aircraft including No. 4 Group Halifaxes. Large areas of the eastern half of the city were left in flames. The late Sergeant Jeff Kirby, navigator with Flight Lieutenant Jimmy Steel's 76 Squadron crew, recalled in his diary notes the scene over Frankfurt:

'150 to 200 searchlights over the target and plenty of light flak. We also saw over eighty fighter flares on the run out. Fires were very well concentrated. Saw three kites get coned at once over the target and one more on the run in. One kite shot down by fighters. Mannheim and Ludwigshafen could be seen with numerous fires, there being a diversionary attack on these towns. One "Morale Buster" burst right in front of our nose and lit up the sky like daylight.'

After a two week break from operations to Germany, 4 Group went back into action again on the night of 22/23rd October when 130 Halifaxes from the Group joined the main force for another strike at Kassel. The marking was accurate and the bombing well concentrated, and by the time the last of the main force was leaving the city a fierce fire-storm was developing. It was clear from photographic reconnaissance taken after the raid that the city of Kassel had been dealt a severe blow. Many buildings were completely destroyed, large areas within the city's residential districts being particularly badly hit. In addition the Henschel aircraft factories, at the time preparing for full scale production of the V-1 flying bomb, were seriously damaged. That night for the first time, Bomber Command used broadcasts from radio stations in England designed to give false instructions to the German night fighters. Code named *Corona*, the broadcasts proved only partially successful as forty-three bombers were shot down. 4 Group lost thirteen Halifaxes, each of the Group's squadrons losing at least one crew.

Bad weather at the end of October prevented the squadrons from operating until the night of 3rd November.

Smiling 76 Squadron crews pose for the Press photographers before boarding their transports, 22nd October 1943. That night Bomber Command raided Kassel and paid a heavy price. Although the city was left in ruins with nearly 10,000 casualties, the raid cost Bomber Command forty-three aircraft including thirteen Halifaxes from 4 Group. *Fred Hall*

Further scenes at Holme-on-Spalding Moor as 76 Squadron crews prepare to leave for Kassel, 22nd October 1943. *W. Day*

Enlarged D-shaped fins were introduced at the end of 1943 as a final solution to the rudder stall problem. 'E-Easy' of 78 Squadron is photographed on a daylight air test from its base at Breighton, late 1943. *Guy Lawrence*

Flight Lieutenant Jimmy Steele of 76 Squadron prepares to take-off for Kassel in Halifax Mk.V series 1 (Special) DK168 'H', 22nd October 1943. *Fred Hall*

'We hope this hurts' is the message these 77 Squadron crews are sending to Berlin, suitably inscribed on 1,000lb HE bombs. Elvington, Winter 1943. *M. Holliday*

Pilot Officer Matthew Holliday with non-regulation scarf. *M. Holliday*

That night the target was Düsseldorf. Over at Holme-on-Spalding Moor, home of No. 76 Squadron, the day had begun like any other with preparations for the forthcoming night's activities. Sergeant Fred Hall, navigator with Flight Lieutenant Jimmy Steele's crew, has reason to remember what started as a normal day:

'In the morning I met the rest of the crew at the Met Lecture, after which I went out to our new aircraft and made my usual inspection. From there I went back to the Navigation Section to prepare maps and charts as we had been told we were on operations that night. The rest of the lads went about their business and after lunch, I returned to the billet to change into my flying clothes. There were no signs of the rest of the crew, so I presumed that they had taken the aircraft up on a local air test. It was a reasonably pleasant day, but from a flying aspect the weather was not so good. A thickish haze persisted, mixed with several areas of very low cloud and I was aware that all the aircraft seemed to be having difficulty in landing. However, I attended the navigators briefing and I can remember thinking Düsseldorf would be our first really short trip. It wasn't until 2.30, when I went to collect my parachute, that I was informed our aircraft had crashed.'

Flight Lieutenant Jimmy Steele and five other members of his crew were all killed when their Halifax crashed near Market Weighton whilst on an air test. Also killed was Miss Dorothy Robson, known to crews as 'Bombsight Bertha'. Miss Robson toured airfields in her travelling workshop fitting and testing bombsights. On this particular afternoon she had taken off with Flight Lieutenant Steele to test the bombsight on his Halifax. Sadly 'the girl with the laughing eyes', as she was sometiimes called, died with the rest of the crew.

Meanwhile, over at Elvington, Pilot Officer Matt Holliday, a newly arrived flight engineer with No. 77 Squadron, was patiently listening to the Engineer Leader complaining of how difficult it was to make up crews when someone was ill. Matt Holiday was not due to fly that night, his place with Flight Lieutenant Cadman and crew was to be taken by the Engineer Leader himself:

'I was making the appropriate noises and commiserating with him on his difficulties when he suddenly looked me in the eye and said, "Will you go?" Assuming what I hoped was a nonchalant air I said, "Of course". I hadn't flown in anger for many months and here I was about to be thrown in at the deep end on my second day on the unit.

'I was to be Flight Engineer to one of the flight commanders, Squadron Leader Badcoe, and the aircraft was to be 'C' JD385, take-off 17.00 hours.

'All went well until about a quarter of an hour's flying time from the target when, as we were gently weaving along, the words "Fighter, fighter, starboard, go go go", resounded through the intercom. With a sickening lurch we dived down and to the right, then up and to port, whilst I could see tracer bullets shooting between me and my instrument panel. Within seconds down and starboard again, and up and then to port in correct fighter evasion drill, the fighter still sticking with us until suddenly I was jammed up in the astrodome, unable to move. The aircraft had stalled and we were upside down and dropping rapidly. The bag in which I carried my equipment slowly rose up and went leisurely down towards the rest position. This is it, I thought, and then remembering an H. G. Wells film I had seen recently, it reminded me of the glass going across the room in "The Invisible Man".

'As we were plunging to earth at a tremendous speed, and unable to move, expecting the end at any second, I have often thought since that time that such mundane thoughts were not in keeping with tales of one's past life rushing through one's mind when death is imminent.

'Suddenly we were on an even keel. Squadron Leader Badcoe had managed to get his feet up on the instrument panel and with a superhuman effort he had succeeded in regaining control. We had fallen from 24,000 feet to 9,000 feet and all loose equipment had made the inside of the aircraft a shambles. The navigator, in particular, had the difficult task of trying to sort out maps, flight plan and his navigation equipment in the darkness.

'Checking on all crew positions and finding everyone, and everything in good order, the skipper decided to press on towards Düsseldorf. I checked the engines and fuel state and, deciding that as the Flight Engineer's log was in a torn and crumpled condition, I would have to calculate on the fuel gauges. I then began to cogitate on our reception over the target area. We would be bombing late, everyone else would have left for home and we would be sitting ducks for the flak.

'In the event we gained sufficient height and found the target brightly lit and the defences swamped by the power of the main force. We bombed and turned for home.

'Shortly after leaving the target area I went aft to check visually that all bombs had gone, and then made my way in the dark to check the flare chute. In the hooded light of the torch I could see that it was empty, so I returned to my position and we closed the bomb doors. Remembering the tracer bullets I had seen passing between myself and the instrument panel, I checked for bullet holes in the side of the aircraft. When I could not find any I realised that what I had seen was the reflection of the tracer bullets going past the aircraft showing in the glass of the gauges – so much for illusion and a vivid imagination.

'Returning over the Wash one of the crew went back to use the Elsan and then called over the intercom, "Hello Skipper, the photo flare is inside the kite!" When the aircraft had turned upside down the flare had fallen from the chute onto the floor. Not thinking of that I had assumed when the chute was empty, that the flare had gone out. In addition, we found that the safety split pin had fallen out. . . if a draught had removed the arming propeller. . .! We opened the door and threw it out over the water.

'Home and Elvington, on the final approach we had to overshoot and the port inner exhaust stubs exploded in a huge flash and bang. Upon examination we found a hole made by a cannon shell in the starboard mainplane, missing by a whisker No.6 petrol tank. "C-Charlie's" back was broken. She'd got us home safely but would now be consigned to the scrap heap. Squadron Leader Badcoe was awarded an immediate Bar to his DFC, and I seem to remember at the crew conference that a general Group signal was read to the effect that when taking evasive action pilots should take precautions to avoid stalling the aircraft. If only the person who drafted that signal had been in our aircraft on the night of 3rd November 1943!'

The night of 18th November 1943 marked the renewal of Bomber Command's campaign against Berlin. That night 440 Lancasters and four Mosquitos were sent against the German capital. Only moderate damage was inflicted on the target which was bombed blindly through cloud. That same night, 122 No. 4 Group Halifaxes joined a force of Stirlings, Halifaxes and Lancasters, from Nos. 3, 6 and 8 Groups, in a major diversionary raid on Mannheim and Ludwigshafen. The town of Mannheim appears to have suffered most with the northern districts being badly hit.

The following night Leverkusen was the target. Again aircraft from Nos. 3, 4, 6 and 8 Groups were employed in a disappointing attack on this small town on the banks of the Rhine north of Cologne. Bad weather kept most of the night fighters on the ground and only five bombers were lost. However, fog was present over many of the bases in England and consequently large numbers of bombers were diverted to other airfields. Flight Sergeant Holdsworth and crew of No. 10 Squadron were diverted to Tangmere airfield because of fog over their home base of Melbourne. Tragically, their Halifax, HX181 'K-Katy', crashed into a hangar on landing and the entire crew was killed. Two other 4 Group Halifaxes were lost in crashes that night plus a Stirling from 3 Group.

Berlin, as well as being the capital city and administrative centre of Hitler's Reich, also housed many important manufacturing complexes vital to the German war effort. To the west of the city centre, in the districts of Spandau and Charlottenburg, there was the huge Siemens electrical works. In the same area, producing naval fire-control equipment and range finders, was the L. Löwe plant. Also in the western side of the city was the vast BMW aero-engine works. In the Treptow and Schöeneweide districts there were three electrical plants run by the AEG concern, an important accumulator factory, zinc smelting plants, the Henschel aircraft works, several

engineering and chemical works, and the largest power station. In the Tegel and Reinickendorf areas, to the north of the city, there were the Dornier and Heinkel aircraft component works, the Argus aero-engine plant and numerous armament works. In the Mariendorf, Tempelhof and Britz districts the most important factories included those of the Daimler-Benz diesel and aero-engine works plus a large number of machine tool and engineering plants near Tempelhof aerodrome.

Air Chief Marshal Sir Arthur Harris had said that 'We can wreck Berlin from end to end'. He had estimated that it would cost between 400 and 500 bombers to achieve his aim of destroying the city. He now set about that task with a fanatical will. The night of Monday 22nd November 1943 saw the largest attack of the war so far against Berlin. That night 764 aircraft struck at the central and western districts of the city. Included in the force this time were some 234 Halifaxes, over fifty per cent from 4 Group. Also included were fifty Stirlings flying their last mission to a German target having borne the brunt of the losses for so long.

The weather over the target was poor with 10/10ths cloud. Nevertheless, the Pathfinders, relying on their H2S sets to locate the aiming point, accurately dropped their yellow and red TIs, set to detonate above the clouds. What followed was the most concentrated and destructive raid so far on Berlin. Damage was extensive, particularly in the Government quarter where many important buildings were damaged. These included the Reich Chancellery, the Foreign Office, a number of foreign legations in the Wilhelmstrasse – including the French and British embassies, and a large number of other government buildings. There was also heavy damage in the western suburbs as the bombing extended outwards in that direction from the city centre aiming point. Among some of the factories destroyed or severely damaged was the Siemens group of plants at Siemenstadt. Also badly hit was Berlin's railway system, with the Potsdamer and Stettiner stations - from which traffic flowed south-west and north of the capital, suffering heavy damage. In addition, no trains were able to enter or leave the Anhalter station for some time because of blocked lines.

Back from Berlin. Warrant Officer Downs, pilot (left) and Sergeants Hendry, navigator and Jupp, flight engineer, show signs of fatigue after the long, exhausting trip to Berlin on the night of 22/23rd November 1943. In the background is their 78 Squadron Halifax Mk.II series 1A, LW318 'R-Robert'. *B. Downs*

Elvington, Winter 1943: the transports arrive to take 77 Squadron crews out to their aircraft. *M. Holliday*

The bad weather over Germany meant that many of the night fighters were grounded, consequently bomber losses were relatively light – twenty-six failed to return.

The press in Britain gave extensive coverage to the opening of Bomber Command's campaign against Berlin. In the 24th November 1943 edition of the *News Chronicle* there were headlines claiming: 'Hitler loses Berlin in 2,300 ton raid', and 'Five times as bad as any raid on London, and in 30 minutes'. *News Chronicle* air correspondent Ronald Walker wrote:

'Sir Arthur Harris has been waiting for the opportunity to 'Hamburg' Berlin. The chance has come, and he has seized it with characteristic boldness. In one night he has given Berlin a blow more than five times greater than the Luftwaffe ever succeeded in dealing out to London'.

In fact the press were on hand at Breighton on the night of 22nd November 1943 and were allowed to interview returning 78 Squadron crews as they arrived from Berlin. The interviews, published in the *News Chronicle* on 24th November, are a good example of contemporary, wartime reporting:

'Shortly after midnight the first of the Halifaxes which had taken off from here (Breighton) was signalled to be approaching. They were well ahead of time.

'One by one they came into land along the strung out lights of the flare path. Lights, white, red and green, which seemed to be attached to huge black shapes, moved slowly past in the darkness. All came home.

'R for Robert (LW318) was the first to land and its crew was the first to tell the remarkable story of how easy it had been to give Berlin its biggest bombing. As it jerked to a halt in the dispersal point the crew jumped down and a medley of accents called to one another. There were two Canadians, one New Zealander, one Australian and three British. The pilot is a Londoner (Warrant Officer Downs). Quite spontaneously he said: "It was wizard. We flew above the cloud all the way. They were certainly shooting the flak up all the way there and all the way back. The kite got hit twice, but nobody got hurt. It was my first time on Berlin. I was surprised. It was so easy. We put our load down in the marked area and did not see a night fighter the whole time."

'Later in the big Nissen hut the crews came straggling in out of the darkness. A Canadian pilot came in followed by a Scottish engineer, an English rear-gunner and wireless operator, a Canadian mid-upper gunner, an American bomb-aimer and a Canadian navigator. "We flew above ten-tenths cloud all the way," said the pilot. "There was slight icing-up, nothing to mention. The temperature fell to about minus 20 degrees. Our navigation was purely by stars. On the way to the target we saw periodic flak. Over the target flak was not very heavy, but what there was was very accurate. There were no night fighters".'

For 78 Squadron the Berlin raid of 22nd November had been largely uneventful. The Squadron had sent eighteen Halifaxes to the German capital of which two returned early, one with oxygen failure and one because of severe icing. The rest of the Squadron were able to reach the target and bomb the primary. All returned safely except Halifax LW319 (Flight Lieutenant Martin and crew), which was damaged by flak over the target and crashed at Coltishall on return. Two 4 Group Halifaxes collided with each other at Barmby Moor, near Pocklington, on return from Berlin. Both crews, one from 77 Squadron and one from 102, lost their lives.

At the end of November 1943 the Halifax-equipped groups operated independently of the main force to carry out attacks on Frankfurt and Stuttgart. The latter attack, on the night of 26/27th November, was a large scale diversionary raid designed to draw the night fighters away from the main force which was targeted on Berlin. Both forces flew a common route across France before diverging near Frankfurt.

Flight Lieutenant Cadman and crew of 77 Squadron photographed with their ground crew at Elvington during the Battle of Berlin, Winter 1943/44. Left to right: three ground crew; Flying Officer McClorry, navigator; Flight Lieutenant Cadman, pilot; Sergeant Batty, mid-upper gunner; Pilot Officer Holliday, flight engineer; Sergeant Trivett, rear gunner; two ground crew; Sergeant Powell, wireless operator; ground crew; Flight Sergeant Clayton, bomb aimer. *M. Holliday*

Life goes on in bomb ravaged Berlin. *IWM, HU10572*

Following an attack on Leipzig, on the night of 3rd December, bad weather prevented No. 4 Group from operating over Germany for the next two weeks. When operations recommenced on the night of 20th December, the target was Frankfurt. This raid was significant as it marked the beginning of a period in which Halifax losses were to rise alarmingly.

That night a small diversionary raid, carried out by Lancasters and Mosquitos on Mannheim, failed in its objective of confusing the German night fighter controller. As a result the main force suffered numerous fighter attacks on the route to and from the target. A Halifax from 51 Squadron, HR868 'B' (Pilot Officer McKenzie), was attacked by a night fighter when some twenty minutes from the target. The tail gunner reported that the port elevator was shattered and was now no more than a broken dangling framework. The fuselage, meanwhile, had begun to fill with fumes and smoke. Despite the damage the pilot was able to maintain control, and as the night fighter appeared satisfied that his one attack was sufficient and had left them, Pilot Officer McKenzie decided to continue to the target. McKenzie's own words best describe what happened next.

'We went on, but on the fringe of the target area we were attacked again. The bomb-aimer, Sergeant Grozier, was wounded and the Halifax again filled with fumes and smoke. The rear gunner called up from the rear turret and said: "You'd better get rid of the bombs. There are flames and sparks and I think there's a fire somewhere aboard".

'As before, the night fighter just made the one attack and then left us. Cannon shells had struck the bomb bay and set fire to a number of incendiaries, and they were burning only a few feet from a 2,000 pounder. The navigator, meanwhile, went to the aid of the wounded bomb-aimer in the nose. He clipped a parachute onto the bomb-aimer and then he and the others tried to release the bombs. Unfortunately the bomb doors would not open fully.

'Two of the crew, the wireless operator and the engineer, then went back into the nose to tend the bomb-aimer. He was found to be suffering from lack of oxygen, having flung off his own helmet and mask. The wireless operator put his own oxygen tube into the wounded man's mouth, and then he, the engineer, plus the mid-upper gunner who had joined them in the nose, took turns to share their oxygen with the wounded bomb-aimer. They were all so short of oxygen that it took them twenty minutes to get the wounded man back from the nose into the rest position.

'When they at last succeeded in getting back, the wireless operator and the mid-upper gunner took off some of their own kit and wrapped it round the wounded bomb-aimer. They attempted to dress his wounds but he died soon after.

'Meanwhile, cold air was rushing in through holes in our damaged fuselage, and the navigator was almost frozen, but he stuck to his job and did wonders.

'Over the sea we tried again to release the bombs, but failed. I told the crew, after we had crossed the English coast, that anybody who chose too could bale out. The navigator answered that he was frozen as it was and didn't intend to get colder by jumping out.

The rest of the crew were unanimous in deciding to stay with the aircraft'.

Over their own base, the crew went to crash positions. In spite of all the damage, plus the added danger of landing with a full bomb load, Pilot Officer McKenzie made a safe landing, despite suffering a burst tyre. The skipper later paid tribute to his crew when he said, 'No captain could have had a finer set of men. Everyone behaved exactly right'. The other members of Pilot Officer Mackenzie's crew were: Sergeant Solomon, navigator; Flight Sergeant Marlow, wireless operator; Sergeant Whittock, flight engineer; Sergeant King, mid-upper gunner; Sergeant Booth, rear gunner.

Meanwhile, the bombing at Frankfurt, despite cloud over the target and the presence of decoy fires and dummy markers, caused considerable damage in the centre of the city. Bomber losses were disturbingly high at forty-one aircraft. Of this number twenty-seven were Halifaxes, nineteen from 4 Group. No. 466(RAAF) Squadron sent sixteen crews to Frankfurt that night. The squadron was operating over Germany for the first time since converting to Halifax Mk.IIIs. Twelve crews reported attacks on the primary, two returned early with malfunctions and two failed to return.

The Halifax Mk.III was the result of mating Bristol Hercules air-cooled radial engines with a Halifax airframe incorporating all the improvements of the Mk.II series 1A aircraft. Performance was dramatically improved and it was decided to place the Mk.III into production. By the end of 1943 Halifax Mk.IIIs began to replace the Mk.IIs in the squadrons of 4 Group.

The half-way point of the momentous Battle of Berlin was reached on the night of 29th December 1943 when 712 aircraft of the main force attacked a cloud covered German capital. Bombing on sky markers, Lancasters, Halifaxes and Mosquitos dropped 1,099 tons of HE and 1,215 tons of incendiaries on the southern and eastern districts of Berlin causing widespread devastation. Successful Mosquito diversions kept losses down to eleven Lancasters and nine Halifaxes (four from No. 4 Group).

Bad weather during the first weeks of 1944 prevented 4 Group from operating, and it was not until the night of 20th January that the squadrons were able to rejoin the fray. That night Berlin was again on the receiving end as Bomber Command mounted its largest raid to date on the battered city. 769 bombers were despatched to Berlin whilst diversionary Mosquitos raided Düsseldorf, Kiel and Hanover. A maximum effort from No. 4 Group saw 154 Halifaxes take off from their Yorkshire bases. This record breaking effort even surpassed that made for the 1,000 raid on Cologne in 1942. Two new squadrons, Nos. 578 and 640, flew their first operations with 4 Group on the Berlin attack. Both had come into being early in January 1944, and were equipped with Mk.III Halifaxes. No. 640 Squadron had been the first to form on the 7th of the month from 'C' Flight of 158 Squadron at Lissett. The new squadron immediately began to work-up for operations under the command of Wing Commander D. J. Eayrs. Seven days later No. 578 Squadron came into being at Snaith when 'C' Flight of 51 Squadron became the basis of the new unit. Under the command of Wing Commander D. S. S. Wilkerson the new squadron took on charge fourteen new Halifax Mk.IIIs on the 16th and began to prepare for operations.

To confuse the German night fighter controller the route to Berlin on the night of 20th January was more northerly than that chosen for previous raids. The bombers were to fly a straight course across the North Sea to a point some twenty miles north of Heligoland. They were then to turn south-east to cross the enemy coast near Büsum before passing over the Kiel canal, then between Hamburg and Lübeck and onto a point directly over the Müritzsee before turning onto a south-south easterly course to approach Berlin from the north-west. The route home was south of Magdeburg, passing between the heavily defended areas of Münster and Osnabrück, before turning north-west to leave the Dutch coast at Schiermonnikoog.

It transpired that the diversionary raids by Mosquitos on Kiel and Hanover failed to conceal the destination of the attack. Consequently the night fighter controller was able to direct large numbers of fighters into the bomber stream soon after it crossed the German coast. Canadian Flight Sergeant Lewis was the pilot of Halifax LW441 'S-Sugar' of No. 640 Squadron, one of eight crews from that unit flying on the Squadron's first operation. They were led by their CO, Wing Commander Eayrs, flying in LW434 'Z-Zebra'. Sergeant Tom Beckett, mid-upper gunner of 'S-Sugar', recalls what happened as they approached Berlin:

'We were attacked by a Ju 88 on the bombing run and were badly shot up. I remember the aircraft went out of control and started to go down. The skipper shouted to get ready to bale out. I was just about to open the rear hatch and dive out but first I thought it best to check with the skipper so I plugged into the intercom and was just in time to hear him call "I think I've got her!" I went back to my turret and we struggled back, surviving two horrendous batterings from predicted flak on the way. We landed at Coltishall with half our incendiaries still on board, a five foot hole in the port wing, the fin and rudder shot away and one dead engine. Needless to say our Halifax was the subject of much examination the next morning by the personnel of Coltishall'.

Of the other seven 640 squadron aircraft, five managed to reach Berlin and drop their bomb loads, consisting of 2 x 1,000 lb and 2 x 500 lb GP bombs plus a mixture of 30 lb and 4 lb incendiary bombs, at or near the aiming point. Two others returned early, one with engine trouble and one with a sick navigator.

No. 578 Squadron, the other new Halifax unit operating for the first time that night, sent six aircraft to Berlin of which, five reached the target and bombed through cloud. The sixth Halifax, LW475 'E' (Flight Sergeant Hill), was shot up by a night fighter and the mission had to be abandoned.

640 Squadron flew their first operation, a night attack on Berlin, on 20th January 1944. Here we see one of the early Halifax Mk.III deliveries from Radlett shortly after arriving at Leconfield, early in January 1944. Left to right: Squadron Leader Renolds; Group Captain Waterhouse; Flight Lieutenant Nicholson; Flight Lieutenant Simons; Flight Sergeant Aitken; Flight Sergeant Roberts.
M. Roberts

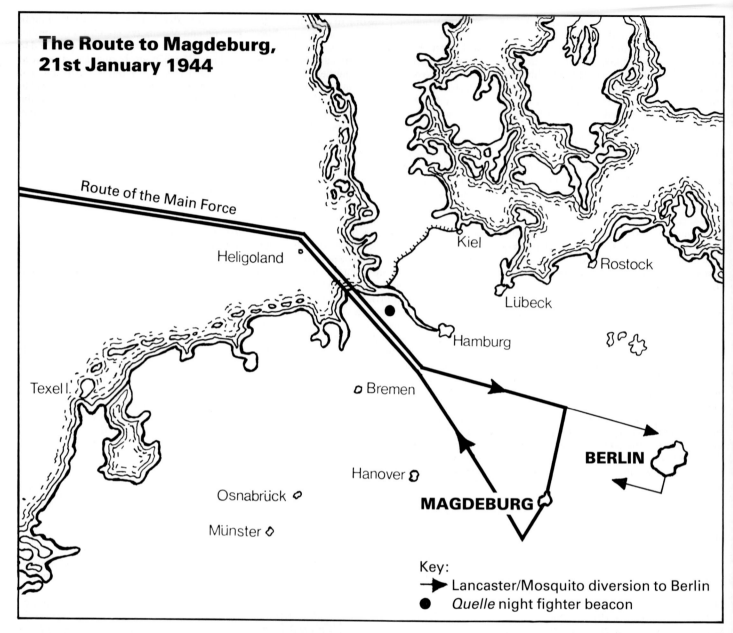

The Route to Magdeburg, 21st January 1944

Route of the Main Force

Heligoland

Kiel

Rostock

Lübeck

Hamburg

Texel I.

Bremen

BERLIN

Hanover

MAGDEBURG

Osnabrück

Münster

Key:
➔ Lancaster/Mosquito diversion to Berlin
● *Quelle* night fighter beacon

The cloud over Berlin prevented accurate post raid reconnaissance but it appears that the German capital suffered only moderate damage. Bomber Command had once more failed to achieve anything like the successful concentration of bombing which had destroyed Hamburg the previous summer. Thirty-five bombers were lost, fourteen of these were 4 Group Halifaxes. 102 Squadron, still operating with the underpowered Halifax Mk.II series 1As lost five crews out of sixteen sent to Berlin.

There was to be no respite for the crews of Bomber Command for on the following night yet another maximum effort raid was planned, this time against Magdeburg, situated some seventy-five miles south-west of Berlin. The bombers' route to the target was designed to deceive the defences into thinking that Berlin was again the target. After crossing the enemy coast close to Hamburg the bombers were to head straight for Berlin.

When some forty miles from the capital the stream was instructed to turn southwards for Magdeburg. At the same time a force of Lancasters and Mosquitos were to continue onto Berlin and drop marker bombs as if to indicate the opening of a major attack. Unfortunately for the bombers' the German fighter controller ordered his night fighters to assemble at the 'Quelle' radio beacon, situated near Cuxhaven, anticipating that Hamburg was to be the target. Unbeknown to the bomber crews radio beacon 'Quelle' was situated directly over the bombers' route to Magdeburg. As the 648 strong force crossed the enemy coast they immediately came under attack from a large number of fully fuelled and armed night fighters. The situation was made worse by Pathfinders dropping route markers south of Hamburg as planned. As a result more and more fighters where drawn to the area were they reaped a rich harvest. Fifty-seven Bomber Command air-

craft were shot down in the running battle that extended from Magdeburg to the coast north-west of Hamburg. Another big effort from 4 Group saw the despatch of 136 Halifaxes from their Yorkshire bases. The night of 21st January 1944 was to be remembered as a night of disaster for the Group as twenty-one Halifaxes and their crews failed to return: Nos. 76, 77 and 102 Squadrons losing four each. In addition numerous aircraft returned with various kinds of damage and wounded crew members. The loss of twenty-one Halifaxes was to be the highest number of aircraft lost by the Group in one night during the whole war. Again it was the Halifax Mk.II and V equipped units that were hardest hit. The replacement of No. 4 Group's earlier model Halifaxes with the improved Mk.III Hercules-engined aircraft was· progressing as rapidly as possible. In the meantime, however, some squadrons would have to soldier on with the more vulnerable Mk.IIs and Vs.

A week after the Magdeburg raid the target was again the 'Big City', Berlin. 432 Lancasters, 241 Halifaxes and four Mosquitos set off for an early morning attack on the Nazi capital, the thirteenth raid of the present Battle of Berlin. No. 4 Group made another big effort supplying 134 of its Halifaxes. One of the seventeen Halifaxes of 102 Squadron that took-off from Pocklington that night was JD165 'S-Sugar', skipper on this occasion was Flight Sergeant Dai Pugh. The following account was taken from Dai Pugh's personal journal kept during his war service:

'On 28th January 1944 we were briefed to fly on operations to Berlin in Halifax JD165, 'S-Sugar'. It was a midnight take-off and the duration of the flight was to be 8½ hours.

'We crossed Denmark, avoiding the flak areas of Flensburg, Sylt and the Kiel Canal, flew over the Baltic Island of Rugen and then south to Berlin. Fifty miles from the target we could see that the raid was already under way and that Berlin was getting a real pasting.

'As we commenced our bombing run we were hit by flak. We jettisoned our bomb load and our aircraft then went into a steep dive. I then gave the order to prepare to bale out. Fortunately I was able to bring the aircraft under control so I quickly rescinded the bale out order and sent the crew back to their stations. The rear gunner, Sergeant Burgess, had suffered concussion when he had been thrown against the side of his turret by the flak burst. When he recovered he changed places with the mid-upper gunner, Sergeant Williams.

'Our flight engineer, Sergeant Perkins, assessed the damage which included severed rudder controls, holed wing tanks and numerous holes in the fuselage. He said to me, "You might feel a draught because there is a bloody great hole in the fuselage behind your head". Without rudder controls all turns had to be made by yawing the aircraft by use of ailerons.

'As we headed north for the Baltic I sounded out the rest of the crew as to our likely options. We had two choices. We could either fly the eighty miles to Sweden and be interned or risk the North Sea crossing for home. Everyone was unanimous on chancing it for home.

'Unfortunately we ran out of fuel when some ninety miles from our coast and we had to ditch in a very rough North Sea. The IFF had been put on distress and an SOS transmitted and acknowledged. As we hit the water, at about 90 mph, the nose broke up, the aircraft went completely under water and the sea poured in through the escape hatch above me. The hatch had been jettisoned before ditching, as per ditching drill. Fortunately the aircraft surfaced almost immediately, due to her empty petrol tanks, and we clambered out onto the wing. We then inflated our Mae Wests and the dinghy and paddled away from "S-Sugar", feeling very grateful for the many "wet and dry" dinghy drills which we had practiced. In fact we had carried out our last

drill only a fortnight before at Bootham Baths in York and we knew exactly what to do. The drill had worked perfectly.

'After a short time in the dinghy we all began to feel sea sick as we bounced about on the waves like a cork. Our hands were so numbed by the cold that we found it impossible to erect the transmitter mast or even undo our sealed emergency rations. We were all beginning to feel pretty uncomfortable when a tremendous wave capsized the dinghy and sent everybody into the freezing sea. Flight Sergeant Jimmy Graham and I finally righted the dinghy and I was first in. I pulled in Jimmy, then Sergeant Cliff Williams followed by Sergeant Albert Cohen, our wireless operator. By this time we were so weak and overcome by the effect of the cold that our efforts to pull in the rest of the crew were in vain. Their soaked flying clothes made them so heavy and it was impossible to help them. Their frozen fingers gradually slipped from the dinghy ropes and they drifted away.

'For three days and two nights we shivered in the rain, sleet and breaking waves, lying in water the whole time with neither food nor drink. The nights were the worst to endure because in daylight there was at least hope of being seen. On the first day a Catalina flying boat flew over us but he failed to see us. We were spotted on the second day by an ASR Warwick who dropped Lindholme survival gear, but the sea was so rough we could not reach it. On the third day another ASR aircraft found us and called up a launch which finally located us, and after a lot of manoeuvring in the heavy sea, managed to come alongside and drag us aboard.'

The four survivors of 'S-Sugar' were landed at Montrose and were taken to Stracathro Hospital, Brechin, all suffering from exposure and shock. Unfortunately the navigator, Sergeant Jimmy Graham, died on the way. The rest spent many weeks in hospital recovering from their ordeal. Only Flight Sergeant Pugh was able to eventually return to his unit where he continued flying as a ferry pilot. Sergeants Williams and Cohen were discharged on medical grounds. Some forty years on, Dai Pugh, a retired school master from Leeds, still flies from his old wartime base of Pocklington as a full time member of the Wolds Glider Flying Club.

The Berlin raid of 28/29th January was one of the most effective of the period and many returning crews reported seeing big fires raging, visible on the return leg over 200 miles away. No. 4 Group lost fifteen out of the forty-six aircraft reported missing.

An all Halifax Mk.III force, drawn from Nos. 51, 158, 466 and 640 Squadrons – comprising some fifty-nine aircraft – joined in another very effective strike at the German capital on the night of 30th January. Bombing through complete cloud cover, 446 Lancasters, 82 Halifaxes and 12 Mosquitos hit the central and south-western quarter of the city. Significantly none of the No. 4 Group force

were lost that night to enemy action, although Pilot Officer Affleck and crew, of No. 640 Squadron, were all killed when their Halifax, LW513 'W', crashed a half mile south of Leconfield whilst attempting to land on three engines. The RAF lost thirty-two Lancasters and one Halifax.

Two weeks of bad weather at the beginning of February 1944 prevented Bomber Command from mounting any major operations until the night of 15th February when once again Berlin was the target. The raid, the fifteenth in the present campaign was carried out by 891 aircraft, the largest force so far despatched to Berlin. 4 Group made its greatest effort to date and despatched 175 Halifaxes, the majority of that force being made up of the improved Mk.IIIs. No. 4 Group were in fact second only to 5 Group in the number of aircraft despatched on the Berlin raid. 5 Group sent a massive force of 226 Lancasters.

**The Berlin Raid 15/16th February 1944
No.4 Group Raid Statistics**

Sqn	Took-off	Early Return	Attacked Primary	Missing
10	18	4	13	1
51	14	-	14	-
76	9	1	7	1
77	20	5	12	3
78	26	8	17	1
102	20	6	12	2
158	15	3	10	2
466 (RAAF)	20	3	15	2
578	14	4	9	1
640	19	1	17	1

One of the nine Halifaxes from 76 Squadron that took off from Holme-on-Spalding Moor for Berlin was LL140 'A-Apple', skipper Flight Sergeant Eaton. When approximately 120 miles from the target, 'A-Apple' came under attack from a night fighter. Wireless operator Sergeant Bob Becker describes what happened:

'I popped my head up into the astrodome and saw the fighter immediately. He was sitting slightly above us firing through our mainplanes, left to right. The port inner was on fire and our mid-upper gunner was in the next second blown from his turret on to the fuselage floor. He seemed not to be seriously hurt, but we were obviously a goner. The rear-gunner was returning the fighter's fire and I think may have hit him because as I went through the forward escape hatch I nearly collided with a twin-engined aircraft that appeared to be burning.'

All of the crew of 'A-Apple' managed to bale out from their doomed Halifax. The mid-upper gunner, Sergeant Upton, came down in a frozen lake and was drowned, all the others were later captured and made POWs. A 578 Squadron crew had a narrow escape that night soon after they left the target. Sergeant Malvern and crew of LW474 'B' were one of nine crews from No. 578 who reached Berlin and bombed the briefed aiming point.

No.4 Group Bomber Command, February 1944

Sqn	Equipment	Airfield
10	Halifax II	Melbourne
51	Halifax III	Snaith
76	Halifax V/III	Holme-on-Spalding Moor
77	Halifax II/V	Elvington
78	Halifax III	Breighton
102	Halifax II	Pocklington
158	Halifax III	Lissett
466 (RAAF)	Halifax III	Leconfield
578	Halifax III	Burn
640	Halifax III	Leconfield

Flight Sergeant Morris, the Canadian navigator of 'B-Bertie', recalls what happened:

'As we left Berlin behind us we suddenly saw to our horror two Fw 190s flying in formation with our Halifax, one on either side and well to the rear. The skipper started to weave, hoping to shake them off, but the fighters stuck with us and made no effort to attack. We flew on like this for the next fifteen minutes, our gunners itching to blast them out of the sky, but nobody daring to in case by chance the German pilots had not seen us.

'Suddenly, the fighters peeled off to left and right, and left us to find our way home. It would seem on reflection, that the German pilots had flown in formation with us completely unaware of our presence. The fact that we could see them, silhouetted against the glow of the target, meant that it was possible that they didn't see us in the darker sky. It is possible that they may have been tracking another aircraft with their radar or perhaps their sets were faulty. Whatever it was we were glad to get home in one piece.'

Other crews were not so lucky. A diversionary raid on Frankfurt-on-Oder failed to draw the night fighters away from Berlin. The German fighter controller was able to accurately plot the bombers route over the Baltic, east of Denmark. It was on the approach route to Berlin that most of the combat took place and the majority of the forty-three bombers were shot down, including fourteen from 4 Group. In addition 640 Squadron lost two Halifaxes which crashed on return. Flight Sergeant Vicary and crew were able to bale out when their aircraft ran out of fuel. Flying Officer Barkley was unlucky, however. His Halifax, LW500 'H', ran into high ground near Scarborough and the entire crew was killed.

The last few months had seen some of the most ferocious air battles of the war as the German night fighter defences strove to save Berlin from destruction. The emphasis of Bomber Command's night offensive now began to swing away from Berlin and by the middle of February 1944 other German cities began to feature in the target lists. It was during this period that the success rate of the German night fighter force reached an unprecedented peak.

On the night of 19/20th February 1944, 561 Lancasters, 255 Halifaxes (140 from No. 4 Group) and seven Mosquitos set off to raid Leipzig. Two Halifax pilots of 78 Squadron,

Pilot Officers Tom Smith and Bernard Downs, had been close friends since they had first met at an OTU in Canada during 1942. As they both took off that night from Breighton, part of a force of seventeen Halifaxes from No. 78, fate had decreed that one of them would not return. Bernard Downs takes up the story:

'When we returned from Canada, Tom and I had been posted to a Ventura squadron at Methwold, Norfolk. We did not stay long however, for in June 1943 we were told that we were to go on a conversion course for heavy bombers. After a brief refresher course in night flying, we went to a Halifax conversion unit at Marston Moor in Yorkshire, where we picked up the additional crew members for the larger aircraft. No. 1652 Heavy Conversion Unit, at RAF Marston Moor, fed squadrons of No. 4 Group, all of which were based in Yorkshire. Tom completed his conversion at the beginning of September 1943 and was posted to No. 78 Squadron at RAF Breighton. Immediately I put in a request to go to the same squadron, and a couple of weeks later followed him to Breighton.

'Breighton, home at that time of No. 78 Squadron, was completed in January 1942 as a typical wartime airfield. It lies some six miles east of Selby between the villages of Bubwith to the north and Wressle to the south. The River Derwent flows to the west.

'The camp was dispersed with a vengeance. Domestic sites were scattered and removed from the messes. Administrative buildings and technical sites were elsewhere. Aircraft hardstandings were dotted around the whole airfield perimeter. Standard accommodation for practically all purposes was the ubiquitious Nissen hut. So, life was primitive and there was little cheer in sight for a hard winter ahead. But for good or evil Breighton was to be our home for a while and we made the best of it with remarkable cheerfulness.

'By the time I arrived, Tom had already started 'ops' which enabled him to greet me with a slightly superior air in addition to vivid accounts of night life over the German Reich.

'By Christmas 1943 Tom and I had both completed a dozen ops. Because of losses, we were already "senior" crews and had long since been allocated our own regular aircraft. I had 'R-Roger' and Tom 'Q-Queenie'. As the aircraft were dispersed in alphabetical order around the airfield (how else would one find them?) we occupied adjacent dispersal points, so our respective crews were the last to reciprocate good wishes with each other before a trip. Also by this time, Tom and I had been commissioned. He was lucky enough to get a spell of leave over Christmas and went home resplendent in his new Pilot Officer's uniform.

'In January 1944 we received the good news that No. 78 Squadron was to be re-equipped with a new version of the Halifax, the Hercules-engined Mark III. On 21st January we operated with the Mark II for the last time and for the next three weeks the Squadron was stood down from ops to convert to the new aircraft. The superiority of this version quickly became apparent. It gave us increased speed, higher altitude and generally improved performance over its predecessor. Indeed, we would now have the edge over our redoubtable sister, the Lancaster. However, because you do not get something for nothing, the improvement was paid for by an increase in fuel consumption which ment a lesser bomb load. Nevertheless, we were delighted with our new charges and anxious to put them to the test.

Warrant Officer Downs and crew of 78 Squadron, in the crew truck after returning from Berlin 23rd November 1943. Left to right: Sergeants Bongard, Garget, Joiner, Sherwin, Hendry; W/O Downs; Sgt Jupp. *B. Downs*

'Saturday, 19th February 1944 started like any other bleak winter's morning in one of the colder parts of north-eastern England. It was dry, certainly, but there was a chill wind and the typical Yorkshire smog obscured every horizon. This day followed the usual routine: check that all crew was fit and available, then report to the Flight Commander by 08.45. Then just wait. At 09.30 the Flight Commander reported to the Squadron Commander the availability of both aircraft and crews. From this meeting there could be three possibilities: no ops, ops on or possible, decision later. On this occasion the Flight Commander came back within half-an-hour, "OK chaps, ops are on tonight."

'From then on everybody and everything had a purpose. Well tried machinery started into motion and a stir of purposeful activity pervaded the whole base. Precisely the same things were happening at dozens of bomber bases throughout Eastern England.'

'This was to be a major attack involving a total of over 800 heavy bombers. Every available aircraft from the Squadron would be used. Crew lists were quickly prepared. Tom was allocated "L-Love", LW367. My own aircraft was unserviceable and would not be ready so I was allocated a spare, "Z-Zebra", LK762. No.78 Squadron scheduled a list of twenty-three aircraft for the attack.

'Preparation for a bombing raid was a deliberate, calculated and cold blooded process that took several hours from inception to commencement. Pre-briefing for captains and navigators was called for at 11.00. (I was delighted with this news because it meant that we should have a late afternoon take off with the prospect of some sleep after midnight). Other crew categories went about their own tasks. Gunners to check turrets and guns. Wireless operators, the radio and radar equipment. Flight engineers double checked the aircraft servicing schedule, fuel load etc. At this stage ground crews were busier than anyone. No praise can be too great for their dedication to the task of maintaining the aircraft, day in, day out, in the most harrowing open air conditions.

'Tom and I walked to the briefing room together. For both of us this would be our fifteenth op, an important landmark which would see us halfway through our tour. We speculated on the possible target. This was at the time when Berlin was receiving more than its fair share of attention, so seemed the possible favourite.

'The briefing room was blacked-out with security guards very much in evidence. At chart tables scattered around the room navigators were sorting out maps, charts, navigational logs and other impedimenta of their trade. A large sheet covered a wall map and blackboard at one end of the room. The room was filled with a tense air of expectancy. There was some desultory conversation and an occasional nervous laugh, but all eyes were attracted to the screening sheet.

'Then the worst happened. The security phone rang to be answered by the Squadron Commander. A brief conversation. He then said, 'Sorry chaps, time on target has been put back. Pre-briefing will now be at 5 pm, with a probable take off about midnight.' Muffled groans of resentment echoed around the room. Maps, charts, and the rest of the stuff were hastily gathered in. But the tension which had already been generated remained and we would now have to live with it for an additional six hours.

'On leaving the briefing room Tom said, "I'll keep an eye on things for you Bern, go and get a couple of hours kip before lunch." I did not need a second bidding and without that necessary couple of hours it may have been a different story.

'We gathered again for the delayed pre-briefing. The navigation leader called for the doors to be locked then carefully removed the screening sheet. On the exposed wall map a red ribbon strip indicated a path to and from central Germany. The accompanying blackboard contained a series of tracks and times. At the head of the board, in large capitals: LEIPZIG 19/2/44.

'The Briefing Officer added detail. In short, the attack of some 800 plus aircraft was directed at the important rail centre which was a junction of lines from all directions. The attack would open at 03.55 with the dropping of Pathfinder markers. The main force would bomb between 03.58 and 04.18. In other words, twenty-three minutes were allowed to get over 800 aircraft across the target area. To ensure a reasonable spread, the main force was divided into five waves, each wave being given a four minute time band. I was allocated to wave four with time-on-target 04.10 to 04.14. Tom was with an earlier wave. All aircraft from No. 78 Squadron were to carry a similar bomb load consisting of one 2,000 lb high explosive and 4,000 lb of incendiaries in small bomb containers.

'The route was to take us eastwards across the North Sea, then south-eastwards, making a feint towards Berlin. A final turn towards the target gave a run-in of some fifty miles. After clearing the target we were to head south west for about thirty miles before turning north west back home. This was standard and, by now, all pretty familiar stuff. The navigators were soon hard at work preparing their logs and charts; bomb-aimers studying target maps and photographs and pilots checking details with all other crew members, although they would not know the target until main briefing at 21.30. Aircraft were being fuelled and bombed-up. Mechanics curing last minute snags. Meteorological forecasters continuously updating information. Control staff checking flarepath and airfield equipment. Parachute section ensuring the standard of safety equipment. Motor transport prepared for crew transportation. Cooks preparing special meals. Everyone had some part to play and all vital to the eventual purpose.

'Throughout the long afternoon and evening Tom remained his cheerful self. Thoroughly and meticulously he checked and rechecked every detail. If he was feeling the strain from the protracted preparations, no sign showed. But, like the rest of us, I think he had a sense of relief when it was time for main briefing.

'Always, main briefing came as something of an anti-climax. By this time all essential preparations had been completed and everyone aware of their task and responsibilities. It did serve, however, to gather all crews together in one place and in good time. The briefing room was crowded to capacity. The air carried a curious mixture of excitement and apprehension. Subdued conversation was broken by sporadic laughter at the wisecracks of irrepressible wags. Until this briefing, for security reasons, ancillary crew members had not known the target location. There had, obviously, been speculation so there was a general sense of relief when Leipzig was revealed as the target instead of the anticipated Berlin.

'There was immediate silence upon the entry of the Commanding Officer together with the briefing officers. Very little time was wasted. A quick run over the route with the stress upon the importance of accurate track and time keeping. The latest weather – a good forecast with no problems anticipated. The bombing procedure to be followed with detail of the target markers being dropped by the Pathfinder Force, warning of danger areas en route. Reminders of the importance of watchfulness, of safety procedures, of fuel economy. We had heard it all before but listened intently anyway. To forget one essential could bring disaster in its train. The odd point of doubt was cleared by "Any questions?" Finally, the Commanding Officer wished us a good trip and good luck: that we would certainly need.

'Tom and I, together with our crews, made our way to the nearby locker room. On went the woollen long johns, an extra sweater, heavyweight pullover and wool lined boots. Check parachute, Mae West, helmet and gloves. The gunners had additional outer clothing with electrically heated gloves and insoles for their boots – and they would need them.

'Usually, Tom and I travelled in the same crew transport to our respective adjacent aircraft, but tonight I was using a stranger from a different dispersal. Tom called his crew together, "OK, eleven o'clock. Time to go." He turned to me with a grin, "Have a good trip, Bern. See you for breakfast." I responded similarly. We gave each other a slap on the shoulder and went out to find the crew transports.

'That was it! Destiny dictated we were not to meet again. I can now recount only my own experiences of the next eight hours, in the sure conviction that Tom's experience would be similar, at least to some point within that period of time.

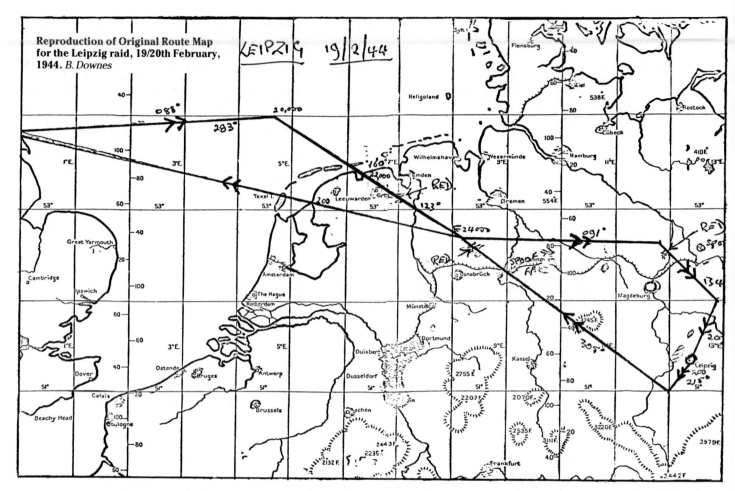

Reproduction of Original Route Map for the Leipzig raid, 19/20th February, 1944. *B. Downes*

'The crew transport made it's way cautiously around the perimeter track. On board was my crew and that of "Y-Yorker". We arrived at my aircraft, "Z-Zebra", and disembarked amid cheerfully reciprocated good wishes. The ground crew were patiently waiting and the Corporal in charge handed me the Form 700 Aircraft Serviceability Log. This, I knew I could sign with confidence and without a second glance as nothing would have been left to chance.

'There was just time for a quick cigarette and a stroll to the edge of the hardstanding for a pee – there would be little chance again for eight hours. Eleven-thirty. Clamber aboard. Plug in the intercom. "Everybody set?" "OK skip" from the six crew. Starting procedure. All engines running smoothly. Instruments functioning. Run-up and check engines – all OK. Switch on navigation lights. Chocks away – thumbs up from the ground crew.

'Eleven forty-five. Ease forward from the hardstanding onto the taxi track. Across the airfield the first aircraft has become airborne and the second is now following. To the uninitiated, an airfield at night is an incomprehensible forest of lights, white, red, amber, green, blue – some bright, some dim, some steady and others flashing. Now the moving lights of taxi-ing aircraft added to the apparent confusion.

'Eleven-fifty. At the runway holding point

pre-take-off check: fuel, flaps, fine-pitch, twenty-seven items all double checked. A short green flash from the Controllers caravan. Turn onto the runway. "Hold your hats, here we go!" Eleven-fifty nine. A long green flash from the caravan. Open throttles. "Z-Zebra" slowly gains momentum as the flarepath lights flash by ever more quickly. The tail lifts off the runway. 100 mph, 115 mph and thirty-three tons of aircraft with a deadly payload takes to the air. It is exactly midnight, and we cross the airfield boundary, still gathering speed in a slow climb.

'As we gain height, the lights of nearby airfields are clearly seen – Holme, Melbourne, Pocklington, Elvington and others. The sky seems full of green, red and white aircraft navigation lights in all directions. Vigilance is essential. A slow climbing orbit around brings us back over base at 6,000 feet. We set off on an eastwards course continuing to climb at 155 mph indicated speed. Ten minutes later we cross the coast at Hornsea. Navigation lights out and double check the black-out security. Except for some faint stars the sky is pitch black. The red glow and short flame from the shrouded engine exhaust stubs seems very bright and is accentuated by the darkness.

'The crew have excellent self discipline and all have faith in each other. Silence on the intercom is rigidly observed unless there is some necessary message to pass. In the nose

Tony Sherwin, the bomb-aimer, has little to do at this stage so he keeps a forward look out. Behind him, navigator Bill Hendry is calculating and re-calculating, as he will be throughout the trip. Bill Garget, the wireless operator, is maintaining a listening watch. Later he will be responsible for dispatching the bundles of "Window". Between times he will come alongside myself to provide an additional pair of eyes. The flight engineer, George Jupp, in a compartment behind me, checks engine instruments and performance. He calculates fuel usage and has duplicate engine controls for fine adjustment. When not otherwise occupied he keeps watch from the astrodome. Further aft are the two gunners, cramped in their respective gun turrets, Bob Dawson and Pat Joiner. Theirs is a cold, thankless task but they need to be doubly alert all the time.

'The time is now 1 a.m. and we are well out across the North Sea. Everything is going smoothly and I attempt to engage the automatic pilot – first snag, it would not engage. This means there will be no relief for me and the aircraft will have to be manually controlled throughout.

'Height now 14,000 feet, still climbing. Engine power has dropped off in the thinner air – time to engage higher supercharger gear. The engines give a slight cough then surge with renewed power. Rate of climb increases again.

'One-forty a.m., now at 20,000 feet and at the first turning point. We turn right on to 120 degrees and increase speed to 160 mph indicated which gives a true speed of about 230 mph. We are still edging up, but very slowly now.

'One-fifty a.m. The navigator warns we shall be crossing the Dutch coast in ten minutes. This is confirmed by some sporadic bursts of flak ahead, together with a few searchlights meandering aimlessly about the sky. The adrenalin is beginning to flow again and everyone doubles watchfulness. Time to start "Windowing". We cross the coast with no problems and shortly fly into Germany. It is as black as ever but the sky is clear. Flak is seen from time to time, one side or the other, presumably aimed at odd aircraft which have strayed off track. Occasionally our aircraft judders slightly as we pass through the slipstream of another ahead of us. Once or twice the gunners catch sight of an aircraft and immediately give warning. Everyone becomes very alert but the sightings prove to be of a friendly nature.

'By 3 a.m. we have reached 22,000 feet, our briefed height. We soon arrive at our next turning point where we turn due east. This course is directly towards Berlin. Everything is going smoothly. The failure of the autopilot is a nuisance, it is the very devil to maintain an accurate course, unrelieved, when the two gun turrets are continuously on the move.

'Once or twice bright flashes are seen on the ground. Almost certainly these are jettisoned bomb loads from aircraft in trouble - possibly engine failure or damage from fighter attack. We continue steadily on our course towards Berlin but at a point some fifty miles short of the city we turn south-east. Simultaneously, Berlin is being attacked by a small diversionary force of Mosquitos with the aim of diverting night fighters to that area. This ploy seems to be working. The hundreds of searchlights surrounding Berlin can be seen clearly but we are already moving in another direction.

'Three fifty-five a.m. Bill Hendry's voice over the intercom, "Turn on to 207 degrees, seventeen minutes run to target." We had no sooner steadied up on the new course than the first of the Pathfinder white target indicators cascaded from the sky to settle on the ground like a giant incandescent mass of cotton wool. A minute or so later down went the first green marker. To this point the way ahead had been black, but now searchlight after searchlight pierced the sky which was already pricked by hundreds of bursting antiaircraft shells.

'More green markers cascaded down and then a red one. Our brief was to bomb the mean centre of the green markers if no red was visible. The fact that a red marker had been dropped suggested that the target was accurately pinpointed. Time now seemed to stand still with the aircraft poised motionless in space. The sky ahead was as bright as day.

Flashes from the ground now denoted exploding bombs and smoke was already beginning to obscure some detail. It was like a maelstrom which we were being sucked towards relentlessly.

'Bill's voice again, "Five minutes to go – it's all yours". Tony Sherwin now took over directions, "Left, left, steady, hold it. Doing nicely skip, three or four minutes I think." In the lightened sky aircraft could be seen all around us steadily going in the same direction. A little to the left some unfortunate was coned in searchlights. If he did not escape within seconds there would be no hope for him. In front and a little below us was a Lancaster. Suddenly a plume of smoke came from it. It then rolled almost lazily on its back and plunged earthwards. The rear-gunner called that another Halifax was under fighter attack behind us but there was nothing we could do to help. Flak was intense. We passed puff-ball after puff-ball of the grey brown residue of shell bursts and some of the acrid smell filtered into the cabin. Still more bombers became visible and there must have been at least a dozen within a couple of hundred yards of us.

'Tony was still giving directions, "hold it steady, skip. Right a bit, OK, bomb doors open, left, left, steady, steady, stea...dy – bombs gone!" "Z-Zebra" lifted perceptibly. Thank God for that. Although nothing was said, the relief felt in the aircraft was almost audible. Sitting for hours on top of a load of high explosive is really not the most comfortable feeling in the world. However, we were still over the centre of a very hostile Leipzig and far from being in the clear. To gain a bit more speed I eased the nose down. This, combined with the weight that had been shed, gave us an extra ten or fifteen miles per hour. The sooner we could get away from this particular hot seat, the better.

'Far below on the ground fires were now raging, partially obscured by steadily rising smoke. The barrage of flak was every bit as intense as during the run-in. Other aircraft were still well in evidence, now all making for the obscurity of darkness which lay ahead.

'Four twenty-five a.m. At last relative security, clear of probing lights and a change of course to the north-west. We were on our way home. Over the intercom came the laconic Australian drawl of the usually taciturn Pat Joiner, "Jeeze, that was a hot bastard."

'Since leaving the target we had lost some 2,000 feet in picking up increased speed. As we were briefed to return at 24,000 feet, I now set about making good the deficit. Then an unusual thing happened. A little ahead of us on the port side a bright parachute flare appeared. Shortly, another similar flare, this time to the starboard. Others began to appear, and soon they had formed into two vast lanes, perhaps some fifteen miles apart, and in line with our course. Before long we were flying down an immense airborne flarepath obviously being laid by high flying aircraft on either side of the bomber stream.

This was a completely new tactic to us, and a very unnerving one. A two-fold purpose seemed evident. Firstly, any aircraft in close proximity to a flare would become visible. Secondly, and more importantly, the parallel line of flares would provide an accurately defined area in which night fighters could operate with benefit.

'The problem with any new tactic is deciding how to handle the situation. The instinctive urge was to "stuff the nose down" and increase speed which would have meant losing height. However, at 24,000 feet we were "on top of the pack" and I reasoned it would be counter productive to join more aircraft at a lower height. It would have been possible to turn at right angles to get outside the lines of the flares. This would have meant isolation from the essential protection of the bomber stream by becoming vulnerable to radar defences. The only course of action I saw open was to use every available ounce of power to try and climb above the area of greatest risk, at the same time keeping equidistant from the flares on either side.

'Slowly we edged upwards, 25 then 26,000 feet. The avenue of flares continued but the higher we went the further they were below us. Anxiety was now beginning to take its toll with the crew. My own flying of the aircraft was becoming ragged and I seemed unable to hold a steady course – to the intense irritation of the navigator. The ever-swinging gun turrets became an increasing burden. The unfamiliar higher altitude undoubtedly had an effect and the intense cold really began to bite. The outside temperature was 40 degrees below zero, although the cabin heaters were going full blast they were barely able to keep cabin temperature very much above freezing.

'George Jupp was getting agitated. His calculations were showing that, due to the heavy increase in fuel consumption, because of the additional power being used, we could find ourselves in difficulties. This was another quandary, but, if needs be, I knew we could later make for a Norfolk airfield some fifty miles closer than base. All the while the interminable flares maintained their threat on either side. They seemed to continue for hours although, in fact, they were with us for about fifty minutes and stopped as suddenly as they began. We were now at 27,000 feet and, I guess, just at about the limit of the aircraft's altitude. From time to time a large flash from the ground would be seen, almost certainly the result of an aircraft crashing. We remained unmolested and were having a clear run.

'Five-thirty a.m. At 20,000 feet crossing the Dutch coast just north of Texel Island. Now we could really "stuff the nose down" and pick up speed across the North Sea. As the altitude decreased the heating picked up to provide warmth for cold, cramped limbs. The tension which had been with us for the past hours reduced dramatically. My own personal problem was to remain awake for the next hour or so.

19 year old flight engineer Sergeant George Barrett of 158 Squadron was the only survivor when Halifax LW501 'M', was shot down by a Ju 88 whilst on the way to Leipzig on the night of 20th February 1944. Nowadays, George Barrett is a member of the five-man organising committee for the 4 Group reunion. *G. J. Barrett*

The night of 19/20th February 1944 was a night of disaster for Bomber Command. The diversionary raids planned for that night – a mining operation by Stirlings in Kiel Bay and a Mosquito attack on Berlin, failed to lure the night fighters away from the main force. Fighter interceptions began to take place soon after the bombers crossed the Dutch coast. The attacks continued, and grew in intensity, all the way to Leipzig. In addition, many aircraft arrived at the target early due to a change in the forecast winds. As a result, these early arrivals had to orbit the target until the Pathfinders arrived. With so many aircraft milling around over the target it was not surprising that many fell victim to flak. Seventy-eight bombers were shot down, the heaviest Bomber Command loss of the war so far. No. 4 Group lost sixteen Halifaxes.

The Leipzig Raid 19/20th February 1944
No.4 Group Raid Statistics

Sqn	Took off	Early Return	Attacked Primary	Missing
10	17	1	14	2
51	15	-	15	-
77	14	-	10	4
78	17	5	9	3
102	19	5	12	2
158	15	3	9	2*
466 (RAAF)	14	3	10	1
578	12	2	10	-
640	17	-	15	2

* One Halifax from No. 158 Squadron crashed soon after take-off.

'Six-thirty a.m. 4,000 feet crossing the coast just south of Hornsea. Over the R/T the first aircraft to arrive back at Breighton was calling for landing instructions. A quarter of an hour later we too were circling base waiting to land. Dawn was showing on the eastern horizon. At ten past seven the wheels of "Z-Zebra" touched the runway with a gentle jolt.

'Back at dispersal were the welcoming ground crew anxious to ensure all had gone well. By a quarter to eight we were back in the briefing room for interrogation. Faces were cheerful and there was a general air of elation. We were greeted with a mug of steaming hot coffee, laced with rum if we wished. Some

aircraft were still arriving back and the 'State' board was slowly filling with landing times. No sign yet of Tom's aircraft.

'We completed interrogation by eight-thirty and were free to go. The sky above now quiet. No further entries were being made on the State board which indicated that five aircraft had yet to be accounted for. Later there was news that two of these had landed elsewhere. Perhaps news of the others would follow. However, I made my way back to the billet with a heavy heart, not prepared to think about the unthinkable. At nine a.m. I collapsed into bed.

'It was mid-afternoon before I awoke. Across the room the empty bed told its own story. I dressed wearily and made my way to the mess still hopeful that some good news might be forthcoming. Hopes were quickly dashed when the Squadron Commander saw me and said, "Sorry, old chap, there's no news of Tommy Smith."

'I arrived back at the billet late and a little worse for drink. It was shattering to find that already the RAF Police had been to collect Tom's personal effects for safe keeping.'

Pilot Officer Tom Smith never returned. He lies buried with the other members of his crew in a cemetery in Holland.

The week of 19-25th February 1944, known as 'Big Week', saw the most concentrated period of air operations to date by the Allied air forces. In an attempt to smash the German aircraft industry, the RAF and the US Army Air Force dropped 19,000 tons of bombs and flew over 8,000 sorties against numerous German towns containing fighter aircraft manufacturing plants and their associated industries.

It was at this time that the increasing losses being sustained by the squadrons equipped with the Halifax Mk.IIs and Mk.Vs forced these units to be permanently suspended from taking part in bombing operations against targets in Germany. The following figures show how the Halifax Mk.IIs and Mk.Vs of No. 4 Group had suffered during the period of the 'Battle of Berlin', from November 1943 to February 1944. †

1943/44	Sorties	% Missing against German targets
November	1,191	3.8
December	713	8.1
January	544	11.4
February	269	10.8

†Source: *The Strategic Air Offensive Against Germany, 1939-45 (HMSO), 1961.*

Reconnaissance photograph taken after the Bomber Command attack on Stuttgart 20/21st February 1944. Smoke is seen pouring from the wrecked plants of Rober Bosch, manufacturers of magnetos and ignition equipment.

The ban on operations against German targets was to only affect three squadrons within No. 4 Group: Nos. 10, 77 and 102. The rest of the Group had, by the end of February 1944, already converted to the Halifax Mk.III. Whilst the Mk.II and V-equipped units waited to be converted they took part in an extensive sea mining campaign in addition to attacks on French targets.

Meanwhile, during 'Big Week', 4 Group sent medium strength contingents of Halifaxes to Stuttgart on 20th February, Schweinfurt on the 24th and Augsburg on the night of the 25th. During the attack on Stuttgart the important Bosch factory, which supplied components for the German aircraft industry, was badly damaged.

With the emphasis of the air offensive now swinging away from Berlin, the coming of March 1944 saw the initial phase of Bomber Command's campaign in support of the preparations for *Overlord*, the invasion of Hitler's Fortress Europe.

The intense period of operations carried out by RAF Bomber Command in the second half of 1943, particularly the bitterly fought campaign against Berlin, resulted in some of the heaviest bomber losses of the war. From June to the end of December 1943 Bomber Command despatched 39,275 night sorties for the loss of 1,420 bombers. As we have seen, losses amongst the Halifax squadrons had become critical. How was it then that any crew was able to survive this intense period of high losses? Flight Lieutenant Bill 'Titch' Day of No. 76 Squadron has no doubt that the main ingredient for survival was teamwork – plus a large helping of 'lady luck'. Bill Day, nowadays committee chairman and secretary of the biennial No. 4 Group Bomber Command Reunion, completed a tour of operations as a rear-gunner with 76 Squadron during the period June 1943 to March 1944.

'I remember the occasion of my passing out parade from No. 2 Air Gunnery School, Dalcross, Scotland in October 1942 and saying to myself – eighteen and a half, what happens next? I was soon to learn. Posted to No. 10 OTU, Abingdon, there to meet up with my crew.

'On my arrival at OTU I was selected by a Sergeant, Ian Inglis, a clean cut dedicated pilot always immaculately turned out. As his rear-gunner I was over the moon to be part of his crew. There was also Sergeant Frank Francis, the thirty-three year old bomb-aimer. What a wise man and such a steadying influence. He became 'father' of the crew and was always there with advice and constructive suggestions.

'As navigation and navigational exercises were a top priority for Bomber Command crews, we were sent on detachment to RAF St Eval, Coastal Command in March 1943. Operating Whitley aircraft, we carried out eight and nine hour anti-submarine and shipping patrols. Some navigational exercise! Our navigator, Sergeant Wal Wallis, rose to the challenge. Flying 45 degrees to track, three course winds, astro shots, with the assistance of Frank – a wizard with the sextant, and myself taking drifts in the rear turret I can truly state that it was out from Bishops Rock and back to Bishops Rock. We were certainly learning the trade.

'In May 1943 we were posted to No. 4 Group Bomber Command, No. 1663 HCU Rufforth,

'Having once more proved our abilities for operational duties, we were posted to No. 76 Squadron, RAF Linton-on-Ouse. What a beautiful peacetime airfield. Just the job – having heard that the great Leonard "C" was about, but before we could settle down we were told "pack up your troubles in your old kit bag" and move out to Holme-on-Spalding Moor. June 1943, what a dump – Nissen huts, mud, but settle down we must and settle down we did to the job in hand. Air testing the aircraft for operational fitness, each member carrying out his duties and learning a little more of each others duties for the sake of emergencies.

'What a lucky chap I was to be part of such a crew, with a pilot like Les Falgate; bomb-aimer Frank Francis; navigator Wal Wallis; flight engineer Ray Dewey; wireless operator Ian Evans and mid-upper gunner Geoff Jennings. I was more than confident that we could make it and our first operation on Cologne proved that. The crew carried out their duties with a quiet confidence. The operations that followed were the major battles of Hamburg, Peenemünde, Hanover, Kassel, Frankfurt and Berlin. During these operations we all respected the rules laid down by our pilot for each member of the crew to follow his set procedure. After testing the intercom and securing all hatches before take off, the only members allowed on the intercom were navigator/pilot when climbing for operational height and course for the target, the rear gunner giving occasional reports on activities in the vicinity of our aircraft, the navigator reporting ETA for target, the bomb-aimer/pilot on the run-in to the target for release of bombs. The wireless operator would be listening out and the flight engineer dropping "Window" through the flare chute. On release of bombs the bomb-aimer would help the gunners by keeping watch for night fighters. The pilot would not suffer any idle chat over the intercom during operations, vigilance was the name of the game.

'There comes a time during a tour of operations when a crew becomes a little tired and careless and this could prove fatal, but as I already have said we had Frank, father of the crew to keep old man gloom away and also our pilot, Les, to keep us on top form. I don't wish to imply that it was all work and no play for our crew. Of course we joined in with the fun on stand down from operations, visiting the pubs, village dances, cinemas, theatre and Betty's Bar in York (known to everyone as the Briefing Room), and taking our ground crew members out for a few pints now and again. They were part of our salvation, the boys who kept us flying. My most sincere thanks, however, are reserved for my fellow crew members. Not only for their companionship, sense of humour, dedication, endurance but above all for their courage. How could one ever doubt that with such belief in one another we would return to be the "Lucky Ones!".'

Above: **Flight Sergeant Les Falgate and crew in front of their 76 Squadron Halifax Mk. V series 1 (Special), Holme-on-Spalding Moor, Summer 1943.** *W. Day*

Some were young, very young. Sgt Bill Day, 19 year old rear gunner with No.76 Squadron, 1943. *W. Day*

The 'Inglis crew' learning the trade on Whitleys. Left to right: Frank Francis; Taffy Evans; Ian Inglis; Bill Day; Wally Wallis. *W. Day*

Sergeant Ian Inglis in the cockpit of a 10 OTU Whitley. He was killed when the Halifax in which he was flying as second pilot was shot down over the Ruhr. *W. Day*

there to convert from the old loveable Whitleys to the four-engined Halifax bomber. What a treat, big stuff carrying out all the necessary exercises required to prove each and every member of the crew was competent and fit for operational duties.

'At last – our first operational squadron – 'Shiny Ten', RAF Melbourne; but not so shiny for us, Sergeant Ian Inglis our pilot was lost over Dortmund flying with an experienced crew acting as second pilot. It was practice at

that time that pilots had to complete two operations with an experienced crew before taking his own crew. Ian was sadly missed. For the rest of us it was back to 1663 HCU Rufforth to await a fresh pilot. He soon arrived, from a low-level Boston squadron. Converting Sergeant Les Falgate, our new pilot, in every sense of the word, wasn't so difficult and we were soon on the same wavelength. Thanks to Frank's diplomacy Les turned out to be every bit as conscientious and dedicated as Ian.

Chapter Fourteen

The Transportation Plan

One of the prerequisites of the *Overlord* plan was the dislocation of the enemy's transport system behind the planned invasion areas, particularly his railway network. With the invasion set to take place in early June 1944, the Allied Air Forces commenced in March 1944, a ninety day campaign to isolate the Normandy and Channel coasts of France by destroying the French and Belgian rail network. Known as the 'Transportation Plan' it was envisaged that seventy-two rail and road targets in France, Belgium and Germany would be attacked in an all out assault by the Allied Air Forces right up to the day of the invasion. Targets were to include railways, rolling stock, marshalling yards, repair and maintenance facilities, roads and bridges.

The systematic attack on communications was designed to prevent the Germans from bringing up reserves to attack the beach head in the vital days following 'D-Day'. But at the same time it was at all costs essential to avoid revealing, by the choice of targets, the exact location where the invasion was to take place. For this reason the Allied bombers, initially, attacked communications targets in the north of France and around the Paris area, convincing the German High Command that the probable landing zone would be the Pas-de-Calais.

The new phase opened with an attack on the marshalling yards and locomotive repair depot at Trappes, south-west of Paris, on the night of 6th March. The all-Halifax raid was carried out by 136 aircraft from No. 4 Group, 119 from No. 6 Group with marking by six 'Oboe'-equipped Mosquitos. In clear conditions over 1,200 tons of bombs were dropped causing extensive damage to railway tracks, installations and rolling stock. Trappes remained out of action for five weeks.

The following night the railway yards at Le Mans were bombed by over 300 aircraft, including 121 from No. 4 Group. Despite the presence of thick cloud cover over the rail yards, a highly successful attack took place. For the second night running there were no aircraft lost.

The need to avoid causing casualties to friendly civilians was paramount when attacking the small French and Belgian rail targets. The fact that casualties were kept to a minimum during the campaign was due in no small part to the vital role played by the Master Bomber in keeping the bombing and marking accurate.

Inevitably there were occasions when civi-lians were killed and injured as happened during an attack on the rail yards at Le Mans on the night of 13/14th March. Although the bombing was reported to be very accurate, many crews actually seeing their bombs bursting amongst railway lines and engine sheds, over a hundred French civilians became casualties. Damage to the rail yards was severe with many lines cut. One Halifax failed to return from the raid – Warrant Officer Withers and crew of 78 Squadron.

The main force went back to Germany again two nights later with a long distance trip to Stuttgart. Crews reported thick cloud on the outward route, in places clouds were three to four miles high, and there was severe icing. Despite clearer conditions over Stuttgart, the Pathfinder's marking was well short of the target, and as a result many bomb loads fell in open country well to the south-west of the city centre. Five Halifaxes from No. 4 Group were lost. In addition, in two separate crashes, involving returning aircraft from 578 Squadron, eight men were killed.

The city of Frankfurt suffered its heaviest bombing of the war so far when Bomber Command flew over 1,600 sorties in two massive attacks on the nights of the 18th and 22nd March. During the first attack over 3,000 tons of bombs were dropped causing widespread destruction and heavy loss of life. Over 55,000 people were made homeless. No. 4 Group despatched 114 Halifaxes for the first attack of which eighty-nine successfully bombed Frankfurt. Flight Sergeant Noyes's No. 76 Squadron Halifax was one of eight aircraft from the Group that failed to return. His Halifax, LK657 'G-George', was shot down over Frankfurt and crashed into an apartment building. Four crew members were able to bale out, one of them landing on the roof of an undamaged apartment building. By lowering himself onto a balcony he was able to force his way into a flat and down the stairs to the basement where he took shelter with a bemused German family.

In the second attack, four nights later, Frankfurt suffered further severe damage. Crews reported that the ground markers were clearly visible and highly concentrated and as a result the bombing was very accurate. Late arrivals reported seeing smoke from many fires rising up to 4,000 feet above the city and the glow of the fires could be seen over a hundred miles away. The night fighters arrived late on the scene, having been drawn to the north by diversions. Nevertheless, they achieved some successes over and near the target. Sergeant Street, rear gunner with Warrant Officer Ashton's 10 Squadron crew, recalls that their Halifax was attacked six times by a Ju 88 over Frankfurt.

'The fighter pilot must have been a new boy because we were helpless. He set us on fire and we were unable to hit back because all our guns were frozen up. In the end he just let us escape. Our luck was in that night.'

Others were not so lucky. Flight Sergeant Eric Sanderson, of 578 Squadron, was rear gunner with Flying Officer Atkins crew and flying that night in Halifax LW540 'R-Robert':

'On 22nd March we were on the Battle Order to attack Frankfurt. We were the senior crew on the Squadron, having completed twenty-seven ops, so on this flight our Station Commander, Group Captain Marwood-Elton, was to fly with us as second pilot.

'The flight out went as normal. We made a turning point at Hanover and started our run down to Frankfurt. Shortly after, I saw a Ju 88 slide beneath us. The skipper immediately took violent evasive action by corkscrewing and making steep diving turns to both port and starboard. Unfortunately it was to no avail as the German pilot followed our every move whilst he pumped cannon shells into our bomb bay and wing roots.

'With both starboard engines and fuel tanks ablaze, and a bomb bay full of burning incendiaries, the skipper realised it was hopeless and gave the bale-out order. I took the usual rear-gunners escape route by tipping out backwards from the turret. Suddenly, as I fell out through the open turret doors, I discovered to my horror that I was held fast by my legs trapped inside the turret. As the burning Halifax spiralled down there was I, surrounded by flames, being dragged down with it. I tried unsuccessfully to get back into the turret. Finally, completely exhausted, I gave up. I had earlier considered pulling the rip cord of my parachute, but the thought of injuring my legs as I was ripped from the turret made this idea unacceptable.

'As I hurtled down with the burning Halifax I finally decided that with only seconds to live I would risk losing my legs and pull the rip cord. As the parachute snapped open there was a very loud bang and I came out of the turret like a cork out of a bottle. I had baled out at only 500 feet and I was still swinging violently when I was dragged through the tops of some very tall trees. Soon after, I lost consciousness.

German villagers pose near the wreck of Halifax Mk.III LW540, 'R-Robert' of No.578 Squadron, just a few days after it was shot down at Steinringsburg, near Frankfurt on the night of 22nd March 1944. *E. Sanderson*

'In the morning the police came and took me to the police station in the nearest town. There I was re-united with Group Captain Marwood-Elton, my pilot and bomb-aimer, all having baled out without injury. Later that morning we were taken under guard to the railway station where we boarded a train. A few stops down the line we were joined by our navigator, mid-upper gunner and engineer, all of them unhurt except for a few cuts and bruises.

'We had to change trains at a town called Giessen, the first and only place I saw by name. There we were joined by over a dozen American aircrew, some badly wounded. From Giessen we travelled to Frankfurt and then to Dulag Luft. The journey from Frankfurt station to Dulag Luft was via public tram, and with the city still burning from our raid, we had a somewhat rough passage. On our arrival at Dulag Luft the wounded were separated and together with the American wounded I was taken to Hohemark Hospital and from that moment for me the war was over.'

In 1978 Eric Sanderson returned to the village of Guntersdorf, near Frankfurt, for a happy reunion with the villagers who treated a wounded British airman with such kindness that night in 1944. Later he was introduced to the pilot of the Ju 88 night fighter that had shot his Halifax down, night fighter ace, Hauptman Heinz Rokker, together with his radio man Oberfeldwebel Carlos Nugent.

The final act of the Battle of Berlin took place on the night of 24/25th March 1944. That night Bomber Command despatched 811 aircraft on the last major attack against the German capital by the RAF. Unexpected high winds on the outward leg of the bombers route to Berlin soon posed early problems. The winds, blowing from the north-west and reaching speeds of well over 100 mph, caused many aircraft to be blown off course, whilst others overshot the target. Worse still, on the return flight the strong winds caused the bomber stream to become scattered as aircraft drifted further and further south of track. A scattered bomber stream, with its protective curtain of 'Window' reduced, quickly becomes vulnerable, particularly to flak and searchlights. The result that night was that in the clear conditions over Germany many aircraft were picked off by radar predicted flak as they drifted unexpectedly into heavily defended areas. Some bombers were even shot down as far south as the Ruhr and of the seventy-two aircraft lost, at least fifty fell to

'When I awoke I was flat on my back. I was sure that I was dead as I was surrounded by complete darkness and utter silence. When, after what seemed ages, I saw a star and soon after heard the faint sound of an aircraft I realised that I was still alive. My next thought was for my legs. After first making sure that I could move my head and arms, I tried to move my legs but no way would they move. I didn't even have any feeling in them. My immediate thought was that they had been ripped off.

'With great difficulty, I managed to sit up, but all I could see was a tangled mass where my legs should have been. With one trembling hand I felt down and found, much to my relief, that the tangled mass was in fact my parachute harness and Mae West. They had both been ripped down my body as I was dragged through the trees during my descent.

The harness was so tightly wrapped around my legs that I had lost all feeling in them. Once more I enjoyed the feeling of utter relief, and at once started to strip off my equipment and take stock of my injuries and surroundings. I found that my face and hands were badly burnt and that I was unable to walk.

'Close by I could see our aircraft burning and soon I heard voices. I began calling for help and I was quickly surrounded by several men with rifles and very long bayonets. I could see by the light of their torches that they were not soldiers. After making sure that I was unarmed, they carried me to the nearest village where I was taken into a house and kept there for the night.

'The daughter of the house washed and dressed my wounds, and during the night most of the village came into the house to have a look at me.

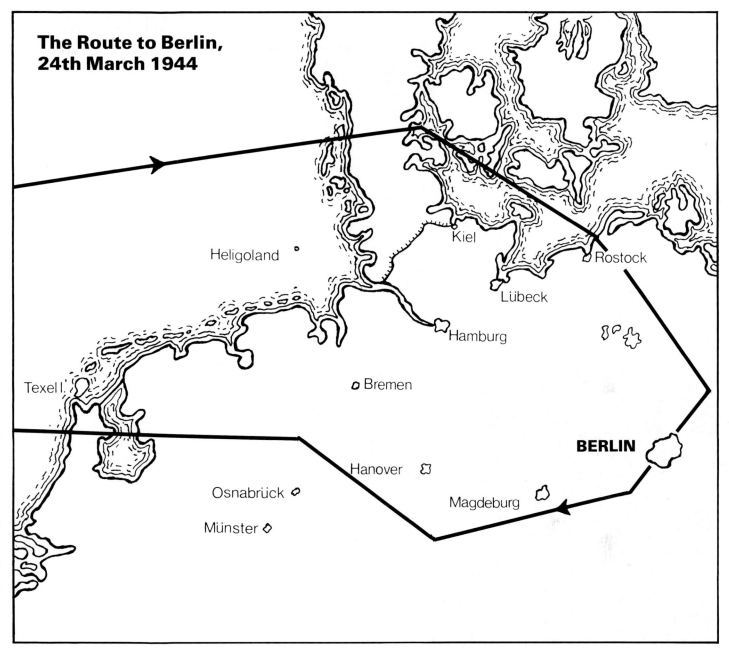

**The Route to Berlin,
24th March 1944**

Heligoland

Kiel

Rostock

Lübeck

Hamburg

Texel I.

Bremen

BERLIN

Hanover

Osnabrück

Magdeburg

Münster

the guns of the Luftwaffe's flak arm. The rest were victims of the night flighters. No. 4 Group lost fifteen Halifaxes plus two which crashed on return killing both crews. No. 78 Squadron came off worst losing six crews of which twenty-eight were killed and fifteen made POWs.

One of sixteen crews from 76 Squadron that left Holme-on-Spalding Moor that night for Berlin was that of Flying Officer Roy Bolt. His navigator that night was Pilot Officer Fred Hall:

'The flight plan was a long leg over the North Sea to Denmark, hitting the island of Romo south of Esbjerg. The winds across the North Sea had been forecast at 45 mph, whereas I had calculated them at nearer 90 mph. I had obtained some good Gee fixes and we hit the Danish coast on track as was confirmed by the bomb-aimer.

'Our route took us across the mainland of Denmark to Haderslev thence south-east over Langeland island to Wustrow, which lies north-east of Rostock on the German Baltic coast. This part of the trip indicated the wind from the north had further increased causing me to give the plot an alteration of course to port to avoid flying over the defences of Rostock.

'My mind went back to 13th August 1938, my wedding day. My wife and I had set of from Tilbury on our honeymoon for the Hook of Holland. From there we travelled by train via Lübeck to Timmendorfer Strand on the Baltic coast, a small seaside resort between Rostock and Lübeck. Who would have thought that in such a short time a world war would be upon us and that I would be flying over what had been a peaceful sea shore – now a hostile country.

The attack on Berlin on the night of 24/25th March 1944 was the last major raid on the German capital by the Royal Air Force.

'On the south-east leg into Berlin I warned the skipper that due to the ferocious wind from the north we were going to be over the target ahead of ETA. We bombed through cloud but did not see any results although there was plenty of flak about. Due to the strong winds I amended my courses to fly on the legs away from the target veering north of track. As we flew westwards the wireless operator advised that his radar set showed that most of the stream were off to port and flying over the Ruhr. We flew across the middle of Holland unmolested and eventually arrived back at base, the first aircraft to do so!'

Flying Officer Roy Bolt with his air and ground crew, 76 Squadron, Holme-on-Spalding Moor, late 1943. Left to right: ground crew; Flying Officer Tony Walker, rear gunner; Sergeant Cal Rathmell, bomb aimer; Sergeant Jack Bates, flight engineer; Flying Officer Roy Bolt, pilot; Sergeant Joe Josey; wireless operator; Sergeant Harry Van-den-Bos, mid upper gunner; Pilot officer Fred Hall, navigator; ground crew. Their Halifax is Mark V LK912 ''N', shot down with another crew on a trip to Magdeburg in January 1944. *Fred Hall*

Wing Commander R.C. Ayling briefs No.51 Squadron crews for the Nuremburg Raid, 30th March 1944. Group Captain N.H. Fresson, Snaith's Station Commander, sits in the front row. No.51 Squadron were fated to lose six Halifaxes that night with the loss of thirty-five men killed and seven PoWs. *IWM, CH12598*

Top: **Halifax Mk.III, LW473 'F-Freddie' of 578 Squadron, about to receive its bomb load at Burn, Spring 1944. 'Freddie' took part in the disastrous Nuremburg raid on the night of 30/31st March 1944. Flight Sergeant Henderson and crew were attacked by a night fighter and lost an engine but managed to return safely.** *W. McDonald*

Halifax Mk.III LV857, photographed here on an air test prior to delivery early in 1944, finally met its end on the way to Nuremburg on the night of 30/31st March 1944; Sergeant J. Binder and his entire 51 Squadron crew were killed. *Handley Page Ltd*

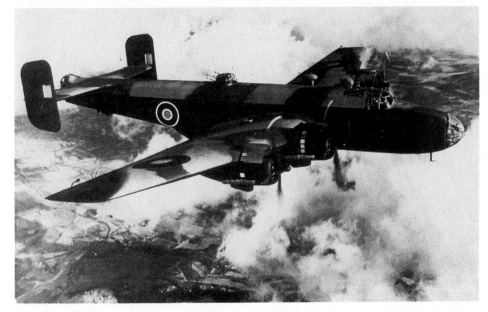

Harris had not been correct when he had predicted that the 'Battle of Berlin' would cost Bomber Command up to 500 aircraft. The actual losses during the period were 625. His hopes of forcing an early German surrender by destroying Berlin, were also over optimistic. Although Berlin had suffered immense damage during the campaign nothing like a 'Hamburg' style effect, in terms of concentration, was ever achieved. Berlin continued to function as the major administrative and arms producing centre of the German Reich despite the bombing. The decisive factors in the battle had been the increasing effectiveness of the German defences combined with a decline in efficiency of the bomber force caused by adverse weather, continued operations at maximum range, and increasing losses.

Successful raids were carried out at the end of March 1944 by Halifaxes of 4 Group against marshalling yards at Aulnoye and Paris-Vaires as well as the Krupps works in Essen. The Essen raid was particularly successful as the raiding force was able to completely outwit the German fighter controller. After approaching central Germany over the Zuider Zee the bomber force suddenly made a sharp turn to the south to attack Essen. Meanwhile, the night fighters, having assembled well to the east anticipating a strike at targets in central Germany were left too far to the east to intercept the main stream.

The night of 30/31st March 1944, however, would be remembered as the night the RAF received a bloody nose. That night 572 Lancasters, 214 Halifaxes and 9 Mosquitos took-off to bomb Nuremburg. The raid was to be the last major deep penetration attack into Germany by the RAF before the bomber force switched over to operations directly associated with the forthcoming invasion of Normandy. As the 120 Halifaxes from No. 4 Group left from their Yorkshire bases to form up with the rest of the bomber stream assembling midway over the North Sea, none of the crews could have foreseen what lay ahead of them that night. Some among them, particularly the experienced crews with many operations behind them, would perhaps have been feeling uneasy about the choice of route for the outward leg to Nuremburg. This required the bombers to fly a dead straight line for 220 miles across enemy

territory before the final turn towards Nuremburg. Normally on a deep penetration raid there would be a number of 'dog legs' or changes of course, particularly on the outward route, to confuse the German fighter controller.

As the bomber stream commenced that long, straight leg things started to go wrong. The forecast layer of high cloud, that would have given the bombers some protection, never materialised. As a result the bomber stream lay exposed in the clear cold air bathed in the light of the rising half-moon. In addition, many of the bombers began to trail long white condensation trails which glowed in the moonlight pointing the way to Nuremburg. The German fighter controller, meanwhile ignored the diversions, which included a mining sortie off Heligoland by twenty Halifaxes from Nos. 77 and 102 Squadrons, and assembled his fighters at two radio beacons (Ida and Otto) astride the bombers route to Nuremburg.

By the time the bomber stream crossed into Germany it had lost its cohesion due to incorrect forecast winds and the scene was now set for the greatest night air battle of the war. The main clash took place near the 'Ida' radio beacon, north-east of Bonn, and from there to Nuremburg a running battle of ferocious dimensions developed.

The first 4 Group victim of the night occurred some ten miles north-east of the 'Ida' beacon when a Halifax of 78 Squadron was shot down by a night fighter. Sergeant Horton and his entire crew were killed. They were on their first operation. Some twenty-five miles further east Flight Lieutenant Coverley and crew of 76 Squadron became the second 4 Group Halifax to fall when they were attacked from below by a Ju 88 using upwards-firing cannons. With his starboard wing a mass of flames and rudder and elevator controls severely damaged Coverley bravely remained at the controls of the doomed Halifax while the rest of the crew made their

escape. Only when he was certain that all had left the burning aircraft did Coverley bale out himself. Sadly the flight engineer, Sergeant Motts, was killed when his parachute caught fire. The rest of the crew survived.

Another crew from 76 Squadron were not so lucky. So swift was the attack, carried out from below by night fighter ace Oberleutnant Martin Becker, that Squadron Leader Clack's Halifax exploded within seconds of being hit. Mid-upper gunner Flight Sergeant Edwards was the only survivor.

Over the next 150 miles, and before the bomber stream made its planned turn to the south to approach Nuremburg, another eleven Halifaxes from the Group were shot down. Ten fell to night fighters and one to flak. In the 'gin clear' conditions scores of bombers could be seen going down in flames. Others were seen to explode and shower to earth in a mass of fiery fragments. Night fighters from all over Germany were fed into the stream lured by the sight of the many blazing wrecks that marked the bombers route.

Snaith Station Commander, Group Captain N.H. Fresson is joined by other officers on the balcony of the control tower as they await the return of 51 Squadron from Nuremburg. The searchlight piercing the night sky is to show the cloudbase. Note the ambulance and crash tender crews standing by. *via W. Baguley*

The slaughter continued unabated all the way to Nuremburg. Sergeant 'Timber' Wood was mid-upper gunner aboard a No. 578 Squadron Halifax named 'Excalibur', (Pilot Officer Cyril Barton). 'Excalibur' carried on its nose an emblem depicting a hand emerging from the base of a cloud and grasping the legendary sword of King Arthur. The journey to Nuremburg had been uneventful until seventy miles short of the target when 'Excalibur' came under attack as 'Timber' Wood recalls:

'As we approached the target Cy Barton told us to keep a sharp look-out for fighters.

We were making a steep bank to port, so as to check the area below us, when suddenly there was a series of sharp bangs. A voice called out an evasive command order to the skipper and then our Halifax shuddered, dipped into a slight dive and the intercom went dead. When I heard the evasive action call I rotated my turret and fired blindly to the rear. Only one of my Brownings operated, the others were frozen solid.

'As Cy took the required corkscrew action I managed to fire a long burst with my single gun at a Ju 88 which I had spotted beneath us. Although with our intercom u/s we had no way of speaking to each other, we did have an emergency system of communication. By pressing a button it was possible to send messages on an inter-call light. Using this method we were able to pass instructions to the pilot whilst under attack.

'Meanwhile the Ju 88 reappeared on our port beam, so I punched off a series of dots. This was the signal for Cy to resume his corkscrew action, beginning with a diving turn to port. During this time a Me 210 joined the fight from upfront. I saw its tracer fly harmlessly over our heads to the rear, then caught a brief glimpse of its silhouette as it sped past on our starboard side. Fortunately our tormentors suddenly left us as quickly as they had appeared and we were able to resume level flight.'*

'Excalibur' had been badly damaged during the attack but even more serious was the loss of the navigator, bomb-aimer and wireless operator. They had wrongly interpreted the signal lights as an instruction to bale out and had left the aircraft at the height of the attack. With his aircraft badly damaged and his navigational team now having gone, Pilot Officer Barton faced a perilous situation. Nevertheless, determined to press home the attack he flew on until the target was reached and released the bombs himself.

The next series of disasters to befall the crew of 'Excalibur' came shortly after they had turned for home. Firstly the starboard inner propeller, which had been vibrating badly, flew off. 'Timber' Wood recalls that moment:

'The propeller eventually became detached from the engine; it was glowing red hot and flew up and away like a giant Catherine wheel.'

Even more worrying was the discovery that two fuel tanks had been holed and that fuel was leaking away. On account of the petrol leakage Pilot Officer Barton elected to make for the Norfolk coast rather than return with the main stream which would be making landfall over the Isle of Wight.

Other crews, having battled their way to the target, now faced the prospect of a long and dangerous flight home. Flying Officer Fred Hall, navigator with Flight Lieutenant Roy Bolt's No. 76 Squadron crew, recalls the eventful journey :

'We had trouble with the DR compass on the outward leg but we could not check it out because of all the fighter activity going on around. Being in the last wave of the attack we could see the target well lit-up some miles away.

'A minute after dropping our bombs we were raked by cannon and machine gun fire. The starboard wing, bomb-bay and fuselage were on fire and the starboard inner engine was put out of action. My plotting table was covered with debris caused by a cannon shell passing through the wireless set to the left of my head. Apparently a fighter had closed in underneath us unseen and we had been attacked without any warning.

'The mid-upper gunner and flight engineer tried to tackle the flames with fire extinguishers but didn't make much progress. The skipper then decided to dive the aircraft and try and blow out the flames. After two attempts the flames went out.

'As we settled on a new course for home we again came under attack, this time from dead astern. Fortunately our rear-gunner Sergeant Harry van den Bos was alert and on his instructions the skipper was able to take evasive action just at the right moment. As the German fighter passed about fifty yards over our tail he received the combined fire of both our gunners. He appeared to be hit, turned over and went down seemingly out of control.

'Meanwhile, Sergeant Jack Bates, our flight engineer, had noticed that our fuel was being eaten up and it was presumed that a fuel line had been severed during one of the fighter attacks. It was touch and go for the next couple of hours but we managed to reach Tangmere were we ended up at the side of the runway due to a burst tyre. The next morning the station engineering officer reported our aircraft was a complete write-off and he couldn't understand how we had been able to get back.'

Cyril Joe Barton the only member of a Halifax crew to be awarded the Victoria Cross.
via W. Baguley

The wreckage of Pilot Officer Cyril Barton's Halifax, LK797 *Excalibur* in the yard of Ryhope Colliery. One miner was killed and another was injured when LK797 struck the end of a row of cottages. *IWM, HU4021*

For Pilot Officer Cyril Barton and the remaining crew members of 'Excalibur' there was still a long way to go. Unsure of their position and with fuel reserves dangerously low they groped blindly towards home in the darkness. Sergeant 'Timber' Wood recalls going forward into the nose of the aircraft to see if he could get any of the navigational aids to work and try and plot their position:

'Cy had always insisted that each crew member should have some experience of the other's work in the aircraft and on the ground I had achieved some success on the 'Gee' set. Unfortunately the Gee-box must have suffered the same fate as the radio, which was shattered, and despite all my efforts I was unable to make it work. The underside of the navigators desk was badly holed and the maps inside the drawer had been torn to shreds by exploding cannon shells.

'It was still dark when we crossed the enemy coast and we then spent a long time over water. Someone suggested that if some searchlights we had avoided earlier on our flight back were surrounding Frankfurt, as we thought at the time, then since we were now heading due west we should be flying down the English Channel and making for the Atlantic. So in the circumstances Cy decided that we should turn north. Had we but known it, we were at that moment not twenty minutes from the emergency aerodrome at Woodbridge in Suffolk.

'We maintained the new course until we crossed some lights on the sea, which we took to be convoy marking lights. At this point Cy returned to the westerly heading. The grey of dawn, meanwhile, became brighter and we could make out a Beaufighter flying past. Using the Very pistol we hurriedly fired off the distress signal, but the Beaufighter pilot, having identified us, flew on into the morning mist and out of sight. Like all Allied aircraft we carried an IFF set, but this was out of action. We realised later that the Beaufighter had been sent out to intercept an unidentified aircraft approaching the coast; once he had recognised us, he naturally left us alone.

'As we neared the coast we saw barrage balloons being raised, and although our radio and intercom were not working we could still pick up the distinctive 'squeaker' sound the balloons emitted. The ground defences, however, failed to recognise us and we were fired upon. As a result, Cy turned on a reciprocal course and flew back out to sea. In the nose I connected the Aldis lamp, signalled SOS and a message to say that we were friendly. That stopped the firing and I immediately made my way back, carefully avoiding the open escape hatch. Just as I reached the cockpit Cy called to me 'Get aft quickly' he shouted, 'we're going to crash'. The fuel pipes from one of the petrol tanks had been severed during the attack. When our flight engineer Maurice Trousdale switched over tanks the fuel ran out instead of into the engines causing both port engines to stop. I rushed back into the fuselage, climbed over the rear spar and had

just settled in the crash position when the first bump came and I was knocked out.

'When I came round it was the sound of Maurice Trousdale, urgently requesting Fred Brice to "Get off me bloody leg!" I looked over and saw Fred trying to get out of the fuselage through the escape hatch above the crash position.

'On our final descent, despite strenuous efforts, Cy was unable to avoid the end of a row of houses; one was demolished and its neighbour slightly damaged. Our momentum carried the Halifax into the yard of Ryhope Colliery near Sunderland, on the Durham coast. On impact "Excalibur" broke up into several parts. The section carrying Maurice, Fred and myself came to rest at the foot of a hill. Cy survived the crash for thirty minutes. He was briefly conscious before he died and his last words were concern for the rest of us.'*

Pilot Officer Cyril Barton was posthumously awarded the Victoria Cross in May 1944, the only Halifax crew member to receive this award during the entire war. 'Timber' Wood, along with the flight engineer, Maurice Trousdale, and the rear gunner, Fred Brice, all received the Distinguished Flying Medal.

No.4 Group aircraft lost on the Nuremburg raid March 30th/31st 1944

Unit	Serial	Captain	Casualties	Cause
10 Sqn	LV881	P/O Regan	5 k, 3 pow	NF
51 Sqn	LV777	S/Ldr Hill	7 k	Flak
51 Sqn	LV857	Sgt Binder	7 k	NF
51 Sqn	LV822	F/Sgt Wilkins	7 k	NF
51 Sqn	LW537	F/Sgt Stembridge	2 k, 5 pow	NF
51 Sqn	LW544	F/Sgt Brougham	5 k, 2 pow	NF
51 Sqn	LW579	P/O Brooks	7 k	CoR
76 Sqn	LK795	F/Lt Coverley	1 k, 6 pow	NF
76 Sqn	LW628	F/Lt Bolt	none	W/o
76 Sqn	LW647	F/O Greenacre	5 k, 2 pow	NF
76 Sqn	LW696	S/Ldr Clack	7 k	NF
78 Sqn	HX421	F/Lt Hudson	6 k, 1 pow	NF
78 Sqn	LK762	Sgt Horton	4 k, 3 pow	NF
78 Sqn	LV899	P/O Topping	7 k	NF
158 Sqn	HX322	F/Sgt Brice	6 k, 1 pow	NF + Flak
158 Sqn	HX349	S/Ldr Jones	2 k, 5 pow	Flak
158 Sqn	LW634	F/Sgt Hughes	5 pow, 2 esc	Flak
158 Sqn	LW724	W/O MacLeod	6 k, 1 pow	NF
578 Sqn	LK797	P/O Barton	1 k, 3 inj	CoR
578 Sqn	LW478	S/Ldr McCreanor	7 k	CoR
578 Sqn	MZ505	F/Sgt Pinks	7 k	NF
640 Sqn	LW500	P/O Burke	7 k	Flak
640 Sqn	LW549	F/O Laidlaw	4 k, 3 pow	NF
640 Sqn	LW555	F/O O'Brien	7 k	NF

24 Halifaxes lost, 117 men killed, 37 pow's, 3 men injured.
Key: k - killed, pow - prisoner of war, esc - escaped, CoR - Crashed on Return, NF - Night-fighter, inj - injured, W/o - written off.

Information source for the above table from *The Nuremburg Raid* by Martin Middlebrook: Allen Lane, 1973.

*Extracts from: *Raider* by Geoffrey Jones: William Kimber, 1978.

Sombre scene at Snaith as Flight Lieutenant A.G. Golding and crew are de-briefed after the raid on Nuremburg. *via W. Baguley*

As the post-raid reports began to filter through to Bomber Command Headquarters it soon became apparent that something approaching a disaster had occurred during the previous nights attack on Nuremburg. When the figures for aircraft missing were obtained it was found that ninety-five bombers had failed to return; a further twelve had crashed and some thirty-four had suffered serious damage. No.4 Group lost twenty Halifaxes plus three that crashed on return and one that was damaged beyond repair. No.51 Squadron had come off worst, suffering the loss of five Halifaxes missing plus one that crashed on return killing the entire crew. Altogether the Squadron lost thirty-five men killed, plus seven who were made POWs.

The Nuremburg Raid 30th/31st March 1944 - No.4 Group Raid Statistics

Sqn	Took-off	Early Return	Attacked Primary	Missing
10	13	4	8	1
51	17	3	8	5+1 crash
76	14	1	10	3+1 W/o
78	16	4	9	3
158	16	4	8	4
466 (RAAF)	16	4	12	-
578	12	3	8	1+2 crash
640	16	1	12	3
Mining Diversion				
77	10	-	10	-
102	10	-	10	-

No.158 Squadron was another unit that was hit badly. Included in the list of missing crews from the Squadron was that of Squadron Leader S.D. Jones, DFC. Jones and his crew were on the twelfth operation of their second tour. Flying in a borrowed aircraft ('G-George' HX349, normal mount of Flight Sergeant Joe Hitchman) - they were shot down by flak on the long outward leg. Meanwhile, Flight Sergeant Joe Hitchman and crew had flown to Nuremburg and returned safely in a new aircraft, LV907 'F', christened *Friday the 13th*. With a fuselage painted with superstition-defying ill omens, such as a skull and crossbones, an inverted horseshoe and a legend that read 'As ye sow, so shall ye reap', *Friday* went on to complete a record 128 operational sorties by VE-Day (see Appendix H).

The Nuremburg disaster resulted in a complete re-think of the RAF's night bombing offensive. For the time being the German night fighters had gained the upper hand and in the early spring of 1944 they stood at the pinnacle of their success. Deep penetration raids by RAF Bomber Command were now halted as the pressing demands of operation *Overlord*, the invasion of Normandy, were now a first priority.

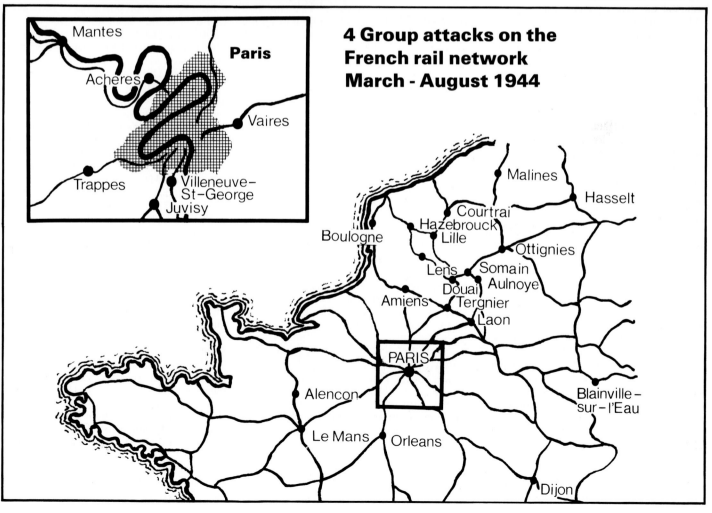

4 Group attacks on the French rail network March - August 1944

No.4 Group Attacks on the French Rail Network

Target	Date of Attack
Trappes-Paris	March 6th, May 31st, June 2nd
Le Mans	March 7th, 13th
Amiens	March 16th, June 12th
Aulnoye	March 25th, April 27th
Courtrai (Belgium)	March 26th
Vaires-Paris	March 29th, July 18th
Lille	April 9th
Villeneuve-St-Georges	April 9th, 26th
Tergnier	April 10th, 18th
Ottignies	April 20th
Montzen (Belgium)	April 27th
Acheres-Paris	April 30th
Malines (Belgium)	May 1st
Mantes	May 6th
Lens	May 10th
Hasselt (Belgium)	May 12th
Boulogne	May 19th
Orleans	May 22nd
Juvisy-Paris	June 7th
Alencon	June 8th
Massy (Road/Rail Bridge)	June 11th
Douai	June 14th
Laon	June 22nd
Blainville sur l'eau	June 28th
Hazebrouck	August 6th
Dijon	August 10th
Somain	August 11th

Bomber Command's attacks on communications began in earnest in April 1944. The Directive, issued on 17th April, by the Deputy Supreme Commander Sir Arthur Tedder, indicated the direction that the Allied Air Forces were to follow in the coming weeks. Bomber Command's mission was 'To destroy and disrupt the enemy's rail communications, particularly those affecting the enemy's movement towards the *Overlord* lodgement area.' And when weather conditions were favourable 'RAF Bomber Command will continue to be employed in accordance with their main aim of disorganising German industry.'

The new phase got off to an unauspicious start with attacks on rail yards at Lille and Villeneuve-St-Georges, south of Paris, on the night of 9th April. Joining with aircraft from Nos. 3, 6 and 8 Groups, 4 Group despatched 111 Halifaxes to Lille and forty-nine to Villeneuve. Widespread and serious damage was inflicted on both rail yards but the price in civilian casualties was high. Unfortunately, at both targets, some of the bombing strayed onto nearby French railway workers housing estates causing severe damage and over 500 deaths.

The following night, 4 Group was sent to rail yards at Tergnier, the 156 strong force of Halifaxes being supported by ten Pathfinding Mosquitos. This time bombing was highly accurate and the yards were severely damaged. The German night fighters appeared to have been up in some strength during this night and ten Halifaxes were lost. Pilot Officer Horace Pearce was skipper of a Halifax from 77 Squadron, one of fifteen from Elvington detailed for the attack on Tergnier:

'Operational aircrews were allowed leave every six weeks and we arrived back from a period of leave on the morning of 10th April to discover that we were on operations that night. We were assigned LL126 'W', a Mk.V Halifax. After the usual procedures we took-off at 20.55 hours with a load of bombs which consisted of five 1,000 lb and ten 500 lb high explosive. The route out was south over England to Newbury, a left turn to pass over Selsey Bill and across the French coast at Cap d'Antifer.

'At the target there was haze at low-levels, but no cloud. Red target indicators went down and Gordon Edwards, our bomb-aimer, identifying the target area by the light of the flares, called for "Bomb doors open". After a few corrections, came the remark "Steady", then "Bombs away", followed a little later by "Photoflash – close bomb doors."

'The route from the target comprised two left turns, bringing us parallel to the incoming route, and to pass south of Amiens and north of Dieppe. At 00.09 hours, flying at 11,000 feet, in the vicinity of Amiens our rear-gunner, Sergeant Ivor Hancocks, reported three fighter flares dropping astern, and at the same time, saw aircraft navigation lights on the port bow 1,500 feet below and climbing on a reciprocal course. At this moment we were subjected to a barrage of heavy flak. I took immediate evasive action until clear and then resumed our course, only to be told by the rear-gunner that a twin-engined fighter was on the port beam down at 700 feet below. The fighter appeared to be showing a nose light as he came in to attack us, climbing and turning as he did so. At this time the moon, which was three quarters full, was on the starboard quarter astern of our aircraft. Visibility was still good above and hazy below. The enemy fighter came in from the port quarter, the rear-gunner reporting, "Enemy range 400 yards and closing. Nose light out, prepare to go". Immediately I could hear the chatter of machine gun fire from the rear turret. At the same moment the fighter also opened fire but his tracers passed over us. I was still waiting the order to corkscrew when the rear-gunner stopped firing, and I wondered if he had been hit. Sergeant Fred Archbold, our flight engineer, set off to go back to the rear turret to see what the score was. Meanwhile, the rear-gunner came over on the intercom with, "Resume course, he won't bother us anymore." To my question "Whats going on back there Taffy? Do I corkscrew?" The rear-gunner replied, that the enemy fighter closed to within 300 yards, at which point he (the rear-gunner) opened fire. At a range of 200 yards his fire caused the fighter to explode.

'The attack, which lasted only a few seconds, was witnessed by the mid-upper gunner who was unable to fire his guns because the Halifax's fin and rudder were in his line of fire.'

The rear-gunner, Sergeant Ivor Hancocks, was awarded an immediate DFM for his exploit in ensuring the safety of his aircraft and fellow crew members.

Tergnier was again bombed on 18th April by a mainly Halifax force of 171 aircraft as Bomber Command's offensive against rail targets now began to gather momentum. No. 4 Group crews reported a highly concentrated attack with sticks of bombs seen to burst right across the railway tracks. Six aircraft from the Group failed to return.

For maximum effect, rail experts selected the best locations for aiming points during the campaign against the French rail system; a campaign in which No. 4 Group now began to play a leading role. Rail yards, depots and workshops at Ottignies, Laon, Villeneuve-St-Georges, Aulnoye, Montzen and Acheres were all subjected to crippling attacks during April by medium strength forces of Halifaxes supported by small numbers of Pathfinders. Interspersed with the French attacks No. 4 Group took part in two heavy main force raids; on Düsseldorf on 22nd April and Karlsruhe two nights later. The night fighters were up in some strength on both nights and bomber losses were heavy. Squadron Leader Somerscales of 76 Squadron was flying in the vicinity of Maastricht on the way to Düsseldorf when his aircraft came under attack. It is not known whether Somerscale's Halifax was attacked by a nightfighter or flak. The first intimation to the crew that they were under attack was when they heard a loud crack. Within seconds the port wing of the Halifax was ablaze and the order to bale out was given. Four members of Somerscale's crew were able to bale out successfully before the aircraft exploded. The pilot and mid-upper gunner were killed in the explosion. The wireless operator, Flying Officer Reavill, had been about to hand the pilot his parachute when the aircraft exploded. The next thing Reavill knew was that he came to and was aware of a falling sensation. Fortunately he was able to pull the rip cord of his chute in time as he almost immediately hit the ground. He was later captured by the Germans along with two other members of his crew. The bomb-aimer, Flying Officer Wingham, along with the navigator, Flying Officer Lewis successfully avoided capture and returned to England after four and a half months. Squadron Leader Somerscales and crew were on the third operation of their second tour.

In the first weeks of May 1944 the build-up to the invasion continued with 4 Group carrying out attacks on locomotive sheds at Malines in Belgium, marshalling yards in the Gassicourt suburb of Paris and coastal gun emplacements near Dieppe and Cherbourg. On the night of 12th May the important rail junction and marshalling yard at Hasselt in Belgium was attacked by a 111-strong force from Nos. 4 and 8 Groups. Sergeant Les Harris, bomb-aimer with Flight Sergeant Laurie Lavelley's 10 Squadron crew, recalls that during that night there was intense fighter activity.

'At our briefing we were detailed to bomb Hasselt, and to fly to the target at approximately 8,000 feet. We soon discovered that on this particular night the German night fighters were very busy. On the outward leg we saw several bombers burst into flames before spiralling down to explode with a sickening orange flash on the ground. On this trip I sat in the nose to keep an eye out for fighters. As we neared the target I suddenly spotted a Focke-Wulf Fw 190, about fifty or sixty feet away, flying upwards across our path. The Halifax carried only a light Vickers gas-operated gun in the nose; really only of value as a scare gun. In that instant I realised that I would give our position away if I fired at the enemy; even though he was a perfect target. Fortunately, we were not seen and the enemy fighter disappeared into the darkness.'

Others were less fortunate that night. For Pilot Officer 'Lew' Lewis and crew of 640 Squadron, the Hasselt raid was to be their twentieth trip of their first tour. Sergeant Stan Beckett was in the mid-upper turret of MZ562 'A-Apple' that night:

'For some time after we had crossed the enemy coast we had been getting warning 'pips' on the Monica set, indicating that we were being trailed by a night fighter. Although we hadn't seen any fighters 'Lew' was taking no chances and he did several 'corkscrews'. Suddenly, and without warning, we were showered with cannon shells from below. They exploded into the wing tanks which immediately caught fire. Lew, from his position in the cockpit, was probably unaware of the extent of the fire, which was quickly consuming the wings. He said he would try and dive and put out the flames. I dropped out of the turret, put on my chute and crawled towards the rear door as I was convinced that we'd had it. I opened the door and was sucked out by the slipstream. As my chute jerked open it almost collapsed as our kite hit the deck and blew-up. I hung for only a few seconds before I found myself flat on my back surrounded by exploding ammunition.'

F/Lt Roy Bolt and crew being de-briefed by the 'Colonel', 76 Squadron Intelligence Officer, on return from Ottignies, 21st April 1944. Seated left to right: F/O Fred Hall, navigator; Intelligence Officer; Sgt Joe Josey, wireless operator; F/Lt Roy Bolt, pilot; P/O Cal Rathmell, bomb aimer; Sgt Harry Van den Bos, mid-upper gunner; P/O Jack Bates, flight engineer. *Fred Hall*

The marshalling yards at Villeneuve-St-Georges, Paris come under attack from Halifaxes of 4 Group on the night of 26/27th April 1944. *S. Pickles*

Five 'Aussies' and two 'Pommies': crew of 466 (RAAF) Squadron 'U-Uncle', return from a daylight air test, May 1944. Left to right: Sgt Morres, flight engineer from London; P/O Heare, bomb-aimer from Sydney; F/Sgt Flett, wireless operator from Sydney; Sgt Page, pilot from Sydney; Sgt Beldin, rear-gunner from London; P/O Reynolds, navigator from Sydney; Sgt Charlesworth, mid-upper gunner from Melbourne. *L. Charlesworth*

Pilot Officer Pearce (5th from right) of No.77 Squadron with his air and ground crew in front of their Halifax Mk.V LK744 'Y' after return from Lens, 10th May 1944. No.77 Squadron finally converted to the improved Mk.III Halifax shortly after moving to their new base at Full Sutton in May 1944. *H. V. Pearce*

Sergeant Beckett was lucky to escape from the doomed Halifax which had quickly lost height after being attacked, despite the brave efforts of the pilot to maintain control. Sergeant Beckett and the rear-gunner, Sergeant Everson, were the only survivors from 'A-Apple'. Their quick reactions had saved their lives. Both were captured soon after landing and spent the rest of the war as POWs.

Marshalling yards at Boulogne and Orléans were bombed on the 19th and 22nd May before 4 Group joined in a heavy main force attack on rail yards at Aachen on the night of the 24th. The railway yards and the town itself were badly hit and nearly 15,000 people were made homeless. Over the target the bombers ran into a murderous barrage of flak and there was considerable night fighter activity. An additional hazard confronted some of the returning bombers as they passed Antwerp. At that time the port was under attack from Lancasters and Mosquitos and it was their target illuminators that served to light-up bombers returning from Aachen. Of the twenty-five bombers that failed to return eleven were Halifaxes from 4 Group; including five from 158 Squadron.

No.10 Squadron crews, returning from an attack on a large military camp at Bourg-Leopold on the night of 27th May, found their base at Melbourne shrouded in fog. The fact that all the Squadron's aircraft were able to land safely was due to the use of a new fog dispersing system (FIDO) being used operationally for the first time at Melbourne. FIDO (Fog Investigation and Dispersal Operation) was used for the first time in November 1943 at Graveley and had been developed to aid night landings when visibility was poor. Lengths of perforated tube had been laid either side and across one end of the main runway. Petrol was then pumped through the tubing and when ignited the resulting blaze would disperse the fog and allow aircraft to land safely. Another airfield in Yorkshire equipped with FIDO became operational under No. 4 Group at this time. Carnaby, situated on the Yorkshire coast south-west of Bridlington, was designed as a Bomber Command Emergency Landing Ground - one of three such sites, the others being at Woodbridge and Manston. All three were situated at or near the coast and were equipped to handle aircraft in difficulties. All three ELGs had a single 3,000 yard runway with a 500 yard overrun at each end. In the short time that Carnaby was operational the airfield recorded over 1,500 emergency landings and the station's emergency services were responsible for saving the lives of countless aircrews.

With *Overlord*, the invasion of Normandy, only days away 4 Group sent ninety-nine Halifaxes, supported by eight Pathfinder Mosquitos, to attack the important radio listening station at Ferme-d'Urvill, near Cherbourg, on 2nd June. The station, operated by the German Signals Intelligence Service, was located near the invasion coast and it was important that it was destroyed before D-Day. Operating that night for the first time with 4 Group were twelve Halifax Mk. Vs of the newly formed No. 346 'Free French' Squadron. No. 346 (Guyenne) Squadron had formed at Elvington on 16th May 1944 under the command of Lt Col G. E. Venot and was the first of two 'Free French' bomber squadrons which were to serve within 4 Group. The other French squadron was No. 347 (Tunisie) which formed at Elvington later in June. Both units had French Officers and aircrew, many of whom had previously served in North Africa.

The attack on Ferme-d'Urvill proved disappointing, cloud frustrating 4 Group's efforts to destroy this important target. Of the twelve French crews from 346 Squadron detailed to attack the radio listening station, eleven were able to bomb the markers. Captain Baron in Halifax LL131 returned early with a faulty Gee set.

The following night 4 Group were out in force again this time sending 105 Halifaxes to attack the marshalling yards at Trappes, south-west of Paris, and a further sixty-three aircraft to raid coastal gun batteries in the Pas de Calais. The attack on the gun batteries was part of the D-Day deception plan. The raid on Trappes was carried out in clear, moonlit conditions and was to prove costly.

The German night fighters were able to take full advantage of the clear conditions and they ravaged the Halifaxes. Fifteen were shot down. No. 158 Squadron lost five crews; 76 and 640 lost three each. Flying Officer Doug Morison from Calgary, Alberta, was pilot of a Halifax Mk.III from 77 Squadron. Doug Morison had reason to recall the events of that night:

'Quite suddenly, as we approached the target area, but while still some distance away, the sky lit up and we could see the area ahead and below becoming increasingly bright as flares and marker-flares exploded into action.

'As we closed in on the target and began our bombing run, we could see aircraft above and below and on both sides of us. The cloud, smoke, flares and markers below us and the aircraft all around us presented a most impressive sight. A few verbal course commands over the intercom from our bomb-aimer, Flying Officer Jack Dye, and we heard the familiar "Bombs Away". We cleared the target and then made a turn to starboard to head for home. Suddenly the urgent voice of the rear-gunner, Scotty MacRitchie, shattered the steady drone of the engines, "corkscrew port!" I responded immediately as tracer laced overhead. We continued evasive action until Scotty gave instructions to level out. About two minutes later there was a blinding flash and an explosion; smoke, dust and pieces of aircraft flew in all directions. We began to corkscrew to port but soon realised it was too late for this fighter pass.

'A quick check revealed the port inner engine to be on fire and a large gaping hole in the side of the fuselage above the navigators table. Our flight engineer, Sandy Moodie, announced he was shutting down the port inner and activating the fire extinguisher button. The fire was soon out. I then initiated a crew check and all replied "okay" except bomb-aimer Jack Dye who reported that he had been hit. Jack was still lying in the bomb-aiming position, so navigator Tommy Melvin assisted him to the rest position aft of the wireless operators table. A short examination of Jack's injuries disclosed multiple shrapnel wounds to his legs and back from the cannon shell that had exploded over the top of him. Tommy stopped the bleeding and made Jack as comfortable as he could before returning to his navigator's position.

In the meantime I had adjusted course according to the magnetic compass since the gyro compass was acting up. A further check of the aircraft revealed that all the flight instruments had been knocked out and all our charts as well as the navigator's bag had been sucked out of the hole in the fuselage. By this time we had left the brightly lit target behind us and were feeling more comfortable with the darkness all around us as we continued on our northerly heading.

'After a period of time, perhaps thirty or forty minutes, the wounded bomb-aimer asked if we would move him up to the second pilots station which he normally occupied during take-offs and landings. He was moved into the seat beside me just as we emerged from under cloud cover. Above us we could see the stars shining clearly overhead. Jack asked what course we were on and I replied that we were flying due north by the magnetic compass. His quick reply was, "we are not flying north, we are going due east; look, the North Star is directly off our port wing!" Sure enough, we were heading straight for the heavily defended Ruhr Valley. A rapid calculation by Tommy Melvin based on an estimate of present course, time and speed indicated that we would need to alter course 120 degrees to port to reach England. This eventually turned out to be very accurate considering that he had no charts or instruments to work with.

'Eventually, after what seemed like an eternity, we crossed the coast line and before long saw the welcome shores of England. We knew we would need identification to enter England but our list of 'colours of the day' had been lost with the navigator's bag. We fired off several white signal flares as we crossed the coast hoping our fighters would identify our Halifax as friendly. We broke radio silence to request an emergency landing and received landing clearance. At least one fighter could be seen following us. Drem lights came on below us and we began a descent without any flight instruments to guide us.

'As we circled trying to judge our height, the runway lights came on, This helped and soon we lined up for a landing, not knowing

Flight Lieutenant Doug Morison (RCAF) and crew of 77 Squadron on completion of their first tour, 20th November 1944. Back row, left to right: Sgt Moodie, flight engineer; F/Lt Morison, pilot; F/Sgt Steward, bomb-aimer; F/O Smith (RCAF), navigator. Front row: F/Sgt MacRitchie (RCAF), rear gunner; F/Sgt Puchalski, mid-upper gunner; W/O Johnson (RCAF), wireless operator. *D. Morison*

our airspeed or height and flying on only three engines. Our first approach failed as we came in a bit too high and too fast. The next approach we got down okay just stopping as we reached the end of the runway. We later learned that we had landed at West Malling aerodrome – a fighter field with short runways.

'An ambulance rushed up to where we stopped to assist the injured. Jack Dye insisted on walking unaided to the ambulance, where he turned, saluted and was then whisked away. We never saw him again – he died two hours later, a gallant man who had saved our lives.'

Just after midnight at Full Sutton airfield, on 6th June 1944, and only minutes before the Halifaxes of 77 Squadron were about to start up, a staff car containing 'Top Brass' came round to each dispersal point and told each crew in turn that it was vital that their targets be destroyed; for today was 6th June, D-Day. Pilot Officer Horace Pearce was skipper of one of those crews charged with an important mission.

'Up to that time, it had been just another coastal battery to be bombed. We had flown similar trips for a few weeks now. We had suspected it was something of a special operation because, at main briefing, great emphasis had been placed on the fact that routes, turning points and heights had to be adhered to rigidly. In fact it was to be a very tight operation.'

Bomber Command had been tasked with the destruction of coastal batteries all along the invasion coast, only hours before the Allied Armies were due to land on the five

Normandy beaches. Over 1,000 bombers would drop nearly 5,000 tons of bombs in those first hours of D-Day, striking the first blows against the ramparts of Hitler's Atlantic Wall. No. 4 Group's targets were the gun batteries at Maisy – commanding the landing site of the US 1st Army, Utah Beach, and the battery at Mont Fleury, one mile inland from Gold Beach where elements of the British 2nd Army would be landing at 07.30 that morning.

As the first Halifaxes of No. 4 Group left their Yorkshire bases there was an early set back at Full Sutton as Pilot Officer Horace Pearce recalls:

'Take-off was marred by "C-Charlie", NA511, failing to get airborne, just after 01.00. When it reached the end of the runway after its take-off run it went straight on across a field and blew up. The rest of us were kept waiting for a possible change of runway but in the event we were sent off the same runway to fly over the burning aircraft with the fear of bombs exploding under us.'

The Halifax crew which had the dubious honour of being the first RAF casualties of D-Day, was that skippered by Flying Officer Stan Baldwin. They had left their dispersal at Full Sutton shortly before 01.00 and the D-Day trip was to be the crew's first operational mission.

Top: **Crew of Halifax Mk.III, MZ697 'L' of 77 Squadron, on a sunny 5th June 1944. Left to right seated: Sgt Archbold, engineer; F/Sgt Kendal, navigator; F/Sgt Morgan, wireless operator; P/O Pearce, pilot; F/Sgt Brooks, mid-upper gunner. Back row: F/Sgt Edwards, bomb aimer; Sgt Hancocks, rear gunner.** *H. V. Pearce*

Above and left: **Wreckage of NA511 'C-Charlie' of No.77 Squadron photographed in a field, half a mile from the end of the runway at Full Sutton. 'Charlie' suffered an engine failure on take off and was almost completely destroyed. Miraculously, Flying Officer Stan Baldwin's crew escaped with their lives, the worst injured being the bomb-aimer who lost an eye. These photographs were taken on 6th June 1944, some ten hours after the crash, and show parts of the fuselage, engines and bombs scattered over a wide area.** *A. Schofield and A. Porter*

Pilot Officer Art Porter, from Burnaby, British Columbia, was 'C-Charlies' navigator:

'Our starboard outer engine packed-up when we were about 100 feet up and seconds after leaving the runway. The pull on the port side swung us over until our starboard wing was pointing to the ground. The skipper had to cut the port outer and then made a beautiful job of bringing us in straight and level but we took out two hedges. By the time we stopped we were no longer an aircraft, just a pile of junk. Both wings broke off and all four engines were scattered over several fields. The fuselage had broken in two and was on fire in three or four places.

'Luckily we all escaped. Four of us: Bill Graham, wireless operator; Arthur Schofield, engineer; Arthur Inder, mid-upper gunner and myself were all in the crash position behind the main spar. The nose section had broken off in the crash so the four of us were able to jump out through the gaping hole where we joined the skipper who had managed to scramble out of the burning cockpit. Realising that there was only five of us I said to the skipper "Where's Dave?" Dave Lettington was our bomb-aimer and he had been sitting next to the pilot on take off. Poor Stan Baldwin couldn't tell me as he was still dazed having been badly knocked about in the crash. I then heard Bill Graham, our wireless operator, say "Where's Larry?" Larry Goodchild was our rear-gunner who we knew would be still in his turret somewhere in the wreckage. We then began a frantic search amongst the scattered sections of fuselage, many of which were still blazing furiously. We found Dave Lettington unconscious in the shattered nose section and soon after we were able to free Larry from his turret. Both had miraculously escaped serious injury.

'With all the burning fuel and bombs scattered about we knew pretty soon something was going to go off with an almighty bang so we made a quick exit from the scene towards a nearby ditch. We had gone about twenty feet when one of the bombs went off. I will never know whether we were knocked down by blast or whether we threw ourselves down. We could hear oxygen bottles and other stuff whacking into the ground around us. I yelled "cover your heads!" and each of us shoved heads under someone else's legs.'

Just before dawn on that historic morning as the Lancasters and Halifaxes approached the Normandy coast some of their crews were fortunate to catch a glimpse of the huge armada of Allied shipping that was closing on the invasion beaches. Otherwise thick cloud contrived to hide the approaches to the coast and the bombers' targets.

At the Mont Fleury coastal battery, Squadron Leader Watson – 'B' Flight Commander of 578 Squadron, had just dropped his bombs and was about to leave the target area when his Halifax, MZ513 'K-Katy', was struck by a bomb from another Halifax. Watson's flight engineer, Flight Sergeant Middleton, was in the astrodome at the time of the incident:

'Immediately after bombs-gone I noticed an aircraft above us release its bombs. At the time I calculated that the first bombs would pass our aircraft but suddenly there was a large explosion on the port side. The forward hatch was blown open and a fire developed almost immediately between the port engines. As the skipper turned for home the fire seemed to go out but after a short while it started up again.'

As the wireless operator, Flying Officer Onions, sent out a distress call Middleton went for his own and the pilot's parachutes. The Halifax, in the meantime, had come down to 9,000 feet and the port wing was trailing a banner of fire.

The situation now became critical as a fuel tank exploded in the port wing. Squadron Leader Watson immediately ordered the crew to "Get out quickly, I can't hold it

much longer", as he pulled the Halifax to starboard in an attempt to keep the flames from the burning wing away from the fuselage.

Flight Sergeant Middleton, after attempting unsuccessfully to fix up the pilot with his parachute, was ordered to bale out which he did at approximately 1,000 feet.

'It was very dark and I hit the sea almost immediately. There was a strong wind blowing and I was unable to detach my parachute. As a result I was dragged head first and then feet first through the water. It was three or four desperate minutes before I was able to release my harness. I was in the water for about twenty minutes before I saw a dark object which transpired to be a boat. I held up my lighted torch and yelled. Fortunately the boat's crew saw my light and threw me a lifebelt. I then became unconscious.'

Flight Sergeant Middleton was picked up by an American LCT and landed on the Normandy coast some hours later. Two other members of the crew of 'K-Katy': bomb-aimer Flying Officer Heffernan and wireless operator Flying Officer Onions, were rescued from the sea. The brave pilot and the rest of the crew were lost.

In the days following the invasion, Bomber Command concentrated on disrupting enemy communications behind the Normandy battle area. No. 4 Group Halifaxes took part in heavy attacks on railway centres and lines of communication over the next ten days. Targets at St Lô, Chateaudun, Juvisy, Alencon, Amiens and Douai all figured prominently in the destinations visited by the Group as Bomber Command attempted to block the flow of reinforcements to the beach head.

Right: **Crew of Halifax NA511 'C-Charlie' of 77 Squadron that had a remarkable escape when their aircraft crashed soon after take-off in the early hours of 'D'-Day. Left to right: P/O Art Porter (RCAF), navigator; P/O Dave Lettington, bomb-aimer; Sgt Larry Goodchild, rear gunner; Sgt Arthur Inder, mid-upper gunner, F/O Stan Baldwin, pilot; Sgt Bill Graham, wireless operator. Missing from this picture is the photographer, Sgt Arthur Schofield, flight engineer.** *A. Schofield*

Bottom, right: **Happy air and ground crew at Lissett, June 1944. Note unusual stripes on undercarriage legs.** *L. R. Harman*

Below: **Navigator and pilot. Flight Lieutenant Mitchell (left) and Flight Lieutenant Brookie-Hunter, 51 Squadron, Snaith 1944.** *via W. Baguley*

Juvisy Railway marshalling yards near Paris, before the Bomber Command attack of 7th June 1944.

Juvisy after the raid. All lines are cut and the whole area is severely cratered.

A Tactical Bomber Group

In the early morning of 13th June 1944 four strange aircraft were tracked flying at high speed above the sleeping countryside of Kent and Sussex. One by one they dived into the ground and exploded. The flying bomb offensive had begun.

Allied intelligence had known for some time that the Germans had been developing pilotless aircraft designed for attacks on Britain. Photographic reconnaissance of north-western France had revealed numerous launching sites under construction throughout the latter half of 1943 and in the early months of 1944. Attempts had been made to disrupt this activity by bombing the construction sites. These attacks were mainly carried out by medium bombers and fighter bombers of the RAF and US Army Air Force. The disruption caused by these attacks however, was only partially successful. Although many of the so-called 'Ski-sites' (named after the ski-shaped buildings that housed the flying bombs prior to launching) had to be abandoned, the Germans now developed a new system of launching site known as 'Modified Sites'. These were very difficult to detect as they were often hidden in orchards and farm yards and were very heavily camouflaged. In the spring of 1944 construction of the new sites went ahead in north-western France largely undetected by Allied intelligence.

When the new 'Modified' launching sites were finally discovered, in May 1944, the Allied air forces were fully committed to the preparations for the imminent *Overlord* operation. There was little chance at this late stage of diverting substantial numbers of aircraft to attack these new sites. Now with the opening of the flying bomb offensive the threat had become a reality.

The Allied air forces, within ten days of the invasion of Normandy, were forced to divert some of their energies to reducing the threat from the flying bombs. The heavy bombers of RAF Bomber Command and the US Eighth Air Force were now ordered to carry out attacks on the large number of launching sites and their associated supply depots in the Pas de Calais.

Opposite page: **Air and ground crew of LK830 'N-Nuts' of 578 Squadron pose in the warm June sunshine at Burn.** *E.Jarvis*

'V' Weapons Sites attacked by No.4 Group June - August 1944

Location	Target Type	Date of Attack
Domleger	V1 Supply Site	June 16, July 4
St Martin l'Hortier	V1 Supply Site	June 17, July 1, 4, 5, 6
Siracourt	V1 Launch Site	June 22
Oisemont Neuville au Bois	V1 Supply Site	June 23, July 1
Noyelles en Chausée	V1 Launch Site	June 24, Aug 1
Le Grand Rossignol	V1 Launch Site	June 24
Montorqueil	V1 Launch Site	June 25
Mont Candon	V1 Launch Site	June 27, July 17
Marquise Mimoyeques	V3 Launch Site	June 27, July 6
Wizernes	V2 Launch Site	June 28
Croixdalle	V1 Launch Site	July 6
Chateau Bernapre	V1 Launch Site	July 9
Les Catelliers	V1 Launch Site	July 9, 23
Ferme du Forestel	V1 Launch Site	July 12
Thiverney	V1 Launch Site	July 12
Les Hauts Buissons	V1 Launch Site	July 12, 23
Les Landes	V1 Launch Site	July 14, Aug 9
Nucort	V1 Launch Site	July 15
Bois de la Haie	V1 Launch Site	July 17, Aug 9
Acquet	V1 Launch Site	July 18
Ardouval	V1 Launch Site	July 20
Forêt du Croc	V1 Launch Site	July 25
Ferfay	V1 Launch Site	July 25, Aug 11
Forêt de Nieppe	V1 Launch Site & Storage Site	July 28, 29 Aug 2, 3, 5, 6, 11
L'Hey	V1 Launch Site	Aug 2
St Philibert Ferme	V1 Launch Site	Aug 8
Coqureaux	V1 Launch Site	Aug 9
Wemaers Cappel	V1 Launch Site	Aug 11
Watten	V2 Launch Site	Aug 25, 27
La Pourchinte	V1 Storage Site	Aug 31
Lumbres	V1 Storage Site	Aug 31

The offensive against the 'Noball' (V-Weapon sites) targets opened on the night of 16th June with attacks on four sites in the Pas de Calais area by 405 bombers. 4 Group were targetted on a flying bomb supply site at Domleger, north-east of Abbeville. Forty-eight Halifaxes from Nos. 10, 76, 78 and 346 Squadrons carried out a highly successful attack and the Domleger site was later abandoned.

That same night Halifaxes from Nos. 77, 102, 158, 466 and 640 Squadrons joined 147 Lancasters for an attack on the Fischer-Tropsch synthetic oil plant at Sterkrade in the Ruhr. On arrival at the target area crews were confronted by thick cloud and heavy flak as Pilot Officer Horace Pearce from No. 77 Squadron recalls:

'At the target there was 10/10ths cloud extending up to 16,000 feet. At first it was difficult to find an aiming point as only glows from the target indicators could be seen, deep in the cloud. However, on the bombing run, green TIs exploding at a higher level were identified and in conjunction with the glow in the clouds an attack was made from 20,000 feet. Heavy flak was intense above and below, but at 20,000 feet there was slightly less action.'

The action that Horace Pearce was referring to was a fierce battle for survival between bombers and night fighters. The enemy pilots found conditions ideal as they hunted for Halifaxes and Lancasters starkly silhouetted against the searchlight lit cloudbase. Thirty-one bombers were shot down that night, eleven from No. 4 Group. No. 77 Squadron lost six and No. 102 Squadron lost five Halifaxes.

In the afternoon of 22nd June, ninety-nine Halifaxes took-off for what was 4 Group's first daylight operation for over two and a half years. This was to be an attack on the huge concrete flying bomb shelter, under construction at Siracourt, in the Pas de Calais. Crews experienced great difficulty identifying the target through the broken cloud and many bombed on Gee fixes. Many Halifax crews reported seeing a Halifax hit by flak over the target and tumble in flames. This was LW116 of No. 466 (RAAF) Squadron with Squadron Leader McMullum and his all-Aussie crew aboard. Only four parachutes were seen. Later that night 4 Group sent 100 Halifaxes out in support of an attack on marshalling yards at Laon and Rheims.

At the end of June 1944, with the battle to enlarge the beachhead in Normandy in full swing, the squadrons of 4 Group entered into a hectic period of operations. Targets were changed at short notice and crews on occasions flew two sorties in one day. The battle against the flying bombs was stepped-up with attacks on launching sites and supply depots at night and during the day.

The daylight missions presented crews with unfamiliar problems and dangers as the constraints of flying in tight formation took their toll of pilots more familiar with flying in a stream at night. Bomb-aimer Flight Sergeant Arthur Smith, on his first operation with his 10 Squadron crew, recalls an incident which was witnessed by the whole of the Group as they prepared to bomb a flying bomb site on the morning of 25th June 1944:

'V' Weapon sites attacked by 4 Group
June - August 1944

Key:
- ■ Launch Site (V-1)
- + Supply Site
- ● Forward Storage Depot
- × Launch Site (V-2)
- ⊙ Long range Gun (V-3)

'It was a fine Sunday morning, the day of our first bombing operation. We were flying at 16,000 feet in a stream of 100 Halifaxes on the run up to the target, Montorqueil flying bomb site in the Pas de Calais. There had been a little heavy flak just below us when crossing the coast. At the turning point before the target, more flak at our height was avoided by turning in front of it. Now the sky was clear as we prepared to bomb, when suddenly our skipper exclaimed over the intercom, "Did you see that?" as a Halifax in front and slightly above us blew up like a giant firework, disintegrating into fragments of burning wreckage and a big ball of smoke through which we flew before completing the bombing run. We learnt later that this aircraft was hit by one of the bombs dropped from another aircraft above it.'*

The unfortunate victim that day over Montorqueil was a Halifax from 102 Squadron. It was struck in the starboard wing by a 500 lb bomb and immediately rolled over as the damaged wing was torn off. There followed a

violent explosion as the shattered fuel tanks ignited. This incident led to a reappraisal of daylight formation flying within No. 4 Group and as a result on future daylight attacks the Halifaxes were instructed to fly in loose vic formations to avoid the dangers of collisions and being hit by bombs.

No.4 Group Bomber Command, July 1944

Sqn	Equipment	Airfield
10	Halifax III	Melbourne
51	Halifax III	Snaith
76	Halifax III	Holme-on-Spalding Moor
77	Halifax III	Full Sutton
78	Halifax III	Breighton
102	Halifax III	Pocklington
158	Halifax III	Lissett
346	Halifax V/III	Elvington
347	Halifax V/III	Elvington
466 (RAAF)	Halifax III	Driffield
578	Halifax III	Burn
640	Halifax III	Leconfield

Despite the intensive bombing campaign against the flying bomb sites the deadly missiles continued to arrive over London. By 21st June 1,000 bombs had been fired at the capital and by the end of the month the number of those killed had risen to 1,769 persons. Damage, particularly south of the River Thames, was severe.

In addition to the flying bomb menace, the Germans were busy constructing vast underground concrete bunkers to launch other fiendish weapons at London. These included the A4 Rocket – the V-2, a twelve ton missile which could carry a one ton warhead 200 miles. Over 6,000 slave labourers from the occupied countries had been hard at work since late 1942 building the bunkers in northern France that would house the new weapon. Another secret weapon, potentially more lethal than the flying bombs or the A4 rockets, was the V-3, a multiple-charge long range gun capable of firing a continuous barrage of six inch calibre shells into London from its fifty smooth bore barrels.

No. 4 Group struck at two of the new secret weapon construction sites within two days at the end of June 1944. During the afternoon of 27th June 105 Halifaxes from the Group, supported by Pathfinder Mosquitos and Lancasters, attacked the vast V-3 long range gun bunker at Marquis Mimoyecques, between Calais and Boulogne. That night a further 104 Halifaxes bombed a flying bomb launch site at Mont Candon near Dieppe.

The following morning 103 Halifaxes from 4 Group bombed the V-2 rocket bunker at Wizernes, near St Omer. Here the Germans were constructing a one million ton concrete dome in a hillside overlooking a quarry. Safe under the protection of the reinforced concrete dome they would be able to assemble and launch their deadly rockets with impunity. Although the subsequent No. 4 Group bombing failed to make any impression on the concrete dome, the attack did succeed in seriously disrupting work on the site by destroying construction equipment and by severely cratering the whole area. It was left to Lancasters of No. 617 Squadron, led by Wing Commander Leonard Cheshire, to finally destroy the site a week later using their six ton 'Tallboy' bombs.

During the night following the attack on Wizernes over 200 Halifaxes from Nos. 4 and 6 Groups bombed rail yards at Blainville and Metz. These were to prove costly raids with twenty bombers lost. No. 4 Group lost eleven Halifaxes, 102 Squadron being particularly badly hit losing five crews out of twenty despatched. Flight Lieutenant Ned Fuery from Queensland, was pilot of LK832 'H' 'Honkytonk 6th', one of nineteen Halifaxes from 76 Squadron on their way to Blainville that night:

'We were flying at 8,000 feet some time before reaching the target. We had seen several bombers going down from fighter attacks so we were all keeping a sharp look-out for trouble. When it came we were surprised that it came from the moon lit side. Our rear gunner, Sergeant Jock Davidson, reported seeing an Me 109 closing from the port quarter. I ordered the flight engineer to keep a close watch on the dark side in case the attack from the light side was only a decoy (a not uncommon night fighter tactic). However, the Me 109 pressed home his attack. During my evasive corkscrew manoeuvre our two gunners were able to get a good concentration on the fighter and sent him down on fire. The action was later confirmed by another crew at de-briefing. We lost three crews that night on a target that was considered to be a 'piece of cake'. This was my crews 26th trip.'

Top: **Pilot Officer Joe Hitchman with his air and ground crew on completion of their tour, 158 Squadron, 22nd June 1944.** *J. Hitchman*

Two happy groups of airmen from 51 Squadron, 1944. *Centre:* **Flying Officer Duckworth with air and ground crew.** *Below:* **Flight Sergeant Longmore and crew.** *via W. Baguley*

209 FSN. 25-6-44 // 18000' ⟶ 125° 0929.
MONTORGUELL. M. 13, 500 GP. C. 34 SEC: S/LD WELCH W. 77.

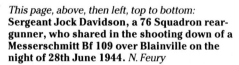

This page, above, then left, top to bottom:
Sergeant Jock Davidson, a 76 Squadron rear-gunner, who shared in the shooting down of a Messerschmitt Bf 109 over Blainville on the night of 28th June 1944. *N. Feury*

V-1 Flying Bomb sites proved difficult targets to bomb accurately, even in daylight. This is Montorgueil in the Pas de Calais under attack from 4 Group on 25th June 1944. *S. Pickles*

Goofy's Gift **- HX356 of 158 Squadron at Lissett, June 1944. Note the light colour of the forward undercarriage legs, possibly an aid to ground crews for marshalling aircraft into their respective dispersals.** *J. Hitchman*

On 22nd June 1944 the giant V-1 bunker at Siracourt was attacked by 4 Group Halifaxes. Conventional bombing of these huge concrete structures proved largely unsuccessful and it was left to 617 Squadron, led by Group Captain Leonard Cheshire, to destroy the bunkers using *Tallboy* **'earthquake' bombs.**

Opposite page; from the top:
A Halifax silhouetted over the Flying Bomb supply site at St Martin l'Hortier on 5/6th July 1944. *IWM, C4462*

The 'V-3' (multiple-charge long range gun) site at Marquise Mimoyecques comes under attack from 4 Group Halifaxes on 6th July 1944. At the right of the photograph is the village of Mimoyecques. Just in front of the nose of the Halifax is the loop line leading into the underground site directly from the Paris to Boulogne railway.

Crew hut at Full Sutton, 1944. Home for crews of 77 Squadron. *A. Porter*

V-weapon supply and launch sites dominated the target lists in the opening week of July 1944. Large forces of Lancasters and Halifaxes of RAF Bomber Command, together with B-17s and B-24s of the US Army Air Force, kept up a relentless bombardment in the launch areas both day and night. Sites at St Martin-l'Hortier, Oisemont, Domleger, Croixdalle and Marquise Mimoyecques were all attacked by Halifaxes during that week.

By the beginning of July the Allied armies were poised to break-out from their lodgement area in Normandy. There remained one obstacle to the planned drive to the Seine, the City of Caen. To the north of the city Montgomery's armies were seriously congested between the town of Caen and the coast. To relieve the pressure Montgomery decided to launch an assault on Caen from the north (Operation *Charnwood*) by three divisions numbering 115,000 men. *Charnwood* was to commence on the morning of 8th July and for the first time was to be preceded by a preparatory bombardment by nearly 500 heavy bombers of RAF Bomber Command. The bomber's targets were a series of fortified villages north of Caen. Because of fears of bombs falling short onto the forward British positions the bombers' aiming point was to be some 6,000 yards in front of the British front line. The target area was a rectangular box two and a half miles long by one mile deep and took in the northern outskirts of Caen. Unfortunately this target area failed to encompass the main German defensive positions. They were situated too close to the British forward positions to be neutralised by area bombing.

The attack took place in the late evening of 7th July, the ground assault itself was to take place at 04.20 hours the following morning. As the massive force of 467 bombers, including eighty-eight Halifaxes from No. 4 Group, swept in to strike at the northern edge of Caen, British troops were treated to the awe inspiring spectacle of an area bombing attack. However, although the bombing appeared to be highly concentrated – it seemed from the watchers in the British lines that no enemy troops could have survived the bombardment – the attack had in fact been largely unsuccessful. Few Germans had been killed in the bombing which had fallen in areas unoccupied by enemy troops. In fact the city of Caen came off worse, particularly the northern suburbs, which were reduced to rubble.

Meanwhile, a further attack east of Caen, again involving bombers in the tactical role, took place ten days later on 18th July. The attack, code-named *Goodwood*, called for a strong armoured 'left-hook' round Caen from the north-east. Along the left flank of the advance were heavily fortified villages which the Germans had linked into a system of strong points covering each other with defensive fire. On the right flank of the advance there were similarly fortified areas in the factory districts on the outskirts of Caen itself.

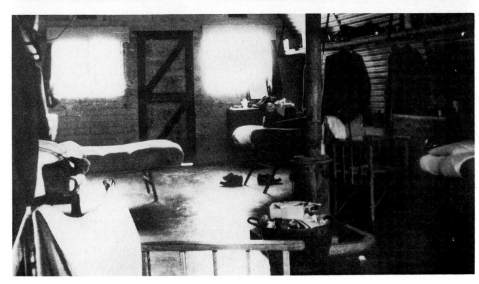

These areas were to be attacked by RAF Bomber Command on the morning of 18th July, shortly before the main ground assault.

At dawn on that morning the first of nearly 1,000 RAF bombers arrived over the villages of Colombelles, Sannerville, Demouville, Monderville and Cagny and commenced dropping the first of over 5,000 tons of bombs. Bomb-aimer Flight Sergeant Arthur Smith of No. 10 Squadron had taken-off with his crew in their Halifax from Melbourne at 04.15 that morning. Their aircraft was just one of over 200 Halifaxes from 4 Group that were taking part in the raid.

'While approaching the French coast many bombers passed us coming back from earlier attacks; we had never seen so many aircraft in the sky at one time. Further ahead the flashes from the guns of our own barrage could clearly be seen on the ground over a wide front. The bombing height of 10,000 feet was uncomfortably low and there was intense heavy flak all the way up to and over the target: we could see and hear it banging all around us. If exploding flak could be heard above the continuous roar of the four engines it was too near for safety.

'The action over the target had to be carefully directed by the Master Bomber to ensure the safety of our own troops and we could hear his calm instructions over the RT. I bombed on yellow TIs just visible through a mass of smoke and from my grandstand position in the nose saw one aircraft go down and another burning on the ground. On the way home we met yet more aircraft – American formations going out.'*

* From *Halifax Crew* by Arthur C. Smith, Carlton Publications: 1983.

Flight Lieutenant Harry Keenan – 'Paddy' to all who heard his Belfast accent – was known in 4 Group as 'The Flying Adjutant'. As Adjutant of No.10 Squadron at Melbourne, taking part in operations was not part of his duties, but such was his love of flying that he would often go as an unofficial extra crew member on operational missions. The crews at Melbourne decided that his enthusiasm ought to be commemorated in some way and so they had a brevet specially made for him in London – a half-wing, similar to an aircrew badge, but with the letters 'FA', (short for 'Flying Adjutant') embroidered in the middle. With much mock ceremony Flight Lieutenant Keenan is presented with his new insignia in the Summer of 1944. *M. Keenan*

Navigators' briefing room at Full Sutton 1944. *A. Schofield*

'Hot seat'. Flight Sergeant Ted Page, navigator with 76 Squadron, sits astride a 500lb bomb at Holme-on-Spalding Moor, July 1944. *N. Feury*

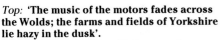

Top: 'The music of the motors fades across the Wolds; the farms and fields of Yorkshire lie hazy in the dusk'.
A 10 Squadron Halifax climbs away from Melbourne, past the gaunt silhouette of the old windmill at Seaton Ross. *A. Porter*

Above: The Full Sutton softball team (all Canadians), Summer 1944. *A. Porter*

Centre right: Halifax Mk.III HX323 *Charlie's Aunt* of No.10 Squadron at its dispersal at Melbourne, July 1944. *A. C. Smith*

Bottom right: Breighton ground crews pull on 'G' George's engine covers after carrying out a routine inspection. *L. Broadhurst*

Above: **A mass of craters surround the fortified village of Sannerville near Caen, after the Bomber Command raid of 18th July 1944. Over 5,000 tons were dropped on the German positions by a force of 942 aircraft, including over 200 Halifaxes from 4 Group.**

Top left: **Flight Lieutenant Horton's No.578 Squadron Halifax pictured over the rail yards at Hazebrouck, 6th August 1944. Note the target indicators bursting over the centre of the target.** *IWM, MH9936*

Centre: **A 78 Squadron Halifax Mk.III comes into land at Breighton after a daylight operation in the summer of 1944. No.78 received its first Mk.III's in January 1944. The absence of an H2S blister on this example suggests the work of the censor.** *G. Carver*

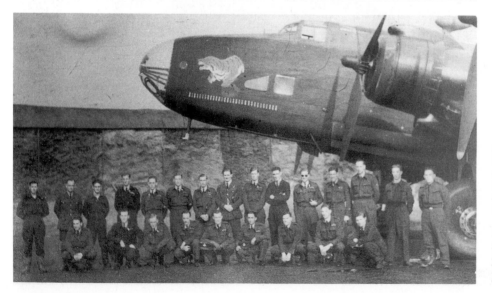

Bottom: **An unidentified Halifax with air and ground crews of 'C' Flight, 51 Squadron, at Snaith, 1944. The nose painting is that of a Tiger plus the mission tally displaying thirty-one operations.** *via W. Baguley*

On 9th August 1944, 147 Halifaxes from No.4 Group struck at a fuel storage dump hidden in the Forêt de Mormal. Flying Officer Rigby's bombing picture reveals numerous bomb bursts in and around the forest as the raid reaches its climax. *S. Pickles*

No.4 Group Halifaxes go in low to blast the marshalling yards at Somain, 11th August 1944. This bombing picture was taken at 8,000ft by Flight Lieutenant Walker in 'C' of 77 Squadron. The bomb load details are also included in the bottom of the photograph. *S. Pickles*

Yellow target indicators (TIs) burst over German troop positions in Normandy during the Bomber Command attack of 14th August 1944. Although the bombing proved to be generally accurate, some Canadian troops were killed when bombs fell in Allied positions . *S. Pickles*

On the 15th August 1944 over 1,000 aircraft of Bomber Command attacked nine night fighter airfields in Belguim and Holland. This is Eindhoven at the height of the attack, photographed from 14,800 feet, at 1208 hrs by Flight Sergeant Murrell in 'P' of 77 Squadron. *S. Pickles*

Above: WAAF's on parade!
Smart turn out of WAAF's at Snaith in August 1944. They are being inspected by Air Commandant Lady Welsh, AOC WAAF. The occasion was the presentation of the Bomber Command 'Sunderland Cup' to the WAAF's of Snaith. *via W. Baguley*

Below: A Halifax of 466 (RAAF) Squadron Halifax comes home to Driffield, summer 1944. A censor has removed the mid-under H2S radome from the original wartime photograph. *L. Charlesworth*

LL599 'E-Easy' of 462 Squadron (RAAF), overflying the Yorkshire countryside. A wartime censor has removed the mid-under gun blister. The underbelly gun positions were a popular addition to the Halifax's defensive capability. The flexible 0.5in Browning machine gun mounted in the perspex blister gave the Halifax a measure of protection from sneak attacks from below. When H2S radars became available the ventral guns were deleted, the space being occupied by the H2S scanner and its protective blister. *RAAF Official*

'Free French' officers at Elvington working out details of a forthcoming operation. Many of the original aircrew of the two Elvington based French Squadrons had previously served with the French Air Force in North Africa. *via W. Baguley*

At 07.45 hours British tanks of the 11th Armoured Division thundered forward, preceded by an intense artillery bombardment. They quickly took the German front line positions, defended by troops still stunned by the pounding inflicted by the RAF. Unfortunately, later in the day, the attack ran up against stiff opposition and began to falter. Heavy rain on the following day brought the attack to a standstill, and although Montgomery's forces had advanced five miles into the enemy's positions, they had failed to overrun them.

With the battle around Caen still raging, and much hard fighting still to come, Bomber Command continued its offensive against the V-weapons – an offensive that was now in its fourth week. In addition, oil plants and oil storage depots were attacked throughout July. On the night of 20th July, 152 Halifaxes from 4 Group, supported by thirteen Mosquitos and four Lancasters from the Pathfinders, bombed the Bottrop/Welheim synthetic oil refinery in the Ruhr. A successful attack, in which heavy damage was inflicted on the plant, was marred by the loss of nine Halifaxes – six of those lost were from 578 Squadron including two which collided with each other over Balkholme, Yorkshire, on return. The following day crews at Burn were mourning the loss of thirty-six of their comrades.

On the night of 23rd July, No. 4 Group was out in force attacking targets in Germany and France. Over a hundred of the Group's Halifaxes attacked flying bomb launch sites in north-western France whilst a similar number joined 629 Lancasters in a highly successful raid on Kiel. The following night Stuttgart suffered its worst raid of the war as 4 Group Halifaxes, together with a strong force of Lancasters, struck at the city for the first in a series of raids that would leave vast areas of the city devastated.

The hectic period of operations continued into August with the Halifaxes of 4 Group attacking V-weapon supply depots and launch sites before the Group once more

returned to a tactical role in support of Montgomery's armies. Once again the heavy bombers of the RAF were required to blast a path for the 21st Army Group this time as they drove down the road to Falaise. The raid was planned for the night of 7th August and would involve over 1,000 Lancasters and Halifaxes attacking five aiming points in direct support of a night attack by armoured forces. Unfortunately thick smoke and dust in the target area prevented nearly half the bombers from dropping their loads and the Master Bomber was left with no choice but to order most attacks to be cancelled.

On 9th August the whole of No. 4 Group were out in force again attacking a variety of targets in France. These included V-1 sites at Les Landes, Bois-de-la-Haie and Coquereaux in addition to a large fuel storage depot hidden in the Foret-de-Mormal. No. 466 (RAAF) Squadron were allocated the V-1 launch site at Coquereaux that day, despatching eighteen of their Halifax Mk.IIIs. Flight Sergeant Richard Shallcross, an Australian wireless operator with Pilot Officer Palmer's crew, recalls feeling uneasy about the briefed bombing height which required the Halifaxes to go in at between 8 and 10,000 feet:

'Just before take-off I remember talking to Flight Sergeant Pat Burrow who was skipper of the Halifax in the next bay to us, "X-Xray". I mentioned to him that I didn't like the idea of us bombing from below 10,000 feet in daylight where we would be vulnerable to the light flak. Pat replied jokingly, "Don't worry mate, just follow me in as we run up to the target and you'll be alright". Pat's confidence was infectious. He had already completed 21 ops and was skipper of the youngest crew on the Squadron.

'Over the target I sat next to the pilot and had a grandstand view of the attack. As we commenced our bombing run we came under fire from very accurate light flak. Suddenly, the Halifax immediately in front of us on our port bow, was hit in the starboard wing which burst into flames. As we crossed behind the blazing aircraft I saw it was "X-Xray", Pat Burrow's aircraft. By coincidence we had followed Pat onto the target. Flames quickly began to consume the starboard wing of Pat's Halifax and we knew that they were a gonner. Bravely, the pilot was able to maintain height long enough to enable five of his crew to escape. Unfortunately Pat Burrow and his flight engineer went down with their blazing Halifax and were killed. This incident had taken place at very close quarters and it brought home to me, at that early stage in my tour, what could be in store for me in the future. It also highlighted one of the many countless acts of devotion and self-sacrifice made by young pilots which went unrecognised and unrecorded.'

Railway targets occupied the squadrons of No. 4 Group on the 10th and 11th August. The railway junction and yards at Dijon were heavily damaged on the 10th whilst on the following day Somain marshalling yards were bombed from 8,000 feet.

The Allied armies were now closing in on the beleaguered German 7th Army trapped in the Falaise pocket and once more the heavy bombers were called in to assist Montgomery's forces. On 14th August over 800 RAF bombers were detailed to attack, in daylight, German strongpoints in preparation for Operation *Tractable*, an attempt by Canadian armour to break through the German lines at Falaise and link-up with the advancing American 3rd Army. No. 4 Group Halifaxes successfully bombed several strongpoints in the German front lines, some located within 2,000 yards of the forward Canadian positions.

The next day 1,000 heavies of RAF Bomber Command hit nine German night fighter airfields in Belgium and Holland. No. 4 Group sent over 200 Halifaxes to attack Tirlemont and Eindhoven and in clear visibility they left both airfields with their runways and dispersals severely cratered.

The port areas of both Keil and Brest were raided during August before a switch was made to oil targets with an attack on a synthetic oil plant at Sterkrade on the night of 18th August. 210 Halifaxes from No. 4 Group, supported by Pathfinders, carried out a highly successful raid. All the Halifaxes returned safely.

Pressure on the German oil industry continued with another raid on an oil plant by No. 4 Group on 27th August, this time in daylight. Such was the superiority of the Allied air forces in the summer of 1944, particularly in daylight, that they were able to mount an operation which, only a few months ago, would have been unthinkable. 216 Halifaxes of No. 4 Group, accompanied by fourteen Mosquitos and thirteen Lancasters of the Pathfinders, bombed the Rhein-preussen synthetic oil refinery at Homberg-Meerbeck.

They were escorted by nine squadrons of Spitfires fitted with long range fuel tanks. Cloud prevented a concentrated attack and there was intense flak over the target. Surprisingly the Luftwaffe failed to make an appearance and all the bombers returned safely. Included in the No. 4 Group force that day were ten Halifaxes of the newly formed No. 462 (RAAF) Squadron, taking part in their first operation to a German target. No. 462 had formed at Driffield only ten days before under the command of the first Australian CO, Wing Commander D. E. S. Shannon, DFC. The squadron had previously operated with Halifaxes in the Middle East from 1942 but had lost its identity in March 1944.

A crew from 466 (RAAF) Squadron in a Halifax of No. 462 (RAAF). Flying Officer 'Rusty' Williams borrows LL599 'E-Easy' for an air test on 26th August 1944. A censor has removed the mid-under gun blister from the original wartime print. This photograph was probably taken on the same day as that on the previous page. LL599 was lost on 23rd October 1944 when she was in collision with a Lancaster on return from Essen. *A. White*

Group Captain Forsyth, CO of 466 (RAAF) Squadron, gives his crews the 'thumbs-up' as they set off for another daylight raid from Driffield in 1944. *L. Charlesworth*

Chapter Sixteen

The Final Offensive

By September 1944 the Allied forces were impatient for the final defeat of Germany. The battle for Normandy had been won, Paris had been liberated and the German armies in the west had been thrown back in disarray towards the German border. In the east the Red Army's summer offensive had pushed the Germans back to the borders of East Prussia and in the process had annihilated sixty-seven German divisions.

In the air the Luftwaffe had lost control of its own airspace during daylight. Now with the overrunning of France a crippling blow had been struck at the Luftwaffe's night fighter organisation. At a stroke much of the enemy's early warning radar systems and forward bases were lost. Although German fighter production was now at its peak a serious shortage of fuel was already hampering operations. The months ahead would see the continuing decline of the Luftwaffe's fighting ability as the shortage of fuel became critical.

The scene was now set for the climax of the RAF's bomber offensive. In the words of the official history of the strategic air offensive, 'By far the greatest part of the strategic damage done by Bomber Command to Germany in the whole war was achieved in the last year of the conflict.'

By the late summer of 1944 No. 4 Group was at the peak of its strength. Now fully equipped with Halifax Mk.IIIs the Group's thirteen operational squadrons were able to despatch over 250 aircraft on a 'maximum effort' operation. In fact the month of August 1944 saw the Group achieve a record total of 3,620 sorties in twenty-two operations. Earlier, in the month of June, 4 Group air gunners had set a Bomber Command record by shooting down thirty-three enemy fighters.

Since March 1944 the Group had played a leading role in the offensive against the French railway system. With the coming of the invasion of France, 4 Group had operated in a semi-tactical role attacking communications, gun emplacements, troop concentrations etc, in support of the Allied armies. All these attacks had been carried out with pin-point accuracy. In addition, the offensive against the V-weapon sites had continued unrelented throughout the summer and was only terminated when the launch sites were overrun by advancing Allied troops in September. No. 4 Group's role in reducing the threat from the V-weapon sites was duly recognised in a note of appreciation from the Air Council received at Heslington Hall in September:

'To convey to you their warm appreciation of the part played by your Command in defeating the enemy's flying bomb attacks on this country. The continuous and heavy bombing of the experimental stations, production plants, launching sites, storage depots and communications which has been carried out by your Command not only imposed on the enemy a prolonged and unwelcome delay in the launching of his campaign but effectively limited the scale of effort which he was able to make. This notable achievement has added one more to the long list of successful operations carried out by Bomber Command.'

With their commitment to the support of *Overlord* having been fulfilled, RAF Bomber Command was now free to resume its strategic bombing campaign against Germany. With the coming of autumn a new directive was issued which stated Bomber Command's priorities for the forthcoming months. First priority would be attacks on the enemy's petroleum industry with special emphasis on petrol including storage. Second priority was the German rail and waterborne transportation systems.

Before the campaign against the German oil industry could get under way Bomber Command was called upon to attack the German garrison stubbornly holding out in the port of Le Havre. During the first week of September the heavy bombers hit the beleaguered port five times. Finally on 11th September the battered German garrison surrendered. The day before 245 Halifaxes from No. 4 Group took part in a massive daylight raid by nearly 1,000 bombers on eight different German strong points at Le Havre. On returning safely to Elvington Lieutenant Colonel Venot and crew, of No. 346 Squadron pulled into their dispersal. Unfortunately, as the bomb doors of their Halifax, NA585, were opened, a hung up 1,000 lb bomb dropped out and exploded killing six of the crew. Venot was seriously injured, for although being blown clear he was badly burned.

Daylight attacks on oil plants were now to be the main feature for the rest of September. In the late afternoon of the 11th, Halifaxes and Lancasters, escorted by fighters, bombed the Nordstern synthetic oil refinery at Gelsenkirchen. A murderous flak barrage greeted the 4 Group Halifaxes as they approached the target. Four of the bombers, two each from Nos. 578 and 51 Squadrons, were seen to go down in flames over the oil plant. One

exploded in mid-air after receiving a direct hit either from flak or 'friendly' bombs. Bombing results were difficult to assess as a smoke screen quickly enveloped the plant at the height of the attack, nevertheless, some crews reported seeing oil storage tanks burning and thick black smoke rising to 10,000 feet.

The following day 4 Group sent 119 Halifaxes out on another daylight, this time to the oil plant at Buer, whilst a further 106 were despatched to Münster. Flight Sergeant Arthur Smith, bomb-aimer with Flying Officer 'Wag' Winter's No. 10 Squadron crew, took part in the Münster attack, the Winter crew's nineteenth trip:*

'At the afternoon briefing, when the curtain was drawn back from the operations board, there was a murmur of consternation from the assembled crews; the target was Münster in northern Germany. A daylight penetration into Germany was a new experience to many of us and not a prospect we particularly relished in view of the possibility of attack by fighters. So far the Luftwaffe had left us alone in daylight over France, probably because we were usually well escorted by Spitfires and Mustangs.

'On approaching Münster, at a height of 18,000 feet, ominous black puffs of smoke were appearing in the sky ahead: the attack was under way. The heavy flak barrage now blossomed around us as we lined up on the target. Visibility was so good that with my eyes glued to the bomb sight graticule tracking up to the target, I only needed to give Wag a few directions on the intercom as I guided him on the final bombing run up to the target. "Right ... left, left ... steady ... steady ... steady ... Bombs Gone!" As I pressed the bomb release button held firmly in my right hand, the Halifax heaved gently upwards, relieved of its lethal burden. I could now take my eyes off the bomb sight to watch the results on the ground more closely where salvo after salvo of bombs sent mushrooms of smoke into the air. We were too high to follow the bombs all the way down, but the intense ground-rippling explosions of the cookies as they struck were clearly evident in the holocaust below. The only noise in our ears was the continuous background roar of the engines which blotted out all else except for speech through the intercom or flak when it was bursting very near.

'We were all still waiting tensely as Wag kept the aircraft on the same steady course for another half minute or so, in order that the

Above: **Shattered German positions in and around Le Havre, the result of heavy assaults by RAF Bomber Command during early September 1944. The Garrison surrendered on September 11th.**

Below: **Senior Officers of 78 Squadron, Summer 1944. Standing left to right: F/Lt Lane,** **Gunnery Leader; F/Lt Fudge, Navigation Leader; F/Lt Griffith, Adjutant; F/Lt Parsons, Bombing Leader; F/Lt Walker, Engineer Leader. Seated left to right: S/Ldr Hyland-Smith, OC 'B' Flight; S/Ldr Kentish, OC 'A' Flight; W/Cdr Markland, No.78 CO; S/Ldr Hurley (RCAF), OC 'C' Flight; S/Ldr Dowden, Station Navigation Officer.** *I. Easton*

automatic camera would give a correct pictorial record of our bombing accuracy. I watched two Halifaxes go down, one with its starboard inner engine on fire, whilst a main undercarriage wheel fell from another as it lost height. Then as we turned away to port, a loud bang shook our aircraft and we were losing height fast in a shallow dive as Wag lost control. A flak shell had apparently hit us aft. Smoke seemed to be coming from the starboard outer engine which Wag immediately closed down and feathered the prop. But then he noticed that there was no power from the starboard inner, and realising he had feathered the wrong engine, he quickly restarted the starboard outer and feathered the inner.

'The fire turned out to be the misty vapour of a fuel leak from one of the wing tanks.

There were one or two shouts of consternation over the intercom during our unexpected descent until Wag managed to level out at about 14,000 feet, and regaining his breath said, "OK everyone, calm down, everything is under control." He then asked the flight engineer to go aft to assess the damage and to see if the rear-gunner was alright as he did not answer over the intercom. The engineer did not get very far, however, he quickly came back to say that the rear of the aircraft was full of smoke and that there was a "bleeding great hole" in the bottom of the fuselage where the H2S blister should have been.

'The rear-gunner was safe, in fact none of us were scratched, but a quick check on the damage revealed that most of the H2S fairing and part of the equipment had been blown off.

The fuselage was heavily peppered with holes, the starboard aileron was u/s, the hydraulics and electrics had partly failed (rendering the gun turrets inoperative except by hand) there was a steady leak from one of the starboard wing fuel tanks, the intercom aft was not working and we were flying only on three engines.

'Our Halifax was unable to keep up with the main stream of returning bombers and gradually lost height as Wag nursed her back over Germany. It was a clear sunlit sky which enabled me to assist the navigator by map reading from the nose. We felt very vulnerable to attack from any prowling fighters for which our gunners were keeping their eyes skinned, but apparently one partly crippled Halifax was not worth their attention. So preoccupied were we with our own troubles that it was some time before we noticed that two Halifaxes seeing our plight had dropped back to keep station with us. At the risk of their own safety, they escorted us until near the Dutch coast which we certainly appreciated.

'The flight engineer had carried out some calculations and manipulations of the fuel cocks, at the same time advising Wag how best to operate the engines in order to economise the fuel which was continually leaking away in a misty trail behind us. In view of the shortage of fuel and condition of the aircraft, it was decided that as we might have difficulty in reaching Melbourne, it would be prudent to land at the emergency landing ground at Woodbridge. The wireless operator was unable to obtain any response from the station on his RT which had also been damaged, so we made a guess at landing direction. The undercarriage had to be pumped down by hand because of the loss of hydraulics. On our first try at landing, the aircraft being difficult to control, Wag could not get properly lined up, so he took us round again. This second time had to be right because the damaged Halifax would not safely make another overshoot on three engines. I was sitting beside Wag, as was usual for landing, to call out the decreasing airspeed and to assist with the throttles if necessary. As we were about to touch down on the left hand side of the runway, I noticed a Lancaster coming towards us from the opposite end on the other side – one of us was landing in the wrong direction! I did not dare say anything over the intercom for fear of causing a minor panic at such a crucial moment, so directly the wheels touched, I gently nudged Wag and pointed frantically at the fast approaching Lanc. Wag calmly nodded and kept the Halifax going straight ahead as it lost speed. I held my breath and hoped that the Lanc would also keep straight on the other side. As the two aircraft drew level the Lanc appeared to burst a tyre and nearly ground looped into us. This was our second lucky escape of the day. We heard later that the bomb-aimer had been landing this Lancaster for his dead skipper.'*

A Halifax over Wanne-Eickel oil refinery. During the late Autumn of 1944, Bomber Command began to concentrate much of its effort on German oil targets. *RCAF*

Attacks by No.4 Group on German Oil Plants and Refineries, June 1944 - April 1945.

Location	Target Type	Date of Attack
Sterkrade	Ruhrchemie Holten	June 16, Aug 18,
	Ruhr Benzin AG	Oct 6, Nov 21,
		Feb 4
Bottrop	Ruhröl AG Welheim	July 20, Sept 30
Wanne Eickel	Krupp	
	Treibstoffwerke AG	July 20, Feb 2, 9
Homberg M'beck	Rheinpreussen AG	Aug 27
Gelsenkirchen	Gelsenkirchener	Sept 11, 13,
	Bergwerke AG	Oct 6, Nov 6
	Nordstern	Jan 22
Buer	Hydrierwerke	
	Scholven AG	Sept 12, Oct 6
Ludwigshafen	IG Farbenindustrie	Jan 2
Dulmen	Lufwaffe fuel	
	storage depot	Jan 14
Bohlen	Braunkohle-	
	Benzin AG	Feb 13
Reisholz	Rhenania Ossag	
	Minerölwerke AG	Feb 20
Kamen	Chemishewerke	
	Essener Steinkohle AG	Feb 24, March 3
Heide	Deutsch Erdöl AG	
	Hemmingstedt	March 7
Bottrop	Matthias Stinnes	
	Stinnessche Zechen	March 15
Harburg	Rhenania Ossag	
	Minerölwerke AG	April 4

Another daylight attack followed on the 13th, again it was a further visit to the oil plant at Nordstern. 102 Halifaxes from No. 4 Group bombed the plant through a thick and very effective smoke screen. Crews were unable to see the markers owing to the haze and the Master Bomber's instructions to 'Bomb reds, overshoot reds, undershoot reds' etc, understandably caused confusion. Over the target there was intense flak and many aircraft received some form of shrapnel damage. Flight Lieutenant Henderson, pilot of a Halifax from 10 Squadron, remembers how his flight engineer had a narrow escape as their aircraft dodged predicted flak:

'After leaving the target we came down a few thousand feet and as there were many aircraft around I asked the engineer to watch above us. This he did by going into the astrodome. Suddenly, predicted flak started on the port side behind us and the rear gunner gave the order to dive starboard which I did immediately. At that moment a shell exploded directly above the cockpit and blew all the perspex away behind me. I had visions of a decapitated engineer but luckily for him he had stepped down from his position in the astrodome when I dived away from the flak. He was hit by flying perspex but was not seriously injured.'

By the third week of September 1944 the advance of the Allied forces was being impeded by a lack of supplies, particularly petrol, caused by the delay in clearing suitable harbour facilities. The British 2nd Army, having advanced into Holland in support of the abortive Arnhem operation, was desperately short of motor transport fuel. A request was made to HQ Bomber Command for help and it was decided to use Halifaxes to transport the much needed petrol into Belgium. The late Air Chief Marshal 'Gus' Walker was then commander of No. 42 Base which included the stations at Pocklington, Elvington and Melbourne:

F/Lt Doug Morison (RCAF) at the controls of Halifax Mk.III MZ359 'G' of 77 Sqdn, September 1944. In the background is the 6 Group airfield of Tholthorpe, home to the Canadians of 420 and 425 Squadrons. Below the Halifax is Derrings Farm. *Courtesy of Aero Modeller*

A view into the nose compartment of a 462 (RAAF) Squadron Halifax. Prominent in the centre of the picture are the propeller speed control levers, with the supercharger control immediately below. Just discernable in the nose is the Mk.XIV bombsight. *R. V. Jubb*

'I received a telephone call from the duty officer at No. 4 Group HQ relaying the Bomber Command HQ message that the 2nd Army had run out of fuel and that we were to supply them with petrol as soon as possible. I asked what method was to be used and received the reply, 'That's your problem.' I quickly convened a meeting of Station Commanders and operations staff whereupon we decided the only solution was to contact the US Army Air Force to ask for a very large supply of Jerry-cans. Within four hours of my request lorry loads of cans arrived at Pocklington. We packed the fuselages of seventy Halifaxes, drawn from Nos. 77, 102, 346 and 347 Squadrons, with Jerry-cans, tightly strapped of course but all rules regarding the carriage of fuel in aircraft went by the board.

'The Group instruction was that Brussels-Melsbroek airfield was to be used as our destination. I flew out to Melsbroek to make the necessary arrangements. We flew seventy-two sorties per day for a period of eight days from 25th September to 2nd October. In all, 582 sorties were flown (of which I flew four) and 432,840 gallons of fuel were delivered without mishap. We later received a letter of appreciation from Air Marshal Coningham, AOC, 2nd Tactical Air Force.

Flight Sergeant Dai Pugh, of No. 102 Squadron, was one of the Halifax pilots who flew the petrol missions:

'I took part in the transport work of which the Squadron flew 179 return trips and delivered 134,250 gallons. Our route to Belgium took us down the east coast of England, across the Channel and Belgium where we landed gratefully at Melsbroek on the one serviceable runway, the others being cratered. I say gratefully, because the Luftwaffe airfields were only about fifty miles away, and considering that the Halifax fuselage was packed with Jerry-cans of petrol, one cannon shell from a fighter would have meant "instant cremation" for us. The airfield at Melsbroek was a shambles with damaged enemy aircraft scattered around the perimeter.'

With the coming of October, Bomber Command concentrated its efforts in the Ruhr. In a major attack in daylight on 6th October, 240 Halifaxes of No. 4 Group struck at the twin synthetic oil plants at Buer Scholvern and Sterkrade Holten. With a strong top cover of Spitfires the Halifaxes carried out a highly concentrated attack which left both plants with serious damage and oil production disrupted. Seven Halifaxes were shot down by flak.

The following day 238 Halifaxes from 4 Group bombed the German town of Kleve, on the Dutch German border. Kleve was situated on the right flank of the advancing 21st Army Group and therefore posed a threat to the exposed Allied units. Another highly concentrated attack by the bombers left a large portion of the town in ruins.

It was back to a night attack on 9th October for a visit to the Ruhr town of Bochum. 375 Halifaxes, half that number from 4 Group, supported by Pathfinders carried out a scattered attack on the centre of the town. 1,453 tons of bombs were dropped mainly on the southern districts, cloud being responsible for the scattered bombing. No. 462 (RAAF) Squadron suffered their first losses since reforming when Flying Officers Black and Coleman and their crews failed to return.

As a result of a directive, received at Bomber Command HQ on 13th October 1944, Operations *Hurricane I* and *Hurricane II* were carried out on 14th and 15th of October. The object of Operation *Hurricane* was to 'concentrate bombing effort on the vital areas of the Ruhr' and 'to demonstrate to the enemy in Germany generally the overwhelming superiority of the Allied Air Forces in this theatre.'† The demonstration of Allied air power came quickly with a massive daylight raid by Bomber Command on Duisburg on the 14th. Over 1,000 heavy bombers, including 474 Halifaxes, took part in the largest daylight raid so far by the RAF. That same night Duisburg's agony was continued by another 1,000 RAF bombers delivering a record 4,547 tons on the battered city. Squadron Leader Lane of 578 Squadron, reported that 'the whole area of the city was covered by fire and there was two particularly large explosions seen in the dock area.' Sergeant Lewis of 158 Squadron remembers:

'Whole streets were burning like a gigantic mesh. Everything glowed red and yellow and what remained was being systematically stoked by more sticks of high explosives and incendiaries.' The glow from the fires could be seen long after the bombers left the target area, even as far as 200 miles away.

Duisburg's defences, although formidable, appeared to have been overwhelmed by the sheer weight of the double blow. Only twenty-one bombers were lost in the two attacks,

Flight Sergeant Robert Jubb (RAAF) 2nd left back row, with his air and ground crew in front of their Halifax Mk. III 'R-Robert' of 462 (RAAF) Squadron, Driffield, October 1944. Flight Sergeant Jubb and crew were shot down on 2nd November 1944 during a raid on Düsseldorf - their 33rd trip. Six of the crew were made PoWs but Jubb was able to reach the Allied lines. Note mid-under gun position on 'R-Robert', a common fitting on No. 462 Halifaxes at this period. *R. V. Jubb*

Air Commodore 'Gus' Walker in his office at Pocklington. *IWM, CH9326*

mostly falling victim to flak. No. 4 Group lost just one Halifax, an aircraft from 462 (RAAF) Squadron that fell during the night attack. Another crew from 462 had a narrow escape that night. Pilot Officer Cockerill's Halifax was coned by searchlights and badly shot-up by flak as he commenced his bombing run. A nearby burst sent whirling shrapnel fragments smashing into the cockpit wounding Cockerill in his left eye and temporarily knocking him unconscious. The Halifax immediately lost height and for a few anxious moments was out of control. Fortunately the pilot recovered and regained control in time to complete his bombing run. Almost half blind and weak from loss of blood Cockerill bravely remained at the controls and brought his Halifax back to make an emergency landing at Manston. During the final approach to the airfield Cockerill had to rely on another member of the crew to shout out readings from the instruments as he was virtually blind at this stage. Pilot Officer A. J. Cockerill was awarded an immediate DSO.

On the night of 15/16th October, 132 Halifaxes from No. 4 Group took part in a heavy main force strike at Wilhelmshaven. In all 506 heavy bombers took part in the raid, the last major attack on the port. Despite poor visibility, severe damage was caused throughout Wilhelmshaven, particularly in the business and residential areas north of the Bauhafen. Scattered damage also occurred in the dock area, especially in the shipyards. Two Halifaxes from the Group failed to return.

Towards the end of October it was the turn of Essen to receive a demonstration of the destructive power of RAF Bomber Command. On the night of the 23rd 4,538 tons of bombs were dropped by a force of 1,055 Halifaxes and Lancasters. In a further dose 3,684 tons were dropped on the long suffering city, this time in daylight on the afternoon of the 25th. The attacks left widespread damage throughout Essen. The vital Krupps works was badly hit, with over 200 buildings damaged or destroyed. From this date Essen ceased to be the leading centre of German war production.

A double strike at Cologne, on the nights of 30th and 31st October, caused further severe damage to the already battered Rhineland city. No. 4 Group Halifaxes flew almost 400 sorties against Cologne without loss. Many crews reported sightings of 'jet' aircraft during both raids.

There were more reported sightings of jets two nights later when nearly 1,000 Lancasters, Halifaxes and Mosquitos attacked Düsseldorf. Sergeant Joe Premble, a rear gunner with Flight Lieutenant Robinson's 158 Squadron crew, claimed to have shot down two 'jet propelled' fighters that night. Sergeant Premble's claim was supported by his mid-upper gunner, Sergeant Jock Ralph. A Halifax from 462 (RAAF) Squadron came under attack soon after leaving the target. Skipper of the Halifax was Flight Sergeant Robert Jubb from Queensland:

'Our usual aircraft "Z5-R" had been damaged on a previous trip so on this occasion we were flying in the replacement aircraft "Z5-U". Turning off the target at about 16,000 feet we were suddenly hit from below by fire from a Me 262 jet fighter. Our port engines and wing caught fire and our aircraft became uncontrollable. Fortunately, all of the crew managed to get out of the aircraft and were subsequently rounded-up by the Germans. I landed to the south-west of Düsseldorf, and after stealing a brown workers jacket from a washing line, I managed to avoid detection and was able to reach the Allied lines near Aachen.'

It has not been possible to confirm that jet aircraft were operating over Düsseldorf that dark November night in 1944. Certainly the claims of sightings and the reported shooting down of two jets by Sergeant Premble, and another by a rear-gunner from No. 76 Squadron, all seem to indicate that some form of jet-propelled aircraft were operating with the night fighters that night. What is certain is that the night fighter defences were still potent as the loss of eleven Halifaxes and eight Lancasters confirmed. It is possible that a small number of Messerschmitt Me 262 jet fighters, at this time operating in daylight against USAAF bomber formations, did part in unofficial nocturnal operations against RAF Bomber Command. It was not until early 1945, however, that a night fighter version of the Luftwaffe's revolutionary new aircraft would be introduced.

More sightings of jets and claims by Halifax gunners for the destruction of three, possibly four 'jets' were reported on the night of 4th November when aircraft from Nos. 1, 4, 6 and 8 Groups bombed Bochum. Earlier at Burn, home of No. 578 Squadron, twenty-three heavily laden Halifaxes had trundled around the narrow perimeter track to the start point only to find that hazardous crosswinds were making take offs too dangerous and the raid was cancelled. However, 705 Lancasters, Halifaxes and Mosquitos reached Bochum and dropped 3,332 tons of high explosive and incendiaries causing severe damage to the centre of the town. The bombers were met by a far from passive defence network as they ran into the target as Sergeant Arthur Smith from No. 10 Squadron recalls:*

Sergeant Joe Pemble, rear gunner with Flight Lieutenant Jack Robinson's 158 Squadron crew, claimed two 'jet fighters' shot down (confirmed by Sergeant Jock Ralph the mid-upper gunner) whilst on a raid to Düsseldorf, 2nd November 1944. Sgt Pemble's victims were more likely twin piston-engined night fighters as jets did not become operational as night fighters until near the end of the war. *A. J. Ralph*

Halifax Mk.III, MZ296 'L' of No.462 (RAAF) Squadron takes off from Driffield for a daylight attack on the Ruhr. MZ296 was the only casualty to No.4 Group during the massive night attack against Duisburg on the night of 14/15th October 1944. *RAAF Official*

No.466 (RAAF) Squadron, Driffield, 1944.
A. White

'Considerable searchlights on the run-up in cones of five to seven and singly. Barrage flak mostly below. Slight cloud haze over the target. Saw several kites go down burning and hit the ground with explosions. Something blew up in mid-air over the target dropping bags of green, red and white lights, may have been a scarecrow. Saw cookies exploding in nice concentration among red and green markers. The duration of the actual bombing in these mass raids was remarkably short, varying from about a quarter of an hour for 200 or 300 bombers, up to half an hour when a thousand or more were involved. Each individual bomber however, would be in the target area for no more than perhaps five or six minutes, except for the Pathfinders and anyone unlucky enough to have to go round again after doing a dummy run. The aim was to deliver a very large tonnage of bombs in as short a time as possible, thus causing maximum destruction and at the same time swamping the flak defences.'

At the same time as Sergeant Smith's Halifax was negotiating Bochum's defences, Flight Lieutenant Joe Herman and crew, in Halifax LV936 'D' of 466 (RAAF) Squadron, were losing height after successfully bombing the target. Suddenly, Herman's Halifax was bracketed by shell bursts and hit several times causing both port and starboard fuel tanks to burst into flames. Joe Herman knew that if he and his fellow crew members did not act quickly they would all be killed so he shouted 'Bale out! Bale out!' As the rest of the crew hurriedly left the doomed Halifax Joe Herman bravely remained at the controls desperately holding on to what little control was left so that his comrades could escape.

There was now not much time left for the pilot if he was to escape himself. He unfastened his Sutton harness, grabbed the handle in the roof and lifted himself out of his seat.

As he bent down to pick up his parachute pack he saw the starboard wing tear off and almost immediately the Halifax went into a spin. As Joe desperately tried to steady himself in the violently spinning cockpit there came a blinding orange flash as the aircraft exploded. The roof disappeared and he found himself falling through space, minus his parachute and surrounded by a shower of burning debris. Falling some 12,000 feet, Herman suddenly collided with something solid and managed to grasp hold of it. Astonishingly Joe Herman had collided with the legs of his mid-upper gunner, fellow Aussie Sergeant John Vivash. The two had collided with each other at the moment when Vivash's parachute had just opened. With Joe Herman locked onto his gunner's legs the two airmen drifted to earth.

Amazingly, although both men were injured, they survived the inevitable heavy landing only to be captured shortly after by German troops. Flight Lieutenant Joe Herman's remarkable death defying escape remains one of the most bizarre stories of the Second World War.

Others were not so lucky that night over Bochum. Twenty-eight bombers were shot down, twenty-three of them Halifaxes. No. 346 Squadron suffered its worst losses of the war when five of the Squadron's Halifaxes failed to return.

A daylight attack on the Nordstern synthetic oil plant at Gelsenkirchen on the 6th and a massive raid by over 1,000 bombers, in support of an advance by US forces between Aachen and the Rhine, on the 16th were the main features of the first half of November 1944. Both raids were successfully carried out without any losses to No. 4 Group. Despite bad weather at the end of the month, which kept the squadrons of the Group firmly on the ground for almost a week, successful night attacks were carried out against the Ruhr towns of Essen – on 28/29th, and Duisburg on the 30th.

December 1944 opened with heavy raids on communications centres at Hagen, Soest and Osnabrück. At this stage of the war a number of veteran Halifaxes, having survived the fierce battles of the spring and summer, were now approaching their 100th operations. One such aircraft was LV937 'E' *Expensive Babe* of 51 Squadron. An ex-578 Squadron aircraft that had been taken on charge in March 1944, *Expensive Babe* had its '100th' bomb painted on it's nose after successfully returning from the Osnabrück attack on 6th December.

Meanwhile, heavy snow falls and foggy conditions set in during mid-December. The Germans, taking full advantage of the bad weather, launched their offensive in the Ardennes. The German plan, to split the Allied armies in two and capture Antwerp, started well and for a time there was considerable confusion amongst the Allied forward positions. However, the Germans gambled on the weather remaining poor but after a few days conditions improved, and Allied aircraft were able to seriously disrupt the progress of the offensive. This, and a serious lack of fuel, caused the German attack to grind to a halt. At the same time Allied heavy bombers carried out attacks on marshalling yards serving the enemy offensive. No. 4 Group Halifaxes took part in heavy raids on communications targets at Duisburg, Cologne and Bingen at the end of December, causing severe damage and disruption.

On Christmas Eve 338 aircraft from Nos. 4, 6 and 8 Groups attacked the airfields at Lohausen and Mülheim. No. 4 Group were targetted on Mülheim airfield near Essen. The Halifax crews soon discovered that there was to be no 'Christmas Spirit' from the enemy's defences. As they ran into the target the Halifaxes were subjected to a murderous barrage of flak. Sergeant Joe Elvins, flight engineer with Flight Sergeant Sandman's 77 Squadron crew, recalls the events of that Christmas Eve afternoon:

'Over the target we encountered very heavy flak but we were able to get our bombs onto the airfield which appeared to be getting a real pasting. Shortly after leaving the target area a shell burst directly under our port wing setting fire to the port inner engine and showering that side of the fuselage with shrapnel. Fortunately we were able to extinguish the flames in the engine but were unable to feather the propeller which continued 'windmilling.'

'A quick check of the crew revealed that the wireless operator, Sergeant Pat Patterson, was injured. The skipper sent me below to check with Pat. I found him still at his table but in a great deal of pain. He pointed to the back of his right thigh from which protruded a bloody mess. I cut away his trousers but could not determine at the time whether it was bone or a piece of shell fragment that was sticking out from his thigh. Fortunately it was found later to be the latter although the piece of shrapnel had shattered his thigh bone. I dressed his wounds as best I could and gave him an injection of Morphine and, as per the standard drill, marked his forehead with the letter 'M'.

'Back in the cockpit I found the skipper struggling to maintain height and stay on course for home. It was obvious that we would never reach Full Sutton on three engines and having lost much of our fuel we decided to make for Woodbridge emergency 'drome. All the way back I juggled with the controls of the remaining engines to obtain as much power from them as possible. Even so we continued to lose height but fortunately we were able to reach Woodbridge and land safely despite a worsening vibration from the port wing that threatened to tear the wing off.'

Another Halifax crew member with memories of the Mülheim raid is Sergeant Richard Shallcross, an Australian wireless operator with 466 (RAAF) Squadron:

'Whilst on a number of occasions aircraft in which I flew were damaged by flak, this particular raid had an impact which will remain with me forever. Our Halifax ran into heavy radar predicted flak just prior to and on the bombing run. A number of things remain vividly in my memory as I recall the tremendous buffeting of the aircraft as shells burst in close proximity. The huge black shell bursts with their angry red centres. The overpowering stench of cordite. The crashing noise of the shell bursts above the steady drone of our engines. The feeling of helplessness and resignation to death. The feeling of anger and resentment towards the higher command for sending us on a raid on Christmas Eve.

'Our aircraft was holed about fifty times, mostly in the forward section. By a miracle nobody was hit but there was one or two near misses, the closest being the navigator who had a six inch diameter hole blown through his table by a piece of shrapnel. Fortunately the navigator was only shaken but all his maps and instruments were destroyed.'

Halifax Mk.III MZ335 'A', of 77 Squadron at Full Sutton late in 1944. *Real Photographs*

Essen-Mulheim airfield was heavily bombed on Christmas Eve 1944 by 338 aircraft of Nos. 4, 6, and 8 Groups. This view taken in 1945 shows the airfield rendered useless by numerous bomb craters. *S. R. Cook*

Flight Lieutenant Bob Pont of 77 Squadron with his air and ground crew, at Full Sutton, winter 1944. *S. R. Cook*

On Boxing Day afternoon another heavy daylight raid took place, this time on the enemy's communications bottleneck at the Belgian town of St. Vith. Flight Sergeant Arthur Smith, of 10 Squadron, took part in the raid:*

'It was to be an afternoon daylight raid on the little rail town of St. Vith which the Germans had recaptured in their last fling Ardennes winter offensive. Only three aircraft were detailed from 10 Squadron to join the force of several hundred Lancasters and Halifaxes. Our bomb load of eight 250 pounders, three 1,000 and a single 2,000 pounder was lower than usual, so was our allocated bombing height of 14,000 feet. Due to a minor technical fault we took off late but caught up with the main force by cutting off a large corner of the planned route over France. The visibility was so good that from my position in the nose I could clearly see woodlands and railway lines from several directions winding into the large junction in the town, all silhouetted against the snow-covered ground. There was flak on the way into the target when I saw two aircraft going down, one of which was on fire, but only one parachute opened out. We bombed in the middle of a bunch of Lancasters and it was the best concentration of bomb bursts I had ever witnessed, a mass of belching smoke completely obscuring the town.'

The unfortunate Halifax seen to go down over St. Vith that Boxing Day afternoon was that of Flying Officer Woolf (RCAF) and crew of No. 76 Squadron. Woolf's Halifax, MZ740 'R-Robert', received a direct hit in the nose after passing through a heavy barrage of flak. The mid-upper gunner, another Canadian, Flight Sergeant Mason, was the only member of Woolf's crew to escape from the noseless Halifax as it tumbled earthwards.

During a raid on the Kalk-Nord marshalling yards at Cologne on the night of 30/31st December, a Halifax from 640 Squadron had a narrow escape. Pilot of the Halifax was Walter Boyes, from Victoria, British Columbia:

'We had just settled onto our bombing run when we had a really hairy experience. Another Halifax, which I identified by its tail markings as having come from 158 Squadron at Lissett, appeared from nowhere out of the darkness and cut in front of us from our starboard quarter. Just in time I pulled up the nose of our aircraft and he scraped underneath us. I felt a slight juddering and a lifting of the aircraft as we collided.

'We made another circuit of the target and assessed the damage. We had lost our bomb doors and one fin and rudder were wrecked but otherwise we were still in one piece. Still shaking from our narrow escape I decided to have another go at dropping our bombs. Unfortunately on the second run all our bombs failed to come away and it took another circuit of the target area before we were able to release some of the bombs manually. It was a very shaky crew that returned to Leconfield that night.'

The new year of 1945 brought with it the promise of certain victory over Nazism. Hitler had played his last card and lost. His offensive in the Ardennes was spent and his exhausted armies had withdrawn behind the last barrier in the west – the Rhine. In the east the Red Army was poised to commence its fourth winter offensive that would eventually carry the Russians to the very gates of Berlin.

Meanwhile, the heavy bombers of RAF Bomber Command, whilst still committed to the official policy of attacking oil and communications targets, were still being sent on area bombing attacks of German cities. At the end of 1944 No. 4 Group had said farewell to one of its two Australian squadrons, when 462 left to join No. 100 Group on special radio countermeasures and bomber support duties. No. 462 (RAAF) Squadron's first operation with 100 Group was on the night of 1st January 1945 when its Halifaxes flew 'window' and bomb dropping sorties in support of the main force. That same night 105 Halifaxes of 4 Group attacked the Hoesch coking plant in Dortmund. On return many of the Yorkshire bases were affected by fog and landing was particularly hazardous. At Pocklington, where the Halifaxes of 102 Squadron were returning in the early hours, one particular Halifax was finding it difficult to get down in the murk.

Flight Sergeant Dai Pugh, who had flown many operations with 102 Squadron and was now a Ferry Pilot at No. 42 Base, was walking home with his wife that foggy night:

'We had been to the Cinema in Pocklington and were walking home to our bungalow at Allerthorpe when we heard an aircraft approaching the airfield. The Squadron had been out on an operation that evening and fog had clamped down. Most aircraft had managed to get down safely but this Halifax (LW158 'P-Peter') overshot the runway four times. Finally he came in too low, clipped the chimney of a house and crashed into a field near the runway. Because of the fog we were not able to see the crash, only the glow of the flames in the distance. One of the first on the scene of the crash – even before the fire truck, was our popular base commander, Air Commodore 'Gus' Walker, who came tearing along in his car. Even though he had lost his arm earlier in the war, he could still fly and drive far better than most people with both arms. The Rescue Party managed to get all seven members of the crew out of the burning wreckage. Sadly one was found to be dead and the rest were badly injured.'

The following night 351 Halifaxes of Nos. 4 and 6 Groups, led by Pathfinder Lancasters and Mosquitos, wrecked the I.G. Farben chemical factories at Ludwigshafen and Oppau. The defences were in the form of barrage fire which was heavy early in the attack but fell off considerably as the weight of the attack swamped the factory areas. All the 4 Group Halifaxes returned safely.

It was a different story three nights later when the main force attacked Hanover. Despite the Luftwaffe's recent decline its night fighter arm still packed a lethal punch as was proved that night. The German controller was able to correctly identify the target as Hanover early enough to vector large numbers of his fighters into the stream.

One for the album. A 77 Squadron crew pose for the camera before take off, January 1945. *R. Runkie*

* Extracts from *Halifax Crew* by Arthur C. Smith, Carlton Publications, 1983.

As a result twenty-three Halifaxes and eight Lancasters were shot down. Some of that number fell victim to the flak whilst others were lost due to collisions. Flying Officer McLennan and crew of No. 158 Squadron, were on the last leg of their outward journey when their Halifax was involved in a collision with another bomber when some twenty miles from the target. McLennan's navigator, Flight Sergeant Huband describes what happened: ‡

'Suddenly, there was a tremendous crash from underneath, followed by an awful vibration accompanied by ice-cold air which reduced the temperature in the forward compartment to minus 32 degrees centigrade.

'We had been struck by another aircraft. My immediate reaction was to clip on my parachute, jettison the escape hatch below my seat in the navigation department and get out. In fact the bomb-aimer and myself were about to abandon the aircraft which was now going down quite steeply when the skipper called over the intercom, "Stay where you are".'

These few hurried words greatly cheered the bomb-aimer, Pilot Officer Carroll. When the collision occurred his intercom plug, unknown to him, came out of its socket and for several terrifying seconds he thought the nose of their aircraft had broken away from the main fuselage. Without communication and pinned to the floor by the force of the dive, Carroll was convinced he was going to die. Then he saw the navigator struggling with the forward escape hatch and life seemed to offer him one more chance. Huband continues: ‡

'The terrible vibration stopped, and as we came out of the dive we saw the starboard engine fall from its mountings leaving wires hanging and sparks flying in all directions. As our best course of action seemed to lie with remaining with the main stream we held our course and dropped our bombs on the outskirts of Hanover.'

From his position in his turret, McLennan's mid-upper gunner, Sergeant Hibbert, had witnessed the collision. The bomber, which he thought was a Lancaster, was being chased by a night fighter and was undoubtedly corkscrewing when the smash took place. He last saw it spiralling down on fire and out of control.

Meanwhile over Hanover the defences were putting up a storm of fire which the Halifaxes and Lancasters had to battle through to bomb the markers. One of the Halifaxes that successfully rode through that storm and was lined-up on its bomb run was MZ360 'A-Apple' of No. 77 Squadron. 'Apple's skipper that night was Flight Lieutenant Peter Fitzgerald:

'Our bomb-aimer, Bish Parsons, seeing the markers go down, ordered a minor change in course and bomb doors open. It was as black as hell ahead when suddenly the whole of the cockpit roof and front windscreen disappeared. Whatever it was that had hit us, flak, fighter or collision with another bomber, will never be known. What was certain was that

Flying officer Robinson and crew of Halifax Mk. III MZ395 'C-Charlie' were one of three Halifaxes from 158 Squadron shot down over Hanover on the night of 5th January 1945. Back row, left to right, Sergeant Watkins, wireless operator; Flight Sergeant Scarff, engineer: Flying Officer Robinson, pilot; Sergeant Ralph, mid-upper gunner; Flying Officer Topliss, bomb aimer. Front row: Flight Sergeant Belcher, navigator; Sergeant Premble, rear gunner. Watkins, Scarff and Premble were killed that night, but the rest of the crew were made PoWs. *A. J. Ralph*

we were in a bad way with the upper section of the nose severely damaged and intercom, instruments and controls out of action. The blast of wind into the open cockpit was terrific and my helmet and goggles were blown to the back of my head. I removed a glove and, with one hand, tried to put the goggles back over my eyes but without success, losing the glove in the process.

'Meanwhile, the bomb-aimer appeared in the well of the cockpit. I made hand signals to indicate that he should bale out and to pass me my parachute. Without comment he immediately disappeared as flashes and sparks began to explode from behind and below the instrument panel.

'What took place in the next few minutes is uncertain. Our aircraft came down near Steinhuder, some fourteen miles from Hanover, and I must have become unconscious soon after the bomb-aimer disappeared. I was suddenly aware of fire all around me and exploding small arms ammunition. The one thought in my head was that we still had bombs on board and that I had to get away quick. I stood up and removed my helmet to free the oxygen and intercom lines and stepped out of the cockpit. I was surprised that I was able to just step down from the cockpit, but on reflection the forward section of the aircraft must have been on its side. I ran through the noise of the fire and exploding ammunition and when I was clear, rolled onto the snow-covered ground to put out my burning clothes. I looked back at the blazing wreck but there was no sign of the rest of the crew.'

The other members of Flight Lieutenant Fitzgerald's crew were all killed in the crash. Badly burnt, frost bitten and suffering from shock Peter Fitzgerald, after a vain attempt to escape from the scene of the crash, gave himself up to two French conscript workers. He was taken to their billet and handed over to the Germans and spent the rest of the war in hospital recovering from his remarkable escape.

Over Hanover the night fighters began to arrive in increasing numbers. Flying Officer Robinson and crew of No. 158 Squadron had just released their bombs when they came under attack. In his own words Robinson describes the events of the next few minutes: ‡

'The aircraft gave a tremendous lurch to port, and on looking back over my left shoulder I was startled to see a great big hole in the port wing between the inner and outer engines. As I looked the port inner engine burst into flames, closely followed by the port outer. I yelled to the flight engineer to come and give me a hand and we feathered the two port engines and pushed the Graviner buttons. However, it was pretty obvious that it was hopeless as by now flames were coming from the main petrol cocks behind me. We shut off the two port cocks, and I ordered the crew to bale out. The bomb-aimer was still in the nose and he attempted to jettison the main escape hatch. By this time the navigator was helping him, and I called over the intercom for them to pull the hatch in as they couldn't get it jettisoned in the airstream.

'As this was going on the flight engineer and the wireless operator were passing me to bale out, the bomb-aimer and navigator having successfully jumped, and the wireless operator handed me my parachute and clipped it on me. He undoubtedly saved my life, for at that moment the Halifax lost a large part of the port wing and started to spin to the left. I still had power on the two starboard engines in my attempt to hold the aircraft steady, but the next thing I knew I was swinging beneath my parachute.

'I had a bad cut on my forehead, which must have been from the oxygen mask as it pulled away from my face, but I have no recollection of pulling the ripcord. Minutes later I landed with a jolt, and after getting rid of my parachute harness started walking, but I did not get far. I knew I had been burned, and when I saw a farm house I knocked on the door for help. The girl who answered my knock screamed and ran away, and the next thing I knew a man was leading me inside. It was not long before a couple of policemen arrived and I was taken to the military hospital at Bodenwerder.'

Danger still lurked even after crews had left the holocaust over Hanover. Halifax RG367, 'O-Orange', of No. 578 Squadron, had successfully attacked the target at 19.22 hours.

‡ Extracts from *In Brave Company: The History of No. 158 Squadron* by W. R. Chorley and R. N. Benwell, 1977.

Some twenty minutes later, and flying at 13,000 feet, 'O-Orange' collided with another Halifax. The pilot of 'O-Orange', Flight Lieutenant Sledge, describes what happened in his post raid report:

'At approximately 19.40 hours another Halifax was seen behind us simultaneously by the rear and mid-upper gunners, converging from above and behind. This aircraft was diving rapidly and there was no time to take evasive action. His starboard wing and outer engine hit us outboard of our port outer, badly damaging the whole of the wing section, rendering the aileron control useless and at the same time the flaps came down 30 degress. Our aircraft went into a spiral dive to port but by using as much force as possible, full right rudder trim and throttling back on the starboard outer engine, I managed to gain control and level out.

'To get the aircraft back onto heading I throttled back the starboard engines and steered a very rough course with the aid of rudder trim and engines. Near Münster we were engaged by flak and I turned north to try and regain our original track. As the aircraft was so unstable and difficult to control I decided to turn south-west at approximately 52.10 North – 05.30 East to head for our own lines so we could bale out. At Nijmegen we again were engaged by flak and when over the Maas the IFF was switched to distress. The wireless operator tried to contact base but was unsuccessful. The aircraft passed south of Antwerp and when in the Ghent area all the crew baled out from the forward hatch successfully between 10,000 and 13,000 feet.' Flight Lieutenant Sledge and crew later returned safely to Burn.

Another Halifax that failed to return from the Hanover raid was LV952 'F' of 51 Squadron, skippered by Pilot Officer Leach. 'F-Freddies' normal wireless operator was Warrant Officer Eddie Hilton:

'After nine trips we had settled down as a fairly competent crew. We had to ditch our original rear gunner who always became violently sick every time we were airborne. He was replaced by Dan Thomsett.

'During January 1945 I was struck down with a heavy cold and the MO prescribed light duties and a lay off from 'ops' for twenty-four hours. During this period my crew were on ops to Hanover and a wireless operator from the RAAF took my place. His name was Wilson and he only needed to complete this one trip to earn a spell of leave back in Australia. Sad to say it was the last trip for all the crew as they were shot down over Hanover. They were all killed except the rear gunner, Dan Thomsett, who became a POW. They are buried together in Hanover War Cemetery and I have since received photographs of their graves, including that of A. G. Wilson (RAAF), which should of course have been my own grave.'

The important rail junction at Hanau was attacked by aircraft from Nos. 1, 4, 6 and 8 Groups on the night of 6th January with mod-

erate results. Two Halifaxes from 4 Group, one each from Nos. 10 and 158 Squadrons, failed to return. There then followed a week of bad weather over the Yorkshire bases, with low cloud and frequent snow showers preventing the Group from operating. During that week crews went through the frustrating process of being briefed for an operation only to find that it would later be 'scrubbed' due to the weather.

Better weather on 13th January made it possible for an attack to be carried out on the marshalling yards at Saarbrücken. The 274 strong force, of mainly Halifaxes from Nos. 4 and 6 Groups, struck a heavy blow against this important link in the enemy's rail system. Shortly after bombing the target, Flying Officer Wilson of 51 Squadron turned his Halifax, MZ465 'Y', towards home. Suddenly, and without and warning, 'Y-Yorker' collided with another bomber and was left with ten feet of its nose missing. Wilson's unfortunate bomb-aimer and navigator were carried off with the decapitated nose section and perished. Frozen by the icy blast tearing through the shattered nose, Wilson, by a superb piece of airmanship, nursed his crippled bomber back to England. Unfortunately the bomber that collided with Flying Officer Wilson's aircraft, a Halifax from No. 347 (French Air Force) Squadron, LL590, from Elvington, crashed with the loss of three of its crew.

The following night 100 Halifaxes from No. 4 Group, supported by twelve Mosquitos and three Lancasters of the Pathfinders, attacked the Luftwaffe fuel storage depot at Dulmen. Scattered damaged was inflicted on the depot and one Halifax, containing Flying Officer Connop and crew of 578 Squadron, was seen to go down in the target area.

Heavy area attacks took place against Magdeburg and Gelsenkirchen during January before Stuttgart received a double blow on the night of the 28th. No. 4 Group Squadrons were targetted on the railway yards at Konwestheim, north of Stuttgart, and the Hirth aero engine plant in the suburb of Zuffenhausen. Early arrivals over Stuttgart were able to bomb the ground markers which showed up well. However, increasing cloud forced the majority of crews to bomb on sky markers. Some of the bombing was scattered whilst other loads fell around a decoy fire site east of the town. Equipped with target indicator rockets and flares and designed to resemble an industrial area under attack these decoy sites were situated near to potential target areas, particularly large towns and cities, their purpose being to lure bombers away from the main target.

Oil plants at Wanne-Eickel and Gelsenkirchen and a rail centre at Bonn were bombed at night during the first week of February 1945. Also attacked during that week were the towns of Goch and Kleve. The attack on Goch, carried out by 464 aircraft, was in preparation for an advance by the British XXX Corps towards the German frontier in the

Reichswald area. The raid took place in the late evening of the 7th and started well but increasing smoke forced the Master Bomber to call off the attack prematurely. A Halifax from No. 102 Squadron was damaged by a Ju 88 over the target and the crew took to their parachutes. The enemy fighter continued to fire on the crew as they descended. The Halifax rear-gunner, Sergeant Peckham, was so incensed he remained in his turret firing at the fighter until his ammunition was exhausted, then baled out himself. The crew of the Halifax landed safely and later discovered that the Ju 88 that had attacked them had crash landed on a railway line and its pilot had been killed by a train. Retribution had indeed been swift.

As part of the plan to give less experienced officers a chance to gain experience at the highest level there were changes in Bomber Command in February 1945. Some of the longest serving Group Commanders, including Air Vice Marshal Carr of No. 4 Group, were replaced. Air Vice Marshal Carr's successor was Air Vice Marshal Whitley (later Air Marshal Sir John Whitley KBE, CB, DSO, AFC) who had served with distinction within No. 4 Group since 1941. Whitley took up his command on 12th February and just twenty-four hours later he was deeply involved in planning his first operation as Group Commander; a maximum effort night raid on the Braunkohle-Benzin AG synthetic oil plant at Böhlen, near Leipzig. The attack was largely unsuccessful due to bad weather which caused the bombing to be scattered. In addition, severe icing caused problems for most of the 368 strong, mainly Halifax, force. One particular Halifax, that of Flight Sergeant McElwee of No. 466 (RAAF) Squadron, became so badly iced up on the return journey from Böhlen that it became uncontrollable. On three separate occasions the ice laden Halifax turned over on its back and each time McElwee was able to regain control, much to the relief of his terrified fellow crew members. With fuel tanks almost dry McElwee landed his battered Halifax at Juvincourt in France.

At the same time as the Halifaxes of Nos. 4 and 6 Groups were on their way to Böhlen a strong force of Lancasters was carrying out Operation *Thunderclap*, the notorious raid on Dresden. 796 Lancasters from Nos. 1, 3, 6 and 8 Groups dropped between them 1,478 tons of high explosive and 1,182 tons of incendiary bombs which tore the heart out of Dresden. The firestorm that was created was far more destructive than anything seen before or since.

The second phase of *Thunderclap* took place twenty-four hours later and this time Chemnitz was the target. The Halifax groups joined with Lancasters from Nos. 1, 3, 6 and 8 Groups in what proved to be a disappointing attack. 10/10ths cloud over the city thwarted any hopes of a 'Dresden' type concentration, most of the bombs falling in open countryside.

There was more success a week later when 156 aircraft from No. 4 Group brought oil production to a standstill at the Rhenania Ossag refinery in Düsseldorf. The attack, which took place on the night of 20th February, was highly concentrated due to the superbly accurate marking by the Pathfinders. Four Halifaxes failed to return, two each from Nos. 158 and 578 Squadrons.

As February drew to a close, maximum efforts were sent out from No. 4 Group against targets that included Worms, Essen, Kamen and Mainz. The last three attacks took place in daylight and were highly successful.

By March 1945 Bomber Command was able to operate over Germany at night almost without hindrance. Area attacks and precision blows against the oil industry and transportation system were the main feature of the attacks carried out during the month. On the night of 3rd March, 201 Halifaxes of No. 4 Group attacked the synthetic oil refinery at Kamen. The force reached the target unchallenged and carried out a devastating attack that completely halted production at the Fischer-Tropsch plant. As the bombers streamed homewards across the North Sea hundreds of German night fighters left their airfields in Holland and Germany in pursuit. The Luftwaffe was about to launch Operation *Gisella*, a long planned intruder operation against the airfields of Bomber Command. That night at airfields all over Yorkshire, Lincolnshire, Norfolk and Suffolk, just as Halifaxes and Lancasters were about to land, a swarm of avenging Ju 88s and He 219s swept in firing cannons and dropping bombs. The defences were taken completely by surprise as were the unsuspecting bomber crews.

Opposite page, top, then anti-clockwise:
PN167 'C' a Halifax Mk. III of 347 'Free French' Squadron stands in the winter sunshine at Elvington, early 1945. *Miquette*, **with S/C Barbeau at the controls, flew on No. 347's last operation of the war – an attack on Wangerooge on 25th April 1945. The wartime censor has erased the nose transparency, H2S blister and side entrance door.** *IWM, CH14613*

Aircrews of 346 and 347 Squadrons are carefully interrogated after ops. *via W. Baguley*

Air and ground crew of *The Ruhr Xpress*, **466 (RAAF) Squadron, February 1945, Driffield.** *A. White*

Shortly after bombing Saarbrücken on the night of 13th January 1945, Flying Officer Wilson of 51 Squadron turned his Halifax, MZ465 'Y', towards home. Suddenly, and without warning, there was a collision with a Halifax from 347 Squadron and they were left with ten feet of nose missing. The unfortunate bomb-aimer and navigator were carried off with the decapitated nose section and perished. Remarkably, Wilson was able to bring his damaged bomber safely back to England. Flying Officer Wilson (centre) is seen here with the surviving members of his crew.

At Driffield, home base of No. 466 (RAAF) Squadron, eleven Halifaxes had safely returned out of the seventeen that had taken-off earlier for Kamen. The other six Halifaxes were either approaching the vicinity of the airfield or were already in the circuit when the intruders struck. Pilot Officer Schrank and crew in NR250 'N-Nuts', had arrived over Driffield at approximately 00.40 hours whereupon they contacted Flying Control on the R/T. They were instructed to maintain their present height, 1,700 feet, because the runway was in use. A few minutes later, the duty controller instructed the pilot to come down to 1,400 feet and prepare to land. About this time the wireless operator, Flight Sergeant Hadlington, received a coded message which he did not have time to decipher. The message was in fact the word 'Bandits'.

Meanwhile, the navigator, Flight Sergeant Tobin, was just going back to the rest position, prior to landing, and was under the Flight Engineer's seat when the aircraft was surprised by an enemy fighter. All the aircraft's lights were on, and in particular, the tail light completely blinded the rear-gunner, Flight Sergeant Kernaghan, who did not see either the fighter, or the tracer. The mid-upper gunner reported that the tracer came from astern, slightly to starboard, and very slightly below.

Immediately following the attack all lights in the aircraft and on the airfield were extinguished. The pilot was too low to take evasive action and, but for the switching off of the airfield lights, would have tried to land. Instead he tried to gain height, and when the fighter approached again from starboard about three minutes later, he was able to evade successfully with a diving turn to starboard, neither side opening fire. In the first attack, Pilot Officer Schrank's Halifax was damaged at the rear of the fuselage, aft of the mid-upper turret; several holes being blown in the floor and side of the fuselage. The hydraulic system was hit and the undercarriage dropped down. The mid-upper gunner was slightly injured with splinters in his leg, but most serious of all a fire was started, the engine covers being set ablaze. These were always carried in the fuselage in case the aircraft had to land away from base. The aircraft's controls were functioning more or less normally although the R/T and W/T equipment was put out of action, fortunately the intercom still worked.

The engineer, Sergeant Hodgson, was first back to tackle the fire, followed by the navigator and rear-gunner. They attempted to put out the fire but without success, using up all seven fire extinguishers in the process. An unsuccessful attempt was made to open the rear exit, but the heat had buckled the door and it would not open. Finally, the navigator used the axe and pulled the burning engine covers towards one of the large holes, that had been made by the cannon fire, in the catwalk and jettisoned them. Despite the removal of the burning covers parts of the interior of the fuselage were still burning. In

addition, the flames appeared to be spreading to the exterior of the fuselage and, plus the fact that there was now only ten minutes fuel remaining, the pilot ordered the crew to abandon the aircraft. All seven members of the crew left via the front hatch. 'N-Nuts' continued on an easterly course and crashed at Friskney, near Skegness, where it demolished a cottage. It was discovered later that the Halifax had been hit by ten 20 mm cannon shells underneath the rear fuselage and several of the holes were eighteen inches in diameter.

Another Halifax of No. 466 (RAAF) Squadron was on final approach to Driffield that night, just at the moment when the intruders were detected in the circuit. Flying Officer Shelton and crew of NR179 'C-Charlie' were on the alert having seen signs of intruder activity as they came in over the Norfolk coast. As a precaution they had switched their navigation lights off.

After having to overshoot on their first approach, due to an aircraft in front having difficulty in getting down, the crew of 'C-Charlie' prepared to come in for another attempt at landing. On their second approach, and whilst flying at 150 feet, all the airfield lights suddenly went out and the pilot was instructed to overshoot and proceed on a dog leg. Flying Officer Shelton took the aircraft up to 1,500 feet and flew west towards Pocklington. He asked the navigator, Flight Sergeant Pat Hogan, from East Ivanhoe, Victoria, for a course to the nearest airfield. Pat Hogan takes up the story:

'As we overshot for the second time the skipper asked me to go down to the nav table and give him a course for somewhere to land. In my haste to get back to my table, from the rest position which was my normal position during landings, I inadvertently left my parachute behind. It was not long after that the engineer warned the skipper that we had very little fuel left, so it was decided to climb to 4,000 feet in case we had to bale out.

'As we began to climb the bomb-aimer suddenly shouted that a fighter was coming in from the port bow down. The mid-upper gunner swung his guns in the direction of the incoming fighter but was unable to open fire. The next moment the fighter fired on us and all hell broke loose.'

Events then happened with great rapidity and in the opinion of a witness on the ground only thirty or forty seconds elapsed between the bomber being set on fire and the subsequent crash. Cannon shells from the fighter, a Ju 88, set both port engines on fire, blew away the H2S blister and caused a fire in the port side of the fuselage forward of the rear exit door. The aircraft went quickly into a dive to port and the pilot ordered the crew to bale out. Flight Sergeant Pat Hogan, realising his parachute was still where he had left it in the rest position, now made a desperate bid to reach it. The Halifax was now going down in a steep dive and Pat Hogan had to claw his way up the slanting fuselage.

'I finally made it to the rest position and grabbed my parachute and headed for the mid escape hatch. When I got there I found it was open as the mid-upper gunner had already gone out. The engineer, Sergeant Wally Walsh, was standing at the hatch and I went out passed him. The fact that I had left my parachute in the rest position probably saved my life. All of the rest of the crew in the forward section of the aircraft didn't make it.'

The rear-gunner, Flight Sergeant Bullen, was the only other member of the crew to bale out and survive. He had turned his guns to port but had difficulty keeping the turret door open in the slipstream. In addition his right foot became stuck between the knee guard and a box under his seat. By now the aircraft was in a steep dive and flames were all around his turret when he finally extricated himself by pulling his right foot out of his boot. He made a very heavy landing and was knocked unconscious, but sustained no serious injuries.

All the other members of the crew were killed. The engineer, Sergeant Walsh, was the only other member of the crew to leave the aircraft but he apparently left at too low an altitude and was killed. Flying Officer Shelton and crew were on their tenth operation.

At other bases throughout Yorkshire that night the intruders created havoc as they struck, unsuspectingly out of the darkness. At the coastal airfield at Lissett a Ju 188 shot-up Flying Officer Strachan's Halifax as he came into land, mortally wounding the rear gunner.

Top: **Halifax Mk.VI PP171 of 102 Squadron displays its distinctive daylight formation markings – two horizontal red bands painted on each outer tail surface and code letters outlined in yellow.** *S. R. Cook*

Above: **F/Sgt Walsh and crew No.158 Squadron Lissett, March 1945. Left to right back row: F/Sgt Walsh (RNZAF), pilot; Sgt Simpson, rear gunner; Sgt Nicholls, mid-upper gunner; Sgt Broad, bomb-aimer. Front: Sgt Cook, flight engineer; Sgt Eckhoff, wireless operator.** *R. Broad*

Left: **Full Sutton Officers' Mess, 1945.** *A. Porter*

Below: **No.77 Squadron, Full Sutton, early in 1945.** *D. Morison*

Opposite page: **Air and ground crew of *Leapin Lena*, MZ919 'L' of No.10 Sqn, March 1945. Standing left to right: F/O Turville, mid-upper gunner; Sgt Huntley, engineer; F/Lt Giles, pilot; Sgt Stear, wireless operator; F/Sgt Cooke, bomb-aimer; F/Sgt Street, navigator; W/O Bates, rear gunner. Ground crew.** *G. Stear*

In another pass the fighter sprayed the watch office with cannon and machine gun fire. Meanwhile another Halifax from No. 158 Squadron was shot down in the circuit and crashed near Driffield: there were no survivors from Flight Lieutenant Roger's crew. The two French squadrons, based at Elvington, lost three Halifaxes: NR229 'D-Donald' of 346 Squadron crashed near Croft but all the crew escaped; NA680 'H' of 347 came down near Cranwell with the loss of the entire crew whilst NR235 'O', also of 347, crashed near York, though all the crew escaped except the pilot Squadron Leader Terrien. There was considerable disruption as returning bombers were diverted to unfamiliar airfields to avoid the intruder activity. One of the many Halifaxes landing at Carnaby that night was LW587 'A-Apple' of 578 Squadron. Flying Officer Gardner and crew had been forced to land at the Emergency Landing Ground due to petrol shortage. The following day, on its return to Burn, LW578's ground crew proudly painted the '100th' bomb on its nose. Another Halifax from 578, MZ527 'D-Donald', reached the century mark that night. Both Halifaxes survived the war.

It had been a costly night for Bomber Command with at least twenty bombers shot down by the intruders over England. No. 4 Group were the worst hit losing eight Halifaxes with a further six damaged. Twenty-

six aircrew were killed. Operation *Gisella* was the swansong of the Luftwaffe's night fighter arm. It would never be able to repeat a similar operation on the same scale again.

Meanwhile, Bomber Command kept up the pressure on the beleaguered German oil industry. Halifaxes of No. 4 and 6 Groups attacked the Deutsche Erdöl refinery at Hemmingstadt, near Heide, on 7th March. No. 578 Squadron lost two Halifaxes on this raid: Flight Lieutenant Powell crashing his Halifax 'R-Robert' on the west bank of the Kiel Canal and Flight Lieutenant Shaw ditching his aircraft in the North Sea. There was only one survivor from the two crews.

Two record breaking raids, involving maximum efforts from the squadrons of 4 Group, followed each other in quick succession early in March 1945. 1,079 aircraft of Bomber Command, the largest number of aircraft sent to a target so far in the war, tore the heart out of Essen during a huge display of air power on the morning of 11th March. This record breaking effort was followed by a devastating blow on the following afternoon when 1,107 bombers dropped the highest tonnage of the war, 4,851 tons, on the centre of Dortmund. Only five Lancasters were lost in these two highly successful operations.

On the afternoon of the 13th March Halifaxes from 4 Group, operating in concert with the Canadians of 6 Group, struck a heavy blow at the Barmen district of Wuppertal.

Flying their last operation of the war were fourteen Halifaxes of No. 578 Squadron. No. 578 Squadron, were due to disband early in April, the result of a general scaling down of Bomber Command in the last weeks of hostilities in Europe. No.578 Squadron finished the war with a proud record, having completed 2,721 sorties and dropped 9,676 tons of bombs. Forty aircraft were lost in 155 bombing raids.

For the rest of March 1945 the Lancasters and Halifaxes of Bomber Command operated over Germany, mainly in daylight, with little or no interference from the defences. No. 4 Group were involved in attacks on targets which included enemy communications at Homberg on the 14th, Benzol plants at Bottrop on the 15th, an area raid on Witten on the 18th and attacks on railway yards at Recklinghausen and Rheine on the 20th and 21st. On the 24th, as Allied forces crossed the Rhine, 4 Group Halifaxes bombed Sterkrade and Gladbeck. The following day Münster and Osnabrück received a double blow. The month of March had seen 4 Group reach it's peak of skill and accomplishment. During the month the Group had dropped it's record weight of bombs and its loss rate was the lowest in Bomber Command.

April began with a final blow on one of the few remaining oil targets, the Rhenania Ossag Mineralölwerke AG plant at Harburg. This attack, which took place in the evening of 4th

Above: **Hit by flak on the run-in to Gladbeck, MZ759 'Q-Queenie' of No.158 Squadron plunges earthwards, its wing tanks ablaze. The two gunners were the only survivors from W/O Yeoman's crew.** *Chaz Bowyer collection*

Below: **It's all over! Aircrew of 77 Squadron, 1945.** *E.Fallen*

April, was carried out by 327 aircraft of Nos. 4, 6 and 8 Groups, and was highly concentrated. One Halifax crew of 158 Squadron failed to join the other twenty crews that took off from Lissett that evening. Pilot Officer Furniss was just raising the tail of his Halifax as it thundered down the main runway, when a slight swing to port developed. The pilot corrected the swing by applying right rudder and after straightening the aircraft found that he could not bring the rudder bar back to the central position as his foot seemed to have jammed. What had caused his foot to become jammed was a piece of the pilot's bootlace caught in the press stud that held the black-out curtain. This press stud was in a position approximately level with the right rudder pedal when right rudder was applied. As the Halifax careered out of control towards another aircraft running its engines at dispersal, Pilot Officer Furniss applied the brakes in an effort to ground loop the aircraft. His efforts, however, were unsuccessful and his aircraft slewed into the stationary Halifax severely damaging both aircraft.

On the night of the 8th, submarine building yards in Hamburg were bombed through partial cloud cover. A Halifax from No. 466 (RAAF) Squadron, LW172 'F-Freddie', veteran of ninety-six operations, on return from Hamburg was descending through fog on approach to Driffield. Not far from the airfield 'F-Freddie' clipped the top of some trees and then ploughed into a copse at Kirkburn Grange, killing all of the crew.

Two daylight attacks on 11th April rank among the most successful operations carried out by No. 4 Group. Whilst 129 Halifaxes of the Group bombed with extreme accuracy the marshalling yards at Nuremburg, a smaller force immobilised the rail centre at Bayreuth. Both raids were carried out without loss.

April 1945 was the month that Bomber Command ceased strategic area bombing. With victory imminent there was now no need for Bomber Command to prolong a campaign that had continued almost without interruption since May 1940. The priority in the remaining weeks shifted to attacks on naval targets, harbour facilities and the few remaining, undamaged rail and oil centres.

Ten days after the Hamburg raid No. 4 Group were involved in a maximum effort by all groups against the naval base on the island of Heligoland. Over at Holme-on-Spalding Moor, home base of No. 76 Squadron, twenty-six Halifax Mk.VIs were preparing to take-off for Heligoland. It was a beautiful spring morning and one by one the Halifaxes, heavily laden with bombs and fuel, sped down the runway. All was going according to schedule and by 11.30 ten aircraft were away. As the eleventh Halifax, RG622 'I-Item' (Warrant Officer Holmes), commenced it's take-off run, things started to go wrong as it began to swerve from side to side as it went down the runway. Air gunner Sergeant Barker was not flying that day and he was with the usual group of watchers at the edge of the runway waving the aircraft off.

'Ten aircraft had taken off on what was to be a maximum effort when along came 'I-Item'. As the aircraft left the runway it seemed to hang in the air before coming down hard onto the concrete. The undercarriage came off as the aircraft spun round ending up at the side of the runway. Bombs spilled out all over the place and seconds later began to explode. Fortunately, all the crew had managed to scramble clear just as the emergency teams arrived. The exploding bombs left huge craters in the runway and of course the rest of the Squadron never took off.'

The ten Halifaxes from 76 Squadron that did take off that morning went on to join the other 617 Lancasters and 332 Halifaxes that laid waste the naval base, airfield and town on Heligoland. Because Holme-on-Spalding Moor was still out of commission, the contingent from 76 Squadron all made safe returns to Breighton.

Seven days later, on the afternoon of 25th April, 308 Halifaxes, 158 Lancasters and sixteen Mosquitos from Nos. 4, 6 and 8 Groups took off to attack coastal gun batteries on the Frisian Island of Wangerooge. The guns controlled the approaches to the ports of Bremen and Wilhelmshaven and Bomber Command was tasked with their destruction.

As the Halifax crews of 4 Group were rising into the sky on that clear spring afternoon, they were unaware that, for most of them, this would be their last operation of the Second World War. Shortly after 17.00 hours the huge formations appeared over Wangerooge and, despite an intensive and very accurate flak barrage, the bombers carried out a devastating attack. Two Halifaxes from Canadian squadrons were seen to collide on the way into the target as did two Lancasters shortly after bombing.

Meanwhile, the flak barrage reached a crescendo as the 4 Group formation commenced its run-in. As the Halifaxes struggled to maintain formation, amid the dark shell bursts that were staining the sky, two aircraft from 76 Squadron collided. Both Halifaxes broke up and fell into the sea 8,000 feet below. Of the crews of Warrant Officer Outerson and Pilot Officer Lawson there was only one survivor. Skipper of Halifax RG553 'T-Tommy' was Pilot Officer Lawson and somehow he managed to escape from the remains of his spinning aircraft to come down by parachute into the sea. He swam the short distance to the shore and was captured by the Germans. Another Halifax, NP921 from 347 Squadron, was hit by flak on the run-in to the target and fell in flames. There were no survivors.

That same night Lancasters of No. 5 Group attacked an oil refinery at Tonsberg in Southern Norway. The raid was the last time that main force squadrons of Bomber Command attacked the enemy during the Second World War. Five days later Adolf Hitler lay dead in his tomb-like underground headquarters in Berlin.

Top: Heligoland, 18th April 1945. The F.24 bombing camera of F/O Fallen (RCAF), No.77 Squadron, records the scene from 14,000 feet. *E. Fallen*

Centre: **The last of the many. Gun batteries on Wangerooge island are hit on 25th April 1945 in 4 Group's final act of World War Two.** *E. Fallen*

Bottom: **Warrant Officer Walsh and crew inspect the damage to their Halifax PN444 'S' of No.158 Squadron. On a daylight raid to Nuremburg on 11th April 1945, 'S-Sugar' was hit by flak over the target. The flak shell exploded in the port wing and blew part of the aileron away and a considerable portion of the outer end of the wing.** *R. Broad*

No. 4 Group Bomber Command, April 1945

Sqn	Equipment	Airfield
10	Halifax III	Melbourne
51	Halifax III	Leconfield
76	Halifax III/VI	Holme-on-Spalding Moor
77	Halifax VI	Full Sutton
78	Halifax III/VI	Breighton
102	Halifax VI	Pocklington
158	Halifax III/VI	Lissett
346	Halifax III/VI	Elvington
347	Halifax III/VI	Elvington
466 (RAAF)	Halifax III	Driffield
640	Halifax VI	Leconfield

Within twelve days of completing its last operation of the war No. 4 Group ceased to exist as a component of Bomber Command. On 7th May 1945, the day before the German surrender in Europe, No. 4 Group was transferred to Transport Command.

† - see page 165
Bomber Command Directive 'Operations *Hurricane I and Hurricane II'*, 13th October 1944, Appendix 8 *The Strategic Air Offensive against Germany 1939-45,* HMSO, 1961.

Below, top: **Halifax Mk.VII NP763 of No. 346 'Free French' Squadron shows off its daylight tail markings; red trellis work with codes outlined in yellow, French fuselage roundels and fin flash. NP763 took part in 346's last operation of the war, an attack on gun batteries at Wangerooge on 25th April 1945.** *IWM, HU1979*

Chapter Seventeen

The Transport Years

With the defeat of Germany in May 1945 the Halifax squadrons of RAF Bomber Command were deemed surplus to requirements. Many of the Halifaxes of Nos. 4 and 6 Groups ended their days at Rawcliffe or No. 29 Maintenance Unit, High Ercall, where they were either sold off or broken up for scrap. Other Halifax-equipped squadrons were to be used for transport duties pending re-equipment with Dakotas, Stirlings or Liberators. Many of the Lancaster squadrons of Bomber Command were earmarked for 'Tiger Force', then being assembled as the RAF's contribution to the projected air offensive against Japan.

With the prospect of the war against Japan continuing into 1946 the urgent requirement in the spring of 1945 was for the RAF to expand its transport capability. The months ahead would see Britain's communications links severely extended by the continuing war in the Far East and her commitments in Europe, the Mediterranean, the Middle East and India. RAF Transport Command's expanded role was to be a vital one supplying troops, supplies and providing communications to and from these vital areas.

As part of this expansion No. 4 Group was to be transferred to transport duties. At 23.59 hours on 7th May 1945 No. 4 Group came under the control of Transport Command. On that date the Group's former HQ at Heslington Hall was redesignated No. 4 (Transport) Group HQ. No. 4 Group's former AOC, Air Vice-Marshal J. R. Whitley, left to take up an appointment at Allied Command South East Asia in Singapore. The new AOC was to be Air Vice-Marshal H. S. P. Walmsley. The Group's former Halifax squadrons were redesignated as transport squadrons and were organised as follows:

No. 42 BASE
Pocklington: No. 102 Squadron
Elvington: Nos. 346 and 347 Squadrons
(Free French aircrew)
Full Sutton: No. 77 Squadron

Opposite, bottom: **Ex-4 Group Halifaxes await their fate at a Maintenance Unit after the war. In the foreground is Mk.III NA222 'O' of 640 Squadron, with yellow and black chequer board daylight tactical markings and code letters outlined in yellow. NA222 was one of the few late production Halifaxes painted in gloss finish. In the background is another late production Mk.III, RG346 'W' of 466 (RAAF) Squadron. Both were sold for scrap in 1947.** *IWM, HU1980*

No. 43 BASE
Driffield: No. 466 (RAAF) Squadron
Leconfield: No. 51 Squadron
Lissett: No. 158 Squadron

No. 44 BASE
Holme-on-Spalding Moor: No. 76 Squadron
Breighton: No. 78 Squadron
Melbourne: No. 10 Squadron

The stations at Snaith and Burn were placed on a Care and Maintenance basis, the emergency landing ground at Carnaby was retained, while the remaining bomber squadron, No. 640, was disbanded. No. 640 Squadron had ended the war with a proud record – it had flown 2,423 Halifax sorties, had lost forty aircraft and won the 4 Group Bombing Cup trophy for a record five times.

The plan now was for the squadrons of No. 4 Group to exchange their Halifaxes for transport aircraft and the allocation of types was to be as follows: Nos. 51 and 158 Squadrons were to convert to Stirling Vs; Nos. 10, 76, 77 and 78 to Dakota IVs and Nos. 102 and 466 were to re-equip with Liberators. The future of the two 'Free French' squadrons, Nos. 346 and 347, was at that time undecided and for the time being they were to keep their Halifaxes and remain under the control of 4 Group.

During the rest of May and early June of 1945 the squadrons, whilst awaiting the arrival of their new aircraft, were kept busy on cross country flights and running 'Cooks Tours'. The latter were sightseeing flights over the bomb shattered towns of Germany. On these flights non-flying personnel were given the chance to see the results of their labours. Typical of the routes and distances flown in late May and June was this example from 78 Squadron. Route: Breighton, Emden, Bremen, Hamburg, Kiel, Heligoland, Egmond, Cromer, Breighton; distance 859 miles. A maximum of twelve personnel including crew was permitted on each flight. The minimum crew was to include pilot, second pilot, navigator, wireless operator and flight engineer. A maximum of two WAAFs per aircraft was allowed and sufficient dinghy and life saving equipment for twelve had to be carried.

In June the first of the new aircraft began to arrive at the squadrons and crews took the opportunity to carry out their familiarisation flying on cross country flights over Germany. During that month No. 4 Group's role in Transport Command became more clearly

defined. The Group was to be responsible for conversion training within Transport Command – a far cry from its former role as the pioneering night bomber group of RAF Bomber Command. On 1st June the Group took over the following stations and units from No. 44 Group: No. 105 OTU based at Bramcote with satellites at Nuneaton and Bitteswell, No. 108 OTU based at Wymeswold with its satellite of Castle Donington, No. 109 OTU based at Crosby-on-Eden, the Lancaster Finishing School at Ossington, the Heavy Conversion Unit at Riccall and the Bomb Disposal Wing HQ at Doncaster. Early in July Marston Moor was transferred to No. 4 Group along with RAF Broadwell which was formally administered by No. 46 Group.

Units of No. 4 Group Transport Command, July 1945

Unit	Equipment	Average Strength	Airfield
10 Sqn*	Dakota	21	Melbourne
	Halifax	13	
51 Sqn*	Stirling	21	Leconfield
	Halifax	10	
76 Sqn*	Dakota	20	Holme-on-Spalding Moor
	Halifax	12	
77 Sqn*	Dakota	17	Full Sutton
	Halifax	18	
78 Sqn*	Dakota	17	Breighton
	Halifax	18	
102 Sqn	Halifax	22	Pocklington
158 Sqn*	Stirling	24	Lissett
	Halifax	8	
466 Sqn	Halifax	20	Driffield
105 (T)OTU*	Wellington	54	Bramcote
	Dakota	28	
108 (T)OTU	Dakota	32	Wymeswold
109 (T)OTU	Dakota	20	Crosby
1332 HTCU	York C.1	11	Riccall
	Liberator	8	
6 LFS	Lancaster	8	Ossington
	Oxford	3	
	Dakota	2	
1513 BAT Flt	Oxford	8	Bramcote
1516 BAT Flt	Oxford	9	Odiham
1521 BAT Flt	Oxford	7	Wymeswold
1527 BAT Flt	Oxford	8	Prestwick
1528 BAT Flt	Oxford	6	Valley
1529 BAT Flt	Oxford	8	St Mawgan

In addition to the units described in the above table the two French bomber squadrons, Nos. 346 and 347, were still being administered by No. 4 Group although they were under the control of No. 1 Group.

* Units rearming and disposing of one of the types.

At Leconfield at the beginning of June, No. 51 Squadron had received its first Stirling V, the specialist transport version of the famous heavy bomber. The Stirling V was fitted with a streamlined perspex nose, shorn of turrets and painted in green-grey-blue finish. The crew numbered five and as many as forty passengers could be carried. A 9ft 6in x 5ft 1in cargo door was fitted to the starboard rear side, hinged at the bottom so that it opened to form a ramp. This allowed bulky loads to be taken into the rear fuselage. The lengthened nose had a hinged top and loads could be hoisted in by means of a block and tackle. On 16th July, No. 51 flew their first overseas training flights when two Stirlings flew to Castel Benito, Libya. By the end of the month the squadron was making regular flights to India. Meanwhile, the other 4 Group squadron earmarked for Stirling transports, No. 158, began to receive its first batch of Mk.Vs early in June. Early conversion flying was done on 'Cooks Tours' and in July flights to Castel Benito commenced. Throughout the rest of July and August long distance training flights were made to India, usually via St Mawgan.

By August 1945, Nos. 10, 76, 77 and 78 Squadrons had disposed of their Halifaxes and were finishing off their conversion training on Dakotas. Both Nos. 10 and 76 Squadrons moved to RAF Broadwell, Oxfordshire on 6th August, where they were to undertake their final intensive Transport Support Course as both squadrons were earmarked for support duties in India. The other Dakota units, Nos. 77 and 78 Squadrons, had completed conversion and pre-support training exercises under the guidance of Mobile Training Parties during the first twelve days of August. By the end of the month 77 had left Full Sutton for Broadwell to complete support training prior to a move to Allied Command South East Asia. No. 78 Squadron remained at Breighton in preparation for a move to the Middle East.

From the top: **A group of 102 Squadron bomb-aimers at Pocklington, May 1945.** *S.R. Cook*

Dakota Mk.IIIs of 10 Squadron at Melbourne on 6th August 1945, ready to depart on the first leg of their flight to India, whereupon they came under the control of Allied Command South East Asia. Note the (radar?) blisters under the fuselages. *M. Chandler collection*

Air and ground crews of No. 102 Squadron at Pocklington about to set off on a 'Cooks Tour' of former target areas. At the end of hostilities in May 1945, ground staff were given the opportunity to go on flights over Europe to view the results of 5½ years of the air offensive. *S.R. Cook*

Stirling Mk.V PK124 'Q' of 51 Squadron being manoeuvred into position for loading at Mauripur airfield, Karachi. The Transport Command callsign 'last two' is on the nose. *IWM, CI1903*

An unknown crewman beside 512 Squadron Conversion Flight Dakota III KG410 'A', Holme-on-Spalding Moor, August 1945. *W.Baguley*

Standard Syllabus for Transport Support Conversion Units, No. 4 Group, October 1945*

Introduction:
This Syllabus is designed to convert crews to Dakota aircraft and to train them to the standard required to carry out their operational role in Transport Support Squadrons.

Operational Role of Transport Support Squadrons:
The operational role of transport support squadrons falls under two headings –
(1) Air Assault Role
    (a) To deliver on the drop zones and landing zones part of the Main Airborne Forces in men and equipment by parachute or glider.
    (b) To deliver reinforcements in men, equipment and supplies for forces engaged in (a) above.
(2) Air Transport Role
    (a) Flying supplies to forward landing grounds.
    (b) Dropping supplies by parachute or free.
    (c) Evacuation of casualties.

Length and arrangement of course:
(a) The course will last nine weeks and the 'straight through' training system is to be used. Navigators will do their Radar training during this nine week period on Dakotas. Wireless Operators will do a one week course at Ringway as parachute despatchers before joining crew.
(b) Pupils will spend the first week on lectures. Pilots will commence flying conversion at the beginning of the second week and Navigators ground radar instruction.
(c) Lectures will consist of 4 hours instruction on 6 mornings of the week and 3 hours on 5 afternoons.
(d) The following hours are allocated to lectures –

	Pilots	Navigators	Co-Pilots	Wireless Operators
Airmanship General	6	4	5	4
Crew Procedure	19	15	19	15
Intelligence	2	2	2	2
Airborne Operations	10	10	10	10
Link Trainer	10	-	10	-
Meteorology	6	6	6	1
Navigation	12	19	12	2
Technical	11	1	11	1
Armament	2	2	2	2
Night Vision	6	1	6	1
Physical Training	12	12	12	12
Medical	3	3	3	3
Radar	2	24	2	2
Signals	12	13	12	59
Totals	113	112	112	114

* *Source: No. 4 Group Monthly Summary, October 1945 (PRO: AIR 25/107)*

During August 1945 two transport squadrons were transferred from No. 46 Group to 4 Group. On 7th August, 512 Squadron moved to Holme-on-Spalding Moor and on the same day 575 moved into Melbourne; both units had previously been based at Broadwell. On the 19th August both squadrons commenced Dakota conversion and pre-support training with a Mobile Training Party. Training was to be suspended, however, on 24th August when, owing to the cessation of hostilities in the Far East, the future role of many units was changed. Both squadrons had been earmarked for the Far East but their new role was now to be trunk route flying in the Mediterranean and the Middle East. Two other units originally planned as support squadrons in the Far East, Nos. 102 and 466, were reconverted to trunk route flying. Both squadrons would receive Liberators on moving to RAF Bassingbourn early in September.

Early training flights, not surprisingly, produced a crop of accidents. During an intensive programme of day and night flying at Bassingbourn, a 102 Squadron Liberator, KN742, flown by Flight Lieutenant Robinson, crashed on take off and all of the crew were killed in the resulting explosion. On 18th September Liberator KN736 of 466 Squadron, crashed at Cockayne Hartley, six miles from Bassingbourn, during a feathering practice.

Douglas Dakota Mk.IIIs of No.575 Squadron. In the foreground is FZ695 'I9-A', showing signs of a former code (possibly 'W') under the 'A'. This particular machine was one of a batch of 151 such aircraft delivered to the RAF between November 1943 and April 1944, it was transferred to 437 Squadron, RCAF on 22nd April 1946. *IWM, CH18862*

The pilot, Flight Lieutenant McNulty, instructor Flight Lieutenant Spiller and two other members of the crew were killed.

October saw the start of large scale trooping flights by Stirlings of Nos. 51 and 158 Squadrons to the Middle East and India. During the period 15th to 24th October both squadrons took part in Operation *Sketch*, the transfer of 10,000 troops from Brussels to Shallufa and the move of 10,000 Indian troops from Shallufa to Arkonam. Each Stirling carried twenty-four troops with 250 lbs of equipment each.

By the autumn of 1945 many of 4 Group's operational transport units had left or were in the process of leaving the Group. Others, although still being administered by 4 Group HQ at Heslington Hall, were now under the control of 47 Group Transport Command. Such was the case with the two Liberator squadrons, Nos. 102 and 466. Both units had moved to the 47 Group station at Bassingbourn on the 8th September. Similarly, by September, Nos. 51 and 158 Squadrons were operating under control of 47 Group from Stradishall in Suffolk.

Of the Dakota-equipped units Nos. 10, 76 and 77 had moved to India and were now under the control of Allied Command South East Asia. No. 78 Squadron had left Breighton in September for Egypt and was now in 216 Group, Middle East Command. No. 512 Squadron, after carrying out many flights to the Middle East from its base at Holme-on-Spalding Moor, finally transferred to its new base at Qastina in Palestine on 15th October. No. 575 Squadron remained at Melbourne until November preparing for a move to 47 Group and an eventual deployment to Italy in January 1946.

The two 'Free French' Halifax squadrons at Elvington were employed for a time in dumping unwanted bomb stocks into the North Sea. This was followed by detachments to

France for transport duties until finally, in October 1945, both 346 and 347 Squadrons were transferred to French Air Force control. The French squadrons began to depart from Elvington late in October for their new base at Bordeaux. Unfortunately the transfer was not without tragedy. On 29th October the pilot of Halifax Mk.VI RG561 lost control temporarily after a shudder at 800 feet. The starboard outer engine then caught fire and this spread to the airframe. The navigator baled out but as the aircraft was too low, he was killed. The Halifax force-landed at Sheep Walk Farm, Deighton, Yorkshire. Two were killed and eight injured.

No.4 Group Transport Command, 31st December 1945

Unit	Location
4 (Transport) Group H.Q.	Heslington Hall, York
1380 Transport Conversion Unit	Tilstock (Shrops)
1381 Transport Conversion Unit	Desborough (Northants)
1382 Transport Conversion Unit	Wymeswold/ Castle Donington
1383 Transport Conversion Unit	Crosby-on-Eden (Cumbria)
1384 Heavy Transport Conv. Unit	Ossington (Notts)
1332 Heavy Transport Conv. Unit	Dishforth (Yorks)
1333 Transport Support Conv. Unit	Syerston (Notts)
Air Ambulance School (Nursing Orderlies)	Syerston (Notts)
1336 Transport Conversion Unit	Welford (Berks)
1665 Heavy Transport Conversion Unit	Linton-on-Ouse (Yorks)
231 Squadron	Full Sutton (Yorks)
4 Group Communication Flt	Full Sutton (Yorks)
102 Squadron* (Controlled by 47 Gp)	Bassingbourn (Cambs) 47 Gp
17 Aircrew Holding Unit	Snaith (Yorks)
1516 Radio Approach Training Flt	Snaith (Yorks)
Flight Engineers School	Snaith (Yorks)
1508 Acclimatisation Flight	Snaith (Yorks)
1510 Rebecca BABS Flight	Melbourne (Yorks)
1552 Blind Approach Training Flt	Melbourne (Yorks)
1521 Blind Approach Training Flt	Longtown (Cumbria)
1513 Blind Approach Training Flt	Bramcote (Warks)
1 Air Traffic School	Bramcote (Warks)
Transport Command Aircrew Examining Unit	Bramcote (Warks)
Squadron and Flight Commanders School	Bramcote (Warks)
Clerks School	Bramcote (Warks)
1527 Blind Approach Training Flt*	Prestwick (47 Gp)
1528 Blind Approach Training Flt*	Blakehill Farm (Wilts) 47 Gp
1529 Blind Approach Training Flt	St Mawgan (Cornwall) 47 Gp
Redundant Aircrew Unit	Pocklington (Yorks)
Emergency Landing Ground	Carnaby (Yorks)
Bomb Disposal Wing	Doncaster (Yorks)
School of Air Transport*	Netheravon (38 Gp)
Training Area Flying Control*	Nutts Corner, Antrim (Admiralty)

Airfields under Care and Maintenance: Bitteswell, Elvington, Marston Moor, Nuneaton, Ramsbury, Winthorpe

* Lodger Units

Above: **Departing officers of Nos. 346 and 347 Squadrons are presented to the C-in-C Bomber Command, October 1945.** *J. Harding*

Bottom: **A Halifax C Mk.VIII of No.1665 Heavy Transport Conversion Unit, established at Linton-on-Ouse on the 7th November 1945. Note the 8,000 lb capacity freight pannier fitted in place of the bomb bay.** *A. White*

Below: **'Bon-Voyage!' French and RAF personnel, including Air Commodore 'Gus' Walker with foot on handrail, and to his right Air Marshal Sir Norman Bottomley, C-in-C Bomber Command, cram every vantage point on the Watch Office at Elvington to wave farewell to the Halifaxes of Nos. 346 and 347 'Free French' Squadrons as they leave to go home to France in October 1945.** *J. Harding*

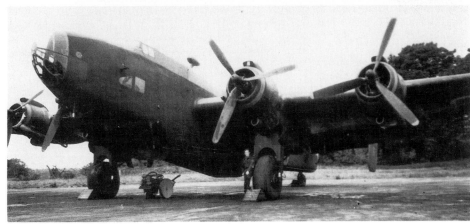

By December 1945 No. 4 Group's former bomber squadrons had all been transferred to other Groups or had been disbanded. No. 4 Group, Transport Command, was now responsible for flying training and ground instruction. In addition the Group now had a new AOC, as from 16th December 1945 Air Vice-Marshal A. Stevens took over from Air Vice-Marshal Walmsley, who had been in command since May. Air Vice-Marshal Stevens was formerly in command of No. 48 Group. Senior Air Staff Officer at Heslington Hall was Air Commodore 'Gus' Walker.

For the next three years No. 4 Group operated purely as a training organisation, supplying qualified crews for the active squadrons of Transport Command. The early months of 1946 were a busy time with demobilisation in full swing. Unfortunately much of the training effort of the Group was wasted as many aircrew had little time to serve in the peacetime RAF after they had completed their conversion courses.

French aircrew load up their Halifaxes before the final flight home to France. *J. Harding*

From June 1946 onwards there was a steady contraction of the training organisation of Transport Command in line with the general pre-war reduction in the size of the RAF. Many units were disbanded and courses closed down. The former bomber airfields were placed on Care and Maintenance or were returned to agriculture. Meanwhile, No. 4 Group had a new AOC in October 1946 when Air Commodore A. P. Revington took over at Heslington Hall. One of his early tasks was to organise the dropping of feedstuffs to beleaguered farmers in the severe winter weather at the beginning of 1947.

By the spring of 1947 No. 4 Group HQ had moved to RAF Abingdon in Oxfordshire, so ending a seven year link with Heslington Hall. The move to Abingdon was part of a long term plan to transfer the future role of No. 4 Group to No. 38 Group Transport Command. Finally, on the 2nd February 1948, No. 4 (Transport) Group was disbanded.

During the war years No. 4 Group squadrons flew 61,577 operational sorties and dropped nearly 200,000 tons of bombs. The cost was heavy with 1,441 aircraft missing and an unknown number lost in crashes. No figures are available for the number of aircrew who were killed on operations. Only the sad and deserted airfields of Yorkshire remain as a memorial to their sacrifice.

Chapter Eighteen

'They Also Served'
A Tribute to the Ground Staff

A typical operational RAF Bomber Station, together with its satellites, housed approximately 2,500 officers, NCOs, airmen and airwomen of which one-tenth comprised aircrew. To keep the station fully operational required a tremendous back-up from the non-flying personnel – the maintenance and administrative staff. These included fitters, riggers, electricians, armourers, transport drivers, parachute and safety workers, fire and crash tender crews, flying control staff, intelligence staff, photographic specialists, meteorological staff, medical teams, stores and equipment personnel, cooks, security staff, airfield defence personnel, waiters and batmen.

This vast army of men and women lived and worked in a self-contained community that was never at complete rest. Day and night, whatever the weather, someone was working.

The ground staff was made up from skilled specialists in a wide variety of fields that essentially were divided into two main groups. The first group included those personnel who were responsible for the maintenance of the aircraft, engines and airframe. Included in this group were the fitters and riggers, instrument makers, electricians, radio mechanics and armourers. The daily maintenance work, the more extensive overhauls, and the repairs to damaged aircraft were carried out by these skilled tradesmen. Each flight, of approximately nine aircraft, was the responsibility of a Flight Sergeant. Each aircraft was entrusted to a Sergeant with, and under his direction, an NCO engine fitter and flight mechanics plus an NCO rigger with three or four riggers. They were assisted by electricians, wireless mechanics, instrument 'bashers' and armourers. Fitters were responsible for checking the engine and all its details and, together with the flight mechanics, they had to examine the cooling system, check magnetos, look for leaks, examine the airscrews and so on. George Ellis Wadsworth was a flight mechanic AC1 at Middleton St George in the winter of 1941/42 and at that time, Middleton was occupied by the Halifaxes of 76 Squadron:

Opposite: **A Halifax Mk.II inside a 'J'-type hangar, summer 1942. The majority of servicing was carried out at dispersals in all weathers, day and night. The type of hangar featured in this photograph narrows the choice of location to either Pocklington or Middleton St George.** IWM, CH6612

'During major inspections each tradesman was responsible for a different part of the engine and my usual job was to check the cooling system. This involved checking the coolant levels, radiators, water joints etc. Each of us had to sign the inspection schedule to confirm that the relevant work had been carried out. The regular daily inspections, the 'DIs', involved minor repairs, replacement of coolant hoses, changing spark plugs etc. During the winter months the engines had to be thawed out before we could start work. The Merlins would normally be covered by heavy rubber covers and we could make use of an engine heater which had a hose that connected to a hole in the base of the cover. This made life a lot easier, but even so, and particularly after a night of heavy snow or frost, conditions could be pretty grim on the dispersals.'

The job of the riggers was to examine the airframe, test the controls and check the metal and fabric control surfaces for damage. In addition tyres were examined for damage and correct pressure. The wireless mechanic tested the receiving and transmitting set, recharged the accumulators, and replaced any damaged coils. He also ran over the wiring and tested the electrical installations. The instrument repairer tested all the aircraft's many delicate instruments. The armourers looked after the guns and tested the gun turrets and bomb releases.

Between five and six armourers under a Corporal, were responsible for the same number of aircraft. The armourer's day would begin with daily inspections and all aircraft guns, turrets and bomb release gear had to be checked as well as wing balloon cable cutters, flares and photoflash equipment. In addition all armourers were expected to help in the bomb dump, handling and preparing bombs and incendiaries – an unpleasant and dangerous task.

Ground crews were immensely proud of their individual aircraft and there often developed a close bond between themselves and the aircrew that flew their charges as Flight Sergeant Arthur Smith of No. 10 Squadron recalls: *

'Our ground crew's daily hours of skilled maintenance and devoted care kept our Halifax flying efficiently and she was always spick and span when we arrived on dispersal for a flight. They would see us off at the start of each raid and were waiting anxiously to welcome us on our return. Bill was the Cor-

poral in charge, working with fitters Mac, Frank and Bobbie. Most ground crew members longed for a flight in the aircraft they tended, and although it was against the rules, occasions did occur when a sympathetic pilot risked bending the rules a little by smuggling one of his ground crew aboard on a training flight.'

Bob Thompson joined 'B' Flight of No. 466 (RAAF) Squadron at Driffield in May 1944 as an engine mechanic at the tender age of eighteen years:

'During most of my time at Driffield I was working on the same two Halifaxes, 'U-Uncle' and 'P-Peter'. During my service I discovered what comradeship was all about. The aircrews had a tremendous amount of faith in us ground crew and we had a great admiration for the fliers. If any of our aircraft failed to return we knew we had lost seven close friends. Similarly if an aircraft returned with dead or injured crew members we had the sad task of removing them from the aircraft.

'When the Squadron took off on a raid all the ground crew were usually there to wave their Halifax off. When the bombers returned it was the 'Duty Crew' that were usually there to meet them. Engine and airframe personnel were on a duty crew every third night at the height of the offensive and it was their job to guide the aircraft into the dispersal points. One particular night I was on duty crew and nearly all our aircraft were down when we were told that the 'Blood Wagon' (Ambulance) was waiting at the end of the runway. Eventually the last aircraft came around the perimeter track with the ambulance following behind. To our horror we saw that it was our Halifax 'P-Peter'; all the other aircraft meanwhile were on their points with engines switched off. I recall that it was a moonlit night and we fully expected to see our Halifax full of holes but as it pulled into the dispersal there appeared to be no obvious signs of damage. It was normal procedure for the pilot to run the engines for a few minutes before shutting down but on this occasion the engines were cut almost immediately. The ambulance, meanwhile, had pulled in close to the aircraft. As I put the chocks under the wheels the crew emerged from the fuselage door and I noticed immediately that one was missing. The ambulance crew came across to the aircraft and we searched the fuselage and found the rear gunner still in his turret. He appeared motionless and in fact he had been dead for quite some time.

'We now had the greatest difficulty in getting him out of the turret. It took the combined efforts of myself, a rigger, the ambulance driver and a doctor to free the body. After a forty-five minute struggle, during which we had to remove part of the turret, our sad job was complete. The doctor, on examining the poor chap, discovered that a tiny piece of shell fragment had passed through the turret bottom and had entered the base of the unfortunate gunner's spine. The metal had gone through his body and had come out at the back of his neck. The only sign of injury was a neat hole at the back of the gunner's neck. The poor fellow had bled to death during the return flight.

'I can remember one particular day when there was an almighty flap on, soon after I'd joined the Squadron. An order came down to us that all the Squadron's Halifaxes were to have their tails painted with distinctive markings. This was to aid formation flying now that the Group was switching over to daylight raids. No. 466 Squadron was to wear three horizontal yellow stripes across the outside of each fin and rudder. All the ground crews

were issued with brushes and tins of aircraft dope, a quick drying paint that smelt of pear-drops. We were told that the job had to be completed before dark. As it was then about 16.00, we estimated that it would take about eight hours to finish all the Squadron so, uncomplainingly, we set too. Later a small utility van called at each dispersal with a supply of cocoa to keep us going. By now it was getting dark and we were painting by torchlight.

'When the job was finally finished one member of the gang had to cycle up to the flight office and inform the NCO in charge, a Flight Sergeant Muzzell, that the work had been done. Later when Muzzell called to inspect the work he blew his top. We had painted the stripes in the wrong sequence. The stripes were painted on horizontally which was correct but the top stripe was yellow instead of black. We had to wash off the yellow and re-start the job all over again. It was 06.00 before the last of us crawled into bed, not that we got much rest because we had to be back on the airfield early that day to prepare the aircraft for an early take off.'

Top left, and then anti-clockwise: **Routine maintenance work being carried out on a Halifax Mk.V series 1 (Special) at a distant disposal 'somewhere in England'.** *IWM, CH10434*

Engine fitters clear a snag on the starboard inner Hercules of *Charlie's Aunt* at Melbourne, summer 1944. As routine maintenance and inspections would normally be carried out in the open, the ground crews' greatest enemy was the weather. *A.C.Smith*

An armourer cleans the nose turret Brownings of a Halifax. *W.Baguley*

Groundcrew of *Vera the Virgin*, No.76 Squadron, Holme-on-Spalding Moor, early 1944. Back row, left to right: unknown armourer; Harry Hill, rigger; George Ellis Wadsworth, flight mechanic; Sergeant Agate, airframe fitter. Front Row from left: unknown electrician; Harry Holcombe, flight mechanic; Ian McCulloch, flight mechanic; unknown armourer. *Vera the Virgin*, MZ516, completed 77 ops before failing to return from Mainz, 1st February 1945. *G.E.Wadsworth*

Linton-on-Ouse armourers servicing the rear turret Brownings of a Whitley V, summer 1940. Lacking both adequate range and hitting power the .303 inch calibre Browning machine guns fitted to the RAF's bombers proved largely ineffective. The bombers best form of defence was concealment. *IWM, CH246*

The second group of ground staff with an equally important role were those men and women who worked in the administrative areas of the station and also provided the services that kept the station operational. Included in this group were the meteorological staff who were responsible for monitoring every possible detail about the local weather conditions. Their weather reports, which included temperatures, visibility, wind direction, barometric pressure etc, were sent to Group headquarters where Met staff collated this and information from other sources to obtain an overall weather picture. Sergeant Tom Allonby served in the meteorological office at No. 4 Group HQ, Heslington Hall, and

it was to his office, that all these weather reports were sent.

'I was not a forecaster, simply a met assistant, but we worked a twenty-four hour non-stop programme. This included hourly weather observations and plotting weather charts at 06.00, noon, 18.00 and midnight. The various weather conditions that we checked were: visibility, temperature, air pressure, wind direction and speed, type of cloud formations (e.g. stratus, cumulus etc), the amount of cloud cover (e.g. four-tenths, ten-tenths etc). Wind direction and speed were of great importance. Not only does the velocity of wind increase with height but it may also change its direction. To check our calculations the wind velocity and direction at various heights was periodically measured. This was done by sending up hydrogen filled balloons. When the balloons were released they travelled at the speed of the wind, their speed varying as they attained different heights. Readings were taken every minute by an observer with a theodolite until the balloon was out of sight. By measuring the speed of the balloon's ascent it was possible to record

the temperatures at various altitudes.

'All the data we received from the Group's airfields came via teleprinter and was in the form of five figure groups. We received hundreds of weather reports each hour from all over the country and these were plotted on the weather charts for the forecasters to use in their crew briefing. It was certainly not all scientific, for example, on the hour, met staff on the stations and at HQ had to go outside and check the weather conditions. If you could see across your airfield then the visibility would be recorded as half a mile. If you could see a factory or church it was one mile, another landmark might be three miles and so on. We used to get weather observations from a dear old village postmistress in the Yorkshire Dales; all useful information to build up an accurate weather picture. What a boon present day met facilities (such as satellite pictures) would have been in our era. Of course the Meteorological Office was simply a part of a vast complex organisation.'

* Extracts from *Halifax Crew* by A. C. Smith, Carlton Publications, 1983.

Chapter Nineteen

'We Also Served'
A WAAF in No.4 Group

The Women's Auxiliary Air Force (WAAF) was formed on 28th January 1939 with the object of replacing officers and airmen with women in certain ground trades and appointments in the Royal Air Force. A vigorous recruiting campaign to expand its numbers was embarked upon and by 1944 nearly a quarter of all ground staff on RAF Bomber Stations were women. Women were employed in a wide variety of duties including watchkeepers, mechanics, cooks, drivers, clerks and by 1944 were a familiar sight at de-briefing as Intelligence Officers.

For many tired bomber crews returning from a raid – often with a damaged aircraft and dead and wounded on board, the first contact with their airfield would be a WAAF wireless operator guiding them safely down. No wonder the crews called them 'Angels'. Although many of the duties carried out by WAAFs were mundane and unglamorous they worked just as long hours as the men and were often in as much danger.

Doris Ikin, (formerly Doris Bayley), was one of the young hopefuls who had joined the WAAF in November 1940. Since her eighteenth birthday she had been eager to get going and 'do her bit' to help the war effort and also to get away from a comfortable but 'dull' home life.

After successfully passing her interview and physical examination, Doris was accepted into the WAAF as a clerk/accounts for which she was paid the princely sum of 1s. 3d per day. After initial training and a spell at Hullavington in Wiltshire, she was posted to Linton-on-Ouse with 4 Group, Bomber Command. Living conditions at Linton-on-Ouse could be grim. Although a pre-war station with reasonably comfortable permanent accommodation, Linton had its share of dispersed hutted sites in which conditions were to say the least, spartan, as Doris Ikin recalls:

'The nissen hutted site on the banks of the River Ouse was to be my home for the next year. The hut in which I found myself held twenty beds and all were occupied by clerks,

both pay and equipment accounts. There was a door and a window at each end of the hut and a loo at the back. The big iron stove in the middle took a great deal of fuel but we were allowed only one bucket full of coal per day, however as we could not light the fire before 16.00 we were able to manage. It was pretty cold for anyone on a day off though, so we usually stayed in bed until lunch time or went into the NAAFI for a warm up.

'The hut was damp, the floor being concrete covered with brown lino which no amount of polishing would shine. We had a small chest of drawers, shared by two girls, and a small mat beside each bed and that was all. After a time we were given empty ammunition boxes for some of our belongings but there were no cupboards.

'Once again bathing became a problem. A

Doris Ikin (formerly Doris 'Bill' Bayley) pictured at the time of her promotion to Sergeant in April 1943. *D.Ikin*

nice big shower hut had been built on the site; his had a couple of dozen cubicles in two rows with concrete floors and shower trays and rough curtains to each. These doubled as decontamination centres in case of a gas attack. The water regulator however was at one end of the hut and I spent one very miserable hour on one of my days off running back and forth from regulator to shower in an endeavour to get water bearable enough in which to take a shower. It was no fun running up and down an unheated hut on concrete floors, stark naked and wet in the middle of a Yorkshire winter. There was an ablution hut with wash hand basins only but as this was some distance from my hut I usually had a quick wash using the water from my hot water bottle in a bucket.

'After a time I was promoted to the pay ledger for Station Headquarters staff. Each day we were given long lists, made out by clerks in the Orderly Room, of leave, deductions from pay for various reasons, promotions and the subsequent raises in pay etc. These were all noted in the ledger and the pay worked out accordingly. Pay day was once a fortnight on a Friday and we were all paid to the nearest two shilling piece. Pay Parade was another ritual you may like to know about. All the camp personnel, apart from W/Os and officers, lined up, buttons gleaming and hats on straight. As each name was called the person had to step forward give the last three numbers of his number and salute. The pay clerk would then give the amount due and ink it in the ledger while the officer paid the money over. It usually worked well unless there were several Joneses or Smiths. I once had difficulty of another kind. It was when I was up north in Yorkshire, a bitterly cold day and the parade was in the open although the pay table at which I sat was under a sort of lean-to. After only a few payments the ink on the nib of my pen froze and I was unable to go on. The parade was held up and we finally had to find warmer quarters. Remember, there was only bottled ink in those days, no biros.

'I found this work quite enjoyable as I like figures but there were many other much more exciting trades open to women. The girls in flying control and the operations room were really in the centre of things. The drivers and later, the mechanics, were more actively engaged in war work but each one of us released an able bodied man for the front line, if nothing else.'

Opposite page: **A WAAF helps to unload petrol from a tanker at the fuel dump at Pocklington. Note the civilian tanker driver.** *IWM, CH6601*

The lower photograph shows a WAAF officer interrogating a tired 405 (RCAF) Squadron crew at Pocklington in 1942. *IWM, CH6634*

Chapter Twenty

'Ops Are On'
The Work of No.4 Group HQ

For the operations staff at No. 4 Group HQ, Heslington Hall, the day would begin with a detailed analysis of the previous night's operations. Teams of photographic interpreters would be examining the bombing photographs taken by the Group's aircraft on the previous night's raid. Reports would then be compiled for despatch to HQ Bomber Command. Meanwhile the teleprinter in the operations room would begin to buzz with the detailed instructions for that night's target.

The decision of which target to be attacked would have been made by Air Chief Marshal Sir Arthur Harris at his regular early morning conference at HQ Bomber Command, High Wycombe. Each conference was attended by the Deputy C-in-C (who was responsible for detailed planning), the Senior Air Staff Officer (who set the operational machinery in motion),

a naval staff officer, the Chief Intelligence Officer, the operations room staff and liaison officers, including those from the US Forces.

At No. 4 Group HQ the initial warning that 'ops are on' would have been received by Wing Commander George 'Tiny' Clapperton, Air 1 for No. 4 Group from late 1942 to 1945. George Clapperton was an experienced bomber pilot having completed two tours of ops with 10 and 78 Squadrons before being posted to 4 Group HQ:

'Each target would be notified to Heslington Hall via scrambler telephone from HQ Bomber Command, High Wycombe. Normally details of the raid were passed to me, although in special cases they were passed direct to the AOC, Air Vice-Marshal Carr or his SASO, Air Commodore Brooke. The target would then be confirmed by a top secret tele-

printer message from HQ Bomber Command giving the following details:
1: The target (usually named by its codeword, i.e. 'Whitebait' – Berlin)
2: The diversionary target if any.
3: Number of aircraft required for 1st and 2nd targets. (This would be a specific number or maximum effort).
4: Time on target. (The period over the target allotted to the Group's aircraft).
5: Bomb load (i.e. the types of bombs to be carried for each specific target).
6: Any other relevant details (i.e. other Groups operating etc).

'When the above information had been confirmed the AOC would call for an operations meeting to discuss what aircraft and squadrons would be taking part in the raid, (each morning the Group's squadrons would notify

Heslington Hall of the number of aircraft available for operations), what routes were to be taken and what bomb loads were to be carried. The meeting was normally held in my office, a room dominated by a large scale map of Europe and the British Isles covering one wall. Officers attending the meeting would be: the AOC, Air Vice-Marshal Carr; the Senior Air Staff Officer, Air Commodore Brooke; myself, Air 1; the Navigation Officer; the Intelligence Officer; the Naval Liaison Officer; the Armaments Officer; and finally the Met Officer (a civilian).

'Ops are on!' Wing Commander George 'Tiny' Clapperton receives the warning from HQ Bomber Command via the scrambler telephone at Heslington Hall. Wing Commander Clapperton was Air 1 at No. 4 Group HQ from 1942 to 1945. *G. Clapperton*

Air Vice-Marshal Carr, AOC No. 4 Group, discusses details of the forthcoming night's operations with his Senior Air Staff Officer Group Captain (later Air Commodore) W. A. D. Brooke. At this stage of the planning of an operation Group commanders could suggest alterations to the planned timing and routeing of a raid. *IWM, CH 9316*

No. 4 Group operations staff at the AOC's morning briefing, Heslington Hall, 1943. On Air Vice-Marshal Carr's left is his Senior Air Staff Officer, Air Commodore Brooke. Next to him is Squadron Leader Robinson, No. 4 Group Navigation Officer. On the AOC's right is Wing Commander, (later Sir Guy) Lawrence, No. 4 Group Training Inspector. Guy Lawrence had completed one tour of operations with No. 78 Squadron before moving to No. 4 Group HQ. He was to return to No. 78 Squadron in 1943 this time as Squadron Commander, and completed another 13 operations before posting to HQ Bomber Command. *Guy Lawrence*

Opposite page: No. 4 Group Headquarters staff in the grounds of Heslington Hall, 1943. Front row from left to right: Wing Commander Peock, Senior Group Medical Officer; Wing Commander Guy Lawrence, Group Training Inspector; Wing Commander 'Tiny' Clapperton, Air Operations; Air Vice-Marshal Carr, AOC No. 4 Group; Air Commodore Brooke, Senior Air Staff Officer; Squadron Leader Firth, Senior Intelligence Officer. Second row: Squadron Leader Robinson, Group Navigation Officer; Wing Commander Walker, Senior Group Signals Officer; Flight Lieutenant Mason-Lewis, Bombing Leader; Squadron Leader Harvey, Equipment; Squadron Leader Grant, HQ Unit Senior Personnel Officer; Squadron Leader Knight, Organisation. Third row; Lieutenant Colonel Johnson, Airfield Defence; Flight Lieutenant Burgess, Signals; Pilot Officer Cain, Armament; Flight Lieutenant Putnam, Group Gunnery Leader; Back row: Flight Lieutenant Pearman, Camp Commandant; Flight Lieutenant Walker, Personnel; Flight Lieutenant Coleman, Administration; Lieutenant Style, Naval Liaison Officer; Squadron Leader Garnder, Flying Control. *Guy Lawrence*

The operations board at No. 4 Group HQ on the occasion of the second 1,000 bomber raid against Essen on the night of 1st June 1942. That night 4 Group despatched 138 aircraft of which 117 bombed the primary and four the alternative target. Nine aircraft were shot down. *G. Clapperton*

'For a normal type of operation the format of the meeting had a familiar pattern. Firstly, the Met Officer would report on the expected weather conditions on the route to, over and back from the target. He would also give a forecast for the conditions over the Group's bases warning of the dangers of fog or low cloud – a regular hazard over the Yorkshire bases. Next came the Intelligence Officer who would give the latest reports of the defences – flak, radar, searchlights etc, in Holland, France and Germany. Bearing in mind the need to avoid any new and existing heavily defended areas, an agreed route would now be marked out on the large wall map by the Navigation Officer so that outgoing and return mileages could be calculated. We had in my office a very simple system of calculating the mileage to and from the target. Two cords, of the non-stretch variety, protruded from the wall map at York, one to be used for the outward journey and one for the return. These cords worked over pulleys to scales in miles on one side of the wall map. The cords would be worked around pins stuck in the map, enabling us to work out the petrol and bomb loads very quickly. For example, a

Halifax Bomb Loads for Use Against Tactical Targets

Target	Bomb Loads Code Name	Bomb Loads Halifax	Fusing Preferred	Fusing Alternative
Marshalling Yards	Normal	9 x 1000 MC/GP 6 x 500 MC/GP	75% .025 25% LD	0.25 with up to 30% T Inst
	Cookie	18 x 500 MC/GP		
Coastal Batteries	Abnormal	9 x 1000 MC/GP 6 x 500 MC/GP	0.25	Nil
	Buffer	18 x 500 MC/GP		
Beach Defences	Patter	18 x 500 MC/GP	No. 44 Pistol Mk.II Nose Inst	Nil
Airfields	Muffle	18 x 500 MC/GP	.025	Tail Inst
	Clatter	18 x 500 MC/GP	No. 44 Pistol Mk.II Nose Inst	Nose Inst
	Normal	9 x 1000 MC/GP 6 x 500 MC/GP	75% .025 25% LD	Nil
	Chisel	18 x 500 MC/GP	25% LD	
Ammo & Fuel Dumps	Rattle	18 x 500 MC/GP	.025	Tail Inst
	Thunder	18 x 500 MC/GP	Nose Inst	Nil
	Crackle	12 x 500 MC/GP 6 x CP No.14	.025	Tail Inst Nose Inst
Hutted Camps	Thunder	18 x 500 MC/GP	Nose Inst	Nil
	Sub Normal	9 x 1000 MC/GP 6 x 500 MC/GP	Tail Inst	Nil
	Rumble	3 x 1000 MC/GP 14 x 500 MC/GP	Tail Inst	Nil
Tank Concentrations Bowzer M/T Parks, Troop Con		18 x 500 MC/GP	No. 44 Pistol Mark II Nose Inst	Nil

Note 1: When Normal, Abnormal, or Subnormal bomb loads are ordered, Halifaxes are, if possible, to carry three ANM -65 bombs with American tails.

Note 2: ANM -59 bombs can be considered equivalent in stowage and performance to British 1000 lb. GP bombs and may be utilised accordingly.

Halifax Mk.V, fully loaded, would fly 0.77 air miles for every gallon of fuel plus 200 gallons reserve. The twin-engined Whitleys and Wellingtons used correspondingly less.

'Once fuel load was known the disposable load for the aircraft could be calculated. A typical tactical bomb load for a Halifax Mk.V might be as follows: nine 1,000 lb and six 500 lb medium capacity general purpose bombs. All bomb stations were capable of carrying small bomb containers for the delivery of incendiaries. I made a number of circular cardboard calculators for quick reference when determining disposable load. These showed track miles to and from the target, amount of petrol required, the number of fuel tanks and finally, bomb load.

'Next it was the turn of the Naval Liaison Officer to give details of any mining operations or information on the movement of naval forces in the general area of the bombers outward and inward routes. To avoid any mistakes by naval gunners, the 'Colours of the day' would be notified to all concerned. Finally, the AOC after a final word about the forthcoming operation, would close the meeting. It was at this stage that changes to the operational plan, subject to approval by HQ Bomber Command, could be made by individual Group commanders.

'Once the planning had been completed all the operational details would be passed to the Group Operations Room. Here the staff would be already working on the details of each of the Group's aircraft. All the individual information of each Squadron's aircraft was displayed on the Operations Room Board and under each Squadron was the following details:
1: Aircraft Call Sign
2: Aircraft Number
3: Time of take-off
4: Time of landing

'On take off, each station would report to the Group Operations Room the time of take off for each aircraft so that it could be marked on the Operations Room Board. On landing the same system would apply.

'During this period it was the job of the Armaments Officer to ensure that each station had the correct bomb loads, fuses etc, relevant to each aircraft. Depending on the type of target to be attacked each aircraft type had a particular bomb load suitable for the task. Each of these bomb loads had their own code name so that it was possible for the Armaments Officer to pass details of bomb loads, fusing etc, to the Group's stations efficiently. The table on the opposite page shows typical bomb loads, fusing and code names for Halifax aircraft attacking tactical targets.

Finally, when all the operational details have been agreed, the 'Form B' is compiled for transmission via the teleprinter room simultaneously to all the Group's stations taking part in the raid. The 'Form B' will contain details of bomb loads, timings, target marking, as well as information of other Groups taking part in the operation.'

Danger, men at work! Holme-on-Spalding Moor armourers manhandle 1,000 lb general purpose bombs in the bomb dump. The date is 22nd October 1943 and the 1,000 pounders are destined for Kassel city centre. *IWM, CH11405*

The Preparations on the Airfields

The warning message that 'Ops are on' would have been flashed to all the Group's stations soon after it was received at Group HQ. Although at this stage the ground staff would not know the identity of the target for tonight, preparations for the raid would be well in hand. In the bomb dumps the armourers, from an early hour, would be toiling to prepare the bombs for the forthcoming raid.

On most airfields the High Explosive bombs were stored in Type 'D' 200 ton open bomb stores. The Type 'D' bomb store comprised four bays separated from each other by earthen traverses. Each bay consisted of a hardcore storage area 47' 6" long and 24' wide and was designed to hold 50 tons of HE bombs. The bombs themselves were stored on wooden battens and each bomb had to be manhandled onto the special bomb trolleys using a block and tackle. There were three main types of High Explosive bomb used by Bomber Command during the Second World War, namely General Purpose (GP), Medium Capacity (MC) and High Capacity (HC). The principal difference between these types lay in their varying charge-weight ratios. The higher capacity bombs had the higher charge-weight ratios and, therefore had thinner and lighter casings. They thus produced a greater blast value but tended to have less penetration and, in some cases, a poorer ballistic performance than their lower capacity equivalents.

Whilst a team of armourers loaded the HE bombs in another section of the dump other armourers would be preparing the incendiaries for loading into the special containers known as SBCs. Lewis Adams was one of those armourers toiling in the bomb dump at Melbourne on most days during 1943:

An AEC Matador fuel bowser pumps fuel at 30 gal/min into a Halifax Mk.I of 76 Squadron at Middleton St George, in the autumn of 1941. The tanker's capacity was 2,500 gallons, which meant that during refuelling operations there would be a constant procession of tankers passing from the fuel dump to the dispersals. Also of interest in this damp autumnal scene is the 78 Squadron Whitley Mk.V standing quietly in the background. At this time No.78 shared Middleton with No.76. *IWM, CH4462*

Engine mechanics filling the wing tanks of a Halifax at Pocklington, 1942. *IWM, CH6619*

'Our day usually began early. First job was loading the incendiaries into the Small Bomb Containers (SBCs). The 4 lb incendiary bombs were stored in boxes containing twenty-five bombs so each box weighed 100 lb. These boxes had to be carried to a central point where the bombs were loaded into the SBCs. Each SBC could hold 90 incendiaries whilst the larger 30 lb bombs were loaded eight to a container. The SBCs then had to be loaded by hand onto the bomb trolleys so in our job you soon developed plenty of muscles. Our next job would be to load the 500 and 1,000 pounders using a block and tackle; more sweating and cursing before the bombs were towed away to the fusing point buildings.'

At the fusing point the transit plugs were removed and the fuses fitted, after which the fuses would be wired to prevent the windmill device from arming the bomb during transit to the aircraft. Safely stowed on the trolleys the bomb and incendiary trains would form up ready for the journey out to the dispersals. Janice Williams was a WAAF tractor driver at Linton-on-Ouse and it was her job to drive one of the Fordson tractors that towed the bomb trains from the bomb dump to the aircraft on their dispersals:

'I had been brought up on a farm so I knew how to handle a tractor. I was only nineteen and I thought that being involved in the war and doing my bit was tremendously exciting. At first I was very nervous at the thought of towing all that high explosive around, but after a while I didn't give it a thought. My most vivid memory of those days was the cold. It was bitterly cold on those wind-swept airfields. And the mud, especially in the bomb dump, it was everywhere. We wore rubber boots all the time but all our clothing, greatcoats, trousers, and gloves became caked in mud. Of course the job had to be done whatever the weather.'

Away from the bomb dumps there would be similar feverish activity going on in and around the fuel storage areas. Here the giant Matador fuel bowsers would each be receiving their 2,500 gallons of aviation fuel before making their ponderous journey around the winding perimeter tracks to the bombers waiting at their dispersals. Refuelling was always time consuming as the bowsers only held enough fuel to fill up one aircraft.

Out on the dispersals the mechanics, fitters and riggers would be swarming over their aircraft working against time to prepare their charges for the coming operation. Occasionally there would be a last minute panic and

Muscle power! Pocklington armourers heave a trolley load of 1,000 pounders into position for hoisting into 'Q-Queenie' of No. 405 (RCAF) Squadron. The presence of nose plugs in the bombs indicates that this load is set for long delay. The airman at the extreme right is fitting the release gear to a Small Bomb Container (SBC). *Chaz Bowyer collection*

Whilst the 1,000 lb MC bombs are hoisted into 'Queenie's' bomb bay, (via the Halifax's own internal winch) an armourer is using a hand winch to lift the SBCs into the wing cells. *Chaz Bowyer collection*

Armourers (of 218 Squadron, 3 Group perhaps) prepare to manhandle a Small Bomb Container onto a bomb trolley. An SBC could hold 90 of the Mk. 1E 4lb Incendiary bombs – the principal fire starting weapon used by RAF Bomber Command throughout the war. *IWM, CH 6272*

a faulty engine would need replacing. In peacetime the task of replacing an engine might have taken a week; in wartime the job would be completed in less than five hours. Everything had to be checked and double checked and faults rectified in time for a test flight. Throughout the morning and early afternoon the ceaseless activity on the dispersals and in the hangars would be accompanied by the constant sound of aircraft engines being tested. The smell of exhaust fumes and spent aviation fuel would hang heavily over the whole airfield.

Meanwhile, on another part of the station, there was activity of a different kind. In the operations room the Station Commander and his team of specialists would be finalising details for the crew briefing. The Flying Control Officer, responsible for the smooth and safe marshalling and take-off of perhaps thirty aircraft, would be checking every detail of his take-off plan. The Meteorological officers would be collating all the latest weather information and the Intelligence staff would be busy preparing target maps, photographs and updating target and route information as it arrived from Group HQ. With the crew briefing due for the early afternoon all these specialists would be working against time to complete their tasks.

Other personnel in a hurry would be the staff of the crew locker rooms busy making sure that each item of the crew's equipment, from lifejackets to socks, was thoroughly checked. In the kitchens WAAFs would be preparing ration parcels for each of the aircrew. Each parcel would contain sandwiches, chocolate, fruit, chewing gum, etc plus a thermos flask of coffee.

Meanwhile out on the dispersals the bomb trains would be arriving. Here there was more hard labour for the armourers as they manhandled the bomb trolleys into the correct position under the aircraft's bomb-bay ready for winching up the bomb load. Prior to winching, bomb carriers which contained the electrical release mechanism, had to be fitted and it was these much abused items of equipment that would cause most problems.

Armourers preparing 250 lb GP bombs for hoisting into the narrow, double bomb bay of a Wellington. *Chaz Bowyer collection*

Larger bombs, like this 1,000 lb medium capacity example, were a tight fit for the Wimpy's bomb bay. *Chaz Bowyer collection*

Some of the staff of the MT Section at Linton-on-Ouse in 1941. *W. Baguley*

Opposite page: **Tea Up! Ground crews queue at the NAAFI refreshment van for a welcome 'cuppa' and a break during preparations for another maximum effort: Elvington, summer 1943.** *IWM CH10595*

Unless the carrier was fitted correctly the bomb release units would fail to operate.

All the bombs would arrive from the dump with safety devices intact and once the load was safely stowed in the bomb-bay, then these could be removed. This was the moment of most danger as the bombs would now be armed. Engine mechanic Bob Thompson remembers a lively incident at Driffield in 1944 involving a Halifax that had just been bombed-up.

'When an aircraft had been bombed-up an electrician had to check the release mechanism to make sure that it was working correctly. This was done by switching the bomb release switch to 'check' – it would normally be set at 'release'. This particular afternoon an electrician failed to make sure that th safety switch was set to 'check' and when he pressed the release button the whole bomb load of 500 pounders fell to the dispersal floor. Fortunately there were no explosions but I think that the four minute mile was broken that day by the ground crew lads who were working on the aircraft.'

Unfortunately there were a number of tragic incidents when bombs exploded during loading. On 28th December 1944 a bomb fell from the rack of a Halifax during bombing-up at Elvington. The bomb exploded setting off the rest of the load which included incendiaries; thirteen were killed and five injured in the incident. An explosion in the fusing shed at Snaith on 19th June 1943 killed eighteen armourers. These incidents underline what a difficult and dangerous task the

armourers faced when handling explosives.

By late afternoon the aircraft would be fuelled, tested, bombed-up and ready for take off. Here and there a busy team of ground crew might be attending to a last minute plug change or curing a persistent oil leak. Meanwhile, the aircrews, their briefing over and having drawn their personal flying kit, parachutes etc, would be gathering at the pick-up point ready for the transports to take them out to their kites. Here the crews would be taking the opportunity to check their gear and inevitably share a joke and a 'fag'. Some would be indulging in nervous chatter and laughter to relieve the tension, whilst others preferred to be alone with their thoughts and fears.

As each crew was dropped off at their respective dispersal they would be greeted by their waiting ground crew. Before he could enter the aircraft the pilot must check that all the engine, cockpit, wheel and pitot head covers have been removed. He must ensure that there are no oil or fuel leaks, that all cowlings, inspection panels are secure and tyres and undercarriage are in order. Preliminary checks having been completed to the pilot's satisfaction the crew would now enter the aircraft to take up their positions and commence checking their own equipment.

When the pre-flight checks were completed the aircraft was ready for start-up. Driffield mechanic Bob Thompson describes start-up procedure for the Halifax.

'When the signal to start up was given the ground mechanic (engines) would plug in the

mobile battery starter. The pilot would then turn the 'Ground/Flight' switch to 'Ground', switch on the master engine cocks and instruct the flight engineer to turn on tanks 1 and 3. The engine mechanic, meanwhile, would board the aircraft and would stand by the pilot ready for start up. At this time the airframe fitter would stand at the front of the aircraft in view of the pilot so as to indicate which engine was to be started first. This was done by pointing at the relevant engine with one hand and rotating his free hand. The pilot would then switch on the ignition and press the starter and booster coil buttons. At the same time and while the engine was being turned, another mechanic would be working the fuel priming pump until such time as the engine fired and picked up on the carburettor.

'Each engine was checked individually and the throttles opened up to 1,000 rpm. Temperatures and pressures and each magneto were checked along with the hydraulic system by lowering and raising the flaps. Minor faults did occur and they had to be rectified before take off but usually it was too late for anything major at this stage.

'As soon as the checks were completed (usually it took about four minutes) the mechanic would hand over the Form 700 for the pilot to sign, indicating everything was in order. The mechanic would then wish the pilot good luck and leave the aircraft making sure that the hatch was secure. The aircraft would be guided from the dispersal by one of the mechanics to join the queue for take off.'

Snaith control tower staff, June 1944. Front row left to right: Meteorology (Met.) WAAF; Flying Officer James; Met. Officer; Squadron Leader Vary, Flying Control Officer; Flying Officer Roderick; Sergeant Whitehead; Met. WAAF. *W.Baguley*

Ground crews 'pre-flight' a Halifax Mk.III of No.347 Squadron at Elvington, 1944. One 'erk' balances on a trolley accumulator as he plugs the power lead into the aircraft's electrical system, whilst others remove wheel and engine covers prior to start-up. *W.Baguley*

Meanwhile in the airfield control tower the flying control staff would be busy logging the progress of each aircraft as it taxied onto the main runway, there to be held by the controller's Aldis lamp awaiting the green for go. Each take off would then be entered onto the control board. As the pilots released their brakes and each bomber accelerated away on its journey into the unknown, there waiting at the end of the runway would be the usual gathering of station personnel to wave each crew off. And, when hours later the bombers return, those same loyal ground staff will be standing by, whatever the weather, to greet the crews, attend to the injured and repair the damage.

Taxying a fully laden Halifax along a narrow perimeter track could be tricky as any slight misjudgement on the part of the pilot could result in the wheels becoming bogged at the side of the track. This could cause chaos to the take off schedule and for this reason towing vehicles were always on hand. For the same reason a stand-by ground crew, along with a spare starter trolley, was positioned at the end of the runway during take offs in case an aircraft stalled and blocked the runway.

The following poem has become a firm favourite with ex-Bomber Command personnel. It was published in Noel Coward Collected Verse *(Methuen, 1984) and is reprinted by permission of Methuen London.*

LIE IN THE DARK AND LISTEN
- by Noel Coward

Lie in the dark and listen,
It's clear tonight so they're flying high
Hundreds of them, thousands perhaps,
Riding the icy, moonlight sky.
Men, material, bombs and maps
Altimeters and guns and charts
Coffee, sandwiches, fleece-lined boots
Bones and muscles and minds and hearts
English saplings with English roots
Deep in the earth they've left below
Lie in the dark and let them go
Lie in the dark and listen.

Lie in the dark and listen
They're going over in waves and waves
High above villages, hills and streams
Country churches and little graves
And little citizen's worried dreams.
Very soon they'll have reached the sea
And far below them will lie the bays
And coves and sands where they used to be
Taken for summer holidays.
Lie in the dark and let them go
Lie in the dark and listen.

Lie in the dark and listen
City magnates and steel contractors,
Factory workers and politicians
Soft, hysterical little actors
Ballet dancers, 'Reserved' musicians,
Safe in your warm, civilian beds.
Count your profits and count your sheep
Life is flying above your heads
Just turn over and try to sleep.
Lie in the dark and let them go
Theirs is a world you'll never know
Lie in the dark and listen.

... We owe them.

Appendix A

The Commanders of No.4 Group 1937-1948

Air Commodore A.T. Harris
12th June 1937 to 24th May 1938
Air Commodore C.H.B. Blount
25th May 1938 to 2nd July 1939
Air Vice-Marshal A. Coningham
3rd July 1939 to 25th July 1941
Air Vice-Marshal C.R. Carr
26th July 1941 to 11th February 1945
Air Vice-Marshal J.R. Whitley
12th February 1945 to 6th May 1945
Air Vice-Marshal H.S.P. Walmsley
7th May 1945 to 15th December 1945
Air Vice-Marshal A.C. Stevens
16th December 1945 to 1st October 1946
Air Commodore A.P. Revington
2nd October 1946 to 2nd February 1948

Appendix B

The Effort and the Cost

Beginning the war with an average of a dozen sorties per operation, No.4 Group reached a record total of 3,620 sorties in twenty-two operations during August 1944. In March 1945 8,294 tons of bombs were dropped on Germany in 2,727 sorties for the low loss of fifteen aircraft. During the whole war a total of 61,577 operational sorties were flown, nearly 200,000 tons of bombs were dropped and more than 7,000 mines laid.

The Cost - No.4 Group Operational Sorties 1939-45

Year	Operational Sorties	Aircraft Missing
1939	246	4
1940	3862	47
1941	5700	205
1942	4957	223
1943	11607	485
1944	25464	402
1945	9741	75
Totals	61577	1441

The *No.4 Group Digest,* for April 1945, provides the following details of all mining (*Gardening*) operations carried out by No.4 Group from October 1942 to April 1945 -
Sorties: Halifaxes 1,836; Wellington 714
Number of mines laid successfully: 6,265
Nights Operated: 193
Mileage flown: 2,169,614
Number of aircraft missing: Halifax 23; Wellington 17

The following record was compiled from the Operational Failures Log kept by the Squadron Engineer Officer / OC Daily Servicing Squadron of No.78 Squadron and shows the typical effort made by a Halifax squadron of No.4 Group during the massive offensive of Bomber command between July 1943 and December 1944.

* During these four months, the unit progressively re-equipped with Halifax Mk.III.

	Det'd	Desp'd	Aborted	Missing	On Target
July 1943	175	174	11	11	163
August	202	197	11	9	186
September	171	167	18	14	149
October	66	61	8	6	53
November*	119	115	5	1	110
December*	62	60	8	5	52
January '44*	45	43	5	2	38
February*	97	84	23	7	61
March	200	170	19	11	151
April	178	175	6	4	169
May	195	193	7	1	186
June	312	306	7	9	299
July	327	320	10	2	310
August	316	310	9	1	301
September	250	244	5	2	239
October	254	240	7	4	233
November	159	151	4	1	147
December	188	182	12	0	170
Total	3316	3192	175	90	3017

Appendix C

The Squadrons of No.4 Group

No.7 Squadron

Motto:	By day and by night
Sqn code:	LT (Munich crisis)
Bases:	
Finningley	Sep 1936 - Sep 1939
Became a Group pool Squadron Jun 1939	
Became No.16 OTU Apr 1940	
Equipment:	
Heyford II/III	Apr 1935 - Apr 1938
Wellesley	Apr 1937 ('B' Flight only)
Whitley II	Mar 1938 - Dec 1938
Whitley III	Nov 1938 - May 1939
Representative serial numbers:	
Heyford II	K4863, K4865
Heyford III	K6873, K6874
Wellesley	K7714
Whitley II	K7233
Whitley III	K8942, K8964, K8978

No.10 Squadron

Motto:	To hit the mark
Sqn codes:	PB (Munich crisis); ZA
Bases:	
Dishforth	Jan 1937 - Jul 1940
Leeming	Jul 1940 - Aug 1942
Melbourne	Aug 1942 - Aug 1945
Broadwell	Aug 1945
St Mawgan	Aug 1945
Transferred to ACSEA India Oct 1945	
Equipment:	
Heyford IA/III	Aug 1934 - Jun 1937
Whitley I	Mar 1937 - May 1939
Whitley IV	May 1939 - May 1940
Whitley V	May 1940 - Dec 1941
Halifax II	Dec 1941 - Mar 1944
Halifax III	Mar 1944 - Aug 1945
Dakota III/IV	Aug 1945 - Dec 1947
Representative serial numbers:	
Heyford IA	K4023 'K', K4027 'A'
Heyford III	K5185, K6879
Whitley I	K7189 'L', K7192 'C'
Whitley IV	K9018, K9026 'O', K9034
Whitley V	P4962, T4143 'J', T4265 'J', Z9119 'C'
Halifax II	R9392 'A', W1057 'X'
Halifax III	NA162 'W', RG442 'E'
Dakota III	KN678

No.35 Squadron

Motto:	We act with one accord
Sqn code:	TL
Bases:	
Leeming	Nov 1940 - Dec 1940
Linton-on-Ouse	Dec 1940 - Aug 1942
Transferred to Pathfinder Force 15 Aug 1942.	

Equipment:	
Halifax I	Nov 1940 - Oct 1941
Halifax II	Oct 1941 - Mar 1944
Representative serial numbers:	
Halifax I	L9489 'F', L9597 'P'
Halifax II	V9978 'A', V9979 'E'

No.51 Squadron

Motto:	Swift and Sure
Sqn codes:	UT (Munich crisis); MH
Bases:	
Boscombe Down	Mar 1937 - Apr 1938
Linton-on-Ouse	Apr 1938 - Dec 1939
Dishforth	Dec 1939 - May 1942
Chivenor (*cc)	May 1942 - Oct 1942
Snaith	Oct 1942 - Apr 1945
Leconfield	Apr 1945 - Aug 1945
Transferred to No.47 Group Aug 1945	
Equipment:	
Virginia X	Mar 1937 - Feb 1938
Anson I	Mar 1937 - Feb 1938
Whitley II	Feb 1938 - Dec 1939
Whitley III	Aug 1938 - Dec 1939
Whitley IV	Nov 1939 - May 1940
Whitley V	May 1940 - Nov 1942
Halifax II	Nov 1942 - Jan 1944
Halifax III	Jan 1944 - Jun 1945
Stirling V	Jun 1945 - Dec 1947
Representative serial numbers:	
Virginia X	K2669
Anson I	K6277 'T'
Whitley II	K7228 'T', K7261
Whitley III	K8937, K9008 'J'
Whitley IV	K9043 'G', K9048
Whitley V	N1406, P4982
Halifax II	LW287 'C', HR946 'T'
Halifax III	MZ319 'B', LL548 'D'
Stirling V	PJ883 'A', PJ945

No.58 Squadron

Motto:	On the wings of the night
Sqn codes:	BW (Munich crisis); GE
Bases:	
Boscombe Down	Mar 1937 - Apr 1938
Linton-on-Ouse	Apr 1938 - Oct 1939
Boscombe Down	Oct 1939 - Feb 1940 (*cc)
Linton-on-Ouse	Feb 1940 - Apr 1942
Transferred to Coastal Command Apr 1942.	
Equipment:	
Virginia X	Mar 1937 - Dec 1937
Anson I	Feb 1937 - Dec 1937
Heyford III	Apr 1937
Whitley I	Oct 1937 - Dec 1937
Whitley II	Oct 1937 - May 1939
Whitley III	May 1939 - Mar 1940
Whitley V	Mar 1940 - Dec 1942

Representative serial numbers:	
Virginia X	K2666
Anson I	K6270
Whitley I	K7211, K7216
Whitley II	K7218, K7260
Whitley III	K8964 'R'
Whitley V	N1428 'B', T4336 'E'

No.75 Squadron

Motto:	Forever and ever be strong
Sqn code:	75
Bases:	
Driffield	Mar 1937 - Jul 1938
Transferred to No.3 Group 11 Jul 1938	
Equipment:	
Virginia X	Mar 1937 - Jul 1937
Anson I	Mar 1937 - Nov 1937
Harrow I/II	Sept 1937 - Jul 1939
Representative serial numbers:	
Virginia X	K2672
Anson I	K6299
Harrow I	K6947 'P'

No.76 Squadron

Motto:	Resolute
Sqn codes:	NM (Munich crisis); MP
Bases:	
Finningley	Apr 1937 - Sep 1939
Became a Group pool Squadron 1 Jun 1939	
Transferred to No.5 Group	
Reformed from 35 Sqn ('C' Flt) May 1941	
Linton-on-Ouse	May 1941 - Jun 1941
Middleton St George Jun 1941 - Sep 1942	
Det in Middle East 12 Jul 1942 - 7 Sep 1942	
Linton-on-Ouse	Sep 1942 - Jun 1943
Holme-on-Spalding Moor Jun 1943 - Aug 1945	
Broadwell	Aug 1945
Portreath	Aug 1945
Transferred to ACSEA India Sep 1945	
Equipment:	
Wellesley	Apr 1937 - Apr 1939
Hampden I	Mar 1939 - Apr 1940
Anson I	May 1939 - Apr 1940
Halifax I	May 1941 - Feb 1942
Halifax II	Oct 1941 - Apr 1943
Halifax V	Apr 1943 - Feb 1944
Halifax III	Feb 1944 - Apr 1945
Halifax VI	Mar 1945 - Oct 1945
Dakota IV	May 1945 - Sep 1946
Representative serial numbers:	
Wellesley	K7714, K7748 'H'
Hampden I	P1269
Anson I	N5000
Halifax I	L9565 'B'
Halifax II	DT550 'B', HR748 'R'
Halifax V	DK134 'Y', LK902 'H'

Halifax III	MZ460 'Q', NA219 'D'
Halifax VI	PP172 'Z', RG497 'S'
Dakota IV	KJ863, KP257 'Y'

No. 77 Squadron

| Motto: | To be, rather than seen |
| Sqn codes: | ZL (Munich crisis); KN |

Bases:

Driffield	Jul 1938 - Aug 1940
Kinloss (*cc)	Apr 1940 - May 1940
Linton-on-Ouse	Aug 1940 - Oct 1940
Topcliffe	Oct 1940 - Sep 1941
Leeming	Sep 1941 - May 1942
Chivenor (*cc)	May 1942 - Oct 1942
Elvington	Oct 1942 - May 1944
Full Sutton	May 1944 - Aug 1945
Broadwell	Aug 1945 - Oct 1945
Transferred to ACSEA India Oct 1945	

Equipment:

Wellesley	Nov 1937 - Nov 1938
Whitley III	Nov 1938 - Oct 1939
Whitley V	Sept 1939 - Oct 1942
Halifax II	Dec 1942 - May 1944
Halifax V	Nov 1943 - May 1944
Halifax III	May 1944 - Mar 1945
Halifax VI	Mar 1945 - Aug 1945
Dakota III/IV	Jul 1945 - Jun 1949

Representative serial numbers:

Wellesley	K8522, L2682
Whitley III	K9015 'R'
Whitley V	Z9306 'S', T4151 'M'
Halifax II	DT666 'F', HR935 'Q'
Halifax V	LL126 'W'
Halifax III	MZ335 'A', MZ715 'Z'
Halifax VI	RG536 'Y'
Dakota III	KP275

No. 78 Squadron

| Motto: | Nobody unprepared |
| Sqn codes: | YY (Munich crisis); EY |

Bases:

Dishforth	Feb 1937 - Dec 1939
Linton-on-Ouse	Dec 1939 - Jul 1940
Dishforth	Jul 1940 - Apr 1941
Middleton St George	Apr 1941 - Oct 1941
Croft	Oct 1941 - Jun 1942
Middleton St George	Jun 1942 - Sep 1942
Linton-on-Ouse	Sep 1942 - Jun 1943
Breighton	Jun 1943 - Sep 1945
Transferred to No. 216 Group Middle East Command	4 Sep 1945

Equipment:

Heyford II	Nov 1936 - Oct 1937
Heyford III	Nov 1936 - Oct 1937
Whitley I	Jul 1937 - Oct 1939
Whitley IV/IVA	Aug 1939 - Feb 1940
Whitley V	Sep 1939 - Mar 1942
Halifax II	Mar 1942 - Jan 1944
Halifax III	Jan 1944 - Apr 1945
Halifax VI	Apr 1945 - Jul 1945
Dakota IV	Jul 1945 - Jul 1950

Representative serial numbers:

Heyford II	K4868
Heyford III	K5193
Whitley I	K7196
Whitley IV	K9017
Whitley IVA	K9050
Whitley V	T4029 'Q', Z6640 'R'
Halifax II	W1015 'V'

Halifax III	MZ361 'D', LV869 'G'
Halifax VI	RG667
Dakota IV	KP233

No. 97 Squadron

| Motto: | Achieve your aim |
| Sqn codes: | MR (Munich crisis); OF |

Bases:

Leconfield	Feb 1937 - Sep 1939
Became an air observers school 7 Jun 1938	
Became a Group pool Squadron in Mar 1939	
Abingdon	Sep 1939 - Apr 1940
Redesignated No. 10 OTU on 6 Apr 1940	

Equipment:

Heyford I/IA/II/III	Sep 1935 - Feb 1939
Anson I	Feb 1939 - Apr 1940
Whitley II	Jul 1939 - Apr 1940
Whitley III	Feb 1939 - Apr 1940

Representative serial numbers:

Heyford I	K3493
Heyford IA	K4034
Heyford II	K4876
Heyford III	K6862
Anson I	N5004
Whitley II	K7239
Whitley III	K9000

No. 102 Squadron

| Motto: | Attempt and achieve |
| Sqn codes: | TQ (Munich crisis); DY |

Bases:

Driffield	Jul 1938 - Aug 1940
Kinloss (*cc)	Apr 1940 - May 1940
Leeming	Aug 1940 - Sep 1940
Prestwick (*cc)	Sep 1940 - Oct 1940
Linton-on-Ouse	Oct 1940 - Nov 1940
Topcliffe	Nov 1940 - Nov 1941
Dalton	Nov 1941 - Jun 1942
Topcliffe	Jun 1942 - Aug 1942
Pocklington	Aug 1942 - Sep 1945
Bassingbourn	Sep 1945 - Feb 1946
Upwood	Feb 46. Disbanded Feb 46

Equipment:

Heyford II/III	Oct 1935 - Oct 1938
Whitley III	Oct 1938 - Jan 1940
Whitley V	Nov 1939 - Feb 1942
Halifax II	Dec 1941 - May 1944
Halifax III	May 1944 - Sep 1945
Halifax VI	Feb 1945 - Sep 1945
Liberator VI/VIII	Sep 1945 - Feb 1946

Representative serial numbers:

Heyford II	K4866
Heyford III	K6900
Whitley III	K8976 'E', K9015 'B'
Whitley V	P5092 'A', T4135 'K'
Halifax II	W1107 'D', HX151 'A'
Halifax III	HX240 'U', MZ772 'P'
Halifax VI	RG502 'Q'
Liberator VI	KN742

No. 104 Squadron

| Motto: | Strike Hard |
| Sqn code: | EP |

Bases:

Driffield	Apr 1941 - Feb 1942
Malta (15 aircraft)	Oct 1941
Home echelon became 158 Sqn 14 Feb 1942	

Equipment:

| Wellington II | Apr 1941 - Jul 1943 |

Representative serial numbers:

| Wellington II | W5437 'Q', Z8345 'S' |

No. 158 Squadron

| Motto: | Strength in unity |
| Sqn code: | NP |

Bases:

Driffield	Feb 1942 - Jun 1942
East Moor	Jun 1942 - Nov 1942
Rufforth	Nov 1942 - Feb 1943
Lissett	Feb 1943 - Aug 1945
Stradishall	Aug 1945 - Dec 1945
Transferred to No. 47 Group 21 Aug 1945	

Equipment:

Wellington II	Feb 1942 - Jun 1942
Halifax II	Jun 1942 - Dec 1943
Halifax III	Dec 1943 - May 1945
Halifax VI	Apr 1945 - Jul 1945
Stirling V	Jun 1945 - Dec 1945

Representative serial numbers:

Wellington II	Z8441 'K', X8577 'T'
Halifax II	R9373 'W', HR757 'M'
Halifax III	LV918 'O', MZ468 'I'
Halifax IV	RG593 'K', PP167 'S'
Stirling V	PJ954, PJ977

No. 166 Squadron

| Motto: | Tenacity |
| Sqn codes: | GB (Munich crisis) |

Bases:

Leconfield	Jan 1937 - Sep 1939
Became an Air Observers School 7 Jun 1938	
Became a Group pool Squadron May 1939	
Abingdon	Sep 1939 - Apr 1940
Merged with No. 97 Squadron and redesignated No. 10 OTU	6 Apr 1940

Equipment:

Heyford III	Nov 1936 - Sep 1939
Whitley I	Jun 1939 - Apr 1940
Whitley III	Nov 1939 - Apr 1943

Representative serial numbers:

Heyford III	K6862, K6886
Whitley I	K7209
Whitley III	K8957, K8960

No. 196 Squadron

| Motto: | Thus we keep faith |
| Sqn code: | ZO |

Bases:

Driffield	Nov 1942 - Dec 1942
Leconfield	Dec 1942 - Jul 1943
Transferred to No. 3 Group 19 Jul 1943	

Equipment:

| Wellington X | Dec 1942 - Jul 1943 |

Representative serial numbers:

| Wellington X | HE167 'A', HE398 'J' |

No. 215 Squadron

| Motto: | Arise, night is at hand |
| Sqn code: | 215 |

Bases:

| Driffield | Sep 1936 - Jul 1938 |
| Transferred to No. 3 Group 25 Jul 1938 | |

Equipment:

| Virginia X | Oct 1935 - Nov 1937 |
| Anson I | Feb 1937 - Nov 1937 |

Representative serial numbers:

| Virginia X | K2330 |
| Anson I | N5030 |

No. 231 Squadron No badge or motto
Bases:
Full Sutton   Jan 1946 - Jul 1946
Disbanded   Jul 1946
Equipment:
Lancastrian C.2   Jan 1946 - Jul 1946
Representative serial numbers:
Lancastrian C.2   VL972

No. 346 (Free French) Squadron
French designation: Groupe 2/23 *Guyenne*
Sqn code: H7
Bases:
Elvington   May 1944 - Oct 1945
Transferred to Armée de l'Air Oct 1945
Equipment:
Halifax V   May 1944 - Jun 1944
Halifax III   Jun 1944 - Apr 1945
Halifax VI   Mar 1945 - Nov 1945
Representative serial numbers:
Halifax V   LL227 'K'
Halifax III   NA121 'D', PN365 'B'
Halifax VI   RG495 'A', RG592 'P'

No. 347 (Free French) Squadron
French designation: Groupe 1/25 *Tunisie*
Sqn code: L8
Bases:
Elvington   Jun 1944 - Oct 1945
Transferred to Armée de l'Air Oct 1945
Equipment:
Halifax V   Jun 1944 - Jul 1944
Halifax III   Jul 1944 - Apr 1945
Halifax VI   Mar 1945 - Nov 1945
Representative serial numbers:
Halifax V   LK728 'D'
Halifax III   MZ984 'G', NA681 'G'
Halifax VI   NP921 'E'

No. 405 (RCAF) Squadron
Motto: We lead
Sqn code: LQ
Bases:
Driffield   Apr 1941 - Jun 1941
Pocklington   Jun 1941 - Aug 1942
Topcliffe   Aug 1942 - Oct 1942
Beaulieu (*cc)   Oct 1942 - Feb 1943
Topcliffe   Mar 1943
Leeming   Mar 1943 - Apr 1943
Transferred to No. 6 Group Apr 1943
Equipment:
Wellington II   May 1941 - Apr 1942
Halifax II   Apr 1942 - Sep 1943
Representative serial numbers:
Wellington II   W4596 'M', Z8344 'F'
Halifax II   W1092 'A', W7710 'R'

No. 408 (RCAF) Squadron
Motto: For Freedom
Sqn code: EQ
Bases:
Leeming   Aug 1942 - Dec 1942
Transferred to No. 6 Group 1 Jan 1943
Equipment:
Halifax V   Oct 1942 - Dec 1942
Halifax II   Dec 1942
Representative serial numbers:
Halifax V   DG231
Halifax II   BB336 'O'

No. 419 (RCAF) Squadron
Motto: Moosa awayita
Sqn code: VR
Bases:
Leeming   Aug 1942
Topcliffe   Aug 1942 - Sep 1942
Croft   Sep 1942 - Nov 1942
Middleton St George Nov 1942
Transferred to No. 6 Group 1 Jan 1943
Equipment:
Wellington III   Aug 1942 - Nov 1942
Halifax II   Nov 1942
Representative serial numbers:
Wellington III   X3344, BJ668
Halifax II   HX189 'J', JD158 'D'

No. 420 (RCAF) Squadron
Motto: We fight to a finish
Sqn code: PT
Bases:
Skipton-on-Swale   Aug 1942 - Oct 1942
Middleton St George Oct 1942 - Dec 1942
Transferred to No. 6 Group 1 Jan 1943
Equipment:
Wellington III   Aug 1942 - Jan 1944
Representative serial numbers:
Wellington III   X3392 'C', X3809 'C'

No. 424 (RCAF) Squadron
Motto: We chastise those who
                     deserve to be chastised
Sqn code: QB
Bases:
Topcliffe   Oct 1942 - Dec 1942
Transferred to No. 6 Group 1 Jan 1943
Equipment:
Wellington III   Oct 1942 - Dec 1943
Representative serial numbers:
Wellington III   X3401 'E', BK435 'U'

No. 425 (RCAF) Squadron
Motto: I shall pluck you
Sqn code: KW
Bases:
Dishforth   Jun 1942 - May 1943
Transferred to No. 6 Group 1 Jan 1943
Equipment:
Wellington III   Jul 1942 - Oct 1943
Representative serial numbers:
Wellington III   X3648 'R', BJ644 'Q'

No. 426 (RCAF) Squadron
Motto: On wings of fire
Sqn code: OW
Bases:
Dishforth   Oct 1942 - Dec 1942
Transferred to No. 6 Group 1 Jan 1943
Equipment:
Wellington III   Nov 1942
Representative serial numbers:
Wellington III   Z1599

No. 427 (RCAF) Squadron
Motto: Strike sure
Sqn code: ZL
Bases:
Croft   Nov 1942
Transferred to No. 6 Group
                     1 Jan 1943

Equipment:
Wellington III   Nov 1942 - May 1943
Representative serial numbers:
Wellington III   X3390, X3752

No. 428 (RCAF) Squadron
Motto: To the very end
Sqn code: NA
Bases:
Dalton   Nov 1942
Transferred to No. 6 Group 1 Jan 1943
Equipment:
Wellington III/X   Nov 1942 - Jun 1943
Representative serial numbers:
Wellington III   X3541 'N'
Wellington X   HZ476 'A'

No. 429 (RCAF) Squadron
Motto: Nothing to chance
Sqn code: AL
Bases:
East Moor   Nov 1942
Transferred to No. 6 Group 1 Apr 1943
Equipment:
Wellington III   Nov 1942 - Sept 1943
Representative serial numbers:
Wellington III   Z1696, BJ908

No. 431 (RCAF) Squadron
Motto: Warriors of the air
Sqn code: SE
Bases:
Burn   Nov 1942 - Jul 1943
Transferred to No. 6 Group Jul 1943
Equipment:
Wellington X   Nov 1942 - Jul 1943
Representative serial numbers:
Wellington X   HE182 'A', HE534 'P'

No. 462 (RAAF) Squadron
No badge or official motto
Sqn code: Z5
Bases:
Driffield   Aug 1944 - Dec 1944
Transferred to No. 100 Group 22 Dec 1944
Equipment:
Halifax III   Aug 1944 - Sep 1945
Representative serial numbers:
Halifax III   LL599 'E', MZ296 'L'

No. 466 (RAAF) Squadron
No badge or official motto
Sqn code: HL
Bases:
Driffield   Oct 1942 - Dec 1942
Leconfield   Dec 1942 - Jun 1944
Driffield   Jun 1944 - Sep 1945
Bassingbourn   Sep 1945 - Oct 1945
Disbanded   26 Oct 1945
Equipment:
Wellington III   Oct 1942 - Nov 1942
Wellington X   Nov 1942 - Sep 1943
Halifax II   Sep 1943 - Nov 1943
Halifax III   Oct 1943 - May 1945
Halifax VI   May 1945 - Sep 1945
Liberator VI   Sep 1945
Representative serial numbers:
Wellington III   X3409
Wellington X   HE152 'L'

Halifax II   W1224
Halifax III   MZ296 'R', NA199 'D'
Liberator VI   KN736

No. 512 Squadron
Motto: Pegasus at war
Bases:
Transferred from No. 46 Group 7 Aug 1945
and based at Holme-on-Spalding Moor
Aug 1945 - Oct 1945
Transferred to the Middle East in Oct 1945
Equipment:
Dakota I/III   Jun 1943 - Mar 1946
Representative serial numbers:
Dakota I   KG625

No. 575 Squadron
Motto: The air is our path
Bases:
Transferred from No. 46 Group 7th Aug 1945
Melbourne   Aug 1945 - Nov 1945
Transferred to No. 47 Group 15 Nov 1945
Equipment:
Dakota III   Feb 1944 - Aug 1946
Representative serial numbers:
Dakota III   KG630

No. 578 Squadron
Motto: Accuracy
Sqn code: LK
Bases:
Snaith   Jan 1944 - Feb 1944
Burn   Feb 1944 - Apr 1945
Disbanded   15 Apr 1945
Equipment:
Halifax III   Jan 1944 - Apr 1945
Representative serial numbers:
Halifax III   LK834 'E', MZ572 'D',
                  NA617 'M'

No. 640 Squadron
No badge or official motto
Sqn code: C8
Bases:
Lissett   Jan 1944
Leconfield   Jan 1944 - May 1945
Disbanded   7 May 1945
Equipment:
Halifax III   Jan 1944 - Mar 1945
Halifax VI   Mar 1945 - May 1945
Representative serial numbers:
Halifax III   LW439 'V', MZ500 'N'
Halifax VI   RG600 'V', RG604 'Z'

NO. 4 GROUP BOMBER COMMAND TRAINING UNITS

No. 4 Group Pool
Nos. 97 and 166 Squadrons became components of an Air Observers School from June 1938, based at Leconfield. In the spring of 1939 both Squadrons became No. 4 Group Pool.
Transferred to No. 6 (Training) Group based at
Abingdon   Sep 1939
Became 10 OTU   Apr 1940
Equipment: Heyford II/III; Whitley I/II/III/V

No. 28 Halifax Conversion Flight
Bases:
Leconfield   Oct 1941 - Dec 1941
Marston Moor   Dec 1941 - Jan 1942
Transferred to No. 1652 CU Jan 1942
Equipment: Halifax I/II

No. 10 Squadron Conversion Flight
Code: ZA
Bases:
Leeming   Feb 1942 - Aug 1942
Melbourne   Aug 1942 - Nov 1942
Transferred to No. 1658 CU Nov 1942
Equipment: Halifax II

No. 35 Squadron Conversion Flight
Code: TL
Bases:
Linton-on-Ouse   Feb 1942 - Sep 1942
Rufforth   Sep 1942 - Feb 1943
Transferred to No. 1663 CU Feb 1943
Equipment: Halifax I/II

No. 76 Squadron Conversion Flight
Code: MP
Bases:
Middleton St George Feb 1942 - Jun 1942
Dalton   Jun 1942 - Aug 1942
Riccall   Sep 1942 - Oct 1942
Transferred to No. 1658 CU October 1942
Equipment   Halifax I/II

No. 78 Squadron Conversion Flight
Code: EY
Bases:
Croft   Mar 1942 - Jun 1942
Dalton   Jun 1942 - Jul 1942
Middleton St George Jul 1942
Riccall   Jul 1942 - Oct 1942
Transferred to No. 1658 CU Oct 1942
Equipment: Halifax I/II

No. 102 Squadron Conversion Flight
Code: DY
Bases:
Dalton   Jan 1942 - Aug 1942
Pocklington   Aug 1942 - Nov 1942
Transferred to No. 1658 CU Nov 1942
Equipment: Halifax I/II

No. 158 Squadron Conversion Flight
Code: NP
Bases:
East Moor   Jun 1942 - Sep 1942
Rufforth   Sep 1942 - Feb 1943
Transferred to No. 1663 CU February 1943
Equipment: Halifax II

No. 405 Squadron Conversion Flight
Code: LQ
Bases:
Pocklington   Apr 1942 - Aug 1942
Topcliffe   Aug 1942 - Oct 1942
Transferred to No. 1659 CU (6 Group) Oct 1942
Equipment: Halifax II

No. 408 Squadron Conversion Flight
Code: EQ
Bases:
Leeming   Sep 1942 - Oct 1942
Transferred to No. 1659 CU (6 Group) Oct 1942
Equipment: Halifax I/II

No. 1652 Heavy Conversion Unit
Codes: GV, JA
Bases:
Marston Moor, with satellites at Burn, Dalton
and Rufforth   Jan 1942 - Nov 1944
Transferred to No. 7 Group Training
Command   Nov 1944
Known as No. 1652 Conversion Unit from
                  Jan 1942 - Oct 1942
Equipment: Halifax I/II/III/V

No. 1658 Heavy Conversion Unit
Codes: TT, ZB
Bases:
Riccall   Oct 1942 - Nov 1944
Known as No. 1658 Conversion Unit from
                  7 Oct 1942 - 1 Nov 1942
Transferred to No. 7 Group Training
Command   Nov 1944
Equipment: Halifax I/II/III/V

No. 1663 Heavy Conversion Unit
Codes: OO, SV
Bases:
Rufforth   Mar 1943 - May 1945
Transferred to No. 7 Group Training
Command   May 1945
Equipment: Halifax I/II/III/V

No. 1665 Heavy Conversion Unit
Codes: FO, OG
Bases:
Marston Moor   Aug 1945 - Nov 1945
Linton-on-Ouse   Nov 1945 - Jul 1946
Redesignated No. 1665 Heavy Transport
Conversion Unit   Aug 1945
Transferred to No. 1332 HTCU Jul 1946
Equipment: Halifax III/V/VI/VII

No. 4 (TRANSPORT) GROUP

The following units were administered by this organisation during the period May 1945 to Feb 1948.
OTUs: Nos. 87, 105, 108, 109
Conversion Units: Nos. 1332, 1333,
                  1336, 1380, 1381, 1382,
                  1383, 1384, 1665
BAT Flights: Nos. 1513, 1516, 1521,
                  1527, 1528, 1529
Rebecca Babs Flt: No. 1510
Lancaster Finishing School: No. 6

For outline histories and illustrations of squadron badges consult *The Squadrons of the Royal Air Force & Commonwealth 1918-88*, James J. Halley, Air Britain, 1988.

(*cc) On loan to Coastal Command during this period.

Appendix D

Airfields of No. 4 Group
1937-1945

ACASTER MALBIS, Yorkshire
(6 miles south of York)
Acaster Malbis opened in January 1942 as a satellite of Church Fenton under Fighter Command. The airfield was rebuilt as a bomber station and re-opened in 1943 under No. 4 Group but never received any operational units. Instead it was used for circuit training by nearby Heavy Conversion Units and as a storage site for bombs. Many wartime buildings remain on the site including the derelict control tower.

BREIGHTON, Yorkshire
(13 miles south-east of York)
Breighton opened in January 1942 as a satellite for Holme-on-Spalding Moor under No. 1 Group. The station was transferred to No. 4 Group in June 1943 and occupied by Halifaxes of No. 78 Squadron until the end of the war. Today many of the wartime buildings have been demolished including the control tower. Light aircraft still use one runway.

BURN, Yorkshire
(3 miles south of Selby)
Burn opened as a bomber station in No. 4 Group in November 1942 and was occupied by the Wellingtons of No. 431 (RCAF) Squadron until their transfer to No. 6 (RCAF) Group in July 1943. After a period of use by Heavy Conversion Units, Burn was occupied by the Halifaxes of No. 578 Squadron who operated from the base from February 1944 until April 1945. Today, the airfield has almost completely disappeared.

CARNABY, Yorkshire
(1¾ miles south-west of Bridlington)
Carnaby opened in March 1944 as a Bomber Command Emergency Landing Ground. Operational under No. 4 Group from June 1944, Carnaby was designed to handle aircraft damaged or in difficulty and was fully operational with emergency services. The airfield presently forms part of an industrial estate.

COTTAM, Yorkshire
(2 miles north of Driffield)
Ready for use by September 1940, Cottam was developed as a satellite for Driffield. However, the close proximity of the North Yorkshire Moors made it unsuitable for flying and no units were ever based at Cottam. Very little remains of this airfield.

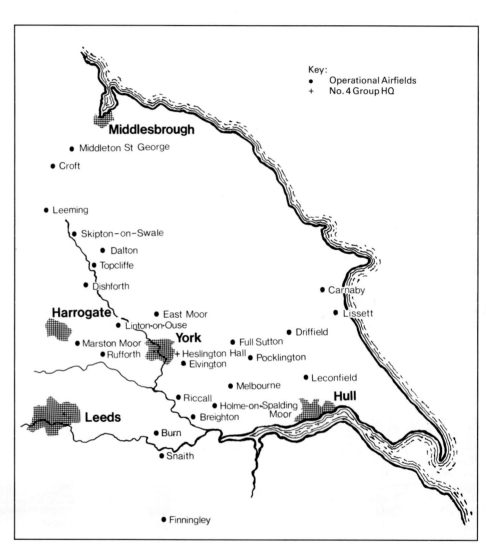

Operational airfields used by No. 4 Group between 1937 and 1945.

CROFT, County Durham
(3 miles south of Darlington)
Croft opened as a satellite of Middleton St George, under No. 4 Group, in October 1941. Whitleys of No. 78 Squadron operated from Croft through to their conversion to Halifaxes in the spring of 1942. Nos. 419 and 427 (RCAF) Squadrons equipped with Wellingtons moved into Croft in September and November 1942. The station was transferred to No. 6 (RCAF) Group on 1 January 1943. Part of the airfield is now used as a car racetrack.

DALTON, Yorkshire
(3½ miles south of Thirsk)
Dalton opened in November 1941 under No. 4 Group and was used by the Whitleys of No. 102 Squadron from Topcliffe until January 1942. On conversion to Halifaxes No. 102 moved out in June 1942. The next No. 4 Group unit to use the station was No. 428 (RCAF) Squadron who formed here in November 1942. On 1 January 1943 the station and its resident squadron was transferred to No. 6 (RCAF) Group. Part of the airfield is now occupied by an industrial estate but many signs of its former wartime use are still visible.

DISHFORTH, Yorkshire
(4 miles east of Ripon)

Dishforth opened under the pre-war expansion scheme in September 1936. The first units to occupy the base were Nos. 10 and 78 Squadrons, two of the original squadrons of No. 4 Group, transferred from No. 3 Group in June 1937. No. 78 moved out in December 1939 and was replaced by No. 51 Squadron. April 1940 saw No. 10 Squadron move to Leeming and July the return of No. 78 Squadron who were to stay until April 1941. In May 1942, No. 51 Squadron was on loan to Coastal Command and the same month saw the formation of No. 425 (RCAF) Squadron, equipped with Wellington Mk.IIIs. Another Canadian unit, No. 426 (RCAF) Squadron, also formed at Dishforth in October 1942 equipped with Wellington Mk.IIIs. On 1st January 1943 the station and its resident squadrons were transferred to No. 6 (RCAF) Group. Dishforth airfield is currently used by the Army Air Corps but remains outwardly much as it did in wartime.

DRIFFIELD, Yorkshire
(26 miles east of York)

Driffield opened as a bomber airfield in No. 3 Group in July 1936. In June 1937 the station and its resident squadrons, No. 75 and No. 215, were transferred to No. 4 Group control. In July 1938 Nos. 102 and 77 Squadrons replaced Nos. 75 and 215. The Whitleys of Nos. 102 and 77 operated from Driffield until August 1940 when the station closed for six months of repair work. After a spell as a fighter station early in 1941 Driffield returned to No. 4 Group use in April when No. 104 and No. 405 (RCAF) Squadrons formed here both equipped with Wellingtons. Also using the base during this period was No. 2 Beam Approach Training Flight and from October 1941 No. 4 Group Target Towing Flight. In February 1942 No. 158 Squadron formed from the home echelon of No. 104 Squadron and began equipping with Wellington Mk.IIs. In June 1942 reconstruction work commenced and it was not until June 1944 that the station was again in use. During that month No. 466 (RAAF) Squadron moved in equipped with Halifax Mk.IIIs. In August more Australians arrived in the form of No. 462 (RAAF) Squadron, who stayed until their transfer to No. 100 Group in December 1944. No. 466 Squadron operated from Driffield until the end of the war. The station is currently used by the Army School of Mechanical Transport and most of the wartime buildings remain in use.

EAST MOOR, Yorkshire
(7 miles north of York)

East Moor opened in June 1942 under No. 4 Group with the arrival of No. 158 Squadron then re-equipping with Halifax Mk.IIs. They were replaced by the Canadians of No. 429 (RCAF) Squadron equipped with Wellington Mk.IIIs, in November 1942. The station and its resident unit was transferred to No. 6 (RCAF) Group on 1st April 1943. The airfield has largely returned to agriculture, but the control tower and a number of dispersed sites still remain.

ELVINGTON, Yorkshire
(7 miles south-east of York)

Elvington opened as a sub station to Pocklington in No. 4 Group in October 1942. That month No. 77 Squadron arrived and began re-equipping with Halifaxes, and stayed until May 1944 when they were replaced by No. 346 (Free French) Squadron who were joined in June by No. 347 (Free French) Squadron. Both squadrons operated from Elvington until the end of the war. Today, part of the airfield is still in use by the RAF but the remainder has been transformed into a museum by The Yorkshire Air Museum. The former wartime control tower has been fully restored and there is a memorial to No. 4 Group in a beautiful memorial garden. An ambitious project is also well underway to build a complete Halifax bomber.

Below left: **Derelict huts on the former technical site at Breighton.**

Below right: **'T2'-type hangar at the north eastern corner of Breighton airfield.**

Bottom left: **The sound of aircraft can still be heard at Breighton: a light aircraft of Hornet Aviation parked near to the former perimeter track where once bomb laden Halifaxes trundled by.**

Bottom right: **Headquarters of the Vulture Squadron flying club, Breighton.**

The photographs were taken September 1986.

FINNINGLEY, Yorkshire
(7 miles south-east of Doncaster)
Finningley opened in No. 3 Group in September 1936. When the station came under the control of No. 4 Group the resident squadrons were No. 7 and 76 equipped with Wellesleys. By September 1939 the station had transferred to No. 5 Group. Today Finningley is a busy RAF station utilised by No. 6 Flying Training School, who are responsible for training aircrew for the RAF's front line squadrons.

FULL SUTTON, Yorkshire
(9 miles east of York)
Full Sutton opened in May 1944 as a bomber station in No. 4 Group. The only unit to occupy the base until the end of the war was No. 77 Squadron. Part of the airfield has now been taken over by industry and few wartime buildings remain; the runways have also disappeared.

Right: **Postwar view of Driffield shows the typical pattern of construction of airfields of the late 1930's expansion period. Grouped on the right of the photograph are the four 'C'-type hangars — Driffield had five 'C'-type hangars but one was destroyed during a German air raid on August 15th 1940 — with brick built administrative, technical and living sites grouped behind. Top left is the bomb dump situated well away from other buildings.** *RAF Museum, 3137*

Below: **Two views of Burn, both taken in September 1986: the water tower and an abandoned Nissen hut.**

HOLME-ON-SPALDING MOOR, Yorkshire
(18 miles south east of York)

Holme-on-Spalding Moor opened under No. 1 Group in August 1941. In June 1943 No. 76 Squadron moved in with Halifax Mk.Vs from Linton-on-Ouse and the station came under No. 4 Group control. No. 76 operated from here until the end of the war. Part of the airfield is now an industrial estate. Holme remains one of the best preserved bomber airfields in Yorkshire with many of the original wartime buildings still intact. The runways, however, have been removed.

LECONFIELD, Yorkshire
(3 miles north of Beverley)

Leconfield opened in December 1936 under No. 3 Group control. In June 1937 the station and its resident squadrons came under the control of No. 4 Group. At that time the station was occupied by Nos. 97 and 166 Squadrons, and became No. 4 Group Training Pool early in 1939 before moving to Abingdon in September. It was December 1942 before any No. 4 Group units operated from Leconfield again, this was when the newly formed Wellington squadrons, Nos. 196 and 466 (RAAF), moved in. In July 1943 No. 196 Squadron transferred to No. 3 Group and in June 1944 No. 466 moved out to Driffield. In the meantime a new Squadron, No. 640, had formed from 'C' Flight of No. 158 Squadron and began operating from Leconfield in January 1944 until the end of the war. Today, Leconfield is the HQ of the Army School of Mechanical Transport, the RAF also operate a Search and Rescue helicopter flight from here.

LEEMING, Yorkshire
(5 miles south-west of Northallerton)

Leeming opened in June 1940 and the following month Whitley Mk.V bombers of No. 10 Squadron arrived from Dishforth. In August No. 7 Squadron formed here with Stirlings but only stayed until October. Also in August the Whitleys of No. 102 Squadron moved in from a bomb-damaged Driffield. No. 102 were on the move again the following month this time to Linton-on-Ouse. In November 1940 No. 35 Squadron arrived from Boscombe Down for the purpose of introducing the new Halifax to squadron service. No. 35 stayed until early December when they moved to Linton-on-Ouse. No. 77 Squadron came to Leeming in September 1941 and remained there until May 1942. In August 1942 No. 10 Squadron moved to Melbourne and their place was taken by the Wellingtons of No. 419 (RCAF) Squadron. More Canadians arrived in the form of No. 408 (RCAF) Squadron from No. 5 Group. They proceeded to convert to Halifaxes and on the 1st January 1943 Leeming and its resident squadrons transferred to No. 6 (RCAF) Group. Leeming is today a major RAF Tornado base.

Three views of East Moor taken in April 1987: the derelict control tower, the WAAF site and one of the last 'frying-pan' dispersals on which Halifaxes stood.

Above: **The memorial to No. 4 Group in the peaceful surroundings of the Memorial Garden at the Yorkshire Air Museum.** *Jenny Blanchett*

Below: **The No.77 Squadron Memorial at the Yorkshire Air Museum, Elvington.** *Jenny Blanchett*

Top: **The former wartime control tower at Elvington, now fully restored, forms part of the Yorkshire Air Museum and Allied Air Forces Memorial.** *Jenny Blanchett*

Above: **Interior shot of the tower: most of the equipment is vintage 1940's.** *Jenny Blanchett*

Below: **Memorial to the French Squadrons Nos. 346 and 347 at Elvington showing recently laid wreaths after the visit of former French airmen in September 1989.** *Jenny Blanchett*

Top: **Marston Moor main gate, guard room, water tower and** *above* **the control tower, in April 1987.**

Below left: **Scene of many an end of tour binge, the College Arms, Linton-on-Ouse, photographed in April 1987.**

Below right: **'C'-type hangars at Linton-on-Ouse, in April 1987.**

Top: **Final resting place for many of the airmen who served from the Yorkshire airfields: Harrogate Cemetery, April 1987.**

Above: **A 'J'-type hangar and twin water tower at Holme-on-Spalding Moor. Holme remains one of the best preserved bomber airfields in Yorkshire with many of the original wartime buildings still intact. This was the scene in April 1987.**

More photographs taken in September 1986.

Top left and right: **Memorial to No.10 Squadron at the entrance to Melbourne airfield.**

Centre right: **The derelict control tower at Melbourne.**

Above: **A 'J'-type hangar at Pocklington.**

Right: **The 'haunted' control tower at Pocklington airfield. Heavily vandalised in later years it has now sadly been demolished.**

LINTON-on-OUSE, Yorkshire
(9 miles north-west of York)

Linton-on-Ouse originally opened in May 1937 under the expansion scheme and in July, No. 4 Group HQ moved in. In April 1938 the first squadrons arrived, Whitleys of Nos. 51 and 58 Squadrons from Boscombe Down. In December 1939 No. 51 Squadron moved to Dishforth and was replaced by No. 78 - No. 4 Group's reserve unit, equipped with Whitley Mk.Vs. In April 1940 No. 4 Group HQ moved to Heslington Hall. In July, No. 78 Squadron, now fully operational, moved to Dishforth and was replaced by No. 77 in August. No. 77 were joined for a brief period by No. 102 during October/November 1940, before that squadron moved to Topcliffe. In December No. 35 Squadron arrived from Leeming with their new Halifaxes and commenced operations on 10th March 1941. The second Halifax unit then formed at Linton in May 1941, No. 76 Squadron re-forming from 'C' Flight of No. 35. In June No. 76 Squadron moved to Middleton

St George. In April 1942 the Whitleys of No. 58 Squadron flew their last mission before transferring to Coastal Command. In August No. 35 Squadron moved to Gravely to join the newly-formed Pathfinder Force and the following month No. 76 and No. 78 returned from Middleton St George. In January 1943 Nos. 76 and 78 moved out and Linton-on-Ouse came under the control of No. 6 (RCAF) Group. Today Linton-on-Ouse is still a busy RAF training station.

LISSETT, Yorkshire
(6 miles south-west of Bridlington)

Lissett opened as a No. 4 Group bomber station in February 1943 when the Halifaxes of No. 158 Squadron arrived from Rufforth. No. 158 operated from Lissett until the end of the war. Lissett airfield has almost completely returned to agriculture and little remains from its former wartime use. There is a memorial to No. 158 Squadron in the village churchyard

Postwar aerial view of Pocklington airfield showing 27 Stirlings dispersed around the site during the period in 1945 when the airfield was used as a modification centre for the Stirling Mk.V. Pocklington opened in June 1941 as a bomber station within 4 Group. The pattern of construction was unusual in that the technical site – comprising two type 'T2'-type and one type 'J'-type hangar – extended into the centre of the airfield almost up to the main runway. Bottom right of the photograph are the bomb stores which comprised dispersed bomb storage areas and fusing point buildings, all protected by earth blast walls. Bottom left is the town of Pocklington.
RAF Museum, 4003

MARSTON MOOR, Yorkshire
(9 miles west of York)
Marston Moor opened in No. 4 Group in November 1941 as a conversion training station for heavy bombers. From the period, January 1942 to June 1945 the station was occupied by No. 1652 Heavy Conversion Unit. Many of the wartime buildings remain in use as the airfield is now occupied by the Home Office Supply and Transport.

MELBOURNE, Yorkshire
(12 miles east of York)
After early use as a satellite for Leeming in 1940 the airfield was reconstructed as a bomber station under No. 4 Group and occupied by the Halifaxes of No. 10 Squadron in August 1942, who continued to operate from here until the end of the war. Little remains of the original wartime installations, the technical site is in use but the control tower is derelict.

MIDDLETON St GEORGE, County Durham
(6 miles east of Darlington)
Middleton St George opened in No. 4 Group in January 1941 and its first occupiers were the Whitleys of No. 78 Squadron from Dishforth. In June 1941 Halifaxes of No. 76 Squadron arrived and in October, No. 78 moved out to Croft to convert to Halifaxes. No. 78 returned in June 1942 but by September of that year both No. 76 and 78 had moved to Linton-on-Ouse. In October No. 420 (RCAF) Squadron moved in from Skipton-on-Swale and the following month, another Canadian squadron, No. 419, came from Croft. On 1st January 1943 the station and its resident squadrons transferred to No. 6 (RCAF) Group. The former wartime bomber station now forms part of Tees-side airport.

POCKLINGTON, Yorkshire
(11½ miles east of York)
Pocklington opened in No. 4 Group in June 1941. The first occupiers were the Wellington Mk.IIs of No. 405 (RCAF) Squadron who moved in from Driffield. The Canadians were to stay until August 1942 when they moved on to Topcliffe – changing places with No. 102 Squadron. No. 102 were to operate from Pocklington until the end of the war. Many buildings are now derelict but the former technical site forms part of a trading estate. The Watch Office, which stood for many years on the north western edge of the airfield, has sadly now been demolished.

RUFFORTH, Yorkshire
(4 miles west of York)
Rufforth opened in No. 4 Group in November 1942 and the first unit to arrive was No. 158 from East Moor. No. 158 stayed until February 1943 when Rufforth became the base for No. 1663 Heavy Conversion Unit, remaining on the station until May 1945. The outlines of the former bomber station are still visible today, although many of the wartime buildings have been demolished.

RICCALL, Yorkshire
(3 miles north-east of Selby)
In October 1942 Riccall airfield opened in No. 4 Group and by the end of the year No. 1658 Heavy Conversion Unit had formed here. No. 1658 were destined to be the sole unit to operate from Riccall, supplying crews for No. 4 Group until April 1945. Most of the airfield site has been returned to agriculture.

SKIPTON-ON-SWALE, Yorkshire,
(3½ miles west of Thirsk)
Skipton-on-Swale opened in No. 4 Group in autumn of 1942 as a satellite of Leeming. The first unit to arrive was No. 420 (RCAF) Squadron in August 1942, moving out to Middleton St George in October. The station was transferred to No. 6 (RCAF) Group on 1st January 1943. A few derelict wartime buildings remain, including the control tower.

SNAITH, Yorkshire
(7 miles south of Selby)
Snaith opened in July 1941 in No. 1 Group. In October 1942 the station was transferred to No. 4 Group with the arrival of No. 51 Squadron, which operated from here until the end of the war. The airfield has now almost completely disappeared apart from the technical site, which is still intact.

THOLTHORPE, Yorkshire
(5 miles east of Boroughbridge)
The airfield at Tholthorpe, no more than just a grass field, opened in No. 4 Group in August 1940 as a satellite of Linton-on-Ouse. Whitleys of No. 77 Squadron used the field from August to December 1940. The airfield then closed for rebuilding as a bomber station and became part of No. 6 (RCAF) Group in June 1943. Little remains today, only the control tower and odd buildings on the technical site.

TOPCLIFFE, Yorkshire
(2½ miles south-west of Thirsk)
Topcliffe opened in No. 4 Group in September 1940, the first unit to arrive being No. 77 Squadron with its Whitley Mk.Vs in October. They were joined by No. 102 in November. Both squadrons moved out a year later when the station closed for rebuilding work. When Topcliffe re-opened in June 1942 the first unit to arrive was No. 102 Squadron with Halifax Mk.IIs. In August No. 102 exchanged bases with No. 405 (RCAF) at Pocklington. That same month more Canadians arrived in the shape of No. 419 Squadron from Leeming and

Top: **Buildings at Snaith in September 1986. They are now used by a local farmer.**

Above: **The butts at Rufforth in April 1987.**

Opposite page, top: **Former meeting place for airmen based on airfields near York was Bettys Bar, nowadays Bettys Cafe and Tea Rooms in St. Helens Square, York. The bar, variously known as 'the Dive' or 'the Briefing Room' was situated downstairs.**
Jenny Blanchett

Two views of Heslington Hall taken in April 1987. The former No. 4 Group HQ now forms part of York University.

Airfields used by No. 4 (Transport) Group May 1945 to February 1948

Bassingbourn	Netheravon
Bitteswell	Nuneaton
Blakehill Farm	Nutts Corner
Bramcote	Odiham
Breighton	Ossington
Carnaby	Pocklington
Castle Donington	Prestwick
Crosby-on-Eden	Riccall
Desborough	Snaith
Dishforth	Stradishall
Driffield	Syerston
Full Sutton	St Mawgan
Holme-on-Spalding Moor	Tilstock
Leconfield	Valley
Leicester East	Welford
Linton-on-Ouse	Wethersfield
Lissett	Winthorpe
Longtown	Wymeswold
Melbourne	

No. 424 formed here equipped with Wellington Mk.IIIs. On 1st January 1943 Topcliffe and its squadrons transferred to No. 6 (RCAF) Group. Today Topcliffe is used by the Army.

THE RAF MEMORIAL
IN
YORK MINSTER

contributed by
Squadron Leader Vernon Noble
PRO No. 4 Group

The RAF Memorial in York Minster, was unveiled by His Royal Highness the Duke of Edinburgh on 1st November 1955. The memorial takes the form of an astronomical clock set in a large oak structure, elegantly carved and with a frieze of bronze seraphs by the sculptor Maurice Lambert RA.

The Monument was designed by Professor A. E. Richardson, President of the Royal Academy, and the clock by the astronomical engineer, Dr R. d'E. Atkinson. The clock faces depict the stars of the Northern hemisphere, revolving once in a sidereal day, and the sun is the Zodiac.

A Book of Remembrance records the names of more than 18,000 young men who lost their lives while serving in squadrons stationed on airfields on and around the plain of York between 1939 and 1945. They came not only from all parts of Britain, but from Canada, Australia, New Zealand, France, Norway, Poland, Czechoslovakia and the Netherlands. These men served in No. 4 Group of Bomber Command (the pioneer Night Bomber Group), No. 6 (RCAF) Group, No. 7 (OTU) Group, units of Fighter Command, and Nos. 16 and 18 Groups Coastal Command. A Turning of the Page ceremony by a contingent from RAF Station Linton-on-Ouse takes place four times each year.

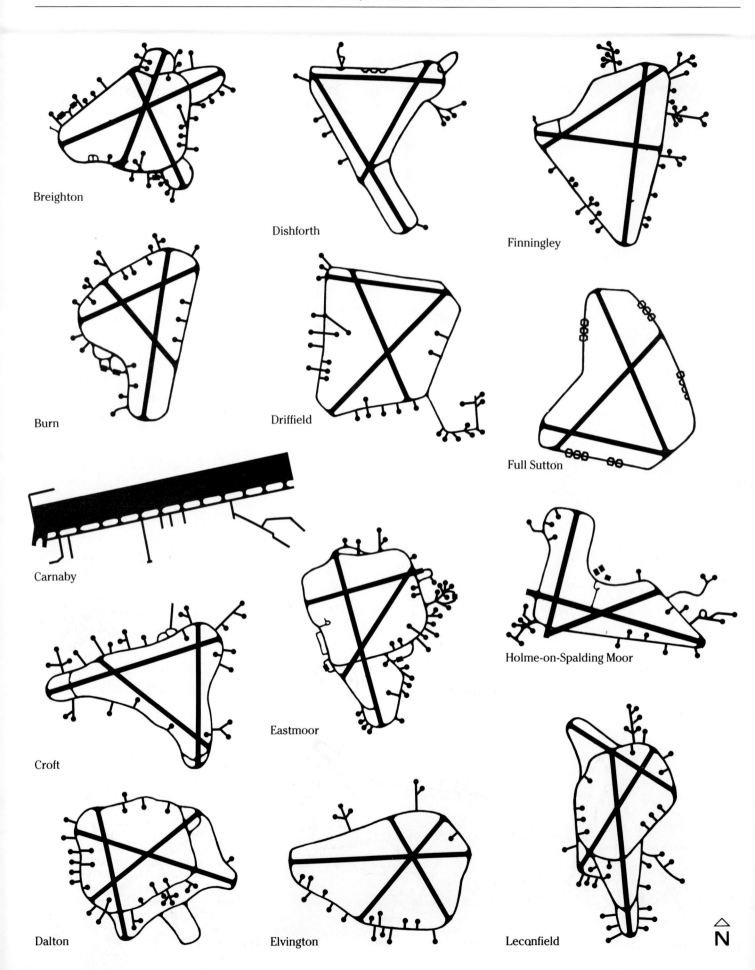

Breighton

Dishforth

Finningley

Burn

Driffield

Full Sutton

Carnaby

Croft

Eastmoor

Holme-on-Spalding Moor

Dalton

Elvington

Leconfield

N

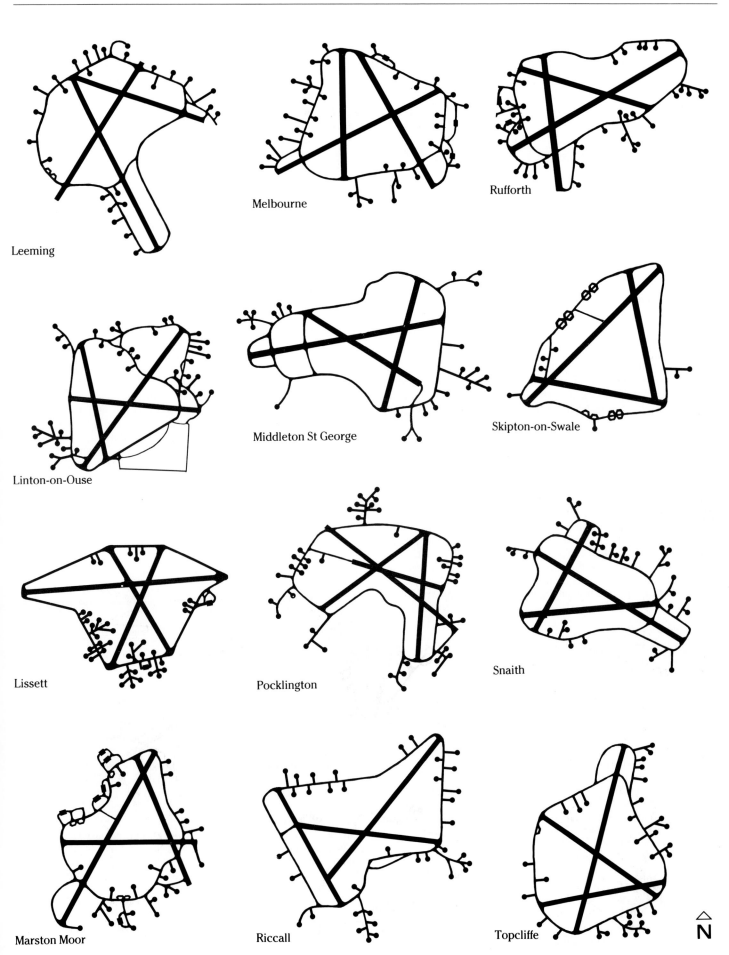

Leeming

Melbourne

Rufforth

Linton-on-Ouse

Middleton St George

Skipton-on-Swale

Lissett

Pocklington

Snaith

Marston Moor

Riccall

Topcliffe

N

Appendix E

Main Aircraft types used by No.4 Group, 1937 to 1948

VICKERS VIRGINIA
Total production of Vickers Virginia bombers was only 126 aircraft yet from 1925 they served with nine front-line squadrons of the RAF in the United Kingdom, the type being finally retired in 1937.

The Vickers Virginia heavy night bomber was developed to replace the Vimy long range bomber, a design on which the Virginia was largely based. The prototype Virginia Mk.I (J6856), was powered by two 450 hp Napier Lion engines and flew for the first time on 24th November 1922. A second machine, the Virginia Mk.II (J6857), flew early in 1924 having a lengthened nose, improved engine installation and other refinements. Armament consisted of a Lewis machine gun in the nose and bomb load was up to 3,000 lb.

Early production examples (Mks III and V) were similar to the prototype in having dihedral on the bottom wings only and a straight leading edge. Virginias began to reach the squadrons early in 1925, No. 9 Squadron receiving Mk.Vs in January. Production Virginias had dihedral on the lower wings only but from the Mk.VI onwards this feature was incorporated on both mainplanes. The Mk.VII featured a redesigned nose, lengthened rear fuselage and outer mainplanes swept back from the centre section.

The Virginia Mk.IX as the first model to incorporate a tail gun position, most Mk.IXs being conversions of earlier models. The last version of the Virginia, also the one built in the greatest numbers (fifty were built and another fifty-three were rebuilds), was the Mk.X which featured an all metal structure with a fabric covering. Earlier models were of wood and fabric. Other modifications included the introduction of Handley Page slots and a tail wheel in place of the skid.

A transport version of the Virginia, known as the Victoria, was developed and served mainly in the Middle East and India.

The No. 4 Group squadrons equipped with Virginias were Nos. 51, 58, 75, 215.

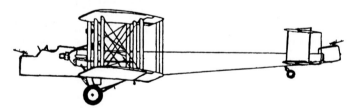

Technical Data (Virginia Mk.X)
Power Plant: Two 570 hp Napier Lion engines.
Performance: Maximum speed 108 mph at 4,920 feet;
    Service ceiling 15,530 feet; Range 985 miles.
Dimensions: Span 87ft 8in; Length 62ft 3in; Height 18ft 2in.
Weight: Empty 9,650lb; Loaded 17,600lb.
Armament: One Lewis machine gun in the nose and twin Lewis guns in the tail; Maximum bomb load 3,000lb.

HANDLEY PAGE HEYFORD
The Handley Page Heyford was the mainstay of the RAF's heavy bomber force during the expansion period and was the last biplane bomber in service with the Royal Air Force. Designed to Specification B19/37 the Heyford four-seat night bomber first flew in June 1930. Heyfords, together with the Fairey Hendon, were earmarked to replace the ageing Virginia and Hinaidi bombers then in service.

The Heyford's configuration was unusual for a biplane as the upper wing was shoulder mounted to the fuselage instead of the lower wing as was more normal. The first production model Heyford Mk.I (K3489) flew in June 1933 and was powered by two 575 hp Rolls-Royce Kestrel IIIS 12-cylinder vee engines. Armament consisted of three 0.303-inch Lewis machine guns, one each in the nose and dorsal positions and one in a retractable ventral 'dustbin' turret. Up to 3,500 lb of bombs could be carried in the centre section bomb bay and on the outer panels of the lower wing. The Heyford's maximum speed was 142 mph at 12,500 feet and range was 920 miles. This was a considerable advance on its predecessors, the Virginia and Hinaidi.

Heyfords first entered service with No. 99 Squadron at Upper Heyford in November 1933. In 1934 Heyfords appeared at the Hendon Air Show and in July 1935 aircraft from Nos. 10 and 99 Squadrons made an impressive appearance in front of King George V at the King's Jubilee Review at Mildenhall. On its formation in June 1937 No. 4 Group had four squadrons equipped with Heyfords. These were Nos. 7, 78 and 97 equipped with a mixture of Mk.IIs and IIIs, and No. 166 with Mk.IIIs. The Heyford Mk.II and III had 640 hp Kestrel VI engines, those on the Mk.II being de-rated. Later Mk.IIIs had four-bladed propellers. A total of 124 Heyfords were delivered to the RAF before production ceased in July 1936. In all, the Heyfords served with eleven first line squadrons from 1933 to 1937. With the arrival of the Whitleys, Heyfords were relegated to various training duties and were finally declared obsolete in July 1941.

The No. 4 Group squadrons equipped with Heyfords were Nos. 7, 78, 97, 102, 166.

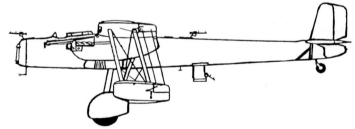

Technical Data (Heyford Mk.I)
Power Plant: Two 575 hp Rolls-Royce Kestrel IIIS engines.
Performance: Maximum speed, 142 mph at 12,500 feet;
    Service Ceiling 21,000 feet; Range 920 miles.
Dimensions: Span 75ft; Length 58ft; Height 20ft 6ins.
Weight: Empty 9,200 lb; Loaded 16,900 lb.
Armament: Three Lewis machine guns in nose, mid upper and ventral 'dustbin' positions. Bomb load varied from 1,600 lb to 3,500 lb.

VICKERS WELLESLEY
On the 12th April 1937, 'B' Flight of No. 7 Squadron, based at Finningley in No. 4 Group, became the nucleus of No. 76 Squadron. Initial equipment of the new squadron was four Vickers Wellesley single-engine medium bombers. No. 76 Squadron thus became the first RAF squadron to be equipped with this unique aircraft.

Designed by Barnes Wallis and Rex Pierson the Wellesley was the first RAF aircraft to employ geodetic construction technique, pioneered by Vickers in the building of their airships. The Wellesley was in advance of other early 1930s designs by featuring long span cantilever, monoplane wings, enclosed cockpit and fully retracting landing gear. The prototype flew for the first time on 19th June 1935 and in September the Air Ministry ordered ninety-six. Between March 1937 and May 1938 a total of 176 Wellesleys were built. In November 1938 Wellesleys of the RAF's Long Range Development Flight broke the World Long Distance Record by flying from Ismailia to Darwin non-stop, a distance of 7,162 miles.

By the outbreak of war Wellesleys had been replaced in the squadrons of Bomber Command by more modern types. Most of the remaining Wellesleys were transferred to the Middle East where they served in the early years of the war.

The No. 4 Group squadrons equipped with Wellesleys were Nos. 76, 77.

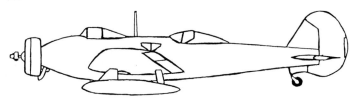

Technical Data (Wellesley Mk.I)

Power Plant: One 925 hp Bristol Pegasus XX engine.

Performance: Maximum speed 228 mph at 19,680 feet; Cruising speed 188 mph; Service Ceiling 33,000 feet; Range 1,110 miles.

Dimensions: Span 74ft 7ins; Length 39ft 3ins; Height 12ft 4ins.

Weight: Empty 6,369 lb; Loaded 11,100 lb.

Armament: One Vickers 0.303 inch machine gun in port wing and one 0.303 inch Vickers K gun in rear cockpit. 2,000 lb of bombs in underwing containers.

HANDLEY PAGE HARROW

The Handley Page Harrow served with two Driffield-based squadrons within No. 4 Group, Nos. 75 and 215, from the late summer of 1937 until July 1938.

Produced to Specification 29/35, the Harrow was based on the earlier HP.51 troop carrier. One hundred were ordered in August 1935 and the first production Harrow Mk.I, (K6933), flew on 10th October 1936. Nineteen of the first Harrow Mk.Is were powered by 830 hp Pegasus X engines. From K6953 onwards Harrows were fitted with 925 hp Pegasus XX engines, power operated nose and tail turrets and were designated Harrow Mk.IIs.

Harrows reached the heavy bomber squadrons of No. 4 Group in August 1937 when No. 215 Squadron at Driffield began to exchange its obsolete Virginias for Harrow Mk.IIs. The following month No. 75 Squadron, also based at Driffield, began to re-equip with Harrow Mk.I and IIs. By December 1937 both squadrons were fully equipped.

The Handley Page Harrow was never more than an interim type evolved during the expansion period to replace the Virginia until more modern types became available. Consequently when the Whitley and Wellington types began to reach the squadrons of Bomber Command Harrows were transferred to transport duties.

The No. 4 Group squadrons equipped with Harrows were Nos. 75, 215.

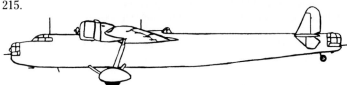

Technical Data (Harrow Mk.II)

Power Plant: Two 925 hp Bristol Pegasus XX engines.

Performance: Maximum speed 200 mph at 10,000 feet; Cruising speed 163 mph at 15,000 feet; Range 1,250 miles.

Dimensions: Span 88ft 5in; Length 82ft 2in; Height 19ft 5in.

Weight: Empty 13,600 lb; Loaded 23,000 lb.

Armament: Four 0.303 inch Browning machine guns, one each in nose and dorsal turrets and two in the tail turret. Up to 3,000 lb of bombs could be carried internally.

ARMSTRONG WHITWORTH WHITLEY

The Armstrong Whitworth AW.38 Whitley first entered service with RAF Bomber Command on 9th March 1937 when the second production Mk.I (K7184) went to No. 10 Squadron at Dishforth. Dubbed the 'Flying Barn Door' because of its angular, slab-sided appearance, the Whitley was destined to become a familiar sight in the skies of the East Riding of Yorkshire.

The Whitley was the outcome of Air Ministry Specification B3/34 which was circulated in July 1934. B3/34 had called for a night bomber/troop transport and at first glance Armstrong Whitworth's Whitley design did bear a resemblance to that company's AW.23 experimental bomber transport. The Whitley, however, marked a departure from Armstrong Whitworth's traditional method of aircraft construction which was to use tubular high-tensile steel with a fabric covering. The new bomber featured stressed skin light alloy monocoque, a method of construction which was to prove time and again its ability to absorb damage. Component parts were reduced to a minimum to simplify production and structural weight was saved by the Whitley's angular design.

Perhaps the Whitley's most noteworthy characteristic was its peculiar 'nose down' attitude in normal flight. When the Whitley design was initiated flaps had not made their universal appearance so in order to reduce landing run the low aspect-ratio wings were given a 8.5 degree angle of incidence. This resulted in the engines having a markedly upwards tilt in relation to the fuselage centre line.

Work commenced on the AW.38 at W. G. Armstrong Whitworth's Coventry plant at the end of 1934. Development was to be rapid with prototype trials commencing only eighteen months after the initial design study. The first prototype made its maiden flight on 17th March 1936 at Baginton. Some seven months earlier in August 1935, the Air Ministry had placed an order for eighty production machines. Such was the pace at which the expansion of the RAF and the re-equipment of its bomber squadrons was taking place that the Whitley had been selected before a single aircraft had flown.

Trials were undertaken at the Royal Aircraft Establishment at Martlesham Heath in the autumn of 1936 and in March 1937 the first Whitleys were delivered to the squadrons. No. 10 Squadron received K7184 on 9th March followed in the same month by K7185 and K7186. By the end of June 1937 No. 10 Squadron had twelve aircraft on strength.

With its turreted armament and retracting undercarriage the Whitley bomber was a tremendous advance on its predecessor, the Heyford. Powered by two Armstrong Siddeley 795 hp Tiger IX radial engines, the Whitley Mk.I had provision for a crew of five comprising pilot, co-pilot/navigator, wireless operator, forward gunner/bombardier, and tail gunner. Armament consisted of two manually operated Armstrong Whitworth nose and tail turrets each fitted with a single 0.303 inch Vickers machine gun. Speeds were, 192 mph at 7,000 feet and 186 mph at 15,000 feet with full load. A total bomb load of 3,365 lbs could be carried in the fuselage bomb bay and underwing cells.

Only thirty-four Whitley Mk.I bombers were completed before production gave way to the improved Mk.II. This mark had Tiger VIII radials with two-stage superchargers, the first RAF aircraft to have this equipment fitted. This boosted performance considerably, maximum speed at 15,000 feet was 215 mph whilst cruising speed at the same altitude was 177 mph. Deliveries of Mk.IIs commenced in January 1938 but production difficulties delayed deliveries and it was not until June 1938 that the forty-sixth, and final Mk.II, was delivered.

With the initial production order for the Whitley Mk.II having been completed attention was now centred around improving the Whitley's armament. This was to be augmented, in the Mk.III, by the addition of a ventral 'dustbin' turret equipped with twin 0.303 inch Browning machine guns. This 'dustbin' would be lowered when required; however, when used it reduced the aircraft's speed considerably. In addition the manually operated nose turret was replaced with a Nash and Thompson powered turret mounting a single Vickers gun. The old manually-operated tail turret was retained.

Eighty Mk.IIIs were produced, the first to be taken on RAF charge being K8937 which was delivered to No. 51 Squadron in August 1938.

Further attempts to improve performance by re-engining the Whitley with Rolls-Royce Merlin IVs, resulted in the Mk.IV version, forty being ordered in 1936. No. 10 Squadron became the first unit to receive Mk.IVs when K9018 was delivered in May 1939. In addition to the change of engines the Mk.IV incorporated a power operated Nash and Thompson tail turret fitted with four 0.303 inch Browning guns. In July 1939 the Mk.IVA was on the production lines. Mk.IVAs differed by having Merlin X engines rated at 1,145 hp.

The final and most important variant of the basic design was the Whitley Mk.V, an order for 302 being placed in 1938. The Merlin X engines were retained but a number of improvements were incorporated. The most noticeable of these were modified fins with straight leading edges and an extension of fifteen inches to the rear fuselage to provide a wider field of fire for the rear gunner. Rubber de-icer boots were fitted to the wing leading edges and fuel capacity was increased. In August 1939 the first of 1,466 Whitley Mk.Vs to be built reached the squadrons. They were to serve in Bomber Command until April 1942 when they were retired. A maritime reconnaissance version, the Mk.VII, was used by Coastal Command and specially adapted Whitleys continued in use with 'special duty' units dropping agents and supplies into occupied territory.

The No. 4 Group squadrons equipped with Whitleys were Nos. 7, 10, 51, 58, 77, 78, 97, 102, 166.

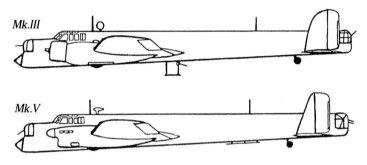

Mk.III

Mk.V

Technical Data (Whitley Mk.V)
Power Plant: Two Rolls-Royce Merlin X engines rated at 1,145 hp.
Performance: Maximum speed 228 mph at 17,750 feet;
   Cruising Speed 210 mph at 15,000 feet; Normal Service Ceiling 17,600 feet; Range 1,500 miles.
Dimension: Span 84ft; Length 70ft 6ins; Height 15ft.
Weight: Empty: 19,350 lb; Maximum overload 33,500 lb.
Armament: One 0.303 inch machine gun in power-operated nose turret and four 0.303 inch machine guns in power-operated tail turret. Maximum boab load 7,000 lb.

VICKERS WELLINGTON
In the early years of the Second World War the Vickers Wellington twin-engined bomber formed the backbone of RAF Bomber Command's offensive against Germany.

Designed to meet Specification B9/32 of 1932 the Wellington was to feature the unique geodetic form of lattice-work construction used on the earlier Wellesley. The prototype Wellington, powered by two 915 hp Bristol Pegasus X engines, was flown for the first time on 15th June 1936 with Vickers' chief test pilot, J. 'Mutt' Summers at the controls. Two months later the Air Ministry ordered 180 Wellington Mk.Is to Specification B29/36. The first production Wellington Mk.I was flown on 23rd December 1937 and was powered by two 1,000 hp Bristol Pegasus XVIII air-cooled engines. Defensive armament consisted of twin 0.303 inch machine guns in Vickers nose and tail turrets plus a single 0.303 inch gun in a ventral, retractable 'dustbin.' Bomb load was up to 4,500 lb. The Mk.I was followed into service by the Mk.IA which had Nash and Thompson nose and tail turrets. The Mk.IC had beam gun positions in place of the ventral turret.

The Wellington's defensive armament was thought to be more than adequate for daylight operations. However, heavy losses in the first months of the war resulted in Wellingtons being switched to night operations only.

As an insurance against supply problems with the Pegasus engines the Mk.II was developed. This variant incorporated all the improvements in the Mk.IA and IC but was powered by two 1,145 hp Rolls-Royce Merlin X engines. The first Wellingtons to reach No. 4 Group were in fact Mk.IIs which were delivered to the newly formed No. 104 Squadron at Driffield in April 1941. These were followed by more Mk.IIs that went to No. 405 (RCAF) Squadron during May.

With the Wellington Mk.III there was another change of engines. This time 1,375 hp Bristol Hercules III engines were fitted along with a new rear turret incorporating four 0.303 inch machine guns. Mk.IIIs began to reach the Canadian squadrons of No. 4 Group which were being formed in the latter half of 1942.

The other Wellington variant that saw service with No. 4 Group was the Mk.X, of which 3,804 were built. This was the last bomber variant and was essentially an improved Mk.III powered by Hercules XVIII engines.

The No. 4 Group squadrons equipped with Wellingtons were Nos. 104, 158, 196, 405, 419, 420, 424, 425, 426, 427, 428, 429, 431, 466.

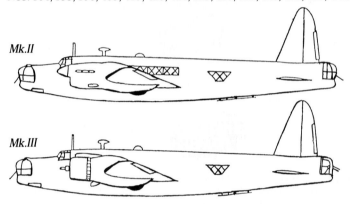

Mk.II

Mk.III

Technical Data (Wellington Mk.II and III)
Power Plant: (Mk.II) Two 1,145 hp Rolls-Royce Merlin X engines.
   (Mk.III) Two 1,375 hp Bristol Hercules III or XI engines.
Performance: (Mk.II) Maximum speed 254 mph at 19,000 feet;
   Service ceiling 23,500 feet; range 1,570 miles.
   (Mk.III) Maximum speed 255 mph at 19,000 feet; Service ceiling 22,000 feet; Range 1,470 miles.
Dimensions: (Mk.II and III) Span 86ft 2in; Length 64ft 7in;
   Height 17ft 5in.
Weight: (Mk.II) Loaded 33,000 lb. (Mk.III) 34,500 lb.
Armament: (Mk.II and III) Eight 0.303 inch machine guns, two in nose turret, four in tail turret and two in beam positions.
   Maximum bomb load 4,000 lb (Mk.II), 4,500 lb (Mk.III).

HANDLEY PAGE HALIFAX
The Handley Page Halifax bomber had its beginnings in Air Ministry Sepcification P13/36, issued in 1936, which called for an all-metal mid-wing medium-heavy bomber, to be powered by two Rolls-Royce Vulture 24-cylinder X-type engines. Two prototypes, designated HP.56, were ordered in April 1937 but an anticipated shortage of Vulture engines led to the design being altered to accommodate four Rolls-Royce Merlins. Redesignated HP.57, the basic design was unchanged, although fuselage length and wing span were increased and all-up weight went up from 26,300 lb to 40,000 lb.

Construction began in January 1938 and that same month one hundred machines were ordered under Specification 32/3. On 25th October 1939 the first prototype HP.57, (L7244), flew at RAF Bicester piloted by Major Cordes. The second prototype flew in August 1940 and the first production Halifax, took to the air on the 11th October that year. Of all-metal stressed-skin construction, the Halifax was specially designed for quantity production. Each major component was made up of transportable sections, the sections themselves being subdivided for ease of manufacture. Four 1,280 hp Rolls-Royce Merlin 10 engines gave the Halifax B.I Series 1 a maximum speed of 265 mph at 17,500 feet. Armament consisted of Boulton Paul nose and tail turrets mounting two and four 0.303 inch Brownings respectively. The early production models were fitted with twin Vickers beam guns. Bomb load was 13,000 lb carried in the fuselage bomb bay and underwing cells.

Within five weeks of the flight of the first production aircraft the first Halifaxes began to enter squadron service with No. 35 Squadron based at Leeming, Yorks. Production aircraft began to arrive throughout the winter of 1940/41 as No. 35 Squadron, now based at Linton-on-Ouse, began working-up for operations. Exactly five months after the first production model flew the Halifax made its operational debut on the night of 11/12th March 1941 when six aircraft of No. 35 Squadron raided Le Havre.

The next Halifax to enter service was similar to the Mk.I Series I except that it was stressed to 60,000 lb loaded, this was the Mk.I Series II. This was followed by the Series III which had increased tankage. Production of the Mk.I was terminated in September 1941 and was superseded by the Halifax Mk.II Series I. This mark was fitted with a two gun 'Hudson' type Boulton Paul mid upper turret and had four 1,390 hp Merlin 20 engines. The earlier beam guns were deleted.

Production of the Halifax mounted and by the spring of 1942 five squadrons of No. 4 Group were fully equipped. Manufacture was spread throughout a number of companies including Handley Page, English Electric at Preston, Rootes at Speke, Fairey at Stockport and the London Aircraft Production Group comprising five companies.

After a spell of operations the Halifax Mk.II was further improved to produce the Series I (Special). Improvements and additions to the Halifax Mk.II had resulted in an increase in all-up weight which began to seriously affect the performance of the already underpowered bomber. With the introduction of the Mk.II Series I (Special) performance was much improved. With this mark the cumbersome mid upper turret and the seldom used nose turret were removed – the nose turret was replaced by a streamlined fairing. Other improvements included the removal of the underwing fuel jettison pipes and the drag producing asbestos exhaust muffs.

Succeeding the Halifax Mk.II Series I (Special) into service was the greatly cleaned-up Mk.II Series IA, powered by four 1,390 hp Merlin 22 engines. The Series IA also had a 'Defiant' type, low-drag dorsal turret fitted with four Browning machine guns and a neat moulded perspex nose mounting a single hand operated Vickers 'K' gun. A 20 mph increase in speed resulted from these aerodynamic refinements. Despite these improvements Halifax losses remained worryingly high. There had, in addition, been a number of inexplicable accidents when Halifaxes had gone into an inverted and uncontrollable spin with, invariably, fatal consequences.

Extensive testing at A&AEE Boscombe Down revealed that rudder stalling was the cause of some crashes. At speeds of 120 mph or less any violent operation of the rudders, coupled with sideslip, could provoke the fatal rudder locking resulting in the aircraft going into an uncontrollable spin. Many Halifaxes lost on operations could well have spun in following violent evasive manoeuvres to escape enemy night fighters. As a cure for the problem larger rectangular fins were introduced onto production Mk.II Series IAs and retrospectively to all aircraft then in service.

Meanwhile, a shortage of Messier undercarriages during the production of the Halifax Mk.II Series I (Special) and Series IA led to the adoption of the Dowty lever-suspension undercarriage. Variants equipped with the Dowty undercarriage system were designated Halifax Mk.V and, except for the landing gear, were identical to the Mk.II.

The next main variant of the Halifax to enter service was the first version to be fitted with engines other than Rolls-Royce Merlins. This was the Mk.III powered by four 1,615 hp Bristol Hercules 16 engines, with an H2S scanner or a ventral gun position housing a single 0.5 inch gun, a retractable tail-wheel and an all-up weight of 65,000 lb. Halifax Mk.IIIs began to reach the squadrons of No. 4 Group at the end of 1943 and by the summer of 1944 had replaced the Group's outmoded Mk.IIs and Vs. The extra power afforded by the Hercules engines boosted the Halifax's performance and at last the aircraft was able to reach its full potential.

The final bomber versions of the Halifax, introduced at the end of the war, were the Mk.VI and VII. The Mk.VI mounted 1,800 hp Hercules 100 engines and had additional fuel capacity. The Mk.VII was similar to the Mk.VI but was powered by Hercules XVI engines.

In addition to its bomber role the Halifax was used by the squadrons of Coastal Command for anti-submarine duties and by Transport Command for glider towing, transport work and supply droppping. In all 6,176 Halifaxes were built for the RAF.

The No. 4 Group squadrons equipped with Halifaxes were Nos. 10, 35, 51, 76, 77, 78, 102, 158, 346, 347, 405, 408, 419, 462, 466, 578, 640, 1652 HCU, 1658 HCU, 1663 HCU, 1665 HCU, 1332 HTCU.

Mk.II

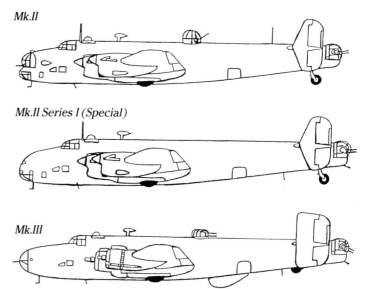

Mk.II Series I (Special)

Mk.III

Technical Data (Halifax Mk.I and III)
Power Plant: (Mk.I) Four 1,280 hp Rolls-Royce Merlin X engines.
(Mk.III) Four 1,615 hp Bristol Hercules XVI radial engines.
Performance: (Mk.I) Maximum speed 262 mph at 17,750 feet;
Service ceiling 18,000 feet; Range 1,030 miles with max bomb load.
(Mk.III) Maximum speed 282 mph at 13,500 feet;
Service Ceiling 24,000 feet; Range 1,030 miles with max bomb load.
Dimensions: (Mk.I) Span 98ft 10ins; Length 70ft 1in; Height 20ft 9ins.
(Mk.III) Span 99ft (later a/c 104ft 2in); Length 71ft 7ins;
Height 20ft 9ins.
Weight: (Mk.I) Empty 36,000 lb; Loaded 60,000 lb.
(Mk.III) Empty 38,240 lb; Loaded 65,000 lb.
Armament: (Mk.I) Ten 0.303 inch machine guns disposed as follows -
two in nose turret, two in port and two in starboard beam positions,
and four in tail turret. Maximum bomb load 13,000 lb.
(Mk.III) Nine 0.303 inch machine guns disposed as follows -
one flexible gun in the nose, four in Boulton Paul mid upper turret,
and four in Boulton Paul tail turret.
Maximum bomb load 13,000 lb.

SHORT STIRLING

The Short Stirling was the first of the RAF's four-engined heavy bombers to see service. Unfortunately this imposing aircraft will always be remembered as a disappointment.

The Stirling was designed by Short and Harland Ltd, the famous flying boat manufacturer, to meet Air Ministry Specification B12/36 of July 1936. The prototype Stirling (L7600) flew for the first time in May 1939. Already, in January 1939, the 'Stirling Group' of companies had been set up to mass produce the new bomber.

In May 1940 the first production Stirling I appeared and deliveries to No. 3 Group commenced in August 1940. The Stirling I was powered by four Bristol Hercules XI 14-cylinder sleeve valve radial engines. Defensive armament comprised two 0.303 inch Browning machine guns in both front and dorsal turrets and four similar guns in the rear turret; bomb load was up to 14,000 lbs.

Peak production of the Stirling was reached in the second quarter of 1943 during which the bomber was being delivered at the rate of eighty machines per month. By that time, however, the Stirling squadrons of Bomber Command were suffering heavy losses. Agile for its size, the Stirling suffered poor climb and altitude performance and by early 1944 was being relegated to glider-tug and transport duties.

The specialist transport version, the Stirling Mk.V, began to appear in September 1944. Powered by Hercules Mk.XVIs the Mk.Vs were designed to carry freight and passengers over long ranges. Two of No. 4 Group's transport squadrons, Nos. 51 and 158, were equipped with Stirling Mk.Vs from June 1945.

The No. 4 Group squadrons equipped with Stirling Mk.Vs were Nos. 51, 158.

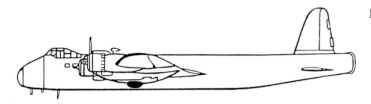

Technical Data (Stirling Mk.V)
Power Plant: Four Bristol Hercules XVI radial engines.
Performance: Maximum speed 280 mph at 6,000 feet;
  Service ceiling 18,000 feet; Range 3,000 miles.
Dimensions: Span 99ft 1in; Length 90ft 6¾in; Height 22ft 9in.
Weight: Empty 43,500 lb; Loaded max 70,000 lb.

DOUGLAS DAKOTA

Over 1,900 Dakotas were supplied to the RAF under Lend Lease and they were to serve on every major battle front. Developed as a military transport from the DC-3 commercial airliner the Dakota entered service with the US Army Air Force in October 1941. Designated C-47 'Skytrain' the type was powered by two 1,200 hp Pratt and Whitney R-1830 Twin Wasp radial engines and had a crew of four. The C-47 could either be used for carrying troops or as a heavy freighter with a reinforced floor and landing gear and a large cargo loading door on the port side.

When No. 4 Group was transferred to Transport Command C-47A and C-47B Sky-trains (known as Dakota III and IV in the RAF) were supplied to four of the Group's former Halifax squadrons, Nos. 10, 76, 77 and 78.

Total production of the Dakota reached over 10,000 and many are still giving good service throughout the world today.

The No. 4 Group squadrons equipped with Dakotas were Nos. 10, 76, 77, 78, 512, 575.

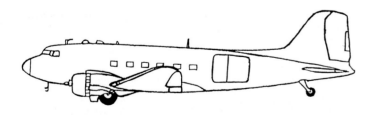

Technical Data (Douglas C-47 Dakota Mk.IV)
Power Plant: Two 1,200 hp Pratt and Whitney R-1830 Twin Wasp radial engines.
Performance: Maximum speed 230 mph at 8,800 feet;
  Cruising speed 185 mph; Service ceiling 23,000 feet;
  Range 1,350 miles.
Dimensions: Span 95ft; Length 64ft 6ins; Height 16ft 11ins.
Weight: Empty 16,976 lb; Loaded 25,200 lb; Typical cargo load 8,600 lb or up to 32 troops.

CONSOLIDATED B-24 LIBERATOR

Built in far greater numbers than any other US aircraft (19,203) the Consolidated B-24 Liberator shared with the B-17 Fortress in the US Army Air Force's daylight bombing offensive against Germany.

Flown for the first time on 29th December 1939 the B-24 was powered by four 1,200 hp Pratt and Whitney R-1830 Twin Wasp radial engines. Its unrivalled range made it ideally suitable for transport and maritime patrol duties as well as the bomber role.

A substantial number of Liberators were supplied to RAF Bomber, Coastal and Transport Commands. Transport versions of the B-24 (Liberator Mks.VI and VIII) were supplied to Nos. 102 and 466 (RAAF) Squadrons, two of No. 4 Group's former Halifax units, for trunk route flying to the Far East.

The No. 4 Group squadrons equipped with Liberators were Nos. 102, 466.

Technical Data (Liberator Mk.VIII)
Power Plant: Four 1,200 hp Pratt and Whitney R-1830 Twin Wasp radial engines.
Performance: Maximum speed 300 mph at 30,000 feet;
  Service Ceiling 28,000 feet; Range 2,290 miles.
Dimensions: Span 110ft; Length 67ft 2in; Height 18ft.
Weight: Empty 37,000 lb; Loaded 65,000 lb.

AVRO ANSON

The Avro 652A Anson, a military development of the Avro 652 six seater commercial aircraft, was designed to meet a requirement for a twin engined shore-based reconnaissance aircraft. The Anson prototype flew for the first time in March 1935. In the July it gained its first production order (to Air Ministry Specification 18/35) and entered service with the RAF in March 1936. Ansons were to serve in the RAF in a variety of roles, including reconnaissance, training and as transports but are perhaps best known for their role as one of the standard trainers for the huge Commonwealth Air Training Plan. The last RAF Ansons were retired in June 1968.

Anson Mk.Is entered service with 4 Group squadrons early in 1937 where they served as an interim type as crews were converted to more modern equipment. When production of the Avro Anson ceased in 1952 just over 11,000 had been built.

The No.4 Group squadrons equipped with Ansons were Nos. 51, 58, 75, 76, 97, 215.

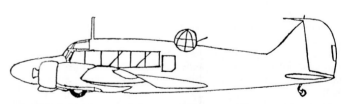

Technical Data (Anson Mk.I)
Power Plant: Two 350hp Armstrong Siddeley Cheetah IX radial engines.
Performance: Maximum speed 188 mph at 7,0000 feet;
  Service ceiling 19,000 feet; Range 790 miles.
Dimensions: Span 56ft; Length 42ft 3in; Height 13ft 1in.
Weight: Empty 5,375 lb; Loaded 8,000 lb.
Armament: Two 0.303 inch machine guns; up to 360 lb of bombs.

Appendix F

What's in a Name?
No.4 Group Nose Art

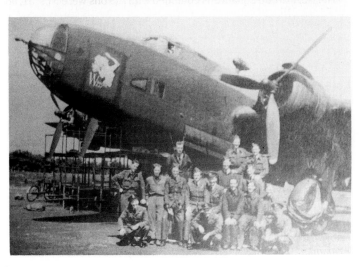

Top left: **Air and ground crew of *Ceylon*, T4261 'S', a Whitley Mk.V of No.102 Squadron, 1941. *Ceylon* was just one of many aircraft that were manufactured for the RAF as a result of donations from individuals, families, companies, overseas countries etc. This example was a gift from the Governor and people of Ceylon.** *W.Baguley*

Centre left: **The date is September 1944 and a proud Warrant Officer Geoff Dowling with air and ground crew pose beneath the partially cropped nose of *Vera the Virgin*, MZ516 'V' of No.76 Squadron, Holme-on-Spalding Moor. *Vera*'s bomb log shows forty-nine operations recorded. Another twenty-eight symbols were added before *Vera* failed to return from Mainz in February 1945.** *G.E.Wadsworth*

Bottom left: **Winsome WAAF, LW497 'W' of No.51 Squadron, with air and ground crew at Snaith early in 1944.** *W.Baguley*

Above: **Flight Lieutenant Jack MacCormack in the cockpit of his No.405 (RCAF) Squadron 'Wimpey' *Dummy Run* at Pocklington on the 14th August 1941. Later that day No.405 took part in a night attack on rail targets at Magdeburg. Fortunately, all the Squadron's Wellingtons returned safely on that occasion.** *Chaz Bowyer*

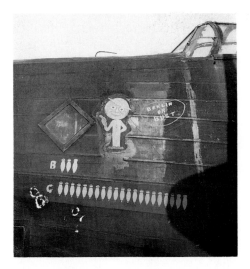

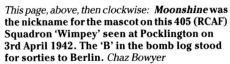

This page, above, then clockwise: **Moonshine** was the nickname for the mascot on this 405 (RCAF) Squadron 'Wimpey' seen at Pocklington on 3rd April 1942. The 'B' in the bomb log stood for sorties to Berlin. *Chaz Bowyer*

Flight Lieutenant Len Broadhurst in Halifax Mk.III LV869 'G-George' of 78 Squadron, Breighton, July 1944. The crest represents four local pubs: The Bowman, The White Swan, The New Inn, and The Seven Sisters. The thirty-seven beer glasses are night operations, the six glasses of milk daylight sorties and the bottle of whisky signifies the 21st operation. After 53 ops, LV869 was lost over Kiel on 15th September 1944. *L. Broadhurst*

Squadron Leader McMullum (centre, back row) with air and ground crew of *U-Again* of 466 (RAAF) Squadron, Driffield, June 1944. The tally shows 37 ops plus one enemy fighter shot down. McMullum's all-Aussie crew failed to return from a daylight trip to Siracourt on 22nd June 1944 in LW116. *R. Thompson*

Appropriately pints of beer were chosen for the mission tally of Pilot Officer Young's and navigator Sergeant Youngers Mk.X Wellington 'Y' *Young/ers* of No. 466 (RAAF) Squadron, Spring 1943. Others are Sergeants Munnoch, Cunningham and Bryant. *S. Freeman*

Captions to photographs on the opposite page:
Top, left: **Sweet Sue**, LW496 'O', a Halifax Mk.III of No. 578 Squadron pictured at Burn late 1944. A veteran of 72 operations *Sweet Sue* survived the war after service with No. 1663 HCU. *Sue's* regular rear gunner Chuck Adams and pilot Jim Bluring are 3rd and 4th from the left, respectively. *C. Adams*

Top, right: Warrant Officer Mickey Jenkins and crew of No. 76 Squadron with their Mk.III Halifax, LW695 'M' *Mickeys Marauders*, taken after they had returned from Villeneuve St. George on 21st April 1944. *A. Hurst*

Bottom: Halifax Mk.II, W7710 'R' *Ruhr Valley Express* of 405 Squadron failed to return from Flensburg on the night of 1st October 1942. The artwork shows a distraught Adolf Hitler being chased by the *Ruhr Valley Express* with the comment, 'Hey Goering, "R-Robert" is here again'. *IWM, CH6614*

Opposite page top left, then anticlockwise: **Another high scoring Halifax from No. 578 was MZ543** *Intuition?* **with a mission tally showing 57 operations. Note 'X' and MZ543 painted on the wheel covers.** *P. Bryant*

Self portrait! Flight Lieutenant Roger Coverley in the cockpit of his Halifax Mk. II W1003 *Roger de Coverley*, **photographed at 1658 HCU Riccall in August 1943.** *H. D. Coverley*

The *Charlie's Aunt* **port side nose mascot of HX323 'C-Charlie', No. 10 Squadron, was the handiwork of her bomb aimer Flight Sergeant Arthur Smith who reproduced one of the popular Varga pin-up girls from the pages of the American magazine** *Esquire. A. C. Smith*

Topsy, **a Mk. III Halifax LK785 of No. 76 Squadron, gets its 43rd bomb motif after returning from Kiel, 24th July 1944.** *Topsy's* **skipper on this occasion was Captain Carl Larson of the Royal Norwegian Air Force, hence the Norwegian flag painted on the nose.** *W. Baguley*

Flying Officer 'Rusty' Williams (RAAF) in the cockpit of his Halifax NP971 'X' *The Ruhr Xpress* **of No. 466 Squadron, February 1945. See page 173.** *A. White*

Nose art on *Goofy's Gift* **of 158 Squadron shows 35 red bombs for night operations and three yellow for daylight raids. The last daylight trip shown was a raid on the V-2 launch site at Wizernes on 28th June 1944. HX356 went on to complete 73 operations.** *J. Hitchman*

50 not out! The names on this unidentified Halifax of No. 578 Squadron, 1944 include 'skipper' Blake, Johnny, Terry, Reg and 'Clueless'. *IWM*

Opposite page, top right: **Flight Sergeant Ned Feury's Halifax Mk. III, LK832 'H'** *Honkytonk 6th*, **pictured at Holme-on-Spalding Moor, July 1944 with air crew Sergeants Page, Davidson, Roberts, Barber, Howley and Allen plus ground crew Corporal Rawlinson and others. The bomb tally is twenty-eight, the large bomb is for D-Day, and the swastika is for one confirmed night fighter. LK832 went on to complete eighty-two operations with No. 76 Squadron and survived the war.** *N. Feury*

This page, top left: **No. 77 Squadron 'L-Love',** *Lassie Come Home*, **shows a tally of 34 night and 11 day operations, Full Sutton, 1944.** *R. Runkine*

Top right: *Achtung! The Black Prince*, **LW648 'A' of No. 76 Squadron on the occasion of reaching its half century, August 1944. Proud crew is that of Flight Lieutenant Watt and includes Nigerian born wireless operator Sergeant Akin Shenbanjo, in whose honour LW648 was named.** *The Black Prince* **completed sixty-six operations before failing to return from Bochum on 4th November 1944.** *A. R. Andrews*

Bottom left: **Flight Lieutenant Jack Watson and three of his crew with** *Zombie*, **Halifax Mk. III MZ399 'Z' of No. 158 Squadron. The flak damage occurred on an operation to Essen on 24th December 1944.**

Bottom right: **Air and ground crew of** *It's That Hank Again*, **Halifax Mk. III MZ341 'P' of No. 462 (RAAF) Squadron, Driffield, October 1944. The crew comprised Australians Pilot Officer Harold Hancock, Flight Sergeant Keith McKay and Ron Lehmann (latter not on photo), plus the Brits – Flight Sergeant Les Holland and Sergeants Andy Hawkins, Don Hulbert and Ken Holmes. Rabbit mascot is** *Flt Lt Albert. D. Hulbert*

Appendix G

No.4 Group
Halifax Tail Markings

It was on the Halifaxes of some of No. 4 Group's squadrons that the distinctive fin and rudder markings were introduced in the spring of 1944, just before D-Day. They are known to have been carried by at least nine squadrons, examples of eight of which are shown in the accompanying illustrations of fin and rudder marking colours. These represent aircraft from the following squadrons: No. 78 (white); No. 102 (red); No. 158 (yellow); No. 346 Free French (red); No. 347 Free French (red); No. 462 RAAF (yellow); No. 466 RAAF (yellow); No. 640 (yellow).

The other squadron whose aircraft sported fin and rudder markings was No. 10, based at Melbourne. This squadron was unusual, however, in that it adopted not just one but a wide variety of such markings, including a large hollow diamond – possibly similar in size and shape to that on No. 347 Squadron's machines; three vertical stripes, and either two or three horizontal stripes. They were applied in white chalk (necessitating frequent re-touching) and like those of No. 78 Squadron (also in chalk or non-permanent white paint), were retained by very few machines much beyond the end of 1944.

The red tail markings were painted in the same dull, almost brick shade of red, as the standard RAF night bomber code letters. Those carried by Nos. 346 and 347 Squadron's Halifaxes however, were of the brighter, more crimson shade used in the traditional French Air Force roundel. The French roundel itself and the fin flash were also carried, of course, but the former only appeared on the fuselage; on the wings the modified (red and blue) RAF roundels were retained.

In addition to fin and rudder markings, Halifaxes of Nos. 102, 346, 347 and 640 Squadrons had their code and individual identification letters outlined in yellow – a practice of several other Halifax and Lancaster squadrons of Bomber Command. The individual identification letters carried on the fins by some squadrons (see illustrations) were similarly outlined. One particular machine of No. 466 (RAAF) Squadron had not only code letters outlined in yellow but the serial number as well; this was a Halifax Mk.VI, RG596 'HD-T' *Trixie*. Halifax Mk.III MZ480 coded 'NP-K', and christened *Klu Klux Klan* of No. 158 Squadron was unusual in having the two yellow fin markings repeated, on a smaller scale and horizontally, around its undercarriage legs; NR133 'NP-J' was similar. Another unusual No. 158 Squadron Halifax was LV917 'NP-C' *Clueless* – its fuselage camouflage scheme had the wavy dividing line between the black sides and the earth and olive green top decking, which went out of fashion on the Halifax, and indeed all the 'heavies', in or about 1942. Yet another unusual No. 158 Squadron machine was NR119 'NP-T', which was seen just after the war wearing No. 462 (RAAF) Squadron's tail markings instead of its own. A further example of this inconsistency. no doubt the result of inter-squadron transfer of aircraft and parts urgently needed as replacements, was RG565 'HD-K' of No. 466 Squadron which in 1945, bore the chequer board markings of the disbanded No. 640 Squadron on its tail.

The above description of Halifax tail markings is extracted from a series of articles on the Halifax by 'Lintonian' that appeared in Air Pictorial *between December 1954 and March 1955.*

Introduced in the spring of 1944 the distinctive 4 Group rudder markings were designed to aid formation assembly during daylight operations. Photographs of Halifaxes sporting the colourful designs are comparatively rare: this No. 466 (RAAF) example, NR169 christened *Waltzing Matilda*, shows the broad horizontal yellow tail stripes carried by 466 from mid 1944 onwards. NR169 survived the war and was purchased by Captain G. H. Wickner to transport his family and other expatriate Australians home. Registered as G-AGXA it was flown to Australia in 1946. *The Aeroplane*

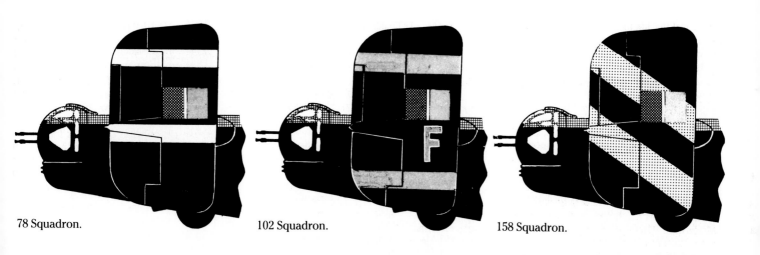

78 Squadron.

102 Squadron.

158 Squadron.

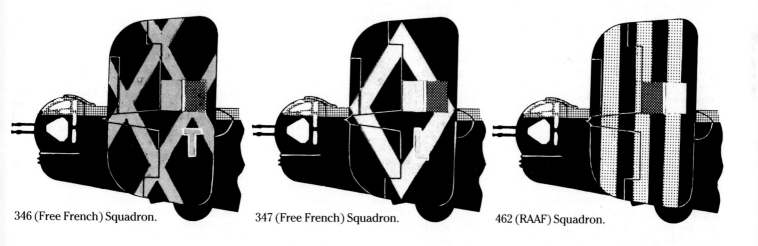

346 (Free French) Squadron.

347 (Free French) Squadron.

462 (RAAF) Squadron.

▨	Red
▨	Blue
▨	Yellow
☐	White
▨	Dark Green
▉	Black

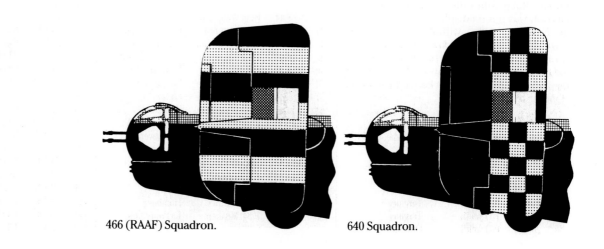

466 (RAAF) Squadron.

640 Squadron.

Appendix H

The 100 Club

When Halifax Mk.III LV907 was delivered to No. 158 Squadron at Lissett in March 1944, its arrival made no particular impact. Fresh from the Handley Page works at Radlett, LV907 was just another issue in the long line of Halifax bombers passing into operational service. Its debut on operations came on 30th March when Flight Sergeant Joe Hitchman piloted LV907 safely to Nuremburg and back. With only the occasional break for maintenance, *Friday the 13th*, as it was now titled, operated throughout the summer and autumn of 1944, until by late October its bomb-log stood at over eighty sorties. For most of November, *Friday* underwent a thorough maintenance check, but had returned to the operational scene by early December. By this time she had safely borne two crews through their tours of duty. Flying Officer C. E. Smith and crew took *Friday* over in the April, and when their tour was completed in early August, Flying Officer D. A. Waterman eagerly took their place. Now with the magical '100' in sight, *Friday* was in the hands of a Canadian crew captained by Flight Lieutenant N. G. Gordon (RCAF). During the evening of 22nd January 1945, this crew took *Friday* to Gelsenkirchen in the Ruhr. On their return the 100th bomb symbol was applied. Flight Lieutenant Gordon paid this tribute to *Friday*:

'We always feel absolutely confident in her. She flies right and she always gets there.'

In late March Flight Lieutenant Gordon and crew completed their tour and the honour of taking *Friday* on its last operation fell to Flying Officer Wheeler. The target, Wangerooge, was the last attacked by No. 4 Group in its long battle against the enemy. Proudly bearing 128 bomb tallies on its nose panels, *Friday*, along with other examples of Allied aircraft, was put on display on Oxford Street in London. Sadly, without any thought towards the future, *Friday* was reduced to scrap soon afterwards. Fortunately, the bomb log panels were salvaged and today these are displayed in the Royal Air Force Museum at Hendon.

Operational record of Halifax LV907 'Friday the 13th'

Opn	Date	Captain	Target
1	30.3.44	F/Sgt Hitchman	Nuremburg
2	9.4.44	P/O Smith	Villeneuve
3	10.4.44	P/O Smith	Tergnier
4	18.4.44	P/O Smith	Tergnier
5	20.4.44	P/O Smith	Ottignies
6	22.4.44	P/O Smith	Düsseldorf
7	24.4.44	P/O Smith	Karlsruhe
8	26.4.44	P/O Smith	Villeneuve
9	27.4.44	P/O Smith	Aulnoye
10	30.4.44	P/O Smith	Acheres
11	1.5.44	F/Sgt Hitchman	Malines
12	8.5.44	P/O Smith	Morsallines
13	10.5.44	F/Sgt Evans	Lens
14	11.5.44	P/O Smith	Colline
15	12.5.44	P/O Smith	Hasselt
16	19.5.44	P/O Smith	Boulogne
17	24.5.44	P/O Smith	Aachen
18	27.5.44	P/O Smith	Bourg Leopold
19	1.6.44	P/O Smith	Ferme d'Urvill
20	2.6.44	P/O Smith	Trappes
21	5.6.44	P/O Smith	Maisy
22	6.6.44	P/O Smith	Chateaudun
23	7.6.44	P/O Smith	Versailles
24	9.6.44	P/O Smith	Laval
25	12.6.44	P/O Smith	Amiens
26	16.6.44	F/Sgt Chilcott	Sterkrade
27	17.6.44	F/Sgt Chilcott	St Martin L'Hortier
28	22.6.44	F/O New	Siracourt
29	23.6.44	F/Sgt Paulson	Oisemont
30	24.6.44	F/Sgt Chilcott	Le Grande Rosignol
31	27.6.44	F/Sgt Chilcott	Mimoyecques
32	28.6.44	W/O Fulker	Wizernes
33	30.6.44	F/Sgt Chilcott	Villers Bocage
34	1.7.44	P/O Smith	Oisemont
35	7.7.44	F/O Montgomery	Caen
36	12.7.44	P/O Smith	Ferme du Forestal
37	18.7.44	P/O Smith	Caen
38	20.7.44	P/O Smith	Bottrop
39	23.7.44	F/Sgt Waterman	Les Catelliers
40	24.7.44	P/O Smith	Stuttgart
41	25.7.44	P/O Fulker	Wanne Eickel
42	28.7.44	F/O Smith	Forêt de Nieppe
43	29.7.44	F/Sgt Waterman	Forêt de Nieppe
44	1.8.44	F/O Smith	Chapelle Notre Dame. DNCO
45	2.8.44	F/Sgt Waterman	L'Hey
46	3.8.44	F/Sgt Waterman	Forêt de Nieppe
47	5.8.44	F/Sgt Waterman	Forêt de Nieppe
48	6.8.44	F/Sgt Waterman	Forêt de Nieppe
49	7.8.44	F/Sgt Waterman	Totaliser III. DNCO
50	9.8.44	F/Sgt Waterman	Bois de la Haie
51	11.8.44	F/Sgt Waterman	Ferfay
52	12.8.44	F/Sgt Waterman	Brunswick
53	14.8.44	F/Sgt Waterman	Tractable 21A
54	15.8.44	F/Sgt Waterman	Eindhoven
55	16.8.44	F/Sgt Waterman	Kiel
56	18.8.44	F/Sgt Waterman	Sterkrade
57	24.8.44	F/O McAdam	Brest
58	25.8.44	F/Sgt Meaden	Brest
59	27.8.44	F/Sgt Harmer	Homberg
60	31.8.44	F/Sgt Meaden	La Pourchinte. DNCO
61	3.9.44	F/Sgt Harmer	Soesterberg
62	9.9.44	P/O Meaden	Le Havre. DNCO
63	10.9.44	F/Sgt Waterman	Le Havre
64	11.9.44	F/O Rees	Le Havre. DNCO
65	12.9.44	P/O Waterman	Gelsenkirchen
66	13.9.44	P/O Waterman	Gelsenkirchen
67	15.9.44	P/O Waterman	Kiel
68	17.9.44	P/O Waterman	Boulogne
69	23.9.44	P/O Waterman	Neuss. DNCO. p/o u/s
70	25.9.44	S/Ldr Salter	Calais. DNCO
71	26.9.44	P/O Waterman	Calais
72	6.10.44	F/O Waterman	Sterkrade
73	7.10.44	F/O Waterman	Kleve
74	9.10.44	F/O Tilston	Bochum
75	14.10.44	F/O Waterman	Duisburg
76	15.10.44	F/O Waterman	Duisburg
77	15.10.44	F/Sgt Harmer	Wilhelmshaven
78	21.10.44	F/O Sinclair	Hanover. DNCO
79	23.10.44	F/Sgt Harmer	Essen
80	25.10.44	F/O Gordon	Essen
81	28.10.44	F/O Waterman	Domberg
82	29.10.44	F/O Gordon	Zoutelande
83	29.11.44	F/O Gordon	Essen
84	30.11.44	Sgt Kaye	Duisburg
85	2.12.44	F/O Compton	Hagen
86	5.12.44	F/O Robinson	Soest
87	6.12.44	F/O Robinson	Osnabruck. DNCO Gee u/s
88	12.12.44	F/O Robinson	Essen
89	18.12.44	F/O Robinson	Duisburg
90	21.12.44	F/O Gordon	Cologne
91	24.12.44	F/O Robinson	Essen Mulheim. DNCO
92	26.12.44	F/O Robinson	St Vith
93	28.12.44	F/O Gordon	Opladen
94	30.12.44	F/O Gordon	Cologne
95	1.1.45	F/O Robinson	Dortmund
96	2.1.45	F/O Gordon	Ludwigshafen
97	5.1.45	F/O Gordon	Hanover
98	14.1.45	P/O Tilston	Saarbrucken
99	16.1.45	F/Lt Gordon	Magdeburg
100	22.1.45	F/Lt Gordon	Gelsenkirchen
101	1.2.45	F/Lt Gordon	Mainz
102	4.2.45	F/Lt Gordon	Gelsenkirchen
103	7.2.45	F/Lt Gordon	Goch
104	9.2.45	F/Lt Gordon	Wanne Eickel
105	13.2.45	F/Lt Gordon	Bohlen
106	14.2.45	F/Lt Gordon	Chemnitz
107	20.2.45	S/Ldr Salter	Reisholz
108	21.2.45	F/Sgt Kaye	Worms
109	23.2.45	F/Sgt Kaye	Essen
110	24.2.45	S/Ldr Salter	Kamen
111	27.2.45	S/Ldr Salter	Mainz
112	2.3.45	F/O Elley	Cologne
113	3.3.45	F/Lt Gordon	Kamen
114	5.3.45	F/Lt Gordon	Chemnitz

115	11.3.45	F/Lt Gordon	Essen
116	12.3.45	F/Lt Gordon	Dortmund
117	13.3.45	F/Lt Gordon	Wuppertal
118	14.3.45	F/Lt Gordon	Homberg
119	15.3.45	F/Lt Gordon	Hagen
120	19.3.45	F/Lt Gordon	Witten
121	20.3.45	F/Lt Gordon	Recklinghausen
122	21.3.45	F/Lt Gordon	Rheine
123	24.3.45	F/O Wheeler	Gladbeck
124	25.3.45	F/O Wheeler	Munster
125	4.4.45	F/O Wheeler	Harburg
126	8.4.45	F/O Wheeler	Hamburg
127	18.4.45	F/Sgt Dargavel	Heligoland
128	25.4.45	F/O Wheeler	Wangerooge*

Three more No. 4 Group Halifaxes passed the century mark: Mk.III LV937 flew with No. 578 Squadron from March to April 1944 as 'LK-X' and 'R'. Transferred to No. 51 Squadron in April, LV937 completed at least 100 sorties as 'MH-J', 'M' and 'E'. It was whilst coded 'E' that she was christened *Expensive Babe*. The *Babe* survived the war and was struck off charge on 18th May 1945. Two other century makers, both from No. 578 Squadron, did their 100th operations together to Kamen on the night of 3/4th March 1945. They were Mk.IIIs LW587 'LK-V', and 'A', and MZ527 'LK-W' and 'D'. Both Halifaxes completed at least 104 and 105 ops respectively. LW587 was struck off charge in September 1946 and MZ527 in April 1945. Another Halifax of No. 158 Squadron LV917 *C-Clueless* is known to have completed 99 operations and probably had the extra op chalked up for luck. One Halifax that ran out of luck was LW172 'F' of No. 466 (RAAF) Squadron. Delivered on 18th May 1944 she completed 96 operations before crashing in fog on return from Hamburg on 9th April 1945.

*Details of the operational record of *Friday the 13th* are taken from *In Brave Company*, the excellent history of No. 158 Squadron, by Bill Chorley and the late Roy Benwell.

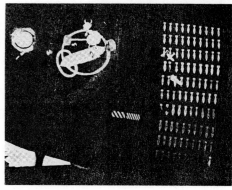

Top: **Friday the 13th**, Halifax Mk.III, LV907 'F' of No. 158 Squadron, pictured having just completed its 117th sortie – a daylight raid on Wuppertal on 13th March 1945. *A.J.Ralph*

Centre left: **100 Today! Flight Lieutenant Kemp and crew in front of *Expensive Babe*, LV937 'E' of No.51 Squadron, on return from *Babe*'s 100th mission, an attack on Osnabruck, 6th December 1944. LV937 survived the war and was struck off charge in July 1945.** *W.Baguley*

Centre right: **Bomb log of Halifax Mk.III LV917 'C' *Clueless* which completed at least ninety-nine operations with No. 158 Squadron. The '100th' bomb may have been added for luck.**

Bottom: **Flight Lieutenant Baer 'buzzes' the control tower at Burn on completion of his tour with No. 578 Squadron, August 1944. His Halifax, MZ527 'W', went on to complete 105 sorties and survived the war.** *IWM, HU4017*

Appendix I

For Valour
Airmen of No.4 Group
Who were Awarded the Victoria Cross

Chaz Bowyer

CYRIL JOE BARTON
'. . displayed unsurpassed courage and
devotion to duty.'

IWM

GEOFFREY LEONARD CHESHIRE
'. . a reputation second to none in
Bomber Command.'

Wing Commander
Geoffrey Leonard Cheshire DSO, DFC
RAFVR, (72021) No. 617 Squadron

This officer began his operational career in June 1940. Against strongly-defended targets, he soon displayed the courage and determination of an exceptional leader. He was always ready to accept extra risks to ensure success. Defying the formidable Ruhr defences, he frequently released his bombs from below 20,000 feet. Over Cologne in November 1940 a shell burst inside his aircraft blowing out one side and starting a fire; undeterred, he went on to bomb the target. About this time, he carried out a number of convoy patrols in addition to his bombing sessions.

At the end of his first tour of operational duty in January 1941, he immediately volunteered for a second. Again, he pressed home his attacks with the utmost gallantry. Berlin, Bremen, Cologne, Duisburg, Essen and Kiel were among the heavily-defended targets which he attacked. When he was posted for instructional duties in January 1942 he undertook four more operational missions.

He started a third tour in August 1942 when he was given command of a squadron. He led the squadron with outstanding skill on a number of missions before being appointed in March 1942 as a station commander.

In October 1943 he undertook a fourth operational tour relinquishing the rank of Group Captain at his own request so that he could again take part in operations. He immediately set to work as the pioneer of a new method of marking enemy targets involving very low flying. In June 1944, when marking a target in the harbour of Le Havre in broad daylight and without cloud cover, he dived well below the range of the light batteries before releasing his marker bombs, and he came very near to being destroyed by the strong barrage which concentrated on him.

During his fourth tour which ended in July 1944, Wing Commander Cheshire led his squadron personally on every occasion, always undertaking the most dangerous and difficult task of marking the target alone from a low level in the face of strong defences.

Wing Commander Cheshire's cold and calculated acceptance of risks is exemplified by his conduct in an attack on Munich in April 1944. This was an experimental attack to test out the new method of target marking at low level against a heavily defended target situated deep in Reich territory. Munich was selected, at Wing Commander Cheshire's request, because of the formidable nature of its light anti-aircraft and searchlight defences. He was obliged to follow, in bad weather, a direct route which took him over the defences of Augsburg and thereafter he was continuously under fire. As he reached the target, flares were being released by high flying aircraft. He was illuminated from above and below. All guns within range opened fire on him. Diving to 700 feet, he dropped his markers with great precision and began to climb away. So blinding were the searchlights that he almost lost control. He then flew over the city at 1,000 feet to assess the accuracy of his work and direct other aircraft. His own was badly hit by shell fragments but he continued to fly over the target area until he was satisfied that he had done all in his power to ensure success. Eventually, when he set course for base, the task of disengaging himself from the defences proved even more hazardous than the approach. For a full twelve minutes after leaving the target area he was under withering fire, but he safely came through.

Wing Commander Cheshire has now completed a total of 100 missions. In four years of fighting against the bitterest opposition he has maintained a record of outstanding personal achievement, placing himself invariably in the forefront of the battle. What he did in the Munich operation was typical of careful planning, brilliant execution and contempt for danger which has established for Wing Commander Cheshire a reputation second to none in Bomber Command.

Geoffrey Leonard Cheshire was born at Chester on 7th September 1917. His father was Geoffrey Cheshire, Professor of Law and Bursar at Exeter College, Oxford.

Whilst studying law at Oxford, Cheshire learned to fly with the Oxford University Air Squadron, joining the RAF Volunteer Reserve as a Pilot Officer in October 1937. He joined No. 102 Squadron in June 1940 flying Whitley bombers, gaining the award of a DSO for bringing a crippled bomber back to base. After completion of one tour of operations Cheshire volunteered for a second tour early in 1941, this time on Halifaxes with No. 35 Squadron at Linton-on-Ouse. During his second tour he was awarded the DFC and a Bar to the DSO.

From January 1942 Cheshire was rested from operations, serving as an instructor at No. 1652 Heavy Conversion Unit, Marston Moor. He began his third tour of operations in August 1942 as commander of No. 76 Squadron, gaining a second Bar to his DSO. In April 1943 he was promoted to Group Captain and given command of the station at Marston Moor. He returned to operations again in October taking over command of the prestigious No. 617 Squadron. It was whilst he was with 617 that Cheshire pioneered the low-level marking of targets, first with the Lancaster and then with the Mosquito. His award of the VC in September 1944 was in recognition of his service to date in Bomber Command, including that with No. 4 Group.

Cheshire ended the war in Europe with a total of 103 operational sorties to his credit. In August 1945 he was sent as an official observer on the second atomic bomb operation against Nagasaki.

After the war Leonard Cheshire spent some time gathering his thoughts before taking an old soldier into his home in Hampshire where he cared for the old man who was dying of cancer. More people came to his home and from that small start the worldwide Cheshire Homes Foundation has grown: there are now 270 in 51 countries, all dedicated to the care of the sick.

In 1989 Cheshire launched the World War Memorial Fund for Disaster Relief. He was also co-founder of the Ryder-Cheshire Mission for the Relief of Suffering. He was awarded the Order of Merit in 1981, and created Baron Cheshire in 1991.

Lord Geoffrey Leonard Cheshire VC, died on 31st July 1992, aged 74.

The full citation to this award appeared in The London Gazette *of 8th September 1944.*

Pilot Officer
Cyril Joe Barton RAFVR (Deceased)
(168669) No. 578 Squadron

On the night of 30th March 1944, Pilot Officer Barton was captain and pilot of a Halifax aircraft detailed to attack Nuremburg. When some seventy miles short of the target, the aircraft was attacked by a Junkers 88. The first burst of fire from the enemy made the intercommunication system useless. One engine was damaged when a Messerschmitt 210 joined in the fight. The bomber's machine guns were out of action and the gunners were unable to return the fire.

Fighters continued to attack the aircraft as it approached the target area and, in the confusion caused by the failure of the communications system at the height of the battle, a signal was misinterpreted and the navigator, air bomber and wireless operator left the aircraft by parachute.

Pilot Officer Barton faced a situation of dire peril. His aircraft was damaged, his navigational team had gone and he could not communicate with the remainder of the crew. If he continued his mission he would be at the mercy of hostile fighters when silhouetted against the fires in the target area, and if he survived he would have to make a four and a half hours journey home on three engines across heavily-defended territory. Determined to press home his attack at all costs, he flew on and, reaching the target, released the bombs himself.

As Pilot Officer Barton turned for home the propeller of the damaged engine, which was vibrating badly, flew off. It was also discovered that two petrol tanks had suffered damage and were leaking. Pilot Officer Barton held to his course and, without navigational aids and in spite of strong head winds, successfully avoided the most dangerous defence areas on his route. Eventually he crossed the English coast only 90 miles north of his base.

By this time the petrol was nearly exhausted. Before a suitable landing place could be found, the port engine stopped. The aircraft was now too low to be abandoned successfully. Pilot Officer Barton therefore ordered the three remaining members of his crew to take up their crash stations. Then, with only one engine working, he made a gallant attempt to land clear of the houses over which he was flying. The aircraft finally crashed and Pilot Officer Barton lost his life, but his three comrades survived.

Pilot Officer Barton had previously taken part in four attacks on Berlin and 14 other operational missions. On one of these two members of his crew were wounded during a determined effort to locate the target despite the appalling weather conditions. In gallantly completing his last mission in the face of almost impossible odds, this officer displayed unsurpassed courage and devotion to duty.

The full citation to this award appeared in The London Gazette *of 27th June 1944.*

Appendix J

Missing

A member of a bomber crew in the Second World War needed to be both quick and lucky to escape from his shot down aircraft. His aircrew training would have taught him to react swiftly in an emergency, but any delay usually proved fatal. If he was among the fortunate few that did manage to bale out then he still faced the prospect of more danger. If he had baled out over friendly territory then there was a chance that, providing he was not seriously injured, he would be able to make contact with an underground organisation that would help him return to England. If he was unlucky to have come down over Germany, and particularly if he was injured, then in all probability he would soon be captured. There were instances of airmen being beaten up and even killed by angry civilians, but such instances were uncommon. As a rule Allied airmen were handed over to the military for interrogation, usually the Luftwaffe, before going on to a POW camp. If they had been injured they were usually well cared for in German hospitals. For many, the prospect of a long imprisonment with an uncertain future, was to lead them to attempt some very ingenious escapes from captivity.

During the course of writing this History of No. 4 Group, I received many stories from airmen who were shot down over enemy territory and were captured. It has not been possible for me to include every story in full because of space limitations. I have therefore decided to include a full account of one airman's experiences.

Flight Lieutenant Desmonde Moss and crew of No. 10 Squadron took-off from Melbourne in their Halifax MZ948 'E-Easy' on the evening of 5th March 1945 for a mission to bomb Chemnitz. There was considerable night fighter activity that night and twenty-two bombers failed to return, one of them was Halifax MZ948, 'E-Easy'. Flight Lieutenant Desmonde Moss was reported missing. This is his story.

'We went to Chemnitz on the night of 5th March 1945, a long, cold journey with cloudy conditions all the way and only a little better over the target area. Our incendiaries were dropped over the target indicators but the 2,000 lb 'Cookie' would not release. We circled and tried to release it in the target area but nothing happened so we set off to return. Our bomb-aimer, Warrant Officer 'Buzz' Webster, and flight engineer, Sergeant Jimmy Tasker, inspected the bomb release

mechanism as closely and as carefully as possible. It's no joke peering through a nine inch diameter hole with a torch, in the face of an icy 200 mph gale, whilst at the same time trying to prise loose a ton of freezing steel and explosive with frost bitten fingers: if you are successful those numb fingers will probably go with the bomb. Buzz reported that the release mechanism appeared to be OK but just did not work, probably ice had formed somewhere inside the mechanism.

'I decided to descend below cloud into warmer air and try again. Several minutes later we levelled off at about 2,000 feet above the sleeping countryside and the boys tried again. Once more, "It looks OK" came the call so the bomb doors were opened and the button pressed - with no result! I tried the jettison release, nothing doing! Jimmy tried again with a screwdriver, then a fire axe but after five minutes could only report that the bomb and bomb slips were working in the airflow. I warned everybody to hold on tight as I threw the Halifax around to try and release the bomb. Eventually there was a crack and a shout of "Hurray, its gone." Bomb doors were closed and then there was a flash from the ground as the Cookie exploded. I opened up to climbing power and we went up through the clouds again into clearer air.

'I levelled off a few hundred feet above the clouds and we got back to normal routine. Suddenly there was a shout from Flight Sergeant Steve Hodgson in the rear turret – "Night fighter attacking!" I saw tracers curving away from below and behind us up to starboard. I started corkscrewing as violently as I could, but it was soon obvious that we had been badly hit. The fuselage filled with smoke and I could no longer hear instructions from the rear gunner. The flight engineer drew my attention to the emergency signalling light from the rear gunner which was flashing. Good for Steve, our rear-gunner, he had stuck to his task and was rewarded by the sight of a Ju 88 going down in flames.

'By this time our port inner engine was blazing out of control, the starboard inner was also on fire as was the rest position area of the fuselage. I could get no reply from any of the gunners – we had one in the mid-under blister on this trip, and we were losing height and were unable to bring the flames under control. I decided we had better get out whilst I could still keep the Halifax reasonably steady. I ordered "bale out" on the intercom

and also tapped out the letter "P" several times on the emergency signal light system in the hope that the gunners would see it and be able to get out in time. I saw the flight engineer pass my seat, wearing his chest-type parachute, and he disappeared past the blackout curtain to the front escape hatch. After a few seconds I tried to follow him but found that my seat harness would not release. Somehow it had jammed. As I struggled to release it the world suddenly exploded!

'I awoke to find myself dangling in my parachute harness a few feet from the ground. I looked up and could see that the canopy was caught up in the branches of a tree. I pulled the straps gently at first, then more and more violently until I dropped to the ground. I then lost consciousness.

'When I at last came to my senses it was morning and I was very hungry and thirsty. My face hurt, I had nothing on my feet and I only had a hazy idea of where I was. I found my emergency kit and discovered that my hair was singed, my eyelashes and eyebrows were gone and the remainder of my face, which had not been covered by the oxygen mask, was raw flesh where all the skin was burnt away. There was only Gentian Violet Jelly in the kit so I applied this liberally to the burned areas of my face and neck, even my eyelids. I ate some of the emergency rations in the kit and then tried to plan my next move. If I had any chance of reaching the Allied lines then I needed to head in a westerly direction, but how could I walk without shoes? Fortunately I still had my flying gauntlets which I put on my feet and tied them on with parachute cord. I picked up my emergency kit and stowed it in my battledress blouse, rolled up the parachute and harness, stuffed them under some bushes and set off heading west, according to my "button" compass.

'After a few minutes walking I came to a rough lane and turned left downhill in search of water. After walking a few hundred yards I was still in trees and no sign of water so I retraced my steps. I now had another problem to worry about. Gentian Violet protects burns alright but it gradually sets hard. I was now having trouble with my eyes and every time I blinked or closed my eyes it was harder to open them again. I struggled on, past my original landing place, being somewhat encouraged by the sound of aircraft engines ahead of me.

'It was now late afternoon and as it grew dark I suddenly stumbled on a abandoned wreck of an aircraft. I gratefully crawled inside the fuselage and went to sleep. I soon awoke, very cold so I found some pieces of cloth which had covered the windows of the aircraft and these helped me to pass the night in fitful sleep.

'In the morning I ate some more of my rations and inspected my surroundings, having to prise open my eyelids and clean off the burn dressing to do so; that awakened me in short order. I found that I was in the wreck of an old Junkers Ju 52, and the fuselage was all there was! I prowled around a bit trying to think. An abandoned aircraft, aero engines heard not far off, all this pointed to an airfield being not far away. In the distance along the lane I could now see in the morning light some more aeroplanes under the trees. They looked like Fw 190s. Perhaps I could steal one and fly home in style. It was not to be. Only a hundred yards away, behind some bushes, was a small guard post. I was seen and arrested.

'I was taken to a First Aid Post in the nearby town of Aschaffenburg where my burns were cleaned and dressed. From there I was escorted to the Oberursel Interrogation Centre by a lone corporal with a big rifle. We went by train to Frankfurt, arriving after dark just as the air raid sirens went. My escort insisted that we descend into the shelter under the railway station, even though I showed him the red candles of the Target Indicators drifting down on to the marshalling yards just a couple of hundred yards off. Down we went, still in RAF battledress with wings plainly showing to join several hundred German civilians in a large cellar. My corporal put me in a corner and stood in front of me with his rifle across his body and carefully loaded it and worked the bolt action to put a round in the breech – making sure everybody saw what he was doing. There were many hands and voices raised but he stood his ground and I left the shelter unharmed.

'We arrived at the Interrogation Centre safely and I was immediately transferred to a large house some half a mile away which was used as a prison hospital. There I received further treatment for several days. The upstairs wards were full and at first I was confined to a small room downstairs by myself. I was visited daily for medical attention, and meals were brought to me. After a day or two I noticed that the door was not always locked after my tray had been brought in so I ventured to explore my surroundings. I found that although the food was brought in from the Interrogation Centre, there was a small kitchen for special diets which was also used as a servery for the main meals and also for the staff meals. If I watched carefully I could slip into this kitchen, after the staff had eaten and whilst they were collecting the empties from the patients upstairs. There I could find plenty of scraps to augment my own some-

what meagre rations. Eventually, when the doctor pronounced me well enough to join the other POWs upstairs, I missed the "extra" rations.

'After a few days I was returned to the Centre for interrogation. The interviewer certainly knew a lot about me and my Squadron and, amazingly, my family. (My father had helped the pre-war RAF in some camouflage experiments). I refused to give anything more than my name, rank and number, so I was soon packed off to one of the cells. There I stayed for several days, sometimes uncomfortably hot but mostly very cold. There was nothing more I had to say to my captors and eventually I left with a party of other RAF types in transit to the camp at Wetzlar.

'Later, as our column was marching down a country road, a lone Thunderbolt made a pass but we saw him in good time and were safe in a ditch before he opened fire. He must have had more important things on his mind as he did not try again. We waited until nightfall in a wooded railway cutting, trying to sleep under the bushes, until about 22.00, when a somewhat rickety train clanked alongside and we were pushed into assorted trucks and vans. After some hours of uncomfortable and intermittent travel we were decanted beside a road and told to march off. We were escorted up a steadily rising dirt road and finally arrived at Dulag Luft. Here we were introduced to 'proper' POW life – long barracks with uncomfortable bunks, palliasses stuffed with very stale straw supported in board frames at intervals - depending on how many boards had been used for fuel in the stoves. Meals were taken in a dining room and consisted mainly of potatoes and concoctions made up from the contents of whatever Red Cross supplies were available. Our captors were no better off, their food was perhaps more plentiful but not as varied. Here I met Flight Sergeant Jock Fowler, our wireless operator. He was in hospital having injured both his ankles when he landed. He told me he had seen Steve Hodgson, our reargunner, but he had already left the camp. Jock, Steve and I were the only survivors of the crash.

'About a week after arriving at Wetzlar we were warned to be ready to leave camp. All POWs who were fit to walk were to be evacuated to a new camp at Nuremburg. Early one morning we were paraded between the barracks, carrying what possessions we still had and each man was solemnly presented with a box of Red Cross goodies to feed him for the journey. Then our numbers and identities were checked, the gates were opened, and out we went, about ninety POWs, mostly RAF and US airmen with a few paratroopers. The column was headed by a platoon of German guards, followed by the main body of POWs three abreast. Another platoon of Germans followed at the rear with a small cart carrying their kit. There was also a file of guards along each side of the prisoners, making the column in effect about seven abreast.

This, of course, completely filled the narrow lanes along which we went, causing some confusion whenever we met any traffic.

'One could not say we marched, although the Major in charge of the detachment tried to keep up a good steady pace. We were as well aware as he of the necessity for speed – the Allied armies were poised on the Rhine and we had to be cleared from the battle area if we were to be any further use as hostages. Consequently we did all we could to slow down our progress. We were not in good enough condition to march to infantry pace, and any hills caused an immediate drop in speed. People got stones in their footwear and had to fall out, until we were shown that the Germans' feet were in no better condition and further excuses would not be accepted. We stopped at mid-day for a meal break, being led into a field and surrounded by our guards. There was a small rivulet where we could get water to drink or wash. Our progress was resumed after about an hour – minus three paratroopers who had mysteriously disappeared – and continued until dusk when we were ushered into a school playground and lined up for a head count. After our numbers had been checked we were led into the single large schoolroom. This was about thirty feet long and fifteen feet wide. On one long wall the windows overlooked the playground, where the baggage cart was parked and a field kitchen set up. The opposite wall was bare and a row of planks had been set up about six feet from the wall and the space between filled with straw. Hot water was eventually provided to go with whatever food we could supply. We slept on the straw as and where we found space.

'When we mustered in the morning we were short of a few more. Of course, no one knew anything about it, so eventually we set off for another day's march. It was a long morning. We were going as slowly as possible, but our guards were getting impatient and we had to keep moving. We finally came to rest in a farmyard in mid-afternoon for a meal. We were allowed to use the farm's copper wash boiler for brewing up and managed to make "Potmess". This consisted of potatoes, oatmeal, broken biscuits, soup tablets or powder, and stale crusty bread. This last item came from the German soldiers who could not resist the smell of our brew up and bartered their half a loaf a man ration for a mess tin full of our "soup". Some of us managed to cat nap but it was soon time to move on.

'As we plodded on through the lengthening shadows, our line straggled more and more, and the Germans got more irritable as they tried to keep our column closed up. They were concerned that we were behind schedule and would have to keep marching after night fall as we were supposed to be catching a train at midnight. We were following secondary roads as main roads were not safe. Anything moving on them was likely to be attacked by roving fighter bombers. Later that night we stopped for a rest, just as we came through a small village. After a few minutes we found out why we had stopped. The German Major had seen a donkey in the village and went back to commandeer it to save his feet. We gave him an ironic cheer as he appeared, then set to work stirring up the guards by saying "it's alright for some". These soldiers were getting a bit fed up with the whole thing anyway and became more friendly as time went on. More people had managed to slip away by now, not all of them POWs.

'I had, by this time, developed a small blister on my foot and I used it as an excuse to limp along as slowly as I dared, gradually dropping back along the column. Several other chaps were doing the same thing, and eventually we found ourselves among the group of Germans with the baggage cart at the rear of the line. From time to time the Major rode up and down the column and the next time he arrived he asked why we were so far behind our comrades. We gave our excuses and suggested that if the pace had to be maintained perhaps we could ride on the cart. He considered the proposal seriously but decided that the horse would not be able to cope with the extra weight. He thereupon beckoned to a Corporal who was limping carefully along behind us and gave him detailed directions with the aid of his field map. Then he told us that we were to follow the rest of the company at our best speed, in the charge of the Corporal and two soldiers, and rejoin the company when they halted for breakfast.

'So now there were four of us left with our three guards, all tired and limping. We carried on slowly for an hour or so, then came to a mutual decision that it was time for a brief rest and review of the situation. Our side consisted of two Americans; a major who spoke passable German and a coloured sergeant still suffering from shell shock sustained when the tank he was driving had suffered a direct hit from a heavy shell, and two RAF men; a sergeant air gunner and myself. Neither of the NCOs could speak German and I knew only a few words of German and the usual "schoolboy" French and Latin. Of the Germans only the Corporal had any knowledge of English, and not much of that, so conversation was slow, hard work. We were all for retracing our steps westward, or at least staying where we were until overrun by advancing Allied troops. We really thought we had convinced our guards and persuaded them to come with us. But the Corporal suddenly decided he was still on duty, loaded his rifle and insisted that we continued to our original destination. The other Germans agreed they had better do the same so up we got and plodded drearily on. The soles of the German Army boots our guards were wearing were of thin cardboard so they were in no state to hurry but insisted we must keep moving.

'In the afternoon we came to an autobahn where the smooth surface made walking easier, although we had to get off the road sometimes when planes came over (and once for a Fw 190 to take off from the roadway). In the late afternoon we left the autobahn at a sign reading Bad Hersfeld, that was where we were supposed to catch a train. Just before dark we stopped for the night in a barn next to a small farmhouse. We slept on hay that night in comparative comfort and woke refreshed to the sounds of the farmyard. A gift of some of our American coffee to the farmer's wife produced boiled eggs and bread for breakfast, so we set off in good heart. The cobbled road was not easy for our aching feet and it was the afternoon when we crossed the *Fulda* river and entered the small town of Bad Hersfeld. We made our painful way to the railway station and our Corporal went off to the Town Mayor.

'The Corporal returned much later with the news that our POW party had left on the train the previous night and there would not be another until midnight. We spent the next hours in a forces canteen behind the station having a welcome meal and chatting with some not unfriendly *Afrika Korps* veterans. The arrival of the train took us all by surprise and we said our goodbyes and hurried out to the platform.

'The carriages had the usual wooden seats on each side of a centre aisle and we were pushed into facing seats with our guards on the inside places. More soldiers crowded into the carriage as it filled up and some of them insisted that we gave up our seats and stand in the aisle. Our escort protested that they could watch us more easily when we were seated together in one small place. The argument grew heated but ended abruptly when cannon shells started smashing into windows, roof and partitions. Everyone for himself! We all scrambled and ran out. I dived across the platform and under a railway wagon. The night intruder, a Mosquito, made another strafing run and then disappeared into the night. I got up and hurried to the side of the tracks but the wall was high and unclimbable. I retraced my way to the station building hoping to pass through unnoticed in the noisy confusion. There were several groups of people talking in the booking hall, obviously discussing the event, so I walked quietly through. Suddenly a hand clutched my jacket and a frantic voice exclaimed, "Captain, Captain, what do we do now?" – in English! It was the shell shocked American sergeant, his nerves upset again. I shook myself free and said quietly, "Don't talk now, just follow a few yards behind me and if I am stopped cross the road immediately and keep on walking." We left the station and walked along the street then turned down a narrow lane. This soon narrowed further into a footpath along the bottom of the railway embankment and was fenced on both sides. Abruptly it turned left and entered a tunnel cut under the railway lines, lit by dim blue lamps and signposted as an emergency air raid shelter. The far end was bricked up. We returned to the station and tried the other direction. After a few yards I was stopped by a Hitler Youth with a large automatic pistol who immediately ordered "Hande hoch!"

'I was taken to the office of the local commander, a very busy man. The area was now under martial law as the Allies had crossed the *Rhine* and the nearby *Fulda* river was the next defence line. He listened impatiently to the Youth's report, gave me a quick look, then said "Todt". I knew that meant "death" and tried to protest, first in English and then in French, that I was an English airman. I carefully showed them my service identity discs hung around my neck. The two Germans examined these and then began a lengthy conversation. The commander suddenly shrugged his shoulders, gave more instructions, and I was taken away to the local jail and locked in an upstairs cell. I huddled on the bare boards of the bottom shelf of a two-storey bunk and eventually fell asleep.

'In the morning a young woman brought a piece of dark bread and a mug of acorn coffee for breakfast. I asked if there was a toilet and was escorted downstairs to a very primitive apparatus. On the way I heard English conversation in one of the downstairs cells and on my return journey I asked in a loud voice if there were any other British there. Two voices replied "Yes" and a few minutes after I returned to my cell I was visited by two Army officers who had been taken prisoner at Dunkirk. They had been in transit from one camp to another and had managed to get away from their escort but had been recaptured in the town. We were allowed to talk for a while before they had to return to their cell.

'That same day the young American sergeant tank driver was brought in and we were allowed to visit him. By the end of the day we arranged with our jailers, two young women who cooked and cleaned for the Police Chief and the jail, that we could have the run of the place so long as we did not try to talk to the occupants of the upstairs front cell who were political prisoners. Some time later some shells landed in the town and the women, who had just brought supper, bolted for safety, leaving the street door open. We were out and off in a moment and ran up the street and across the road at the end into a doorway to decide which way to go from there. A shout from the end of the road told us that we had been seen. The door behind us was not locked so we slipped inside and down some steps into a cellar apparently under the pavement. Heavy footsteps announced the arrival of the men who had seen us, then a voice shouted that we should come up or be blown up. A whispered conference resulted in a decision to risk staying where we were, but a few seconds later, there was a metallic clatter and a hand grenade rolled into sight. We reached the top of the steps well within the five second fuse time. Our captors marched us across the street and lined us up against the wall, then backed off and raised their machine pistols. I thought, this is it, my time has come, when suddenly the old Police Chief came around the corner and demanded to know what the soldiers were doing with his prisoners. He shouted down all protestations that we were deserters and saboteurs and insisted that we were his responsibility. It seemed that our captors were more of the Hitler Youth and that the policeman had known them all their young lives and they were used to him being "their" policeman. Once back in the jail we received a stern lecture and were locked in our cells again.

'A few hours later the two young women ran in, saying that some SS men had heard about us and were coming along to make sure we did not escape again. There was an old sofa in the cell, minus most of its straw stuffing. I managed to climb in from the underneath and arranged the remaining straw as strategically as possible so that the sofa appeared merely to be properly stuffed. My ruse was successful – there was apparently nowhere to hide in the cell and the searchers gave the place no more than a cursory glance before going on to find the political prisoners upstairs. These unfortunates were dragged out and shot before the SS troopers moved on. When we dared to come out of our hiding places the girls came back from the Police Office and told us to come to the cellar under the next house which was used as an air raid shelter. This was the idea of the Police Chief as he told us when he visited us later. He said that the town was not safe for civilians who had all been evacuated as it was expected that the area would be defended fiercely by the SS who were now in command. As the girls were forced labour conscripts he told them to stay with us, it was obvious that he expected we should be free quite soon. He wished us goodbye as he had been told to leave.

'We slept that night on the floor, where I suddenly realised that I was not alone! I scratched furiously, realising that my short stay in the inside of the old sofa had been long enough for its inhabitants to make the most of their opportunity to explore the warm new blood which had suddenly visited them! There was not much sleep anyway. The guns rumbled intermittently throughout the night.

'The following day we were visited by a Frenchman from the local labour camp. He said that attempts would be made that evening to contact the American forces to try to arrange that their assault teams were aware of the position of the nearby labour camp. He came back about midnight with another guide and they led us to the river which we crossed in an inflatable rubber boat, as the bridge had been destroyed. We hauled ourselves across by the rope which had been stretched from bank to bank, being greeted on the Allied side by a very suspicious American sergeant with a very large sub-machine gun. He took us back across the fields to a group of houses and handed us over to some MPs who made us empty our belongings onto a table. We were interrogated by the local Army commander, my "Dog Tags" eventually convinced him that I was not an enemy and the tank driver sergeant had little difficulty either. For the two ex-Dunkirk officers it was not so easy but eventually he believed their stories. We were given food and a room to rest in.

'Eventually, after recounting my experiences to endless intelligence officers, and after treatment for the bites and scratches I had received whilst hiding in the straw stuffing of the sofa, I was returned to England. I was flown from Brussels to a south coast airfield and driven to an interrogation centre in London. I re-told my story and there was an official Court of Enquiry into the loss of "E-Easy". Eventually I was given a leave pass and a travel warrant and I went to my nearest relatives, an uncle and aunt near Reading, and there I was able to telephone my parents and set their minds at rest'.

Bibliography

Action Stations 4 - Yorkshire: B.B.Halpenny; Patrick Stephens, 1982.
Aircraft Crash Log No.2 - HP Halifax: R.N.Roberts.
Aircraft Crash Log No.4 - AW Whitley: R.N.Roberts.
Aircraft of the Royal Air Force since 1918: O.Thetford, 8th edition; Putnam, 1988.
A Most Secret Place, Boscombe Down 1939-45: Brian Johnson & Terry Hefferman; Janes, 1982.
Battle over the Reich: Alfred Price; Ian Allan, 1973.
Before the Storm: Robert Jackson; Arthur Baker, 1972.
Bombing Colours: M.J.F.Bowyer; Patrick Stephens, 1973.
Bomber Command: Max Hastings; Michael Joseph, 1979.
Bomber Intelligence: W.E.Jones; Midland Counties Publications, 1983.
Bombers over Berlin: Alan J.Cooper; William Kimber, 1985.
Bomber Squadrons of the RAF: P.J.R.Moyes; Macdonald, 1964.
Britain's Military Airfields 1939-45: D.J.Smith; Patrick Stephens, 1989.
British Military Aircraft Serials 1878-1987: Midland Counties Publications, 1987.
Cheshire VC: Russell Braddon; Evans Brothers Ltd, 1954.
Confound and Destroy: Martin Streetly; Macdonald and Janes, 1978.
Coningham: Vincent Orange; Methuen, 1990.
Guns in the Sky: Chaz Bowyer; J.M.Dent & Sons Ltd, 1979.
Halifax: K.A.Merrick; Ian Allan, 1980.
Halifax Crew: Arthur C.Smith; Carlton Publications, 1983.
Halifax in Action: Jerry Scutts; Squadron Signal, 1984.
Handley Page Halifax - Merlin Engined Variants: Aerodata, 1979.
History of the German Night Fighter Force 1917-45; Janes, 1979.
In Brave Company: No.158 Squadron History: W.R.Chorley & R.N.Benwell; 1979.
Melbourne Ten: B.J.Rapier; Air Museum York, 1980.
No.578 Squadron History: C.W.Adams; Unpublished.

Pathfinders at War: Chaz Bowyer; Ian Allan, 1977.
Raider: the Halifax and its Flyers: Geoffrey Jones; William Kimber, 1978.
RAF Bomber Units 1939-42: Brian Philpott; Osprey, 1977.
The Battle of Hamburg: Martin Middlebrook; Allen Lane, 1982
The Bomber Command War Diaries: An Operational Reference Book 1939-45: Martin Middlebrook & Chris Everitt; Viking 1985.
The Bomber Offensive: Sir Arthur Harris; Collins, 1947.
The Defence of the Reich: Werner Held & Holger Nauroth; Arms & Armour Press, 1982.
The Flying Bomb: Richard Anthony Young; Ian Allan, 1978.
The Great Raids vol.2: Essen: A/Cdre J.Searby; Nutshell Press, 1978.
The Halifax File: R.N.Roberts; Air-Britain, 1982.
The Handley Page Halifax B.III, VI, VII: P.J.R.Moyes; Profile Publications No.11, 1965.
The Legacy of Lord Trenchard: Wg Cdr H.R.Allen; Cassell, 1972.
The Nuremburg Raid: Martin Middlebrook; Allen Lane, 1973.
The Peenemunde Raid: Martin Middlebrook; Allen Lane, 1982.
The Royal Air Force 1939-45: Denis Richards; HMSO, 1953.
The Second World War vols I, II, III, IV, V: Winston S.Churchill; Cassell 1948-54.
Squadron Codes 1937-56: M.J.F.Bowyer & J.D.R.Rawlings; Patrick Stephens, 1979.
The Squadrons of the Royal Air Force: J.J.Halley; Air-Britain, 1980.
The Squadrons of the Royal Air Force and Commonwealth 1918-1988: James J.Halley; Air-Britain, 1988.
The Strategic Air Offensive against Germany, vols I-IV: Sir Charles Webster & Noble Frankland; HMSO, 1961.
To See The Dawn Breaking, No.76 Squadron History: W.R.Chorley.
Wellington at War: Chaz Bowyer; Ian Allan, 1982.
White Rose Base: B.J.Rapier; Air Museum York, 1980.

Index